Scott Foresman
Assessment Handbook

Reading STREET

Grades 4-6

PEARSON

Glenview, Illinois • Boston, Massachusetts • Chandler, Arizona • Upper Saddle River, New Jersey

ISBN-13: 978-0-328-48899-5
ISBN-10:   0-328-48899-2
6 7 8 9 10 V016 18 17 16 15 14 13 12 11
CC1

Contents

Chapter 7 Collecting, Evaluating, and Reporting Evidence of Learning

Scott Foresman *Reading Street* Assessment

Some Questions and Answers

This *Assessment Handbook* will be a resource throughout the school year. The handbook presents an overview of the Scott Foresman *Reading Street* assessment program, and it provides numerous resources that you may use to best fit your assessment, instruction, and learning goals. In addition, the *Assessment Handbook* may be regarded as a professional development resource. Inside you will find:

- guidance for using a variety of diagnostic, entry-level, progress-monitoring, summative, and classroom-based assessments;
- suggestions for using writing to strengthen learning and to assess learning;
- proven methods and models for assessing, managing, evaluating, and grading student work;
- steps for designing quality assessments in all content areas; and
- instructional strategies for preparing students for state-required assessments.

Scott Foresman *Reading Street* assessments reflect current theories of teaching language and literacy and are aligned with solid classroom teaching practices. Formal and classroom-based assessments, combined with "assessable moments" during instruction, become a continuous cycle in which one is always informing and supporting the other, resulting in a seamless learning program for students.

Following are some commonly asked questions about the Scott Foresman *Reading Street* assessment program.

How was the Scott Foresman *Reading Street* assessment program developed?

The assessment components of Scott Foresman *Reading Street* were developed by a specialized testing organization, Questar Assessment, Incorporated. Scott Foresman authorial and editorial staff guided these development activities, specifying the purposes to be served by each component and their general coverage. In addition, Scott Foresman editorial teams critiqued and approved the test specifications and prototype test items for each program element that were developed by Questar. Finally, Scott Foresman reviewed and provided editorial feedback on all test content. However, the development of all materials was the responsibility of Questar Assessment staff.

Questar Assessment's development team, formerly Beck Evaluation & Testing Associates, Incorporated (BETA), is one of the country's most experienced assessment-development corporations. Over the past twenty years, Questar's test development team has provided standardized test content for a broad range of state and federal agencies in addition to most leading test and textbook publishers. Questar has played key roles in developing large-scale, high-stakes testing programs in over twenty-five states. Questar staff regularly assist state Departments of Education and federal agencies on matters of test development, implementation, and psychometrics, providing such consultation to over thirty-six state Departments of Education. Over the past decade, Questar has developed over 82,000 test items for use in large-scale assessment programs. Most of these programs include the assessment of elementary reading and other language-arts skills.

All test items developed by Questar are written by experienced assessment-development professionals, all with extensive experience in creating test questions in the appropriate content areas and for the targeted grade levels. The development activities in support of Scott Foresman *Reading Street* were directed by Questar senior staff members, and all test items were written specifically for Scott Foresman *Reading Street*.

How will your program help prepare my students for required state and national standardized tests?

In many ways! The Student Editions, Teacher's Editions, and Reader's and Writer's Notebooks are all carefully crafted to teach the knowledge, skills, and strategies students need in order to meet or exceed the standards in all their reading and writing tasks. Many Reader's and Writer's Notebook pages contain items that reflect common standardized test formats, allowing students repeated opportunities to become familiar with question patterns. In addition, the formal entry-level, progress-monitoring, and summative assessments are comprised of literal, inferential, and critical-analysis questions based on the question-answer framework used in instruction and are similar to question types on high-stakes tests used by school districts. Tips on instructional strategies designed to prepare your students for state-required assessments are described in Chapter 1 of this handbook and in Chapter 6, where they are tailored for English language learners. With the preparation provided by Scott Foresman *Reading Street* materials, your students will have experience with a variety of test-taking situations and learn a variety of test-taking skills.

How do I find out where my students are at the beginning of the year?

Finding a starting point for each student can be difficult. Scott Foresman *Reading Street* makes it easier by providing test options and parent and learner surveys to help you get to know your students' skills, abilities, and interests.

Entry-level assessments provide information about where to begin instruction for individual learners. The more you know about your students at the beginning of the year, the better equipped you are to maximize their learning experiences to ensure that they achieve continuous growth in writing, speaking, reading, and listening skills. The group-administered *Reading Street* Baseline Group Test gives you information about the instructional needs of your class and points you to program features that help you meet those needs. The Group Reading Assessment and Diagnostic Evaluation (GRADE) is a norm-referenced formal assessment that may help you determine your students' prerequisite skills and knowledge. The Developmental Reading Assessment (DRA) enables you to make a quick analysis of a student's independent reading level. Student surveys, such as the questionnaire Myself as a Reader and Writer, familiarize you with each student's reading attitudes and interests, while parent surveys, such as My Child as a Learner, give you insights into their literacy habits and behaviors when they are not in school. Chapter 2 of this handbook describes all of the entry-level formal and informal assessment techniques and tools available to you through Scott Foresman *Reading Street*. All entry-level and diagnostic assessment information helps you determine which content standards have been mastered, resulting in appropriate placement and planning for each student in your class.

How do I know that my students are being tested on the right skills?

Scott Foresman *Reading Street* is founded on a carefully crafted scope and sequence of skills, based on the most current research and accepted practices in reading instruction, and systematically aligned with state language arts and reading standards.

This scope and sequence is the basis for both the instructional plan and for the depth and breadth of the Scott Foresman *Reading Street* assessment program. Target skills and strategies are taught in each lesson and then assessed in the Weekly Test. Each target skill is also assessed in the Unit Benchmark Test after it has been taught and reviewed multiple times. This systematic alignment of instruction and assessment ensures that students are being tested on *what* they are being taught, in the way they are being taught.

What is the best way to assess my students? How does your program provide what I need?

Accurate and ongoing assessment enables teachers to monitor students' progress toward achieving the standards, to evaluate classroom instruction, and to help students monitor their own learning. An effective assessment system incorporates a variety of assessment methods—both formal and informal—to help teachers meet those varied purposes.

Scott Foresman *Reading Street* provides a full complement of materials to meet your assessment requirements. For a formal assessment of unit skills and selections, you will find several different tests from which to choose. For classroom-based assessment, the *Assessment Handbook* contains surveys, observation forms, and reporting forms, as well as questioning and observation techniques you can adapt for your classroom needs. These informal strategies will assist you in making student self-assessment, peer assessment, portfolios, and grading more efficient. Also, the Teacher's Editions provide tools for you to make both immediate and long-term decisions about the instructional needs of your students.

How does your program support assessment of my English language learners?

Scott Foresman *Reading Street* recognizes the unique challenges and rewards of teaching and assessing the progress of English language learners. Chapter 6 of the *Assessment Handbook* discusses research-based methods of assessing the strengths and needs of English language learners in your classroom. Scott Foresman *Reading Street* classroom-based assessments reflect those methods as they help teachers monitor progress in the basic reading and expression skills of alphabetic understanding, decoding, sight vocabulary, and grammar, along with measurement of the more complex skills of fluency, comprehension, and vocabulary. The chapter provides guidance on instructional strategies designed to prepare English language learners for standardized tests, including high-stakes tests, as well as advice on appropriate use of accommodations for Scott Foresman *Reading Street* formal assessments.

Will your program help me when I have to assign grades?

Because we know that these are major concerns for many teachers, we devote an entire chapter (7) to record keeping and grading. We recognize that you will be using the *Reading Street* tools to assess students' literacy skills and strategies at the beginning of the year and monitor progress throughout the year. You will be collecting large amounts of information about your students. Access to this data informs sound decision-making relating to the focus of the curriculum, effectiveness of instruction, meaningful feedback to students and parents, and improved achievement, but it is often difficult to manage.

In Chapter 7, you will find guidance for keeping accurate, informative records and sharing details with students, parents, and others. Advice for implementing student portfolios and grading is also provided; you will review how to design scoring rubrics, evaluate student participation in class discussions and group activities, grade oral presentations, and assess individual or group writing.

Add to this the many formal testing opportunities, which are an integral part of the program, and you have an assessment program that gives you the information you need to meet your assessment requirements.

Program Assessment Overview

A variety of assessment instruments, used with fiction and nonfiction selections, allow you to

- determine students' strengths and needs
- monitor students' progress
- measure students' skill and strategy proficiencies
- evaluate the effectiveness of instruction

from the beginning of the school year to the end!

Baseline Group Tests

Weekly Tests

Fresh Reads for Fluency and Comprehension

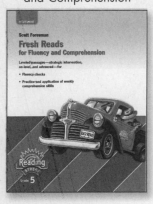

Unit Benchmark Tests

End-of-Year Benchmark Tests

Assessment Handbook

Technology

ASSESSMENT
ReadingStreet.com

Beginning of the Year

Entry-Level Assessments

Baseline Group Test

- Is administered as a placement test to your entire class
- Provides options for group and individual administration
- Identifies your below-level students requiring strategic intervention
- Identifies your on-level students
- Identifies your above-level students requiring challenge
- Helps you use Scott Foresman *Reading Street* features and components to focus instruction on students' needs
- Establishes baseline data

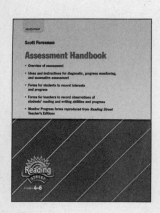

Assessment Handbook for Grades 4–6

Informal, classroom-based assessment tools and techniques, including:

- Student and parent surveys
- Reading, writing, and oral-language teacher checklists
- Learner inventories and profiles

During the Year

Progress-Monitoring Assessments

Teacher's Edition and *First Stop*

- Ongoing assessment
- Success Predictor boxes
- Guiding Comprehension questions
- Think Critically
- Look Back and Write model answers
- Writing scoring rubrics
- Spelling tests
- Weekly assessment for fluency and comprehension

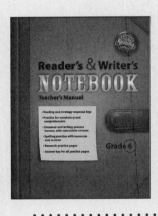

Reader's and Writer's Notebook

- Provides practice pages for all vocabulary, spelling, and comprehension skills
- Grammar and writing process practice and cumulative reviews
- Reading and writing logs
- Helps you identify students needing more instruction

Weekly Tests

- Are multiple-choice tests administered on Day 5 of every week
- Measure students' understanding of each week's introduced vocabulary words, word analysis skills, and comprehension skills
- Help identify students who have mastered each week's words and skills and students who may need intervention

Fresh Reads for Fluency and Comprehension

- Are multiple-choice and constructed-response tests administered throughout the year, each week after students have been taught the comprehension skill lesson

- Give students opportunities to practice the target and review comprehension skills of the week with new selections matched to their instructional reading levels

- Provide checks of oral reading fluency

Unit Benchmark Tests

- Are multiple-choice and constructed-response tests administered throughout the year, at the end of each six-week unit

- Measure students' abilities to apply target comprehension skills and other literacy skills taught during each unit

- Help you make instructional decisions for each student

- Provide feedback about the effectiveness of your instruction and help you plan instruction for the next unit

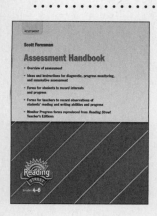

Assessment Handbook for Grades 4–6

Informal, classroom-based assessment tools and techniques, including:

- Questioning strategies
- Teacher observation forms
- Fluency checks
- Retelling and summarizing forms
- Work habits and skills conference records
- Parent observation form
- Self, peer, and group assessment forms
- Student portfolios
- Reading and writing logs and responses

Technology

- Online assessment and data management with diagnostic prescriptions

- Exam View: Test generator with alignment to statewide and district-wide standards and prescriptions

End of the Year

Summative Assessments

End-of-Year Benchmark Test

- Is a cumulative test administered at the end of each grade
- Provides three reading selections
- Tests comprehension skills, vocabulary strategies, written conventions (grammar, usage, and mechanics skills), and writing
- Combines multiple-choice and constructed-response questions
- Provides an integrated approach to assessment

. . . .

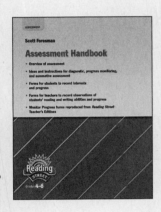

Assessment Handbook for Grades 4–6

Informal, classroom-based assessment tools and techniques, including:

- Summary reports, forms, and checklists
- Student portfolios
- Cumulative folder forms
- Reading and writing logs
- Reading and writing assessment forms
- Guidance with grading

. . . .

Technology

- Online assessment and data management with diagnostic prescriptions
- Exam View: Test generator with alignment to statewide and district-wide standards and prescriptions

Chapter 1

Assessment Literacy

Overview

Classroom teachers make an extraordinary number of decisions every hour of the school day. Four important decisions are:

1. What are the critical understandings and skills that I want students to know and be able to do upon completion of this lesson/unit/grade?

2. How will I know if the students have reached these expectations?

3. What will I do to support those who have not met these standards?

4. What will I do to support those who already have exceeded the standards?

The critical understandings and skills are the **learning targets,** usually based on school, district, and state curriculum standards. The second question is the focus of this introductory section of the handbook: *How will I know? What evidence must I collect?* Scott Foresman *Reading Street* Teacher's Editions and other program resources provide ongoing guidance for implementing intervention techniques for struggling readers and extending and enriching the curriculum for advanced learners. *Reading Street* also offers valuable resources, strategies, and tools for collecting evidence of achievement and encourages educators to be wise about the subject of **assessment**—what it is, when to use it, how to do it, and why it is so important.

What Is Assessment Literacy?

Now, more than ever before, it is important for all teachers and administrators to be "literate" about educational assessment and evaluation. Why? Research tells us that the use of meaningful classroom assessment strategies and tools, such as questioning, observational methods, and student self-assessment, empowers educators, guides instruction, and improves learning.

Further, we cannot ignore that increased demands for accountability at the state and national levels, e.g., *Reading First, No Child Left Behind (NCLB),* and *Adequate Yearly Progress (AYP),* etc., have produced an unprecedented proliferation of testing, and student test performance has become the accountability yardstick by which the effectiveness of schools, districts, states, and even teaching is measured and judged.

To be informed consumers and creators of assessment, individuals must:

- understand the power of assessment in promoting student achievement;

- become knowledgeable about the functions, strengths, and limitations of formal and informal assessment;

- maintain a balance of summative and formative assessments in their classrooms and schools;

- embrace standards of quality as they evaluate and create assessments; and

- use sound assessment practices to design and administer quality classroom-based assessments.

What Is Assessment?

The Latin root of the word "assess" means "to sit beside." This is a much gentler notion of this concept than most of us have, although "sitting beside" a student to confer about the development of a story in progress, to conduct a fluency check, or to observe a group discussion are valuable assessment techniques. What is assessment? *Assessment is simply the gathering and interpretation of evidence about student learning.* There are many methods for collecting information to determine if students have mastered the knowledge and skills, or the learning targets. We can use a variety of formal and informal or classroom-based measures to collect that evidence.

Summative and Formative Assessment

Summative assessments are formal assessment measures, most often regarded as tests or tasks presented to students in order to obtain conclusive evidence about their performance. Tasks are designed to provide samples of individual achievement and are administered, scored, and interpreted according to mostly prescribed conditions. These activities are regarded as **summative** because they come at the *end* of an instructional process and are used to determine placement or assign grades. Examples might be chapter tests, unit projects, culminating performances, and final examinations. (Airasian, 2000)

Standardized tests are summative assessments designed to be administered to large numbers of test-takers. The tests are administered at the same time each year, and testing conditions, such as precise directions, time allowances, and security procedures, are tightly controlled. Test questions are written, reviewed, and revised following tryouts by a representative sample of the population for which the instrument is designed.

Examples of standardized tests are commercially published tests, as well as state assessments, which are now used annually to measure student achievement of standards for reporting and accountability purposes, in compliance with federal *NCLB* legislation and other mandates. These tests are often called "high-stakes," because scores are made very public, and schools and districts are subject to sanctions and embarrassment if they do not make annual *AYP* goals. (Popham, 2004)

Dr. Richard Stiggins distinguishes between assessment *of* learning and assessment *for* learning. Assessments *of* learning are generally formal, summative assessments administered at the end of an instructional period. They answer the question, "How much have students learned as of a particular point in time?" (Stiggins, 2002)

Formative assessment is the process of systematically and continuously collecting evidence about students' learning and monitoring their progress. It is classroom-based assessment *for* learning that helps us *dig deeper* in order to ascertain exactly *how* individual students are making progress toward achievement of the learning targets. These assessments are called **formative** because they are influential in "forming" the process under way and are intended to guide and inform instruction.

Reading Street offers a variety of formal and informal formative assessment techniques. While informal assessment tasks may not be the same type or depth for all students, and may not be recorded in a prescribed, standardized manner, they are not "informal" in the sense of "casual" or "random." Instead, use of informal assessments is the thoughtfully-planned, intentional monitoring of learning embedded within the instructional process, rather than the evaluation of learning at the conclusion of the process.

Examples of formative assessment tools are teachers' questions, observations, checklists, portfolios, homework, student self-assessment, and teacher-student conferences, as well as weekly and unit tests.

Balancing Formative and Summative Assessment

Annually administered tests provide general feedback about student performance related to broad content standards, or achievement targets. These tests are not designed to offer the immediate and ongoing information about achievement that teachers need to make critical instructional decisions. Even once-a-unit classroom tests do not provide sufficient information to improve teaching and increase learning. (Stiggins, 2004)

> "Balance continuous classroom assessment in support of learning with periodic assessments verifying learning."
> (Stiggins, 2004)

To establish and maintain productive, learning-centered classroom environments, teachers rely on a balance of informal assessments *for* learning and formal assessments *of* learning to guide their instruction. They use an array of formative and summative measures *derived from* and/or *aligned with* the content standards and based on their assessment purposes.

Why and when do we monitor progress with formative assessment?

- To diagnose students' strengths and needs
- To elicit prior knowledge for a concept or topic
- To provide frequent feedback to students that is descriptive and helpful, rather than judgmental, as in grades
- To motivate learners to increase effort as they experience incremental successes
- To build students' confidence in themselves as learners
- To help students take responsibility for their learning as they monitor their progress and adjust their goals
- To plan, modify, and regulate the pace of instruction to meet the needs of all students
- To communicate with parents and caregivers (e.g., learning expectations, students' progress in meeting learning targets, and methods of providing support at home)

Why do we obtain evidence with summative assessment?

- To report achievement of content standards, the learning targets
- To document growth over time (e.g., unit-to-unit, year-to-year)
- To assign grades appropriately at the end of a unit, for a report card, etc.
- To validate judgments and decisions about student achievement
- To recommend students for promotion and placement in special programs

- To gauge program effectiveness, note strengths, and identify gaps

- To examine comparative data across schools and districts in order to make programmatic decisions (e.g., establish school improvement priorities, improve curriculum alignment, establish a need for intervention programs, additional resources, etc.)

- To satisfy state and federal accountability mandates, such as AYP

- To inform the public (e.g., taxpayers, business leaders, and legislators)

Evaluating Assessments for Quality

Most textbooks and instructional programs, including Scott Foresman *Reading Street*, have accompanying assessments for teachers to use. The formal and informal measures within *Reading Street* reflect the highest standards of quality and seamlessly align with the instructional program, yet teachers may wish to occasionally construct their own tests and performance assessments for other content areas and interdisciplinary studies. In order to implement fair and sound assessment, teachers are encouraged to consider the following standards for evaluating the quality of commercial assessments and designing their own classroom assessments to augment or replace the textbook measures.

> "...educators need to become sufficiently assessment literate so they can understand and, if necessary, help improve any accountability system that relies on unsuitable achievement tests."
>
> (Popham, 2004)

Know Your Learning Targets

Statewide and district-wide curriculum standards embody the content knowledge and skills we want our students to have, and they are the basis for all of our testing.

- "Unpack" the content standards to identify the underlying knowledge, concepts, processes, skills, and dispositions (e.g., attitudes, values, habits of mind) that become the **learning targets.**

- Translate the targets into student-friendly language.

- Post the targets in the classroom for all to see.

- Discuss the targets with the students at the beginning of the instructional process (e.g., lesson, unit, marking period).

- Review them throughout the process so that students have clear, reachable targets to hit.

Determine the Match

Teachers must carefully scrutinize each test item to ensure that the assessment has **content validity.** To what extent does the assessment measure what it is used to measure? Does the content of the test or task represent a balanced and adequate sampling of the targeted knowledge and skills as they are taught in the classroom? In other words, a recall exercise in which students are to match vocabulary words with their definitions would not be a valid assessment of a vocabulary standard requiring students to use structural analysis and context clues to determine word meanings. Test questions and tasks should be "instructionally sensitive"; that is, they should clearly reflect the learning targets and require students to perform the behaviors as you have taught them.

Consider the Number of Tested Standards

An effective assessment measures only a modest number of important learning targets and measures them well, so that teachers and students are not overwhelmed by the length and complexity of the activity. (Popham, 2004) Assessments are meant to sample components of the learning that takes place in the classroom, so an appropriate test or task must also contain a sufficient number of items related to each sampled learning target. In this way, teachers can be confident that the results will identify target skill areas that have been thoroughly taught and those that need improvement.

Strive for Reliability and Fairness

Reliability: How trustworthy is this assessment? Can I rely on the scores? Will this assessment give me the same results about the same learning targets every time?

Scoring of selected-response tests is considered quite reliable, and two teachers scoring the same set of multiple-choice tests will probably get the same results, barring a small chance of human error.

Although constructed-response assessments may measure more meaningful learning targets, they are considered less reliable because extensive training is needed in order to achieve consistency in scoring. To increase reliability, many states and school districts develop scoring rubrics and train scorers in a thorough, systematic way. Panels of raters score a large number of papers and discuss their scores until they're consistent in their ratings. Some papers are chosen as anchor papers because the raters believe they exemplify score points on the rubric. These papers are then used to guide subsequent scoring sessions, and reliability is improved. This activity can be replicated at the building level as teachers of the same grade level collaborate to design and score performance assessments, such as end-of-unit projects and presentations.

Fairness: Do all students, including those with diverse cultural and linguistic backgrounds, have an equal chance to demonstrate what they know and can do? Have all of them had the same opportunity to learn the content? Are the directions clear? Is the environment comfortable?

Fairness in assessment is compromised when teachers assess knowledge and skills that have not been taught or use assessment formats that do not reflect *how* the learning targets have been taught (e.g., asking for opinions and reasons when the emphasis has been on recall of facts).

Designing Quality Classroom Assessments

Teachers can construct multi-purpose classroom assessments that reflect the standards of quality—validity, reliability, and fairness. Purposes include diagnosing students' strengths and needs; planning, monitoring progress, and adjusting instruction; and providing feedback to students, parents, and others regarding progress and proficiency. The following design questions are intended to guide educators as they plan and build their own assessments:

1. **What learning target(s) based on the statewide and district-wide curriculum standards will you assess?**

2. **For which formative or summative purpose(s) is this assessment being administered?**

   - To detect strengths and needs
   - To motivate learners
   - To assign grades
   - To check progress
   - To group for instruction
   - To collect additional evidence
   - To evaluate instruction
   - Other

3. **Who will use the results of this assessment?**

   - Students
   - Teacher(s)
   - Parent(s)
   - Principal
   - Community
   - Other

4. **What format will the assessment take?**

   It is important to select the format that most appropriately matches the target. For example, you wouldn't create a multiple-choice test to assess students' *use* of action verbs in their writing. Rather, you would assign a constructed-response activity asking them to incorporate action verbs in their text.

   Conversely, you wouldn't use a constructed-response format to assess students' identification of states and their capitals. An activity requiring them to match states and capitals would suffice for this purpose—assessing recall. Constructed responses are valuable because they help us seek insights into students' reasoning behind their answers or evidence that they can apply what they have learned. Possible assessment formats and examples of activities are listed in the table on page 23.

5. What criteria will you use to evaluate performance?

- How will you know it when you see it?

- What does hitting the target look like? What are the qualities?

- Is there one right answer or several possible answers?

- What will you accept as evidence that students have hit the target; that is, that they have acquired the knowledge and skills identified in the content standards?

6. What type of feedback will be provided to guide improvement?

How will results be communicated? How will you tell the story behind the numbers? Will you use a letter grade, a rubric score, written descriptive comments, a checklist, a point on a continuum of learning (such as an oral language behaviors' continuum), or another way?

The most valuable feedback is very specific and descriptive of how the performance hits (or does not hit) the target. Give concrete suggestions rather than vague comments or encouragement, such as "Nice work!" or "You can do better next time!" Share clear examples of successful work with students, and have them compare their work with the model. Allow students opportunities to revise their performances.

Transforming learning expectations into assessment tasks, assigning criteria, designing scoring procedures, and preparing feedback are challenging and time-consuming activities when they are attempted alone. It is a rewarding and collegial experience to collaborate with peers in articulating expectations, designing common assessments, analyzing student work, and selecting anchor/model performances. When educators work together to become assessment-literate, they empower each other with the ability to improve assessment practices and accountability systems in their school districts and states. More importantly, they increase learning for students.

Assessment Design Options

Possible Format	Examples of Tasks	Suggested Scoring/Feedback
Selected-Response	• Multiple-choice • Matching • True-false	One right answer; cut scores and percentages
Short Constructed-Response (written/oral)	• Fill-in-the-blank • Sentence completion • Graphic organizer • Brief response to prompt	One (or few) right answers; cut scores and percentages
Extended Constructed-Response (written/oral)	• Prompt-based narrative, descriptive, expository, and persuasive writing • Retellings • Position with support • Summaries	More than one right answer; scoring with checklists, descriptive criteria, standards, continuum, rubrics, comparative models
Performances	• Oral presentation • Demonstration • Discussion • Role play	More than one right answer; scoring with checklists, descriptive criteria, standards, continuum, rubrics, peer and self-evaluation, comparative models
Products	• Science project • Visual display • Model • Video • Poem, story, play • Log/journal • Portfolio	More than one right answer; scoring with checklists, descriptive criteria, standards, continuum, rubrics, comparative models
Processes	• Strategy applications (e.g., think-alouds, questioning) • Teacher-student conferences • Peer and group assessments • Student self-assessments • Interviews • Inventories • Observations • Book club participation • Surveys of reading or writing behaviors • Portfolio selection slips • Response logs • Reading/writing lists	No one right answer; not necessary to score; collect as additional evidence; provide descriptive feedback to students

What Is the Scott Foresman *Reading Street* Assessment System?

All assessments in the program reflect current theories of teaching language and literacy and are aligned with solid classroom teaching practices. Scott Foresman *Reading Street* offers a "seamless assessment system" at each grade. The formative and summative assessments, combined with "assessable moments" during instruction, become a continuous cycle where one is always informing the other, resulting in a seamless learning program for the students.

Fundamental to this cycle are clear, grade-appropriate, and important learning targets that are aligned with statewide and district-wide reading and language arts curriculum standards.

> To prepare students for standardized tests, teachers should teach "the key ideas and processes contained in content standards in rich and engaging ways; by collecting evidence of student understanding of that content through robust local assessments, rather than one-shot standardized testing; and by using engaging and effective instructional strategies that help students explore core concepts through inquiry and problem solving."
>
> (McTighe, Seif, & Wiggins, 2004)

- At the beginning of each school year, the cycle begins with the administration of entry-level assessments used for screening and diagnosis. They will help you establish a starting point for students and determine the amount of instructional support students will need in order to hit the targets. Informal tools will provide additional information about students' learning styles, confidence, and interests that will help you in designing effective instructional plans.

- During the school year, literacy achievement is checked daily and weekly through formative, progress-monitoring assessments—informal, such as teacher observations, fluency checks, retellings, and conferencing, as well as formal assessments. For example, the Scott Foresman *Reading Street* Weekly Tests assess students' understanding of the skills taught during the week, and the Fresh Reads for Fluency and Comprehension give students opportunities to practice comprehension and build fluency with new selections matched to their instructional levels.

- The Unit Benchmark Tests and the End-of-Year Benchmark Test are formative and summative assessments designed to assess students' understanding of the targeted skills, strategies, and critical thinking skills taught throughout the unit and the school year.

What Are the Assessment Targets?

Reading

What are the reading targets? *Reading Street* emphasizes the reading skills that are described by the National Reading Panel. These reading skills are essential as students learn to become independent, strategic readers and writers.

Oral reading fluency is the ability to effortlessly, quickly, and accurately decode letters, words, sentences, and passages. Fluent readers are able to group words into meaningful grammatical units and read with proper expression. Fluency is an essential component of comprehension and is assessed regularly in Scott Foresman *Reading Street*.

Reading comprehension, the overarching goal of reading, is the active process of constructing meaning from text. It is a complex process in which readers apply their prior knowledge and experiences, use their understandings about text (types, structures, features, etc.), and intentionally employ an array of before-, during-, and after-reading strategies and skills, in order to attain meaning. Effective readers combine their own experiences with their interpretation of the author's intent as they work to make sense of ideas in text.

In Scott Foresman *Reading Street*, students' use of targeted comprehension strategies and skills is monitored continuously on the Weekly Tests and Fresh Reads for Fluency and Comprehension. Students read a variety of engaging, culturally- and age-appropriate narrative and expository texts and respond to appropriate multiple-choice questions designed to assess how they use the comprehension skills in constructing meaning. There are three types of comprehension questions that correspond to the *In the Book* and *In My Head* categories of questions in the instructional program.

- **Literal** questions, which focus on ideas explicitly stated in the text, although *not necessarily* verbatim. In response to these items, students *recognize* and *identify* information which might be found in a single sentence or in two or more sentences of contiguous text.

- **Inferential** questions, which are based on the theme, key concepts, and major ideas of the passage and often require students to *interpret* information from across parts of the text and to *connect* knowledge from the text with their own general background knowledge.

- **Critical-analysis** questions, which are also inferential in nature and focus on important ideas in the selection. Yet they differ from inferential questions in that readers are required to stand apart from the text and *analyze, synthesize*, and/or *evaluate* the quality, effectiveness, relevance, and consistency of the message, rhetorical features (tone, style, voice, etc.), author or character motivation, and the author's purpose or credibility.

Throughout the program, students are guided using scaffolding as they move from literal understanding, to inferential comprehension, and to critical analysis of text.

Vocabulary acquisition and development contribute significantly to overall text comprehension. While extensive reading experiences with varied text types and opportunities for classroom discussion are known to increase word knowledge, *Reading Street* explicitly teaches and assesses vocabulary skills through the study of context meaning, word structure, and dictionary/glossary use.

"Having a strong vocabulary is not only a school goal, it is a characteristic that allows us to participate actively in our world, and it is viewed by those we meet as the hallmark of an educated person."
(Blachowicz, 2005)

- Context clues from the words or phrases surrounding an unknown word help readers identify its meaning or, as in the case of words with multiple meanings, its meaning appropriate to this situation. Context clues include synonyms, antonyms, definitions, explanations, descriptions, and examples that appear within the text surrounding an unfamiliar word. Not only are these textual clues helpful in determining word meanings, but they also assist readers in interpreting phrases, such as idioms, metaphors, similes, and analogies.

- The study of word structure is the analysis of word-meaning elements to make meaning of the word as a whole. Such meaningful elements include word roots, origins (Latin, Greek, Anglo-Saxon), prefixes, suffixes, and compound words. Syllabication generalizations and inflected endings, which change the tense, case, or singular-plural form of words, but do not affect meaning or part of speech, are also taught and assessed.

- The understanding and guided practice in how, why, and when to use a dictionary, glossary, or thesaurus helps to increase students' vocabularies. They become familiar with the organization and format of these important resources and are guided and assessed in their use of the components of an entry, including syllabication, pronunciation, part of speech, etymology, definition, and determination of related words.

Writing

Targeted skills are based on the writing strategies and writing applications strands of state language arts standards. Skills include:

- Writing clear, coherent, focused multiple-paragraph essays

- Logical organizational structure (e.g., chronological, cause/effect, similarity/ difference, posing/answering a question, etc.) with details and transitions that clearly link paragraphs

- Awareness of purpose and audience

- Use of supporting evidence (e.g., facts, details, and examples)

- Interesting word choice and sentence variety

- Narrative, descriptive, expository, and persuasive compositions

- Written responses to literature that demonstrate understanding and careful reading

- Research reports and summaries

- Evaluation and revision of writing

The Unit Benchmark Tests and End-of-Year Benchmark Test require responses to narrative, descriptive, expository, summary, and friendly-letter writing prompts.

Other informal writing assessments are included in *Reading Street*.

- Myself as a Reader and Writer is a questionnaire in which students can reflect on their own reading and writing habits at the beginning of the school year.

- Written retellings demonstrate students' ability to understand narrative and expository text elements and to recall and record information in writing.

- Teacher-student conferences provide insights about students' writing behaviors and strategies.

- Student portfolios, containing draft and final copies of work, give evidence of students' growth and progress in writing.

- Writing logs allow students to monitor their writing growth over time.

- About My Writing is a form in which students can reflect on their writing progress at various points during the school year.

- Writing Strategy Assessments help teachers synthesize information about students' writing progress and use of writing strategies.

Writing Conventions

Skills include:

- Sentence structure, including appropriate use of appositives, participial phrases, independent and dependent clauses, etc.

- Grammar, including use of regular and irregular verbs, coordinating conjunctions, modifiers, pronouns, etc.

- Punctuation, capitalization, and spelling

Skills are assessed in the Unit and End-of-Year Benchmark Tests. The writing scoring rubrics assess sentence structure, fluency, and variety, as well as control of writing conventions.

Speaking and Listening

Skills include:

- Critical listening, thoughtful questions, and relevant responses

- Interpretation of speakers' verbal and nonverbal messages, purposes, and perspectives

- Formal presentations employing rhetorical strategies (e.g., narration, exposition, persuasion, description)

- Organization and delivery of oral presentation with focus, organizational structure, and point of view

- Clarifying and supporting spoken ideas with evidence and examples

- Engaging the audience with verbal cues, facial expressions, and gestures

- Proper phrasing, pitch, and modulation

- Analysis and evaluation of oral and media communication (e.g., persuasive techniques, logical fallacies, and transmission of culture)

Informal assessments that allow you to document students' oral language development throughout the year are oral retellings, teacher-student conference records, ongoing teacher observation, and student portfolios. Student self-assessments are opportunities for students to monitor and evaluate their growth in speaking and listening and to set goals for improvement.

Research/Study Skills

Skills include:

- Understanding and using graphic sources (e.g., charts, maps, diagrams, graphs, etc.)

- Understanding and using reference sources (e.g., dictionaries, encyclopedias, almanacs, library databases, online information, etc.)

- Understanding and using the research process

Skills are assessed informally by having students demonstrate the ability to perform a task involving the use of the skill.

What instructional strategies will help to prepare students for formal assessments and high-stakes tests?

- Use the Scott Foresman *Reading Street* program to continually monitor student progress and refine instruction to reflect your students' needs.

- Use the administration of the formal progress-monitoring and summative assessments as a way to teach test-taking skills.

- Literal, inferential, and critical-analysis questions on the Weekly, Unit, and End-of-Year Benchmark Tests are based on the question-answer framework used in instruction and are similar to question types on high-stakes assessments. Daily practice in answering literal, inferential, and critical-analysis questions will improve student achievement on high-stakes standardized tests.

- Download and examine released items from standardized assessments, reviewing the various item constructions and test vocabulary. Model and discuss the thinking steps involved in responding to multiple-choice and constructed-response items, as well as writing prompts.

- Familiarize your students with the formal language of test directions. Instruct them to listen to, restate, follow, and write test directions.

- Preteach the "language of tests" encountered in directions and test items, including:
  - Question words: *who, what, which, where, when, why,* and *how*
  - Emphasis words: *not, except, most likely, probably, major, both, neither, either, most,* and *least*
  - Action words: *explain, describe, discuss, persuade,* and *support with evidence*

- Encourage students to be careful readers and to check their own work.

- Provide repeated opportunities for practicing all of the techniques above.

References

Airasian, P. W. *Classroom Assessment: Concepts and Applications.* New York: McGraw-Hill, 2000.

Blachowicz, C. L. Z. "Vocabulary Essentials: From Research to Practice for Improved Instruction." *Research-Based Vocabulary Instruction.* Glenview, IL: Scott Foresman, 2005.

Heritage, M. "Formative Assessment: What Do Teachers Need to Know and Do?" *Phi Delta Kappan*, vol. 89, no. 2 (2007), pp. 140–145.

McTighe, J., E. Seif, and G. Wiggins. "You Can Teach for Meaning." *Educational Leadership*, vol. 62, no. 1 (September 2004), pp. 26–30.

National Reading Panel. "Teaching Children to Read: An Evidence-Based Assessment of the Scientific Research Literature on Reading and Its Implications for Reading Instruction." *Reports of the Subgroups.* National Institute for Literacy, National Institute of Child Health and Human Development, 2000.

Popham, W. J. "Instructional Insensitivity of Tests: Accountability's Dire Drawback." *Phi Delta Kappan*, vol. 89, no. 2 (October 2007), pp. 146–150, 155.

Popham, W. J. "Tawdry Tests and AYP." *Educational Leadership*, vol. 62, no. 2 (October 2004), pp. 85–86.

Stiggins, R. J. "Assessment Crisis: The Absence of Assessment for Learning." *Kappan Professional Journal.* http://www.pdkintl.org/kappan/k020sti.htm (accessed May 8, 2005).

Stiggins, R. J. "New Assessment Beliefs for a New School Mission." *Phi Delta Kappan*, vol. 86, no. 1 (September 2004), pp. 22–27.

Vaughn, S. and S. Linan-Thompson. *Research-Based Methods of Reading Instruction, Grades K–3.* Alexandria, VA: Association for Supervision and Curriculum Development, 2004.

Chapter 2 Entry-Level Assessment: What to Do at the Beginning of the Year

Overview

By fourth grade, entry-level assessment becomes complicated by several factors, including the quantity and variety of prerequisite knowledge and skills that students are expected to demonstrate they have achieved by this point in their education. Entry-level assessments determine foci for initial instruction as well as interventions that might be needed for individual students or groups of students. There are many formal and informal assessment tools and practices that determine entry-level skills and provide the type of information needed to make decisions about where to begin instruction for individual learners.

What is the purpose of using entry-level assessments?

Entry-level assessments are used for screening and diagnosis. The results of entry-level assessment tests are reported by specific knowledge and skill areas and can be used to:

- help you get to know your students and find a starting point for good instructional decisions;

- help you gather information about students' knowledge and skills in reading, writing, speaking, and listening at the beginning of the year; and

- gather specific information about students with special learning needs, such as English language learners, students with disabilities, struggling readers, and advanced learners.

What do I want to learn from entry-level assessments?

Learning where to begin instruction is the primary goal of entry-level assessments. The more you know about your students at the beginning of the year, the better equipped you are to maximize their learning experiences to ensure that they achieve continuous growth in writing, speaking, reading, and listening skills. Entry-level assessments identify students who are already proficient and need challenge, as well as those who need additional support and literacy intervention, in areas such as:

- Oral reading fluency

- Reading comprehension

- Vocabulary

- Writing

What types of assessments should be used at the beginning of the year?

Use a variety of assessment practices early in the year to screen and diagnose students' achievement of writing, speaking, reading, and listening skills. Both formal and informal assessments will help you diagnose your students' prerequisite knowledge and skills, as well as gain a personal understanding of your students.

FORMAL ASSESSMENTS

- Formal entry-level assessments provide detailed analyses of students' performance in specific domains. They make available information about the degree to which students have acquired the knowledge and skills, and they identify areas in which additional instruction is needed for particular students.

- Formal entry-level assessments can be used to:
  - assess instructional needs of individual students;
  - focus instruction to meet targeted needs of all of the students in your classroom; and
  - determine what needs to be pretaught or retaught to individual students or groups of students.

INFORMAL ASSESSMENTS

- Informal entry-level assessments provide additional information about areas where instructional support is needed. They also provide useful background information, including knowledge about students' learning styles, confidence, and interests that will help you in designing effective instructional plans.

- Informal assessments, such as conferencing with students and administering inventories, surveys, and checklists at the beginning of the school year, will help you:
  - identify students' interests and attitudes about literacy;
  - assess instructional and motivational needs of individual students;
  - assess instructional needs of the class as a whole;
  - learn specifics about students with particular needs; and
  - make focused instructional decisions.

When do I gather the information?

The best time to administer entry-level assessments is during the first few weeks of the school year. However, it is important to avoid overwhelming students with too much assessment at one time. Plan carefully and spread a variety of assessment tasks throughout the first month of school. Prioritize the tools and tasks in relation to their importance to beginning instructional planning.

What techniques and tools are available?

FORMAL ENTRY-LEVEL ASSESSMENT TOOLS AND TECHNIQUES

- **Baseline Group Test** (See pages 38–39.)
  This Scott Foresman *Reading Street* test, one at each grade level, has both a written multiple-choice format and a one-on-one teacher–student fluency subtest for grades 4 through 6. It enables you to establish baseline data for determining the level of instructional support students need and placing them into instructional groups.

- **Group Reading Assessment and Diagnostic Evaluation (GRADE)** (See pages 35–36.)
  A group-administered, norm-referenced diagnostic reading assessment for grades PreK through adult that provides information about the skills students have mastered and the skill areas in which they need mastery or intervention.

- **Developmental Reading Assessment® Second Edition (DRA2)** (See page 37.)
  This is a set of individually administered criterion-referenced reading assessments for students in kindergarten through grade 8. The DRA2 is used to identify students' independent reading levels in terms of accuracy, fluency, and comprehension.

INFORMAL ENTRY-LEVEL ASSESSMENT TOOLS AND TECHNIQUES

- **Getting to Know You Conference** (See page 40.)
  An individual conversation with a student that explores his or her learning interests, strengths, challenges, and goals

- **Myself as a Reader and Writer** (See page 41.)
  An informal questionnaire that gives your students an opportunity to identify the reading genres and topics that are of interest to them

- **Reading and Me** (See pages 42–43.)
  A survey that assesses your students' attitudes and level of confidence about their reading

- **How Do I Learn** (See page 44.)
  A survey that identifies your students' learning styles and preferences

- **Profile of English Language Learners** (See page 45.)
  A checklist that identifies the strengths and needs of students who are English language learners

- **My Child as a Learner** (See page 46.)
  A survey that provides information about your students' literacy behaviors at home

Want to learn more about entry-level assessment?

If you are interested in learning more about research that discusses the use of entry-level assessment tools and practices, you will find the following resources interesting.

2 • Entry Level

References

Allinder, R. M.; M. Rose; L. S. Fuchs; and D. Fuchs. "Issues in Curriculum-Based Assessment." In *Critical Issues in Special Education: Access, Diversity, and Accountabiity*. Eds. A. M. Sorrells, H. J. Rieth, and P. T. Sindelar. Boston: Allyn and Bacon, 2004.

Buly, M. R., and S. W. Valencia. "Below the Bar: Profiles of Students Who Fail State Reading Tests." *Educational Evaluation and Policy Analysis*, vol. 24 (2002), pp. 219–239.

Chard, D.; S. McDonagh; S. Lee; and V. Reece. "Assessing Word Recognition." In *Classroom Literacy Assessment: Making Sense of What Students Know and Do*. Eds. J. R. Paratore and R. L. McCormack. New York: Guilford Press. pp. 85–100.

Helman, L. A. "Using Literacy Assessment Results to Improve Teaching for English-Language Learners." *The Reading Teacher*, vol. 58, no. 7 (April 2005), pp. 668–677.

Johnston, P. H., and R. Roger. "Early Literacy Development: The Case for Informed Assessment." In *Handbook of Early Reading Research*. Eds. S. B. Neuman and D. K. Dickinson. New York: Guilford Press, 2001, pp. 377–389.

Kame'enui, E. J., R. H. Good, and B. A. Harn. "Beginning Reading Failure and the Quantification of Risk: Reading Behavior as the Supreme Index." In *Focus on Behavior Analysis in Education: Achievements, Challenges, and Opportunities*. Eds. W. L. Heward, et al. Upper River, NJ: Pearson/Merrill/Prentice Hall, 2005.

McMillan, James H. "Essential Assessment Concepts for Teachers and Administrators." In *Experts in Assessment* series. Eds. T. R. Guskey and R. J. Marzano. Thousand Oaks, CA: Corwin Press, Inc., 2001.

Group Reading Assessment and Diagnostic Evaluation (GRADE)

What is it?

GRADE is an accurate, in-depth, and easy-to-use entry-level assessment for pre-kindergarten children through young adult, postsecondary students. It is a normative diagnostic reading assessment that determines developmentally which skills students have mastered and where they need instruction or intervention. GRADE is a research-based assessment that can be group-administered. It was standardized and normed using the most up-to-date methodology.

Why would I use it?

You will want to use GRADE for many reasons.

- It helps you screen your students and determine the strengths and weaknesses of individuals or groups of students in relation to specific skills.

- It helps you determine your students' prerequisite skills and knowledge.

- It allows you to save time through whole-group administration as opposed to individual student administration.

- You can score the assessment and analyze results using information in the teacher manual or scoring and reporting software.

- Students who appear to have significantly above- or below-grade-level reading performance can be given an out-of-level test form.

- Parallel forms offer the opportunity to test up to four times a year.

- Results are linked to specific follow-up instruction and interventions.

- Using GRADE assessment to focus instruction will improve student achievement and help deliver Adequate Yearly Progress gains.

What does it test?

In fourth, fifth, and sixth grades, GRADE assesses essential elements of reading, including:

- Sentence and passage comprehension
- Vocabulary
- Listening comprehension

Administering earlier levels of GRADE to students in grades 4, 5, and 6 will assess their knowledge of phonemic awareness and phonics.

When do I use it?

When GRADE is used as an entry-level assessment, it should be administered by the end of the first month of school. GRADE can be used up to four times a year, with the recommendation that three months be allowed between testing sessions.

How do I use it?

- Give the appropriate grade-level assessment or an out-of-level assessment if you determine the student will perform below or above grade level.
- Analyze students' results using normative tables for converting raw scores to standards scores, stanines, percentiles, normal curve equivalents, grade equivalents, and growth-scale values.
- Use results to plan focused instruction for individuals or groups of students.
- Use activities and exercises that are correlated with the assessment results from the *GRADE Resource Library* and *Head for Success* to plan interventions for students with special learning needs.

Developmental Reading Assessment® Second Edition (DRA2)

What is it?

- The DRA2 is a set of individually-administered criterion-referenced reading assessments for students in kindergarten through grade 8. Modeled after an informal reading inventory, the DRA2 is designed to be administered, scored, and interpreted by a classroom teacher. The DRA2 for grades 4 through 6 identifies a student's independent reading level based on the student's accuracy, fluency, and comprehension.

Why would I use it?

You will want to use the DRA2 for many reasons, including:

- To identify your students' strengths and weaknesses
- To evaluate the phonological awareness and phonics skills of students in grades 1 through 5
- To help you prepare students to meet classroom and testing expectations
- To provide information about your students' reading achievement levels for Adequate Yearly Progress

What does it test?

The DRA2 assesses essential elements of reading and language arts, including:

- Independent reading level
- Reading engagement
- Oral reading fluency (rate and accuracy)
- Reading comprehension
- At the beginning of the school year, to identify students' needs in reading

When do I use it?

The DRA2 can be given twice a year (fall and spring) to provide you with information to guide instruction. It can also be administered at mid-year to identify the needs or skills of students who are challenged readers, to monitor progress, and to provide more instructional guidance.

How do I use it?

- The student completes a reading survey (orally for younger and less proficient students and in writing for levels 28 and up).
- You have an individual reading conference with each student involving the student's reading a text orally.
- As the student reads aloud, you use a text-specific observation guide to record reading behaviors and errors.
- You convert the total number of oral-reading errors to an accuracy score and calculate the student's reading fluency as words correct per minute (WCPM).

2 • Entry Level

Copyright © by Pearson Education, Inc., or its affiliates. All Rights Reserved.

37

Baseline Group Test

What is it?

- A placement test given at the beginning of the school year to establish a baseline for each student

Why would I choose it?

- To identify students who are on grade level, those who need intervention, and those who could benefit from more challenge

- To recognize how best to shape the curriculum to fit the needs of all students

What does it test?

- In grades 4–6, vocabulary words and reading comprehension skills are tested.

- Also included are a graded oral vocabulary test and a passage for testing fluency and/or doing a running record (both optional).

When do I use it?

- At the beginning of the school year, to establish baselines for students and to place them in groups according to their level of ability

- Throughout the year as needed to assess progress and determine instructional requirements of new students

How do I use it?

- The test is designed to be group administered

- Each test includes a table specifying how many correct responses indicate the various levels of mastery (Strategic Intervention, On-Level, or Advanced)

How do I use the results?

- The teacher manual includes charts with percentage scores, an evaluation chart, and an interpretation key that will allow you to place each student in an appropriate instructional group

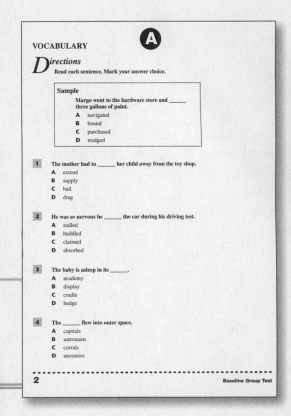

VOCABULARY

Directions
Read each sentence. Mark your answer choice.

> **Sample**
>
> Margo went to the hardware store and _____ three gallons of paint.
>
> A navigated
> B bound
> C purchased
> D trudged

1 The mother had to _____ her child away from the toy shop.
A extend
B supply
C bail
D drag

2 He was so nervous he _____ the car during his driving test.
A stalled
B huddled
C claimed
D absorbed

3 The baby is asleep in its _____.
A academy
B display
C cradle
D hedge

4 The _____ flew into outer space.
A capitals
B astronauts
C corrals
D ancestors

2   Baseline Group Test

Ⓐ Vocabulary words are tested in context.

Ⓑ Students read several passages and answer comprehension questions about them.

Samples are from Grade 5 Baseline Group Test.

READING   Ⓑ

Directions
Read each selection and answer the questions that follow. Mark your answer choice beside the best answer to each question.

One of New York City's Best Mayors: Fiorello LaGuardia

Fiorello LaGuardia's parents were immigrants. Perhaps this was the reason LaGuardia worked so hard to help people from other countries who were moving to the United States. He began his career in public service when he was only seventeen years old, working in many countries in Europe for the United States government. He later had a job on Ellis Island. This was the place where millions of people who were moving to the United States entered the country. LaGuardia had learned five languages, so he was able to help many of the people who didn't speak English.

LaGuardia became a lawyer and helped immigrants, the poor, and workers. He was later elected as a congressman. He also served as a pilot in World War I.

In 1933, he was elected mayor of New York City. He was one of only three modern-day mayors who served three terms in a row. In those twelve years, he brought about major changes. He helped create thousands of new jobs. He had many parks, playgrounds, hospitals, and schools built. He also had roads, tunnels, and bridges built. Under his leadership, New York City built an amazing transportation system. However, LaGuardia didn't let all of his big projects keep him from staying in touch with the people he served. When there was a newspaper strike in New York City and no newspapers were being sold, LaGuardia read comic strips over the radio for the children. Throughout his life, he worked to help others.

1 What did LaGuardia do first?
A served in World War I
B worked in Europe
C served as mayor of New York City
D worked on Ellis Island

GO ON

Baseline Group Test   7

---

2 What is the author's main purpose for writing this selection?
A to tell about Fiorello LaGuardia's life
B to convince people to be more helpful
C to express pride about being an immigrant
D to explain the history of New York City

3 Based on information in the selection, which of the following most likely helped LaGuardia learn so many languages?
A His parents spoke many languages at home.
B He was required to learn languages in school.
C Mayors learn many languages by serving so many people.
D He worked in many European countries as a young man.

4 Which of the following describes one way LaGuardia differed from most other New York City mayors?
A He loved the people he served.
B He made many improvements.
C He served three terms in a row.
D He knew how to fly an airplane.

5 Which word best describes LaGuardia?
A patient
B helpful
C curious
D selfish

6 Which event gave LaGuardia a chance to stay in touch with people?
A migration from Europe
B the transportation system
C the newspaper strike
D serving as a pilot

8   Baseline Group Test

Getting to Know You Conference

What is it?

- A conversation with each individual student at the beginning of the year
- An experience that personalizes learning for both you and your students

What does it show?

- A student's interests
- A student's preference for different literacy experiences
- A student's self-assessment of his or her learning strengths and challenges
- A student's learning goals for the coming year

How do I use it?

- Plan to meet individually with each student for five minutes during the first two weeks of school.
- Before the conference, prepare a list of questions to select from as you conference with each student.
- Highlight the questions that you think might be the most relevant for the particular student being interviewed.
- Questions might include:
  - What was the best book you read last year? What did you like about it?
  - What do you like to read about?
  - During choice time at school, what would you rather do: read, write, or draw? What do you usually read, write, or draw?
  - What did you do last year that you liked the best? What did you like about it?
  - What did you do last year that you liked the least? What didn't you like about it?
  - What do we do in school that is easy for you?
  - What is the hardest thing we do in school?
  - When you don't know how to do something, what do you do? How do you get help?
  - What would you like to do better this year?
- Keep notes of the conference and add them to the student's portfolio or cumulative folder.

Interest Inventory
Myself as a Reader and Writer

What is it?	• An informal questionnaire that gives students an opportunity to tell you about their reading and writing interests
	• A tool that helps students reflect on their reading and writing habits
What does it show?	• Genres and topics that are of interest to students
How do I use it?	• Have students complete the form early in the school year.
	• As an extension, ask students to exchange forms and find classmates with similar interests.
	• Place the completed forms in each student's portfolio as additional information about the student.
	• Consider using the inventory during parent conferences.

A Checklist format is easy for students to complete and for you to interpret.

B Form probes students' interests in specific topics as well as genres.

Form for reproduction is on page 128.

Student Form
Myself as a Reader and Writer

Name **Joshua Engelman** Date **Sept. 12**

	A Lot	Sometimes	Not at All
1. I like to read			
realistic fiction		✓	
fantasy stories (for example, tall tales, myths, science fiction)		✓	
historical fiction			✓
plays	✓		
biographies/autobiographies			✓
nonfiction articles	✓		
other:			
2. The subjects I like to read about most are			
students my age	✓	✓	
sports			✓
famous people			✓
exploration and adventure	✓		
how things work	✓		
things that are funny	✓	✓	
other: **what different jobs are like**	✓		
3. I like to write			
made-up stories		✓	
true stories	✓		
letters	✓		
poems			✓
reports		✓	
plays	✓		
other: **journal entries**	✓		

4. The best book or story I have read in the last year is
What Do Author's Do?

5. The best thing I have written in the last year is a piece about
how my father opened up his own business

Survey
Reading and Me

What is it?

- An in-depth survey to gauge students' feelings about and confidence in their reading

What does it show?

- How students assess various aspects of their behavior as readers
- How students think they read various kinds of materials
- The value students place on reading

How do I use it?

- Administer the survey early in the school year.
- Evaluate students' responses in the four categories that are described on page 43.
- Place the completed forms in each student's portfolio as additional information about the student.

Student Form
Reading and Me ✔

Name **Joshua Engelman** Date **9/30**

Mark the box next to the answer that tells how you feel.

1. How often do you like to read?
- ☐ All of the time
- ☐ Sometimes
- ☑ Not too often
- ☐ Never

2. When I read I
- ☐ always try my best.
- ☑ try my best most of the time.
- ☐ don't try very hard.
- ☐ often give up.

3. In general, when I read I
- ☐ really enjoy it.
- ☐ think it's OK.
- ☑ don't like it very much.
- ☐ dislike it a lot.

4. I think reading is
- ☐ my favorite thing to do.
- ☐ one of my favorite things to do.
- ☑ not one of my favorite things to do.
- ☐ my least favorite thing to do.

5. I read
- ☐ a lot better than my classmates.
- ☐ a little better than my classmates.
- ☑ about the same as my classmates.
- ☐ worse than my classmates.

6. When I am reading by myself, I understand
- ☐ most of what I read.
- ☑ some of what I read.
- ☐ not much of what I read.
- ☐ very little of what I read.

7. I am
- ☐ a great reader.
- ☐ a good reader.
- ☑ an OK reader.
- ☐ a poor reader.

8. I care what other kids think about my reading.
- ☐ never
- ☐ not too often
- ☐ sometimes
- ☑ always

9. I think that reading is
- ☐ very easy.
- ☐ kind of easy.
- ☑ kind of hard.
- ☐ very hard.

10. When I read in school I usually
- ☐ feel good about it.
- ☑ feel OK about it.
- ☐ feel not too good about it.
- ☐ feel terrible about it.

Student Form
Reading and Me (continued) ✔

Mark the box next to the answer that tells how you feel.

11. I talk with my friends about the things that I read
- ☐ all of the time.
- ☐ sometimes.
- ☑ not too often.
- ☐ never.

12. People who read a lot are
- ☐ very interesting.
- ☑ kind of interesting.
- ☐ not very interesting.
- ☐ pretty boring.

13. I think that reading in school is
- ☐ very important.
- ☐ important.
- ☑ somewhat important.
- ☐ not too important.

14. I think that reading at home is
- ☐ very important.
- ☐ important.
- ☐ somewhat important.
- ☑ not too important.

15. I like getting a book for a present.
- ☐ all the time
- ☐ sometimes
- ☑ not very often
- ☐ never

16. I read newspapers
- ☐ very well.
- ☑ pretty well.
- ☐ not too well.
- ☐ not well at all.

17. I read schoolbooks
- ☐ very well.
- ☐ pretty well.
- ☑ not too well.
- ☐ not well at all.

18. I read comics
- ☑ very well.
- ☐ pretty well.
- ☐ not too well.
- ☐ not well at all.

19. I read magazines
- ☐ very well.
- ☐ pretty well.
- ☑ not too well.
- ☐ not well at all.

20. I read storybooks or novels
- ☐ very well.
- ☑ pretty well.
- ☐ not too well.
- ☐ not well at all.

A Items 1–4 probe students' motivation as readers.

B Items 5–10 get at students' feelings about their reading and how they measure themselves against other readers.

C Items 11–15 probe the value that students put on reading.

D Items 16–20 have students assess their abilities at reading different kinds of materials.

Forms for reproduction are on pages 129–130.

Survey
How Do I Learn?

What is it?

- A form to help you recognize students with particular learning styles or preferences

What does it show?

The survey can help you begin to identify:

- students who learn best through sight or mental images (visual/spatial learners);

- students who learn best through body positions and movements (kinesthetic learners); and

- students who learn best through interactions or negotiations with others (interpersonal learners).

How do I use it?

- Have students complete the form early in the school year.

- Use the explanations below to help you begin to identify students with particular learning preferences.

A An (a) response to questions 1 and 2 helps to identify students with strong visual/spatial or interpersonal preferences, respectively.

B Consistent responses to questions 3–5 point out
(a) visual/spatial learners;
(b) kinesthetic learners;
(c) interpersonal learners.

Form for reproduction is on page 133.

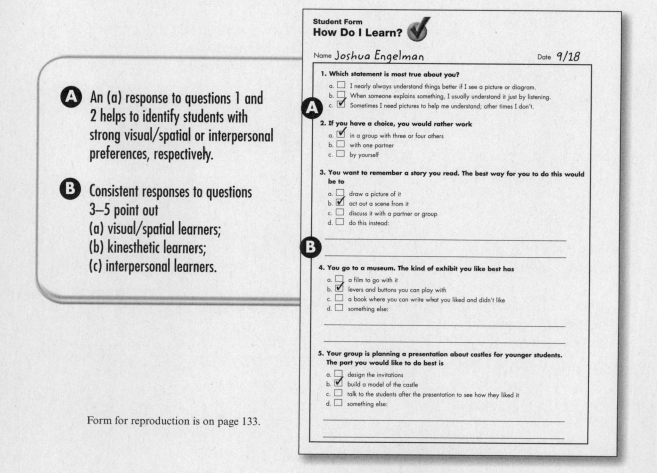

Student Form
How Do I Learn?

Name *Joshua Engelman*   Date *9/18*

1. Which statement is most true about you?
- a. ☐ I nearly always understand things better if I see a picture or diagram.
- b. ☐ When someone explains something, I usually understand it just by listening.
- c. ☑ Sometimes I need pictures to help me understand; other times I don't.

2. If you have a choice, you would rather work
- a. ☑ in a group with three or four others
- b. ☐ with one partner
- c. ☐ by yourself

3. You want to remember a story you read. The best way for you to do this would be to
- a. ☐ draw a picture of it
- b. ☑ act out a scene from it
- c. ☐ discuss it with a partner or group
- d. ☐ do this instead:
_____
_____

4. You go to a museum. The kind of exhibit you like best has
- a. ☐ a film to go with it
- b. ☑ levers and buttons you can play with
- c. ☐ a book where you can write what you liked and didn't like
- d. ☐ something else:
_____

5. Your group is planning a presentation about castles for younger students. The part you would like to do best is
- a. ☐ design the invitations
- b. ☑ build a model of the castle
- c. ☐ talk to the students after the presentation to see how they liked it
- d. ☐ something else:
_____

Survey
Profile of English Language Learners

What is it?
- A form to help identify the strengths and needs of students whose first language is not English

What does it show?
- An English language learner's proficiency with speaking, reading, and writing English

How do I use it?
- Identify students whose English proficiency you are uncertain about.
- Use the criteria on the form to assess students' abilities in the various language areas, noting specific examples.
- Use the form as a rough guideline of where students are in their English language development and where they may need help.

What do I do next?

Scott Foresman *Reading Street* offers your English language learners

- standards-based instruction at all levels of language acquisition—Beginning, Early Intermediate, Intermediate, Early Advanced, and Advanced
- the English Language Learners Handbook with instructional material and comprehensive guidance for teachers and effective, efficient, and explicit instruction for English language learners. Building on the *Reading Street* literacy instruction, the guide uses components such as ELL Posters, ELL Readers, and English Language Support (blackline masters).

Forms for reproduction are on pages 131–132.

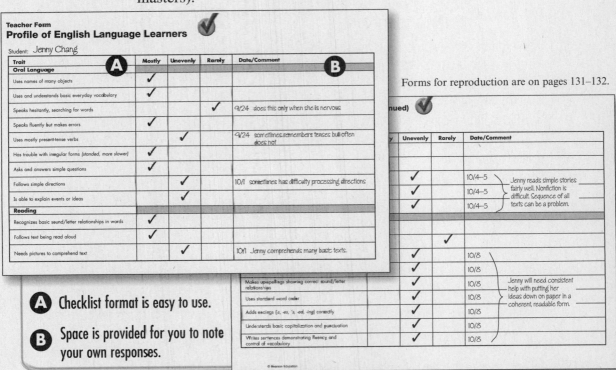

A Checklist format is easy to use.

B Space is provided for you to note your own responses.

Survey
My Child as a Learner

What is it?
- A survey to help you get to know your students better from their families' perspectives
- An opportunity to establish a positive relationship with your students' families from the start

What does it show?
- Student behaviors that families observe at home
- A family's view of a student as a learner

How do I use it?
- Send the survey home at the beginning of the school year with a cover letter explaining the value of family input.
- Place the completed form in each student's portfolio as additional information about the student.
- Discuss it during parent conferences.

(A) Checklist format is quick to complete and easy to interpret.

(B) Comments provide information specific to each student in your class.

(C) Additional comments let families offer information beyond the form.

Form for reproduction is on page 134.

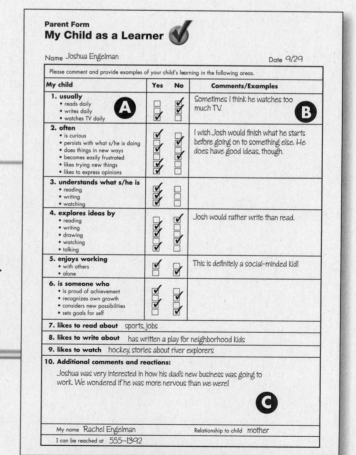

Parent Form
My Child as a Learner

Name Joshua Engelman   Date 9/29

Please comment and provide examples of your child's learning in the following areas.

My child	Yes	No	Comments/Examples
1. usually • reads daily • writes daily • watches TV daily	☐ ☐ ☑	☑ ☑ ☐	Sometimes I think he watches too much TV.
2. often • is curious • persists with what s/he is doing • does things in new ways • becomes easily frustrated • likes trying new things • likes to express opinions	☑ ☐ ☑ ☐ ☑ ☑	☐ ☑ ☐ ☑ ☐ ☐	I wish Josh would finish what he starts before going on to something else. He does have good ideas, though.
3. understands what s/he is • reading • writing • watching	☑ ☑ ☑	☐ ☐ ☐	
4. explores ideas by • reading • writing • drawing • watching • talking	☐ ☑ ☑ ☐ ☑	☑ ☐ ☐ ☑ ☐	Josh would rather write than read.
5. enjoys working • with others • alone	☑ ☐	☐ ☑	This is definitely a social-minded kid!
6. is someone who • is proud of achievement • recognizes own growth • considers new possibilities • sets goals for self	☑ ☑ ☑ ☐	☐ ☐ ☐ ☑	

7. likes to read about   sports, jobs

8. likes to write about   has written a play for neighborhood kids

9. likes to watch   hockey, stories about river explorers

10. Additional comments and reactions:
Joshua was very interested in how his dad's new business was going to work. We wondered if he was more nervous than we were!

(C)

My name Rachel Engelman   Relationship to child mother
I can be reached at 555-1392

| Chapter 3 | # Progress-Monitoring Assessment: What to Do During the Year |

Overview

Assessments designed to monitor student progress take many forms, including weekly tests; unit tests; checklists and rubrics used in self-assessment; and teacher-managed activities, such as collecting and analyzing work samples and observing students while engaged in literacy tasks. Progress-monitoring involves using a variety of formal and classroom-based assessment formats that are characterized by timely feedback aligned with instructional goals. After using entry-level assessments to determine where to begin instruction for individuals and groups of students, it becomes equally important to monitor the progress that your students make throughout the year and the effectiveness of your instruction. The assessments labeled progress-monitoring tools in this handbook provide ongoing feedback on the progress your students make toward achievement of the skills and knowledge described in the strands and domains of the national and state reading and language arts standards.

What are the benefits of progress-monitoring?

- It helps you determine if all students are progressing as expected and helps you focus instruction for individuals and groups of students, as opposed to teaching to the middle performance level in your classes.

- It allows you to determine students' progress in meeting or exceeding national and state reading and language arts standards based on a regular process of observing, monitoring, and judging the quality of their work.

- You can guide student learning better if you have an up-to-date understanding of your students' current performance levels, wasting no time on skills students have already mastered and focusing instead on the areas that need additional attention.

- Frequent use of progress-monitoring assessments gives *all* your students a more equitable opportunity to demonstrate their skills because high standards are most reliably achieved in small, consistent increases that occur over time.

- Because many progress-monitoring assessments are curriculum-embedded and aligned to instruction, they provide feedback on the effectiveness of your instruction.

What are the purposes of progress-monitoring?

- To identify mastery of national and state reading and language arts standards both at the individual student level and at the class level

- To determine when differentiation of instruction is required for individuals or groups of students

- To provide a basis for focused instructional decision-making

- To help you modify or emphasize parts of your curriculum and instruction to reflect the results of progress-monitoring assessments

- To determine report card grades and/or communicate progress to parents

- To encourage student self-assessment and evaluation by helping students learn how to make judgments about the quality of their own work

- To evaluate instructional approaches

- To promote continuous improvement

What are some typical classroom-based activities that might be used to monitor progress?

- Class discussions

- Speeches, oral readings, dramatizations, and retellings

- Drawings, sculpture, and other artwork

- Graphic organizers

- Collaborative activities and projects

- Student response logs

- Student reflective essays

When do I use progress-monitoring assessment activities?

Use the activities throughout the school year to measure students' growth and development. Make assessment part of your classroom culture, an established classroom routine, and a natural step in learning.

> "...quality is the result of regular inspections (assessments) *along the way*, followed by needed adjustments based on the information gleaned from the inspections."
> (McTighe, 1997)

Who should engage in progress-monitoring?

Although you are the primary initiator of progress-monitoring assessments, your students should be given opportunities to engage in ongoing self-monitoring. There are many benefits to involving students in their own progress monitoring. When your students participate in self-assessment practices, they are more likely to develop metacognitive awareness and exhibit self-regulating skills. This means they will become consciously aware of their learning and actively set goals designed to increase their performance. Engaging in self-assessment leads to the development of positive attitudes toward learning. Furthermore, self-assessment emphasizes application of the knowledge and skills identified in the statewide and district-wide reading and language arts standards and promotes higher-order thinking and the development of reasoning skills.

- **How can you help students become better self-assessors?**

  - Model self-monitoring by sharing your thoughts with students as you evaluate and reflect on a project you are doing, such as putting up a bulletin board, writing a note to another teacher, or drafting directions for an assignment you are going to give them.

  - Make the criteria on which students are assessed public so that they can use this information to self-assess.

  - Schedule regular times for self-assessment.

  - Give students opportunities to draft criteria for assessing their own work.

  - Provide opportunities for students to engage in activities that encourage thinking, writing, and talking about their performance.

- **What kinds of activities support self-assessment?**

  - Writing and Reading Conferences with you

  - Writing and Reading Conferences with classmates

  - Reflection journals and cognitive logs

  - Portfolio reviews

  - Use of self-assessment checklists and rubrics

  - Student-led, parent-teacher conferences

What techniques and tools are available?

FORMAL ASSESSMENT TOOLS AND TECHNIQUES FOR MONITORING PROGRESS

- **Weekly Tests** (See pages 54–55.)
  These multiple-choice tests measure students' understanding of each week's introduced vocabulary, word analysis skill, and comprehension skills as applied to a new passage.

- **Fresh Reads for Fluency and Comprehension** (See pages 56–57.)
  These multiple-choice and constructed-response tests allow students to practice comprehension skills with a new selection matched to their instructional reading level. They also provide a check of reading fluency.

- **Unit Benchmark Tests** (See pages 58–59.)
  These tests are designed to measure your students' abilities to apply target comprehension skills and other literacy skills taught in each unit.

INFORMAL ASSESSMENT TOOLS AND TECHNIQUES FOR MONITORING PROGRESS

- **Questioning Strategies** (See pages 60–61.)

  Skillful questioning is an important assessment technique. Your ability to frame and ask powerful questions is an effective way to monitor the learning progress of your students.

- **Ongoing Teacher Observation** (See page 62.)

  Observation of your students allows you to monitor their performance in the context of classroom activities and provide helpful feedback while students are in the process of learning, rather than after-the-fact.

- **Fluency Check** (See pages 63–64.)

  This assessment technique is an individually-administered procedure for recording and analyzing your students' reading rates and reading behaviors.

- **Retelling** (See pages 65–66.)

  These oral or written recountings of narrative or expository text in your students' own words serve as indicators of what they can remember after reading or listening to a text.

- **Work Habits Conference Record** (See page 67.)

  This record sheet can be used when conferencing with students and provides a way to monitor your students' understanding of task completion and time management behaviors.

- **Skills Conference Record** (See page 68.)

  This checklist allows you to capture information about your students' reading, writing, speaking, and listening behaviors, strategies, and proficiencies.

- **Observing English Language Learners** (See page 69.)

  This form allows you to record ongoing observations about your English language learners' progress in developing reading skills.

> "Research on accomplished readers demonstrates that they are planful and aware and capable of online monitoring of their reading."
> (Afflerbach, 2001)

- **Student Self-Assessment** (See page 70.)

  This form provides your students with an opportunity to assess themselves as readers, writers, and learners.

- **Peer Assessment** (See page 71.)

  This form affords your students an opportunity to assess a peer's work and apply what they are learning about the quality of effective reading, writing, and speaking.

- **Group Assessment** (See page 72.)

  This form allows students to assess their collaborative efforts during group work as well as those of other group members.

- **Student Portfolios** (See pages 73–74.)

  Maintaining a portfolio is a process that allows your students to use work samples to document and reflect on their growth in reading, writing, speaking, and listening. See Chapter 7 for descriptions of the Portfolio Guide and the Portfolio Selection Slips.

- **Reading Log** (See page 75.)

  This form allows students to keep track of the literature they have read, as well as rate the quality of the selections.

- **About My Reading** (See page 76.)

  This form encourages your students to describe and evaluate their own reading progress.

- **Writing Log** (See page 77.)

  This form helps students keep track of and reflect on the pieces they have written.

- **About My Writing** (See page 78.)

  This form encourages your students to describe and evaluate their own writing progress.

Want to learn more about progress-monitoring assessment?

If you would like to learn more about how to use progress-monitoring assessment practices in your classroom, you will find the following resources interesting.

References

Afflerbach, P. *Understanding and Using Reading Assessment K–12.* Newark, NJ: International Reading Association, 2007.

Afflerbach, P. "Teaching Reading Self-Assessment Strategies." In *Comprehension Instruction: Research-Based Best Practices.* Eds. C. Block and M. Pressley. New York: The Guilford Press, 2001, pp. 96–111.

Bailey, J. M., and T. R. Guskey. "Implementing Student-Led Conferences." In *Experts in Assessment* series. Eds. T. R. Guskey and R. J. Marzano. Thousand Oaks, CA: Corwin Press, Inc., 2001.

Danielson, C., and L. Abrutyn. *An Introduction to Using Portfolios in the Classroom.* Alexandria, VA: ASCD, 1997.

Gambrell, L. B.; P. S. Koskinen; and B. A. Kapinus. "Retelling and the Reading Comprehension of Proficient and Less-Proficient Readers." *Journal of Educational Research*, vol. 84 (1991), pp. 356–363.

Gambrell, L. B.; W. Pfeiffer; and R. Wilson. "The Effects of Retelling Upon Reading Comprehension and Recall of Text Information." *Journal of Educational Research*, vol. 78 (1985), pp. 216–220.

Good, R. H.; D. C. Simmons; and S. Smith. "Effective Academic Interventions in the United States: Evaluating and Enhancing the Acquisition of Early Reading Skills." *School Psychology Review*, vol. 27, no. 1 (1998), pp. 45–56.

Hasbrouck, J. E., and G. Tindal. "Curriculum-Based Oral Reading Fluency Norms for Students in Grades 2 through 5." *Teaching Exceptional Children*, vol. 24 (1992), pp. 41–44.

Keene, E. O., and S. Zimmermann. *Mosaic of Thought.* Portsmouth, NH: Heinemann, 1997.

Marzano, R. J.; D. Pickering; and J. E. Pollock. *Classroom Instruction That Works: Research-Based Strategies for Increasing Student Achievement.* Alexandria, VA: ASCD, 2001.

Marzano, R. J., et al. *Handbook for Classroom Instruction That Works.* Alexandria, VA: ASCD, 2001.

McMillan, J. H. "Essential Assessment Concepts for Teachers and Administrators." In *Experts in Assessment* series. Eds. T. R. Guskey and R. J. Marzano. Thousand Oaks, CA: Corwin Press, Inc., 2001.

McTighe, J. "What Happens Between Assessments?" *Educational Leadership*, Vol. 54, no. 4 (1997), pp. 6–12.

Morrow, L. M. "Effects of Structural Guidance in Story Retelling on Children's Dictation of Original Stories." *Journal of Reading Behavior*, vol. 18, no. 2 (1986), pp. 135–152.

Moss, B. "Teaching Expository Text Structures Through Information Trade Book Retellings." *The Reading Teacher*, vol. 57, no. 8 (May 2004), pp. 710–718.

Pappas, C. C. "Fostering Full Access to Literacy by Including Information Books." *Language Arts*, vol. 68, no. 6 (October 1991), pp. 449–462.

Raphael, T. E. "Teaching Question Answer Relationships, Revisited." *The Reading Teacher*, vol. 39, no. 6 (February 1986), pp. 516–522.

Wixson, K. K., and M. N. Yochum. "Research on Literacy Policy and Professional Development: National, State, District, and Teacher Contexts." *Elementary School Journal*, vol. 105, no. 2 (November 2004), pp. 219–242.

Wood, K. D.; D. B. Taylor; B. Drye; and M. J. Brigman. "Assessing Students' Understanding of Informational Text in Intermediate- and Middle-Level Classrooms." In *Classroom Literacy Assessment: Making Sense of What Students Know and Do.* Eds. J. R. Paratore and R. L. McCormack. New York: The Guilford Press, 2007, pp. 195–209.

Weekly Tests

What are they?	• Tests designed to measure students' understanding of the skills and vocabulary words of the week
	• Tests consisting of multiple-choice questions
Why would I choose them?	• To assess students' understanding of the vocabulary words, decoding skill, and comprehension skills of the week
	• To monitor student mastery of skills
What do they test?	• Understanding of vocabulary words taught in a reading selection
	• Word analysis skills
	• Comprehension—target and review skills
	• Ability to respond in writing to the "Look Back and Write" assignments in the Student Edition
When do I use them?	• At the end of Day 5 in each week
How do I use them?	• The tests are designed to be group-administered.
How do I use the results?	• To identify students who can successfully construct meaning from a reading selection and to identify which students need intervention
	• To identify the specific vocabulary words, decoding skills, and comprehension skills a student has and has not mastered

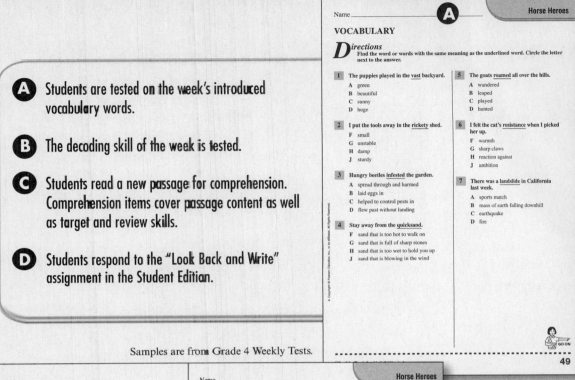

A Students are tested on the week's introduced vocabulary words.

B The decoding skill of the week is tested.

C Students read a new passage for comprehension. Comprehension items cover passage content as well as target and review skills.

D Students respond to the "Look Back and Write" assignment in the Student Edition.

Samples are from Grade 4 Weekly Tests.

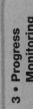

Page 49 sample:

Name _____ **A** Horse Heroes

VOCABULARY

Directions
Find the word or words with the same meaning as the underlined word. Circle the letter next to the answer.

1 The puppies played in the vast backyard.
A green
B beautiful
C sunny
D huge

2 I put the tools away in the rickety shed.
F small
G unstable
H damp
J sturdy

3 Hungry beetles infested the garden.
A spread through and harmed
B laid eggs in
C helped to control pests in
D flew past without landing

4 Stay away from the quicksand.
F sand that is too hot to walk on
G sand that is full of sharp stones
H sand that is too wet to hold you up
J sand that is blowing in the wind

5 The goats roamed all over the hills.
A wandered
B leaped
C played
D hunted

6 I felt the cat's resistance when I picked her up.
F warmth
G sharp claws
H reaction against
J ambition

7 There was a landslide in California last week.
A sports match
B mass of earth falling downhill
C earthquake
D fire

GO ON

49

Page 50 sample:

WORD ANALYSIS

Directions
Find the compound word in each sentence. Circle the letter next to the answer.

8 Heidi's brother is training to be a lifeguard at the beach.
F lifeguard
G training
H beach
J brother

9 I felt bad when I broke the pretty, green flowerpot.
A felt
B broke
C green
D flowerpot

10 The hungriest person at the table always gets the last pancake on the platter.
F hungriest
G person
H pancake
J platter

11 I leaned my elbows on the windowsill and let the summer breeze cool my flushed face.
A elbows
B windowsill
C summer
D flushed

12 Tom raised an eyebrow when he heard the startling news.
F eyebrow
G startling
H raised
J news

B

COMPREHENSION

The Play's the Thing

William Shakespeare is the greatest playwright who ever ... London during the 1500s and 1600s. He wrote more than thir... His plays are still acted today in every country of the world. ... know anything about our theaters today! Things were very di...

Shakespeare's plays were acted out in a London theater ca... was shaped like an open can. It had a roof only around the ed... open to the sky. That center space was called the pit. People ...

50

Page 51 sample:

Name _____ Horse Heroes

pay a penny or two to stand in the pit. These people were called *groundlings* because they stood on the ground to watch the play. Groundlings made every play very lively. They often yelled at the actors. They would boo loudly when a villian came on stage. When two actors fought with swords, they would cheer loudly for their favorite.

For people who could afford higher prices, the Globe had seats. These seats were hard, uncomfortable, wooden benches. They looked just like benches in a gym. Each bench was one step above and behind the row in front of it, so that everyone could see over the people in front. There were three decks, or stories, of seats at the Globe.

There were no electric lights in the 1500s. Fire was the only source of light. Since the Globe was made of wood, fire was dangerous. The actors only used fire when they had to. Plays were always acted during the day. The sunlight came right through the big, open space above the pit. It shone on the stage and the audience. If it rained, the groundlings would get wet. Today, plays are acted in indoor theaters at night. The audience sits quietly in a darkened room. The only lights are the ones focused on the stage.

Shakespeare would never have recognized the sets and costumes in today's theaters. Most theaters spend a lot of money on furniture, design, and costumes. These are very ...

C

GO ON

51

Page 53 sample:

Name _____ Horse Heroes

WRITTEN RESPONSE TO THE SELECTION

Look Back and Write Look back at pages 268–271. What made Gato and Mancha so amazing? Provide evidence to support your answer.

D

The information in the box below will help you remember what you should think about when you write your composition.

REMEMBER—YOU SHOULD

☐ write about why Gato and Mancha were so amazing.

☐ make sure you support your points with details from the text.

☐ use time order words to show the sequence of events.

☐ try to use correct spelling, capitalization, punctuation, grammar, and sentences.

GO ON

Weekly Test 9 Unit 2 Week 4   53

Fresh Reads for Fluency and Comprehension

What are they?
- Tests that give students an opportunity to practice oral fluency and the comprehension skills of the week with a new selection, a "fresh read," matched to each student's instructional reading level
- Tests consisting of multiple-choice and constructed-response questions

Why would I choose them?
- To assess students' abilities to derive meaning from new selections that are at their instructional reading levels
- To retest a student's reading after administering a Weekly Test
- To check a student's reading rate
- To monitor student mastery of *Reading Street* skills

What do they test?
- The target and review comprehension skills of the week
- Comprehension of the reading selection through literal, inferential, and critical-analysis questions
- Reading fluency

When do I use them?
- Throughout the year, each week after students have been taught the comprehension skill lesson

How do I use them?
- One option is for the student to read the passage aloud to you as a fluency check.
- Another option is for the student to complete the pages as extra skill practice.
- Teachers choose which of the three types of reading passages for the week to give to each student: Strategic Intervention (SI), On-Level (OL), or Advanced (A).

How do I use the results?
- To gather additional information about a student's ability to comprehend a passage written at his or her instructional reading level
- To gather additional information about the specific comprehension skills a student has and has not mastered
- To monitor a student's progress in fluent reading

A — First worksheet

Name _____

Read the selection. Then answer the questions that follow.

Why the Raven Is Black

The people of the far north tell this story about Owl and Raven, who were best	16
friends. One day, Raven made a lovely new dress for Owl. Since Raven had been so	32
nice, Owl then began to make a white dress for Raven. Owl worked at night by the light	50
of a lamp that burned heavy oil. Owl tried to measure Raven for the dress, but Raven	67
kept hopping around.	70
"Oh, I'm going to be so beautiful!" Raven cried as she hopped.	82
"Stop that hopping," Owl warned. "You'll knock over the lamp."	92
But Raven would not stand still. Just as owl had predicted, Raven finally knocked	106
over the lamp. The black oil spilled all over the white dress. That is why Raven is black.	124

Turn the page.

Fresh Reads Unit 1 Week 2 SI   7

Second worksheet

Name _____

Read the selection. Then answer the questions that follow.

The Spider Tower

The Zuni people of the Southwest tell an ancient story about a spider who saved a	16
hunter. The hunter was in the desert when suddenly a group of men from another tribe	32
came upon him. They told him he could not hunt on their land, though the desert did not	50
belong to anyone at that time. They chased him into a deep canyon. Outnumbered, the	65
hunter did not want to argue. He looked for a way to escape. He came to a tall narrow	84
pillar of rock. It rose hundreds of feet above the canyon floor like a tower.	99
The hunter thought that the sides of the tower were too smooth to climb. As he got	116
closer, he realized that a rope hung down from the top. As his pursuers drew near, the	133
hunter grabbed the rope and climbed. When he reached the top, he gathered up the rope.	149
The hunter was exhausted by the time he reached the summit of the tower. He	164
collapsed and rested. He could hear the men below. Even when it sounded as if they'd	180
left, he stayed for days, drinking rainwater and eating birds' eggs.	191
When he felt safe again and was about to leave, he suddenly wondered where the	206
rope had come from. He followed it to a huge, strong spider web. In the center of the	224
web sat the spider, who had seen his plight and saved him.	236
The hunter thanked the spider, and then used the rope to descend to the canyon floor	252
and return home safely.	256

Turn the page.

Fresh Reads Unit 1 Week 2 A   11

(A)

Third worksheet

Name _____

(C)

Read the selection. Then answer the questions that follow.

The Cricket and the Mountain Lion

The Native Americans of California tell this story about a cricket who chased away	14
a mountain lion. The mountain lion jumped onto a hollow log and sat down. Before he	30
had settled down, a cricket hopped out of the log and scolded him.	43
"Get off my roof, trespasser!" Cricket yelled.	50
Lion just looked at Cricket. He could not believe that this tiny creature was telling	65
him what to do. He climbed off the log and crouched low on the ground, eye to eye	83
with Cricket.	85
"I am the chief of the whole animal tribe," said Lion haughtily. "I can do as I please.	103
Why, I could crush your house with one paw!"	112
"If you did, you'd be sorry," said Cricket. "My cousin will come after you if you do	129
anything like that."	132
"I am not afraid of any insect," Lion growled. "Tell your cousin to meet us here	148
tomorrow. If he can make me run away, I will never bother you again. If he can't, well,	166
you better get ready to move."	172
The next morning, Lion returned to Cricket's log. As he called out to Cricket, he	187
heard a buzzing in his ear. Suddenly that ear began to sting and itch, and Lion howled	204
in pain.	206
"Meet my cousin, Mosquito," said Cricket.	212
Lion scratched his ear furiously, shook his head, and begged Cricket to make	225
Mosquito leave him alone.	229
"That's enough, Cousin," said Cricket. Mosquito flew out of Lion's ear. Lion	241
bounded away as fast as he could. And he never came back.	253

Fresh Reads Unit 1 Week 2 OL

Questions page

Answer the questions below.

(B)

1 Why did Cricket scream at Lion?
A Lion threatened Cricket.
B Lion crushed Cricket's house.
C Lion sat on Cricket's log.
D Lion made too much noise.

2 What caused Lion's ear to sting?
F Cricket was yelling at him.
G Mosquito was buzzing in it.
H Lion was shaking his head.
J Lion was scratching his ear.

3 What was the effect of Lion's meeting with Mosquito?
A Lion ran away.
B Lion threatened Cricket.
C Lion slapped Mosquito.
D Lion challenged Cricket.

4 How would you describe the change in Lion at the end of the story?
F He became less boastful.
G He became less patient.
H He became more foolish.
J He became more angry.

5 Why do you think people would enjoy a story about a cricket who chased away a lion?

_____
_____
_____
_____
_____
_____

10   Fresh Reads Unit 1 Week 2 OL

Callout box

A Passages of different instructional levels

B Questions on the target skill and review skill of the week

C Opportunity for fluency check

Samples are from Grade 5 Fresh Reads.

Unit Benchmark Tests

What are they?
- Tests designed to measure the students' ability to apply the target comprehension skills and other literacy skills taught during the unit

Why would I choose them?
- To assess students' understanding and use of specific skills
- To identify skill areas in which students need intervention and continued practice
- To know that there are sufficient items per individual skill to track a student's proficiency with that skill

What do they test?
- Unit reading comprehension skills through literal, inferential, and critical-analysis questions
- Vocabulary
- Writing conventions (grammar, usage, mechanics, and spelling)
- Writing—response to prompt
- Reading fluency

When do I use them?
- Throughout the year, at the end of each of the six-week units

How do I use them?
- All portions of the tests are designed to be group-administered except for the fluency passages.
- The fluency passages are to be individually administered.

How do I use the results?
- To identify students who can successfully construct meaning from a reading selection and to identify students who need intervention
- To identify specific skills students have and have not mastered
- As feedback about the effectiveness of your instruction and to help plan instruction for the next unit

Sample A

Directions

Read this selection about planning and building a playground. Then do Numbers 12 through 22.

GRAND OPENING OF TOWN PLAYGROUND

Yesterday afternoon, Pine Lake marked the opening of its new playground. There were balloons, speeches, and a lot of prizes. The people of Pine Lake are proud of their new playground. They are also proud that everybody worked together to build it.

It all started last September in a fourth-grade classroom. The teacher, Miss Green, asked her class to think about Pine Lake. Miss Green wondered how the town could be better. Her students decided that a playground would enhance the town.

Some students drew pictures of a new playground. Others wrote stories about it. Students in other classes got excited about the idea too. They talked to family members about the project. Everyone worked to make the dream come true.

A group of parents met to work on park plans. Mrs. Schein said, "I was sure many people would lend a hand. We sent out a letter asking people to list ways they could help. A lot of people answered the letter. Some said they could build things. Others agreed to pick up supplies. An artist made a poster. Neighborhood businesses gave money and goods."

In January, the town had a planning day. The children had many ideas about the playground. They knew what they wanted. Sue Wing, a builder, wrote down the ideas. She spent the next month drawing the design. Wing said, "Designing the playground was the most fun I have had in years. The kids had such good ideas."

GO ON

Benchmark Test Unit 2 — 7

Grade 4, Unit 2

Samples are from Grade 4 Unit Benchmark Tests.

Sample B

March was building month. Wood, sand, and other goods were ordered. Helpers picked up the supplies and dropped them off beside the lake. Tom Smith used his bulldozer to level the ground at the site.

Last Saturday, the people of Pine Lake built the playground. The weather was warm and sunny. It was a great day for building. Over two hundred people showed up to help. Some people were unavailable, but everybody who was there went to work. By the end of the day, the job was done. Pine Lake had its new playground.

12 What is the main idea of this selection?

F There were balloons, prizes, and speeches at the grand opening.
G Pine Lake needed a new playground for the town.
H Miss Green's class was responsible for the new playground.
J The people of Pine Lake built a new playground together.

13 You would most likely see writing like this in

A a local newspaper.
B an encyclopedia.
C an atlas.
D a sports magazine.

14 What happened in January?

F The idea of a playground was introduced.
G The playground was built.
H The playground materials were ordered.
J The town planned the playground.

15 What did Tom Smith do for the playground?

A He led the parents' group.
B He designed the playground.
C He gave money.
D He leveled the ground.

8

Sample C

PART 2: VOCABULARY

Directions

Mark your answer choice for Numbers 23 through 32.

23 The first selection explained that the blueberry is a *native* plant. What does *native* mean?

A was brought here first by the settlers
B has always been here
C is well-liked by the people who live here
D makes people healthy

24 In the second selection, Miss Green wondered how the town could be better. Her students decided a playground would *enhance* the town. The word *enhance* means

F destroy.
G shrink.
H be costly for.
J improve.

25 *National* Blueberry Month is celebrated in July. What is the base word of *national*?

A nat
B nation
C tion
D al

26 Americans grow about 300 million pounds of [ ] replace *every year* in this sentence?

F yearable
G yearal
H yearful
J yearly

27 Native Americans drank blueberry juice to cu[ ]

A soften.
B increase.
C spread.
D fix.

Sample D

PART 4: WRITING

> **PROMPT**
>
> Both "The All-American Berry" and "Grand Opening of Town Playground" tell about things people know how to make or do. Think of something you know how to do. It could be cooking a meal, throwing a football, building a birdhouse, playing a game, or something else. Write to explain how to do what you know how to do.

> **CHECKLIST FOR WRITERS**
>
> _____ Did I think about something that I know how to do?
> _____ Did I take notes about the activity before I started writing?
> _____ Did I write my explanation in the correct order?
> _____ Did I use words and details that clearly express my ideas?
> _____ Do my sentences make sense?
> _____ Did I check my sentences for proper grammar and punctuation?
> _____ Did I check my spelling?
> _____ Did I make sure my paper is the way I want readers to read it?

16   Benchmark Test Unit 2

A Students read selections in a variety of genres.

B Students respond to multiple-choice and writing questions.

C Vocabulary skills and writing conventions are tested.

D Students produce original compositions relating selections in test to unit themes and writing instruction.

Questioning Strategies

Why is questioning important?

- While asking questions is a routine practice for teachers, it is often overlooked as our most powerful tool for instruction and assessment.

- Artfully crafted questions engage students, focus their attention, stimulate their thinking, facilitate their understanding, and deepen their comprehension.

- Student self-generated questions improve learning and strengthen problem-solving and critical-thinking skills.

How do I use effective questioning strategies?

> "Our questions help us formulate our beliefs about teaching and learning, and those beliefs underlie our instructional decisions."
>
> (Keene & Zimmermann, 1997)

- Selectively choose questions for specific purposes (e.g., recall-level questions about sequence of ideas and analytic questions about the theme of a story).

- Ask questions that represent diverse thinking activities—recall, analysis, comparison, inference, and evaluation.

- Design questions that emphasize both content and the thinking needed to process the content, using such verbs as *list, define, compare, conclude,* and *defend.*

- Remember that when students are asked to analyze information, they will learn more than if asked simply to recall or identify information.

- Listen carefully to students' answers in order to shape skillful follow-up questions.

- Ask probing follow-up questions that help students extend their thinking and clarify and support their points of view.

- Allow wait time because it gives students time to think and provides answering opportunities for those who process more slowly.

- Model question-asking and question-answering behavior and provide repeated opportunities for students to practice generating their own questions.

- Model questioning with a variety of texts and, through reading conferences with the students, monitor their developing use of questioning.

- Guide students in understanding that through their own questions, they can actively regulate their reading and learning.

How does Scott Foresman *Reading Street* support effective questioning practices?

- Questioning strategies are based on a question-answer framework suggesting an interaction among the question, the text to which it refers, and the prior knowledge of the reader (Raphael, 1986).

- Students are taught that answering comprehension questions in class and on tests demands thinking: they have to analyze the questions in order to provide the right answers.

- Students learn that answers to questions can be found **In the Book** and **In My Head.**

- **In the Book** questions can be:

  - **Right There** questions, which are *literal* and focus on ideas explicitly stated in the text. The words in the question may match the words in the passage.

  - **Think and Search** questions, which are also *literal* and require students to locate and integrate information from within different sections of the text.

- **In My Head** questions can be:

  - **Author and Me** questions, which are *inferential* in nature, requiring students to interpret information and connect themes and major ideas with their own background knowledge. The most demanding **Author and Me** questions necessitate use of critical analysis as readers evaluate and justify the purpose, content, and quality of text.

  - **On My Own** questions are not based on the text and can be answered from the students' general background knowledge and experience. These questions are often posed by teachers in order to activate prior knowledge before reading and/or to extend the learning beyond the lesson.

- The Scott Foresman *Reading Street* formal assessments offer students a variety of engaging narrative and expository texts, and students respond to test items designed to assess how they use their comprehension skills in constructing meaning.

- Literal, inferential, and critical-analysis questions on the formal assessments are based on the question-answer framework used in instruction and are similar to question types on high-stakes assessments.

- Daily practice in answering, analyzing, and asking **Right There, Think and Search,** and **Author and Me** questions will improve student achievement on high-stakes standardized tests.

Ongoing Teacher Observation

What is it?

- Observation that occurs in the context of teaching or classroom activities
- A way to check students' progress on a daily or weekly basis
- The basis for developing a concrete plan for dealing with individual students' classroom strengths or needs

How do I make observations?

- Choose one or more students to focus on each day.
- Select the literacy behavior, strategy, or skill that you wish to observe.
- Observe those students as they are participating in classroom activities.
- Using a clipboard, sticky note, customized form, or checklist, note a student's behavior or performance in the targeted skills.
- Include any comments, insights, or other information you regard as significant.
- Develop a record-keeping system that is convenient and informative for you.

Why should I record my observations?

- To remember information when you need to reflect on a student at the end of the day, week, grading period, or year
- As a helpful tool for presenting information to students, parents, and administrators
- For documentation when you need to explain why you've placed a student in a particular group or given a certain grade
- To plan intervention strategies for students needing special attention

Fluency Check

What is it?

- An individually-administered procedure of recording and analyzing a student's specific reading behaviors
- A method of deciding whether a text is at the appropriate instructional level for a student
- A means of determining the level of support a student will need while reading the material

What does it show?

- Teachers who administer regular fluency checks gather evidence about the following:
  - oral reading skills and fluency calculated as words correct per minute
  - decoding and word recognition strategies
  - reading strategies a student uses and how he or she uses them to derive meaning

When do I use it?

- As often as necessary to get a clear and ongoing picture of a student's precise reading behaviors (for example, at the beginning or end of a unit or grading period, or when you need to report progress to interested parties)

How do I use it?

- Use an excerpt from Scott Foresman *Reading Street*, from a trade book, or any other text that is at an appropriate reading level for the student.
- Make one photocopy of the passage for yourself and one for the student.
- Use a watch with a second hand to time the student's reading for exactly one minute.
- Observe the student closely as he or she reads aloud and note the miscues or errors that are made.

3 • Progress Monitoring

**How do I use it?
(continued)**

• Use the following notations and symbols for errors:

– **Last Word Read ( ])** – Put a bracket after the last word the student reads in one minute.

– **Mispronunciation/misreading (/)** – Write the student's pronunciation of the word.

– **Substitutions** – Write the substituted word above the text word. Cross out the text word. If it is a nonsense word, write it phonetically.

– **Self-correction (sc)** – Write *sc* in a circle next to the corrected word/text; this is not considered an error.

– **Insertions (∧)** – Write the text word/phrase and the inserted word/phrase. Mark each insertion with a caret. Include any repetitions of words.

– **Omissions** – Circle the word(s) or word part(s) omitted.

The formula is:

Total number of words read in one minute – Number of errors = Words correct per minute

Teacher Form
Retelling

What is retelling?

- A post-reading recall of what students can remember from reading or listening to a particular text
- An oral or written recounting of narrative or expository text in a student's own words
- A reminder for students that the purpose of reading is to make sense of text

What does it show?

- A holistic view of a student's understanding of text
- Students' ability to understand narrative text elements and author's purpose and to connect stories to personal experiences and other texts
- Students' ability to understand expository text—the relationship of main ideas and details, organizational structure, author's purpose, and inferences—and to connect texts to personal experiences and prior knowledge (Moss, 2004)
- Oral and written language development

What does the research say?

- Several researchers (Gambrell, Koskinen, and Kapinus, 1991; Gambrell, Pfeiffer, and Wilson, 1985; Morrow, 1986) have found that using retellings improves student understanding of text.

How do I do it?

- In preparation:
  - Have students attempt to retell narrative or expository texts only after you have taught and modeled the procedure and students understand the task.
  - Have students practice in groups before retelling for assessment purposes.
  - Teach text structures (narrative and expository) separately to avoid confusing students.
- Oral retellings should be administered individually. Written retellings can be administered individually or in a group.
- For oral retellings, read the passage aloud to the student or have the student read the selected text. Remind the student to remember everything he or she has heard or read. Then ask the student to tell you everything about what was read. Use prompts, such as "Can you tell me more about that?"; "What happened next?"; and "What else do you remember?" At the end of the retelling, use follow-up questions (e.g., main idea, author's purpose, personal response, etc.) to gain a deeper understanding of the student's comprehension.

3 • Progress Monitoring

How do I do it? (continued)

- For written retellings, read the text aloud to students or ask them to read it silently. Remind the students to remember everything they can. Immediately after reading, have students write out what they remember about the text.

How do I use the Retelling Forms?

- Record your scores and observations on either the narrative or the expository checklist. Try to record at least one narrative retelling and one expository retelling from each student per unit.

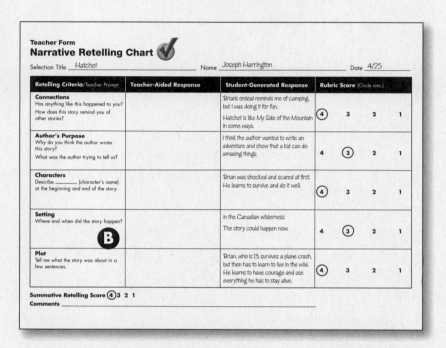

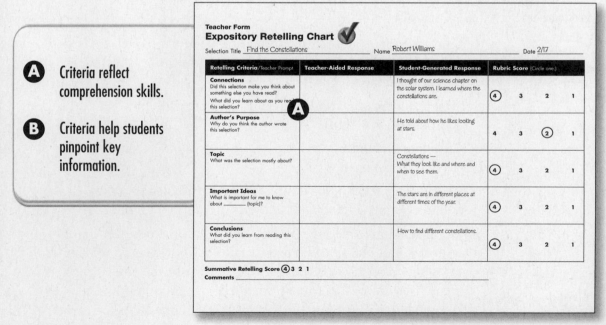

A Criteria reflect comprehension skills.

B Criteria help students pinpoint key information.

Forms for reproduction are on pages 135–136.

Teacher Form
Work Habits Conference Record

What is it?
- A means of assessing a student's understanding of tasks and time management behaviors

What does it show?
- A student's ability to set priorities and manage time
- A student's behavior toward problem-solving tasks

How do I use it?
- Plan to confer with each student at least once per grading period.
- Use the form for frequent, ongoing, informal conversations about the student's ability to manage time, set priorities, identify resources, follow directions, and articulate task completion processes.
- Tailor each conference to the student's needs, interests, and abilities; encourage him or her to take an active role.

A Did the student understand the assignment's purpose and procedures? Did he or she follow directions?

B Was the student able to decide which parts of the assignment had to be done first?

C Did the student allot time appropriately and use the time productively?

D Did the student know when it was time to seek help? Did he or she seek out the right resources (books, peers, teacher, and so on)?

E Was the student able to clearly articulate how he or she carried out the assignment, as well as the goals set in the process?

Teacher Form
Work Habits Conference Record

Student Erika Sato

Use the key at the bottom of the page to assess student's performance.

Date	Understands tasks	Sets priorities	Uses time appropriately	Solves problems effectively	Seeks help when needed	Completes tasks on time	Can explain process/ project effectively	Comments
9/20	2	2	3	2	1	2	1	Needs to bring more of herself to discussion group.
10/24	2	2	3	2	2	2	2	Doing more independent thinking.
	A	**B**	**C**		**D**		**E**	

4 Does more than expected	3 Does what was expected	2 Does less than expected	1 Does not fulfill the assignment or does not complete the assignment

Form for reproduction is on page 137.

Teacher Form
Skills Conference Record

What is it?
- A means of focusing and recording results of conversations with a student about his or her reading, writing, speaking, and listening

What does it show?
- A student's behaviors, strategies, and proficiencies in the areas of reading, writing, speaking, and listening

How do I use it?
- Plan to confer with each student at least once per grading period.
- Use the form for frequent, ongoing, informal conversations about the student's progress, strengths, and areas for improvement.
- Tailor each conference to the student's needs, interests, and abilities; encourage him or her to take an active role.

A Specific criteria in each area show particular strengths and needs.

B Comments can be made to record student's behavior or a specific concern.

C Checklist covers the continuum of student's skill growth.

Form for reproduction is on page 138.

Teacher Form
Skills Conference Record   Grade 4

Student: Elisa Ramsey   Teacher: Ms. Sills

		Proficient	Developing	Having Difficulty	Not showing trait
Reading Comments:	Sets own purpose for reading	✓	☐	☐	☐
	Predicts and asks questions	✓	☐	☐	☐
	Retells/Summarizes	✓	☐	☐	☐
	Reads fluently	✓	☐	☐	☐
	Understands key ideas in a text	☐	✓	☐	☐
	Uses decoding strategies	✓	☐	☐	☐
	Makes text connections	☐	✓	☐	☐
	Other:	☐	☐	☐	☐
Writing Comments: Elisa is working on using more specific language.	Follows writing process	✓	☐	☐	☐
	Develops central idea with details	☐	✓	☐	☐
	Organizes ideas logically	☐	✓	☐	☐
	Reveals purpose with voice	☐	✓	☐	☐
	Expresses ideas with word choice	☐	✓	☐	☐
	Uses varied sentence structure	☐	☐	☐	☐
	Uses language conventions appropriately	✓	☐	☐	☐
	Other:	☐	☐	☐	☐
Speaking and Listening Comments:	Follows instructions	✓	☐	☐	☐
	Asks questions	✓	☐	☐	☐
	Answers questions	✓	☐	☐	☐
	Paraphrases	✓	☐	☐	☐
	Participates in discussions	✓	☐	☐	☐
	Makes eye contact with audience	☐	✓	☐	☐
	Other:	☐	☐	☐	☐

Teacher Form
Observing English Language Learners

What is it?
- A form to record your ongoing observations about how English language learners process what they read

What does it show?
- How English language learners use strategies to make sense of materials they read
- Students' growth and development in processing what they read

How do I use it?
- Work with students individually as they read a new selection.
- Record your observations about how students deal with new words and concepts.
- Continue to review and record students' behaviors periodically as needed.
- Consider using the information on the form in parent conferences.

A Behaviors identify common strategies for success in reading a new language.

B Space is provided to record students' development over time.

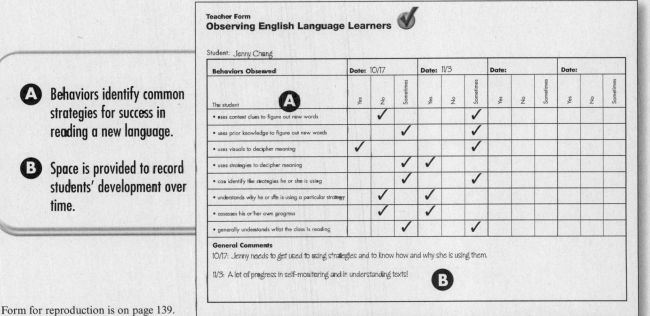

Teacher Form
Observing English Language Learners

Student: Jenny Chang

Behaviors Observed	Date: 10/17			Date: 11/3			Date:			Date:		
The student	Yes	No	Sometimes	Yes	No	Sometimes	Yes	No	Sometimes	Yes	No	Sometimes
• uses context clues to figure out new words		✓				✓						
• uses prior knowledge to figure out new words			✓			✓						
• uses visuals to decipher meaning	✓					✓						
• uses strategies to decipher meaning			✓	✓								
• can identify the strategies he or she is using			✓			✓						
• understands why he or she is using a particular strategy	✓			✓								
• assesses his/her own progress	✓			✓								
• generally understands what the class is reading			✓			✓						

General Comments

10/17: Jenny needs to get used to using strategies and to know how and why she is using them.

11/3: A lot of progress in self-monitoring and in understanding texts!

Form for reproduction is on page 139.

3 • Progress Monitoring

Student Form
Student Self-Assessment

What is it?

- A form that allows students to assess their own growth as readers, writers, and learners
- An opportunity for students to make some of their own decisions and become more independent learners

What is the purpose?

- To help students recognize their own strengths and weaknesses
- To help students set their own goals for improvement

How is it used?

- Students assess themselves or a piece of work at least once per grading period.
- Confer with students about their self-evaluations, goals, and progress.
- Place the forms in students' portfolios and share them at parent conferences.

A Students select the work, project, or time frame to be assessed.

B Students assess their own growth as learners by positively reflecting on some of their successes.

C Students reflect on things they still want to learn or improve.

D Students think about how they would like to work on or improve their learning.

E Students set future learning goals related to this or other projects.

Form for reproduction is on page 140.

Student Form
Student Self-Assessment

Name: *Tyrone Harris*   Teacher: *Ms. Danowitz*   Date: *2/20*

A Work/Project I'm Assessing: *my speech for Black History Month*

Things I Did Well **B**	Things I Need to Work On **C**
1. Got everyone interested in my topic right away	1. Being comfortable when I talk to the whole class
2. Told how hard Frederick Douglass's life was	2. Talking louder

How I Will Work on Them **D**	My Goals for the Future **E**
1. Ask Ms. Danowitz, Dad, and Rev. Johnson for tips on how to talk in public and how to relax.	1. Give a speech to the class without anyone knowing I'm nervous.
2. Practice giving a talk at home and making sure evryone can hear me.	2. Read more about African American leaders.

Student Form
Peer Assessment

What is it?
- A form that allows students to evaluate and comment on each other's work
- A way to help students become aware of and value different points of view

What does it show?
- Constructive feedback that students provide to their peers
- Different perspectives students have on their peers' work and/or performance

How do students use it?
- Students should assess a piece of a peer's work at least once per grading period.
- Students might keep this form in their portfolios and use it during peer conferences.

A Students assess their peers' work and/or performance in a positive way by reflecting on some of the things they like best.

B Students suggest things that their peers might want to work on and/or improve.

C Students have the opportunity to make suggestions that their peers might not have considered for improving their work and/or performance.

Form for reproduction is on page 141.

Student Form
Peer Assessment

My name is Rob Santez   Date 10/20

I'm looking at Kathy Noonan   's work.

The work I am looking at is "My Dad and Me"

A Things I Especially Like About Your Work	**B** Things I Had Trouble Understanding
You don't use hard words when you write. Your story about you and your dad cleaning the garage was excellent.	How the garage door got unstuck

C Suggestions
You should write a comic strip for the school newspaper based on your stories about your dad.

Student Form
Group Assessment

What is it?
- A form that allows students to assess their work in groups
- A way for students to evaluate both their own contributions to group work and those of other group members

What does it show?
- Group members' evaluation of their own work on a project
- How members view the work of the group as a whole
- Areas of the project that succeeded and failed, as well as goals for the future

How do students use it?
- Students may use the form to evaluate any assignment or project in which several students participate.
- Students should evaluate their own roles and contribute to an assessment of the whole group's work.

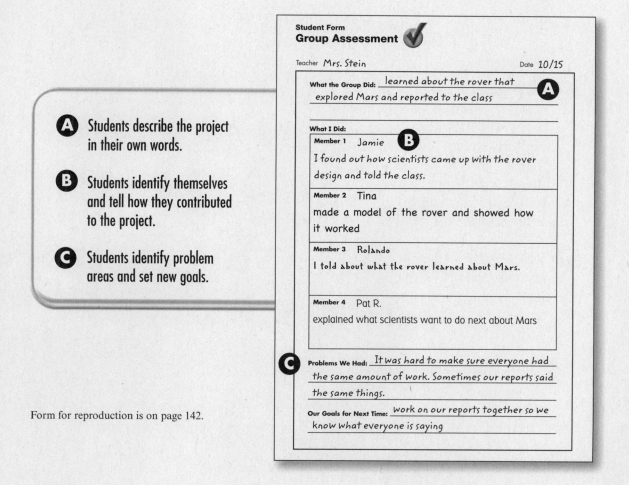

A Students describe the project in their own words.

B Students identify themselves and tell how they contributed to the project.

C Students identify problem areas and set new goals.

Form for reproduction is on page 142.

Student Form
Group Assessment

Teacher *Mrs. Stein*   Date *10/15*

What the Group Did: *learned about the rover that explored Mars and reported to the class* **A**

What I Did:

Member 1 *Jamie* **B**
I found out how scientists came up with the rover design and told the class.

Member 2 *Tina*
made a model of the rover and showed how it worked

Member 3 *Rolando*
I told about what the rover learned about Mars.

Member 4 *Pat R.*
explained what scientists want to do next about Mars

C **Problems We Had:** *It was hard to make sure everyone had the same amount of work. Sometimes our reports said the same things.*

Our Goals for Next Time: *work on our reports together so we know what everyone is saying*

Student Portfolios

What is a portfolio?	• A teacher-guided process in which students collect representative samples of their own reading, writing, speaking, and listening as a means of demonstrating growth over time
	• A method of documenting growth by using the actual products students create during normal day-to-day learning
	• A way to encourage students to feel ownership of their learning

What is the purpose of a portfolio?

Portfolios may accomplish any or all of the following:

- Demonstrate students' growth and progress
- Show students' strengths and needs
- Help you make instructional decisions about students
- Encourage students to assess their own growth and progress and to set new goals
- Make it possible to share evidence of students' growth during parent conferences
- Compile representative samples of students' work that you can pass along to their next teachers

What goes into a portfolio?

- Chapter 7 provides a full description of forms to use for organizing portfolios throughout the year.
- Possible items to include in Student Portfolios are:
  - Drawing or writing projects that students have done at school or at home
  - List of books students have read
  - Works in progress
  - Audio recordings of students reading or performing
  - Video recordings of students presenting projects or performing
  - Photographs of group projects and products
  - Student work samples suggested in the Scott Foresman *Reading Street* Teacher's Editions

How do I help students choose samples for their portfolios?

- At the beginning of the school year, explain the process of developing a portfolio.
- Show models of portfolios and sample entries. Explain that portfolios should include:
  - a wide variety of materials
  - samples that demonstrate learning experiences

3 • Progress Monitoring

How do I help students choose samples for their portfolios? (continued)

- – pieces that show growth or improvement over time
- – materials that indicate that students have challenged themselves to try something different
- – self-assessments and future learning goals

- Periodically set aside time for students to examine their work and think about which pieces they would like to include in their portfolios.

  - – Ask students to complete a Portfolio Selection Slip that can be attached to each piece of work selected for inclusion in the portfolio.
  - – Ask students to briefly describe the work sample, the rationale for including it, and a reflection on the quality of the work (for example, *What I Chose, Why I Chose It,* and *What I Like About It*).

- Encourage students to include other documentation of literacy growth and progress, such as journal entries, inventories, writing drafts and revised copies, reading and writing logs, and peer assessments of portfolio work.

How do I involve the family in the portfolio process?

- At the beginning of the year, send home a letter to parents informing them about portfolios.
- Share students' portfolios during parent conferences as students explain the contents, how projects were developed, and how portfolio pieces were selected.
- While viewing portfolios with parents, point out students' strengths and progress over time.

What can I do at the end of each grading period?

- Hold portfolio conferences toward the end of each grading period to help students reflect on the contents of their portfolios.
- Have students decide which pieces to take home, which pieces to keep in their portfolios, and which pieces to lend to you to update their Portfolio Guides.

What can I do at the end of the school year?

- Hold final conferences with students to help them reflect on their portfolios and decide what to save and what to eliminate.
- Have students decide what to take home and what to pass along to their next teachers (for example, the pieces they are most proud of or the ones that show the most growth).

Student Form
Reading Log

What is it?
- A form to help students keep track of the literature they have read

What does it show?
- Literature students have read and how they evaluate what they read
- A student's reading growth over time

How do students use it?
- Students can list *Reading Street* text selections or trade books, as well as pieces of literature they have selected on their own.
- Students may put this form in their portfolios as a way of documenting what they have read.

Student Form
Reading Log

Name _Kathy Noonan_

Dates Read	Title and Author	What is it about?	How would you rate it?	Explain your rating.
From _9/12_ to _9/18_	Stuart Little by E.B. White	a fantasy about a brave mouse named Stuart	Great 5 4 ③ 2 1 Awful	Some of the words were hard, but the story kept my interest. It was kind of weird.
From _9/12_ to _9/18_	Yeh — Shen by Ai-Ling Louie	a Chinese Cinderella story	Great 5 ④ 3 2 1 Awful	Beautiful story and nice pictures. The story has a happy ending.
From ___ to ___			Great 5 4 3 2 1 Awful	
From ___ to ___			Great 5 4 3 2 1 Awful	
From ___ to ___			Great 5 4 3 2 1 Awful	

A Students list titles and authors of selections they have read.

B Have students circle the rating they would give each selection. Students should give a reason or two to explain or support their ratings.

Form for reproduction is on page 143.

Student Form
About My Reading

What is it?	• A way for students to describe and evaluate their own reading progress
What does it show?	• Students' assessments of their own reading abilities and attitudes • Students' evaluations of reading selections that they particularly liked
How do students use it?	• Students complete the form at various points during the year, but at least once each grading period. • Students should keep completed forms in their portfolios and periodically review them to assess progress over time.

A Students evaluate their reading strengths and weaknesses.

B Students describe a specific reading selection that they enjoyed.

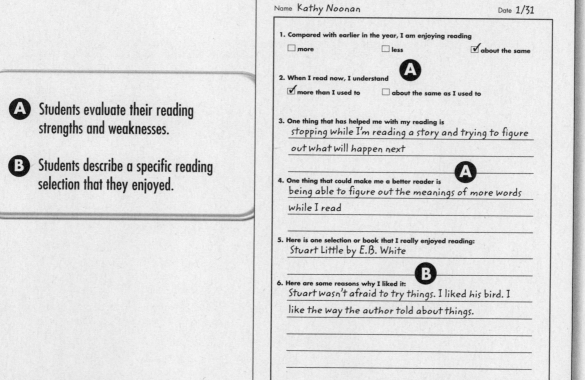

Form for reproduction is on page 144.

Student Form
Writing Log

What is it?
- A form to help students keep track of and reflect on the pieces they have written

What does it show?
- Titles and genres of compositions students have written
- Students' feelings toward their writing and what they liked or disliked about each piece

How do students use it?
- Students can make notes on their Writing Logs during any stage of the writing process for any pieces they choose.
- Students may put this form in their portfolios as a way of keeping track of what they have written.

A Students list pieces of writing by genre—for example, personal narrative, sports story, folk tale, biography, and so on.

B Have students circle the rating they would give each selection.

C Encourage students to assess their own writing and to point out the strengths of the piece.

Student Form
Writing Log

Student _Sami Smith_   Date _10/20_
Teacher _Ms. Brewer_   Grade _4_

Date	Title **A**	Type of Writing	How I felt about this piece **B**	What I liked or disliked **C**	Put in Portfolio
10/20	My Camping Trip	Narrative	④ 3 2 1	I described everything on the trip.	✓
11/15	Chimpanzees	Expository	4 3 ② 1	I couldn't find information.	
			4 3 2 1		
			4 3 2 1		
			4 3 2 1		
			4 3 2 1		

Key
4 = Excellent
3 = Good
2 = Fair
1 = Poor

Form for reproduction is on page 145.

Student Form
About My Writing

What is it?	• A way for students to describe and evaluate their own writing progress
What does it show?	• Students' assessments of their own writing abilities and attitudes • Students' evaluations of original pieces of writing that they thought turned out well
How do students use it?	• Students may complete the form at various points during the year, but at least once each grading period. • Students should keep completed forms in their portfolios and periodically review them to assess progress over time.

A Students evaluate their writing strengths and weaknesses.

B Students assess an original piece of writing.

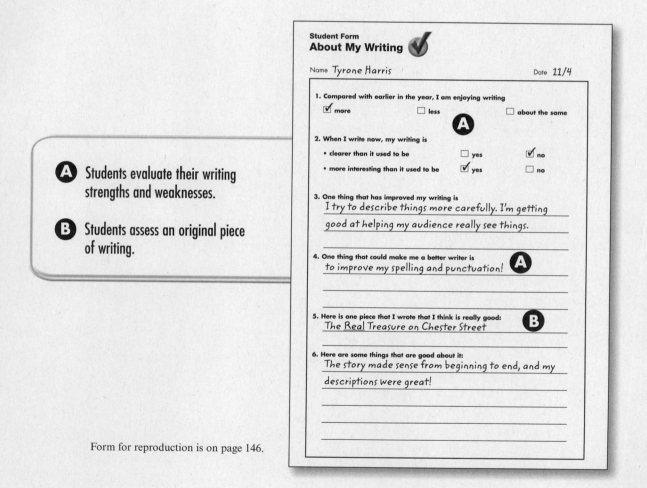

Student Form
About My Writing

Name _Tyrone Harris_   Date _11/4_

1. **Compared with earlier in the year, I am enjoying writing**
   ☑ more   ☐ less   ☐ about the same   **A**

2. **When I write now, my writing is**
   • clearer than it used to be   ☐ yes   ☑ no
   • more interesting than it used to be ☑ yes   ☐ no

3. **One thing that has improved my writing is**
   I try to describe things more carefully. I'm getting good at helping my audience really see things.

4. **One thing that could make me a better writer is**
   to improve my spelling and punctuation! **A**

5. **Here is one piece that I wrote that I think is really good:**
   The Real Treasure on Chester Street **B**

6. **Here are some things that are good about it:**
   The story made sense from beginning to end, and my descriptions were great!

Form for reproduction is on page 146.

Chapter 4

Summative Assessment: What to Do After Instruction Has Taken Place

Overview

Summative assessments are formal assessments used to determine how well students have met or exceeded state reading and language arts curriculum standards. They are designed to document long-term growth in the development of literacy skills and include state-required assessments as well as Scott Foresman *Reading Street* assessments and tests developed by school districts. They focus on yearly and end-of-year standards and outcomes.

What are the benefits of summative assessments?

Summative assessments help you determine if all students are making expected academic growth and provide you with information to:

- determine your students' progress in meeting or exceeding state reading and language arts curriculum standards;

- gather information in a systematic way to validate judgments and decisions about learning;

- standardize opportunities for each student taking the test;

  - Each student receives the same directions.

  - Each test is scored by the same criteria.

- give feedback to your students that enables them to learn about their own literacy development; and

- continually refine and modify instruction in your classroom to meet the needs of your students.

What is the purpose of using summative assessments?

Summative assessments are used for measuring long-term growth. The results of summative assessments can be used to:

- determine the degree to which your students have achieved the goals defined by a given standard or group of standards; and

- gather specific information about students with particular needs, such as English language learners and students with disabilities.

What do I want to learn from summative assessments?

Summative assessments provide you with information about how well your students have mastered the content of previously taught lessons. They include feedback on student achievement of standards in the following grade level strands of national and state reading and language arts standards.

- Reading comprehension
- Systematic vocabulary development
- Written language conventions (e.g., sentence structure, grammar, punctuation, capitalization, spelling)
- Writing ability
- Reading fluency

What type of assessments should be used as summative assessment?

- Use formal assessments that provide a detailed analysis of how well your students have mastered the knowledge and skills described in the national and state reading and language arts standards.

When do I gather the information?

- Summative assessments should be given at the end of the year.

What techniques and tool are available?

FORMAL ASSESSMENT TOOL AND TECHNIQUES FOR SUMMATIVE ASSESSMENT

- **Scott Foresman *Reading Street* End-of-Year Benchmark Test** (See pages 82–83.) A group-administered, summative assessment is used to determine your students' growth in mastering the content in the national and state reading and language arts standards and to document achievement of skills taught throughout the school year

INFORMAL ASSESSMENT TOOLS AND TECHNIQUES FOR ASSESSMENT

- Additional classroom-based assessment forms can be found in Chapter 7. These include:
  - Reading Strategy Assessment
  - Writing Strategy Assessment
  - Cumulative Folder Form

Want to learn more about summative assessment?

If you are interested in learning more about research that supports the use of summative assessment tools and practices, you will find the following resources interesting.

References

Afflerbach, P. "Teaching Reading Self-Assessment Strategies." In *Comprehension Instruction: Research-Based Best Practices*. Eds. C. Block and M. Pressley. New York: Guilford Press, 2001, pp. 96–111.

Guthrie, J. T. "Preparing Students for High-Stakes Test Taking in Reading." In *What Research Has To Say About Reading Instruction*. Eds. A. E. Farstrup and S. J. Samuels. Newark, DE: International Reading Association, 2002, pp. 370–391.

Howell, K. W., and V. Nolet. *Curriculum-Based Evaluation: Teaching and Decision Making*, 3rd Ed. Belmont, CA: Wadsworth and Thompson Learning Company, 2000.

Johnston, P., and P. Costello. "Principles for Literacy Assessment." *Reading Research Quarterly*, vol. 40, no. 2 (2005), pp. 256–267.

Marzano, R., et al. *Classroom Instruction That Works: Research-Based Strategies for Increasing Student Achievement*. Alexandria, VA: ASCD, 2001.

Pearson, P. D.; S. Vyas; L. M. Sensale; and Y. Kim. "Making Our Way Through the Assessment and Accountability Maze: Where Do We Go Now?" *The Clearing House*, vol. 74, no. 4 (2001), pp. 175–182.

Shepard, L. "The Role of Classroom Assessment in Teaching and Learning." In *Handbook of Research on Teaching*, 4th Ed. Ed. V. K. Richardson. Washington, DC: American Educational Research Association, 2001, pp. 1066–1101.

Valencia, S. W. "Inquiry-Oriented Assessment." In *Classroom Literacy Assessment: Making Sense of What Students Know and Do*. Eds. J. R. Paratore and R. L. McCormack. New York: The Guilford Press, 2007, pp. 3–20.

Wixson, K. K., S. W. Valencia, and M. Y. Lipson. "Issues in Literacy Assessment: Facing the Realities of Internal and External Assessment." *Journal of Reading Behavior*, vol. 26, no. 3 (1994), pp. 315–337.

4 • Summative

Scott Foresman *Reading Street* End-of-Year Benchmark Test

What is it?	• A multiple-choice and constructed-response test designed to measure your students' mastery of state reading and language arts curriculum standards • A means to document your students' long-term growth
Why would I choose it?	• To evaluate your students' end-of-year mastery in specific reading and language arts skills • To identify skill areas in which students need intervention and continued practice • To document academic growth
What does it test?	The grades 4, 5, and 6 End-of-Year Benchmark Tests include subtests for the following grade-level strands: • Reading comprehension • Vocabulary • Writing conventions—usage, mechanics, grammar, and spelling • Writing application—response to a prompt • Oral reading fluency
When do I use it?	• At the end of the year
How do I use it?	• The test is designed to be group-administered. • The fluency check is to be administered individually.

How do I use the results?

- To document and record individual student growth in cumulative skills taught during the school year
- To diagnose and record individual student needs for the next year
- To inform and improve the delivery of curriculum and instruction
- To provide guidance for teacher teams in the next school year who plan interventions for students who need additional support
- To provide helpful feedback to students and parents
- To help determine students' overall grades
- To guide parents in working with their students during vacation, so learning continues throughout the summer months

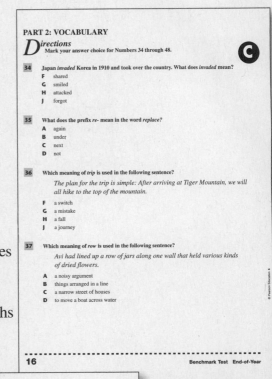

PART 2: VOCABULARY

Directions
Mark your answer choice for Numbers 34 through 48.

34 Japan *invaded* Korea in 1910 and took over the country. What does *invaded* mean?
- F shared
- G smiled
- H attacked
- J forgot

35 What does the prefix *re-* mean in the word *replace*?
- A again
- B under
- C next
- D not

36 Which meaning of *trip* is used in the following sentence?
  The plan for the trip is simple: After arriving at Tiger Mountain, we will all hike to the top of the mountain.
- F a switch
- G a mistake
- H a fall
- J a journey

37 Which meaning of *row* is used in the following sentence?
  Avi had lined up a row of jars along one wall that held various kinds of dried flowers.
- A a noisy argument
- B things arranged in a line
- C a narrow street of houses
- D to move a boat across water

16   Benchmark Test End-of-Year

Samples are from Grade 4 End-of-Year Benchmark Test.

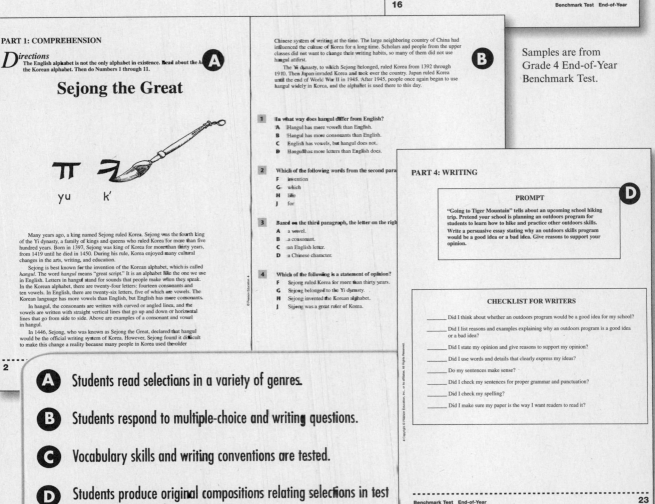

PART 1: COMPREHENSION

Directions
The English alphabet is not the only alphabet in existence. Read about the history of the Korean alphabet. Then do Numbers 1 through 11.

Sejong the Great

ㅠ   ㅋ
yu   k'

Many years ago, a king named Sejong ruled Korea. Sejong was the fourth king of the Yi dynasty, a family of kings and queens who ruled Korea for more than five hundred years. Born in 1397, Sejong was king of Korea for more than thirty years, from 1419 until he died in 1450. During his rule, Korea enjoyed many cultural changes in the arts, writing, and education.

Sejong is best known for the invention of the Korean alphabet, which is called *hangul*. The word *hangul* means "great script." It is an alphabet like the one we use in English. Letters in hangul stand for sounds that people make when they speak. In the Korean alphabet, there are twenty-four letters: fourteen consonants and ten vowels. In English, there are twenty-six letters, five of which are vowels. The Korean language has more vowels than English, but English has more consonants.

In hangul, the consonants are written with curved or angled lines, and the vowels are written with straight vertical lines that go up and down or horizontal lines that go from side to side. Above are examples of a consonant and vowel in hangul.

In 1446, Sejong, who was known as Sejong the Great, declared that hangul would be the official writing system of Korea. However, Sejong found it difficult to make this change a reality because many people in Korea used the older

2

Chinese system of writing at the time. The large neighboring country of China had influenced the culture of Korea for a long time. Scholars and people from the upper classes did not want to change their writing habits, so many of them did not use hangul at first.

The Yi dynasty, to which Sejong belonged, ruled Korea from 1392 through 1910. Then Japan invaded Korea and took over the country. Japan ruled Korea until the end of World War II in 1945. After 1945, people once again began to use hangul widely in Korea, and the alphabet is used there to this day.

1 In what way does hangul differ from English?
- A Hangul has more vowels than English.
- B Hangul has more consonants than English.
- C English has vowels, but hangul does not.
- D Hangul has more letters than English does.

2 Which of the following words from the second para[graph]
- F invention
- G which
- H like
- J for

3 Based on the third paragraph, the letter on the right
- A a vowel.
- B a consonant.
- C an English letter.
- D a Chinese character.

4 Which of the following is a statement of opinion?
- F Sejong ruled Korea for more than thirty years.
- G Sejong belonged to the Yi dynasty.
- H Sejong invented the Korean alphabet.
- J Sejong was a great ruler of Korea.

PART 4: WRITING

PROMPT

"Going to Tiger Mountain" tells about an upcoming school hiking trip. Pretend your school is planning an outdoors program for students to learn how to hike and practice other outdoors skills.
Write a persuasive essay stating why an outdoors skills program would be a good idea or a bad idea. Give reasons to support your opinion.

CHECKLIST FOR WRITERS

_____ Did I think about whether an outdoors program would be a good idea for my school?

_____ Did I list reasons and examples explaining why an outdoors program is a good idea or a bad idea?

_____ Did I state my opinion and give reasons to support my opinion?

_____ Did I use words and details that clearly express my ideas?

_____ Do my sentences make sense?

_____ Did I check my sentences for proper grammar and punctuation?

_____ Did I check my spelling?

_____ Did I make sure my paper is the way I want readers to read it?

Benchmark Test End-of-Year   23

A Students read selections in a variety of genres.

B Students respond to multiple-choice and writing questions.

C Vocabulary skills and writing conventions are tested.

D Students produce original compositions relating selections in test to unit themes and writing instruction.

4 • Summative

| Chapter 5 | # Writing as Learning and Assessment |

Overview

Writing is an important component of the state reading and language arts curriculum standards. Writing facilitates learning by providing a means through which students can develop complex thinking and express depth of understanding. As you design writing instruction, you will not only want to consider how to assess the development of writing, but also how your students use writing as a tool for demonstrating knowledge and skills.

Writing as Learning

The process and products of writing are in themselves educative. The act of writing helps your students organize and clarify their thoughts. It helps them discover meaning and express what they understand about a topic or concept. Writing gives your students an opportunity to explore thoughts and deepen their understanding. When your students write down their ideas and then have an opportunity to rethink and revise them, they also have an opportunity to expand their thinking. During this process, their ideas are extended and refined, especially if you are able to give students opportunities to participate in writing conferences in which they share their drafts with you and their peers. Some activities that give your students opportunities to learn as they write are:

- Making lists of ideas as they brainstorm information on a specific topic
- Creating concept maps
- Completing graphic organizers
- Describing what they have learned in logs or journals
- Taking notes as they use media, listen to lectures, or research topics
- Writing responses to literature and analyzing literary texts
- Writing reports
- Reflecting on what they have learned while completing projects
- Writing observations and lab reports during science investigations

Writing as a Demonstration of Knowledge and Skill

Because writing illustrates thinking, it provides you with an opportunity to assess what your students have learned during or following instruction. Constructed responses, whether short (e.g., two or three sentences describing how they solved a mathematics problem, a short paragraph describing the causes of a historical event) or extended (e.g., multiple paragraphs identifying and supporting themes found in a piece of literature), are very effective forms of assessment. The checklists and rubrics used to evaluate constructed-response items allow you to provide clear feedback to your students so that they can improve their performance.

Assessment and Evaluation of Writing

Writing assessment is an essential part of a comprehensive writing program. In order to ensure growth in writing, a balanced approach to assessment is needed—one that includes entry-level, progress-monitoring, and summative assessments. Through the combination of these assessments, you will gain an in-depth view of your students' knowledge and skill in using the stages of writing (e.g., pre-writing, drafting, revising, editing, postwriting). The assessments labeled progress-monitoring tools in this handbook provide ongoing feedback on the progress your students make toward achievement of skills and knowledge.

What are the benefits of a balanced approach to writing assessment?

- Using a balanced approach to writing assessment allows you to collect data throughout the year and respond specifically to the learning trajectory of your students.

  - Entry-level writing assessments, given at the beginning of the year, help you diagnose where to begin writing instruction for individual students and help you plan specific instructional activities designed to meet the learning needs of each of the writers in your class.

  - Progress-monitoring assessments, given throughout the year, help you determine if all students are making expected progress toward the goal of writing multiple-paragraph compositions.

  - Summative assessments at the end of the year determine how well your students have learned the writing skills you have taught and how well how your students have met or exceeded statewide and district-wide curriculum standards.

- You can guide your students' writing development better if you have an up-to-date understanding of their current performance levels—wasting no time on skills they have already mastered and focusing instead on the areas that represent the next step in their growing writing proficiency or areas that need additional attention.

- Because high standards in writing achievement are most reliably achieved in small, consistent increases that occur over time, a balanced approach to writing assessment affords you the opportunity to monitor and adjust curriculum and instruction as needed to maximize the writing improvement for all students.

- Providing feedback to students about their performances on writing assessments will help them develop skills required to successfully complete writing tasks (e.g., constructed-response questions in mathematics, science, social studies, and English language arts) included in high-stakes assessments.

What are the purposes of writing assessment?

- To promote continuous improvement in your students' successful use of the writing process and language conventions
- To identify mastery of state curriculum standards both at the individual student level and at the class level, which address:
  - Organization and focus
  - Penmanship
  - Research and technology
  - Evaluation and revision
  - Written language conventions (sentence structure, grammar, punctuation, capitalization, spelling)
- To determine when differentiation of instruction is required for individuals or groups of students who have not demonstrated mastery in writing
- To provide a basis for focused instructional decision-making, mini-lessons on the writing process and skills, and feedback to be shared during writing conferences with your students
- To encourage student self-assessment and evaluation by helping students learn how to make judgments about the quality of their writing
- To determine report card grades and/or communicate progress to parents
- To evaluate instructional approaches and modify curriculum to reflect results from writing assessments

When do I use writing assessments?

- Use entry-level writing assessments at the beginning of the year to gather baseline data regarding students' writing proficiency levels.
- Use progress-monitoring writing assessments throughout the school year to measure students' growth in developing writing proficiency.
- Use summative writing assessments to determine students' proficiency levels in the area of writing at the close of each grading period and at the end of the year.

5 • Writing

How do I help students assess their own writing?

Self-assessment is very important to your students' writing development. Although you are the primary evaluator of your students' writing, you should give your students opportunities to engage in ongoing self-assessment and peer assessment. The benefits are many—such assessments will help them analyze their writing and the writing of their peers, set goals for improvement, and evaluate their performance in achieving the goals.

- **How can I help students become better self-assessors?**
  - Model self-monitoring by sharing your thoughts with students as you evaluate and reflect on a writing project you are doing.
  - Make the criteria on which students are assessed (e.g., checklists, rubrics) public so that they can use this information to self-assess.
  - Schedule regular times for self-assessment.
  - Give students opportunities to draft criteria for assessing their own work.
  - Provide opportunities for students to engage in activities that encourage thinking, writing, and talking about their writing.

- **What kinds of activities support self-assessment?**
  - Writing conferences with you
  - Writing conferences with classmates
  - Reflections about writing goals and progress in achieving the goals
  - Reviews of student portfolios
  - Use of self-assessment checklists and rubrics
  - Student-led parent-teacher conferences

The Role of Rubrics in Assessing Writing

Rubrics play an important role in assessing writing. They identify criteria upon which writing is evaluated, and they identify levels of performance. Using rubrics helps you and your students in many ways:

- Rubrics help you focus your students' attention on elements of quality writing, especially if you share the rubrics with them before they begin writing.

- Rubrics help you achieve consistency when evaluating your students' work.

- Rubrics allow you to provide focused feedback to students so that they can improve their writing.

- Rubrics help you identify objectives for individuals and groups of students.

- Your students will become better writers by using rubrics to guide their self-assessment.

- Peer assessment will be more effective when students have rubrics to guide their analysis of writing samples.

There are several types of rubrics:

- Some rubrics are general and describe the features of good writing that can be applied to a variety of genres.

- Some rubrics describe the features of a specific type or genre of writing.

- Some rubrics are holistic, assessing writing on how well the parts (e.g., ideas, organization, voice, conventions) interact to create a quality piece of writing.

- Some rubrics are analytic, assessing the individual characteristics of writing that serve as criteria for assessing the quality of a piece of writing.

A general four-point writing rubric is included in this chapter.

For guidance in creating your own rubrics, see page 121.

5 • Writing

What techniques and tools are available?

ENTRY-LEVEL ASSESSMENT TOOL

- **Myself as a Reader and Writer** (See page 41.)
  An informal questionnaire that gives students an opportunity to share information about their writing interests.

PROGRESS-MONITORING ASSESSMENT TOOLS AND TECHNIQUES

- **Unit Benchmark Tests** (See pages 58–59.)
  These tests are designed to measure your students' abilities to apply target comprehension skills and other literacy skills. Included in each assessment is a writing prompt that elicits a narrative, expository, persuasive, or friendly-letter response.

- **Ongoing Teacher Observation** (See page 62.)
  Observation of your students allows you to monitor their performances in the context of classroom writing activities and provide helpful feedback while students are in the process of learning, rather than after the fact.

- **Skills Conference Record** (See page 68.)
  This checklist allows you to capture information about your students' writing.

- **Student Self-Assessment** (See page 70.)
  This form provides your students with an opportunity to assess themselves as writers.

- **Peer Assessment** (See page 71.)
  This form affords your students an opportunity to assess a peer's work and apply what they are learning about the quality of effective writing.

- **Student Portfolios** (See pages 73–74.)
  Maintaining a portfolio is a process that allows your students to use work samples to document and reflect on their growth in writing.

- **Writing Log** (See page 77.)
  This form helps students keep track of the pieces they have written, as well as rate the quality of their own writing.

- **About My Writing** (See page 78.)
  This form encourages your students to describe and evaluate their own writing progress.

SUMMATIVE ASSESSMENT TOOL

- **End-of-Year Benchmark Test**
  (See pages 82–83.)
  A group-administered, summative assessment used to determine your students' growth in mastering the *Reading Street* content. Additionally this test documents achievement of skills taught throughout the school year. The Writing subtest requires students to write to a prompt based on one of the reading passages on the test.

Want to learn more about writing assessment?

If you would like to learn more about how to use writing assessment practices in your classroom, you will find the following resources interesting.

References

Bromley K. "Assessing Student Writing." In *Classroom Literacy Assessment: Making Sense of What Students Know and Do*. Eds. J. R. Paratore and R. L. McCormack. New York: The Guilford Press, 2007, pp. 227–245.

Calfee, R. C. "Writing Portfolios: Activity, Assessment, Authenticity." In *Perspectives on Writing: Research, Theory, and Practice*. Eds. R. Indrisano and J. R. Squire. Newark, DE: International Reading Association, 2000, pp. 278–304.

Fisher, D., and N. Frey. *Checking for Understanding: Formative Assessment Techniques for Your Classroom*. Alexandria, VA: Association for Supervision and Curriculum Development, 2007.

Glazer, S. M. "A Classroom Portfolio System: Assessment Instruction." In *Classroom Literacy Assessment: Making Sense of What Students Know and Do*. Eds. J. R. Paratore and R. L. McCormack. New York: The Guilford Press, 2007, pp. 227–245.

Spandel, V. *Seeing with New Eyes: A Guidebook on Teaching and Assessing Beginning Writers*. Portland, OR: Northwest Regional Educational Laboratory, 1998.

Spandel, V. *Creating Writers Through 6-Trait Writing Assessment and Instruction*. Boston: Allyn and Bacon, 2000.

Vacca, R. T., and J. L. Vacca. "Writing Across the Curriculum." In *Perspectives on Writing: Research, Theory, and Practice*. Eds. R. Indrisano and J. R. Squire. Newark, DE: International Reading Association, 2000, pp. 214–232.

Zamel, V. "Writing: The Process of Discovering Meaning." *TESOL Quarterly*, vol. 16, no. 2 (1982), pp. 195–209.

Four-Point Scoring Rubric—Grades 4–6

4 The writing—

- *Clearly* addresses the writing task.

- Demonstrates a *clear* understanding of purpose.

- Maintains a *consistent* point of view, focus, and organizational structure, including paragraphing when appropriate.

- Includes a *clearly presented* central idea with relevant facts, details, and/or explanations.

- Includes sentence variety.

- Contains *few or no* errors in the conventions of the English language (e.g., grammar, punctuation, capitalization, spelling). These errors do **not** interfere with the reader's understanding of the writing.

3 The writing—

- Addresses *most* of the writing task.

- Demonstrates a *general* understanding of purpose.

- Maintains a *mostly consistent* point of view, focus, and organizational structure, including paragraphing when appropriate.

- Presents a central idea with *mostly* relevant facts, details, and/or explanations.

- Includes *some* sentence variety.

- Contains *some* errors in the conventions of the English language (e.g., grammar, punctuation, capitalization, spelling). These errors do **not** interfere with the reader's understanding of the writing.

2 **The writing—**

- Addresses *some* of the writing task.

- Demonstrates *little* understanding of the purpose.

- Maintains an *inconsistent* point of view, focus, and/or organizational structure; may lack appropriate paragraphing.

- *Suggests* a central idea with *limited* facts, details, and/or explanations.

- Includes *little* sentence variety.

- Contains *many* errors in the conventions of the English language (e.g., grammar, punctuation, capitalization, spelling). These errors **may** interfere with the reader's understanding of the writing.

1 **The writing—**

- Addresses *only one part or none* of the writing task.

- Demonstrates *no* understanding of purpose.

- *Lacks* a clear point of view, focus, and/or organizational structure; may contain inappropriate paragraphing.

- *Lacks* a central idea but may contain *marginally related* facts, details, and/or explanations.

- Includes *no* sentence variety.

- Contains *serious errors* in the conventions of the English language (e.g., grammar, punctuation, capitalization, spelling). These errors interfere with the reader's understanding of the writing.

5 • Writing

Student Portfolios

What is a portfolio as it relates to writing?

- A teacher-guided process in which students collect representative samples of their own writing as a means of demonstrating growth over time

- A way to encourage students to feel ownership of their writing

What is the purpose of a portfolio as it relates to writing?

- Portfolios may accomplish any or all of the following:

  - Demonstrate students' writing progress

  - Show students' writing strengths and needs

  - Help you make instructional decisions for each student's writing

  - Encourage students to assess their own growth and progress in writing and to set new writing goals

  - Make it possible to share evidence of students' writing growth during parent conferences

  - Compile representative samples of students' writing that you can pass along to their next teachers

Which writing pieces go into a portfolio?

- Chapters 3 and 7 provide full descriptions of techniques and forms to use for compiling and organizing portfolios.

- Possible writing pieces to include in Student Portfolios are:

  - Drawing or writing projects that students have done at school or at home

  - Works in progress

  - Examples of pre-writing activities

  - Examples of first drafts

  - Examples of revision at the paragraph, multi-paragraph, and self-composition levels

  - Documentation of peer assessment

  - Documentation of self-assessment

  - Examples of a variety of genres, including:

    - Narratives

    - Written responses to literature

    - Expository reports and research reports

    - Summaries

    - Persuasive letters or compositions

How do I help students choose writing samples for their portfolios?

- At the beginning of the school year, explain the process of developing a portfolio.

- Show models of portfolios and sample writing entries. Explain that portfolios should include:
  - a wide variety of written works
  - samples that demonstrate learning experiences in writing
  - pieces that show growth or improvement in writing over time
  - materials that indicate that students have challenged themselves to try something different with their writing
  - self-assessments and future learning goals in the area of writing

- Periodically set aside time for students to examine their writing samples and think about which pieces they would like to include in their portfolios.

What can I do at the end of each grading period?

- Hold writing conferences toward the end of each grading period to help students reflect on the written pieces they have placed in their portfolios.

- Have students decide which pieces to take home, which ones to keep in their portfolios, and which ones to lend to you to update their Portfolio Guides.

What can I do at the end of the school year?

- Hold final conferences with students to help them reflect on their writing and decide which pieces to save and which to eliminate.

- Have students decide which writing samples to take home and which to pass along to their next teachers (for example, the pieces they are most proud of or the ones that show the most growth).

5 • Writing

Assessing the Progress of English Language Learners

Chapter 6

Overview

Classrooms throughout the United States are populated with students representing diverse cultures, ethnicities, and languages. This diversity offers rich benefits to learners, but also places enormous demands upon teachers, who are expected to guide *all* students with vastly different literacy and learning abilities toward achievement of state reading and language arts curriculum standards.

English language learners pose unique challenges to educators. Teachers must monitor language acquisition of these students in an ongoing, systematic way, in addition to assessing their understanding of concepts, skills, and strategies. This chapter is designed to assist teachers of English language learners in recognizing the assessment challenges, utilizing appropriate assessment accommodations, preparing students for high-stakes tests, and implementing classroom-based strategies for assessing the strengths and needs of English language learners.

What are the unique challenges in assessing achievement of English language learners?

- Many English language learners may quickly master *social* English, the conversational language skills and conventions used in everyday interactions with classmates. These same learners frequently encounter difficulty with the *academic* English found on formal assessments.

- The structure of academic English is complex, e.g., fiction and nonfiction text structures; paragraph organization; and syntax, including prepositional phrases, introductory clauses, and pronoun references. There are structural analysis constraints at the word, sentence, paragraph, and text levels.

- The vocabulary of academic English consists of specialized meanings of common words, abstract concepts, multiple-meaning words, and words based on Latin and Greek roots. (Bielenberg, 2004/2005)

- The topics and concepts of comprehension passages are frequently unfamiliar, and the purposes of assessment tasks divorced from real-life contexts can be difficult to perceive.

- Formal assessments often fail to reflect the diverse cultural and linguistic experiences of English language learners and then have limited value for helping teachers select appropriate instructional strategies. (Garcia, 1994)

How are Scott Foresman *Reading Street* assessments sensitive to the needs of English language learners?

- Both formal and informal classroom-based *Reading Street* assessments help teachers monitor growth in the basic reading and expression skills of alphabetic understanding, decoding, sight vocabulary, and grammar, along with measurement of the more complex skills of fluency, comprehension, and vocabulary.

- Reading comprehension test passages reflect diverse ethnic content and cultural experiences.

- Texts are matched to the age, interest, and background knowledge of students.

- Most assessment tasks are embedded in contexts with which students have familiarity. The comprehension assessments are generally based on themes and topics explored in instruction; vocabulary is assessed within the context of the passage; and writing tasks relate to main ideas of the texts.

- The language of the test directions and assessment items is straightforward and unambiguous.

What instructional strategies will help prepare my English language learners for formal assessments?

- Preteach the "language of tests" encountered in directions and test items, including:

  - Question words, such as *who, what, which, where, when, why,* and *how*

  - Emphasis words, such as *not, except, most likely, probably, major, both, neither, either, most,* and *least*

  - Action words, such as *explain, describe, discuss, persuade,* and *support with experience*

- Teach use of context clues to interpret meaning of unfamiliar terms.

- Highlight and discuss routinely the *academic* language, vocabulary, syntax, and narrative and expository text structures encountered in textbooks and trade books.

- Coach students in oral and written retelling and summarization, so they develop a "sense" of text types, features, conventions, and organization. English language learners relate to the concrete nature of expository text, and expository summarization helps to familiarize them with common text structures, such as sequence, description, classification, compare/contrast, cause/effect, and problem/solution.

- Provide regular opportunities for meaningful oral language experiences in which English language learners participate in discussion of important topics and perform the activities required on tests, such as explaining, describing, and stating and supporting opinions. Encourage them to use vocabulary that will support academic language development.

- Read aloud, think aloud, and model the purposeful and strategic behaviors of effective readers, speakers, and writers of English.

- Provide repeated opportunities for practicing all the techniques above.

6 • English Learners

What accommodations are appropriate to use with the Scott Foresman *Reading Street* assessments?

- Accommodating the needs of English language learners ensures fairness and full participation in formal assessments. A general rule of thumb is to use the same accommodations in testing situations as used in instruction. For instance, if students receive part of their instruction in their first languages, then it is appropriate to translate test directions and comprehension questions into the students' first languages.

> "Accommodation in assessment allows students to best demonstrate their reading development and achievement."
> (Afflerbach, 2007)

- Other acceptable accommodations might include the following:

  - providing additional testing time and allowing frequent or extended breaks

  - administering the tests at times most beneficial to students

  - administering the tests in small groups or in one-on-one settings

  - reading test directions to students in English (or in the students' first languages, if this is possible), and repeating as often as needed

  - simplifying the language and sentence structure of test directions

  - requesting that students restate and clarify test directions in their own words

  - discussing the pictures and any graphics, such as maps, to ensure that students can interpret them

  - allowing the use of bilingual, word-for-word translation dictionaries

  - reading test passages to students in English, and repeating as often as necessary, when listening comprehension is being assessed

  - reading comprehension questions orally in English or in the students' first languages

  - allowing students to respond orally to questions or dictate answers for transcription

  - permitting students to draw pictures to demonstrate their thinking and learning

- In providing accommodations to students, it is important not to compromise the intent of the assessment. It is never appropriate to read aloud the *reading* comprehension passages or the vocabulary and grammar questions to students in English or their first languages. These practices alter the constructs of the assessments. For example, the reading comprehension assessments are designed to measure both word recognition and understanding, so reading the selections to students actually changes the intent of the test.

- While the language-specific modifications above may be most appropriate for English language learners, many of the listed accommodations are also beneficial for students with learning and reading disabilities and other special needs. The use of appropriate accommodations in assessment ensures that all students have fair and equal opportunities to demonstrate evidence of learning and achievement.

- Following the administration of the formal assessments, note which accommodations were used, and interpret scores with that information in mind.

What are the *best* ways to assess the strengths and needs of English language learners?

- Through informal and on-going classroom-based assessment, teachers can observe, monitor, and judge the quality of student work.

- Multiple assessments mirror the learning process, while single assessments capture one moment at a time, much like the difference between an album of photographs and a single snapshot.

- Ask students frequently to communicate orally or in writing their understanding of concepts and processes. In this way, teachers are provided with instant insight about students' thinking and depth of learning.

- Observing small, consistent increases in learning over time is most reliable. The goal is continuous improvement.

- Frequent monitoring addresses learning in progress, allows for correction of misconceptions as they occur, and provides helpful feedback to English language learners.

- Teaching students to self-assess their reading progress helps to build independence in language and learning. For example, encourage them to monitor their progress by comparing work samples and voice recordings over time.

- Authentic assessment activities enhance, rather than diminish, instructional time, because they are inseparable from instruction. Activities include classroom observation, language-experience stories, storytelling or writing, voice recordings of oral reading, reading-response logs, and journals. (Garcia, 1994)

- Scott Foresman *Reading Street* provides many resources to help you tailor instruction and assessment for all your students; administer and score entry-level, formative, and summative assessments; interpret scores; and make decisions based on test results.

What are examples of classroom-based assessment techniques and tools?

- **Profile of English Language Learners** (See pages 103–104.)
  A checklist that identifies the strengths and needs of students who are English language learners

- **Observing English Language Learners** (See page 105.)
  A form that allows you to record ongoing observations about your English language learners' progress in developing reading skills

References:

Afflerbach, P. *Understanding and Using Reading Assessment K–12*. Newark, DE: International Reading Association, 2007.

Bielenberg, B., and L. W. Fillmore. "The English They Need for the Test." *Educational Leadership*, 2004, pp. 45–49.

Garcia, G. E. "Assessing the Literacy Development of Second-Language Students: A Focus on Authentic Assessment." In *Kids Come in All Languages: Reading Instruction for ESL Students*. Eds. K. Spangenberg-Urbshat and R. Pritchard. Newark, DE: International Reading Association, 1994, pp. 180–205.

Lenters, K. "No Half Measures: Reading Instruction for Young Second-Language Learners." *The Reading Teacher*, vol. 58 (2004), pp. 328–336.

Moss, B. "Teaching Expository Text Structures through Information Trade Book Retellings." *The Reading Teacher*, vol. 57 (2004), pp. 710–718.

Zwiers, J. "The Third Language of Academic English." *Educational Leadership*, vol. 62, no. 4 (2004), pp. 60–63.

Survey
Profile of English Language Learners

What is it?

- This checklist helps to identify the strengths and needs of students whose first language is not English. Complete this profile at the time the student enters your classroom and update it periodically throughout the school year.

What does it show?

- An English language learner's proficiency with speaking, reading, and writing English

How do I use it?

- Identify students whose English proficiency you are uncertain about.
- Use the criteria on the form to assess students' abilities in the various language areas, noting specific examples.
- Use the form as a rough guideline of where students are in their English language development and where they may need help.

What do I do next?

Scott Foresman *Reading Street* offers many instructional resources to advance the achievement of your English language learners.

- Standards-based instruction addresses all levels of language acquisition—Beginning, Early Intermediate, Intermediate, Early Advanced, and Advanced levels of English-language proficiency.
- The English Language Learners Handbook and the English language learner student materials together provide before-, during-, and after-reading support for English language learners to allow them to successfully participate in and progress through the daily lessons of the basic program with their peers.

6 • English Learners

What do I do next? (continued)

- The English Language Learners Handbook offers instructional material and comprehensive guidance for teachers and effective, efficient, and explicit instruction for English language learners, with scaffolded comprehension and vocabulary development. It builds on the *Reading Street* Student Editions and on literacy instruction in each Teacher's Edition. The guide uses program components including ELL Posters, ELL Readers, and English Language Support (blackline masters) for activities that engage students with the English language, literature, and comprehension skills.

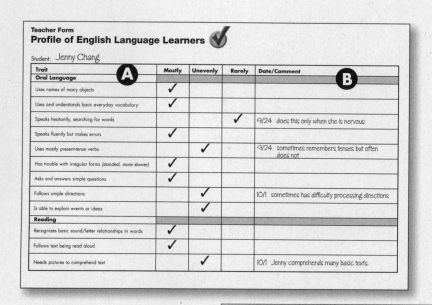

Teacher Form
Profile of English Language Learners ✓

Student: Jenny Chang

Trait	(A) Mostly	Unevenly	Rarely	Date/Comment (B)
Oral Language				
Uses names of many objects	✓			
Uses and understands basic everyday vocabulary	✓			
Speaks hesitantly, searching for words			✓	9/24 does this only when she is nervous
Speaks fluently but makes errors	✓			
Uses mostly present-tense verbs		✓		9/24 sometimes remembers tenses but often does not
Has trouble with irregular forms (standed, more slower)	✓			
Asks and answers simple questions	✓			
Follows simple directions		✓		10/1 sometimes has difficulty processing directions
Is able to explain events or ideas		✓		
Reading				
Recognizes basic sound/letter relationships in words	✓			
Follows text being read aloud	✓			
Needs pictures to comprehend text		✓		10/1 Jenny comprehends many basic texts.

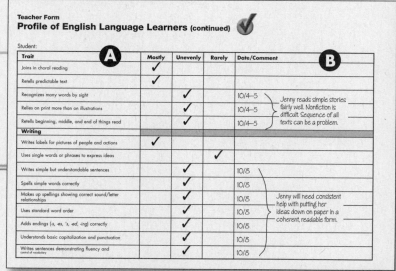

Teacher Form
Profile of English Language Learners (continued) ✓

Student:

Trait	(A) Mostly	Unevenly	Rarely	Date/Comment (B)
Joins in choral reading	✓			
Retells predictable text	✓			
Recognizes many words by sight		✓		10/4–5
Relies on print more than on illustrations		✓		10/4–5
Retells beginning, middle, and end of things read		✓		10/4–5
Writing				
Writes labels for pictures of people and actions	✓			
Uses single words or phrases to express ideas			✓	
Writes simple but understandable sentences		✓		10/8
Spells simple words correctly		✓		10/8
Makes up spellings showing correct sound/letter relationships		✓		10/8
Uses standard word order		✓		10/8
Adds endings (-s, -es, 's, -ed, -ing) correctly		✓		10/8
Understands basic capitalization and punctuation		✓		10/8
Writes sentences demonstrating fluency and control of vocabulary		✓		10/8

Jenny reads simple stories fairly well. Nonfiction is difficult. Sequence of all texts can be a problem.

Jenny will need consistent help with putting her ideas down on paper in a coherent, readable form.

(A) Checklist format is easy to use.

(B) Space is provided for you to note your own responses.

Form for reproduction is on pages 131–132.

Teacher Form
Observing English Language Learners

What is it?	• A form to record your ongoing observations about how English language learners process what they read
What does it show?	• How English language learners use strategies to make sense of materials they read • Students' growth and development in processing what they read
How do I use it?	• Work with students individually as they read a new selection. • Record your observations about how students deal with new words and concepts. • Continue to review and record students' behaviors periodically as needed. • Consider using the information on the form in parent conferences.

A Behaviors identify common strategies for success in reading a new language.

B Space is provided to record students' development over time.

Form for reproduction is on page 139.

Teacher Form
Observing English Language Learners

Student: Jenny Chang

Behaviors Observed	Date: 10/17			Date: 11/3			Date:			Date:		
The student	Yes	No	Sometimes	Yes	No	Sometimes	Yes	No	Sometimes	Yes	No	Sometimes
• uses context clues to figure out new words		✓				✓						
• uses prior knowledge to figure out new words			✓			✓						
• uses visuals to decipher meaning	✓					✓						
• uses strategies to decipher meaning			✓	✓								
• can identify the strategies he or she is using			✓			✓						
• understands why he or she is using a particular strategy		✓		✓								
• assesses his or her own progress		✓		✓								
• generally understands what the class is reading			✓			✓						

General Comments

10/17: Jenny needs to get used to using strategies and to know how and why she is using them.

11/3: A lot of progress in self-monitoring and in understanding texts!

Chapter 7

Collecting, Evaluating, and Reporting Evidence of Learning

Overview

Information about the three levels of assessment, entry-level (diagnostic and screening), progress-monitoring, and summative assessment, explained in Chapters 2–4, suggests that teachers will be compiling large amounts of information about students. Access to this data informs sound decision-making related to the focus of curriculum instruction, effectiveness of instruction, meaningful feedback to students and parents, and improved achievement.

Teacher Record Keeping

Learning goals are met by shaping effective instruction and assessment to meet the needs of each student. Checking for understanding contributes to improved instruction and learning. The evidence of this learning can be collected on a variety of record forms.

Why collect evidence of learning?

- A roadmap of each student's learning is created by keeping records of learning from classroom assessment, including:

  - the Scott Foresman *Reading Street* Baseline Group Test, entry-level (diagnostic) inventories, and surveys (Chapter 2)

  - progress-monitoring discussions, logs, journal entries, essays, portfolios, projects, and Scott Foresman *Reading Street* tests (Chapter 3)

  - summative measurements, such as state-required tests, the Scott Foresman *Reading Street* End-of-Year Benchmark Test, and district tests (Chapter 4)

- Pace, content, and type of instruction may be adjusted after evaluating the student's collected evidence of learning to see that learning goals are met.

How do I collect evidence of learning?

- Collect records of the students' learning throughout the year—at the beginning of the school year, daily, weekly, after clusters of instructional time such as units, and at the end of the year.

- Collect a variety of records of students' learning (e.g., notes from observations, responses to questions, checklists, portfolios, self-assessment, rubric and test scores, and grading).

- Collect key indicators about skills and concepts (e.g., words correct per minute, recognition of multiple meanings, summaries of readings).

Tools and Techniques for Teacher Record Keeping

- **Teacher Summary Reports** (See page 115.)
  compilations of assessment data that help describe students' growth in reading, writing, speaking, and listening

- **Reading Strategy Assessment** (See page 116.)
  a checklist that allows you to synthesize the information you have gathered about each student's knowledge and use of reading strategies

- **Writing Strategy Assessment** (See page 117.)
  a checklist that allows you to synthesize the information you have gathered about each student's knowledge and use of writing strategies

- **Cumulative Folder Form** (See page 118.)
  a cumulative record of students' reading progress that can be placed in their permanent files and follow them from year to year

How do I share assessment information?

- Assessment information is shared in two ways, communication and grading. Communication of assessment information may occur as written remarks or as conversation in which the quality or level of learning is discussed.

- Conferences provide excellent opportunities to convey assessment information and to maintain ongoing communication between teacher and student, teacher and parent, and student and student.

  - Teacher-student conferences can be part of your classroom routine and allow you time to learn about the unique learning needs and successes of individual students in your class.

  - Teacher-parent conferences are held formally during regularly scheduled school conference days, but they can also be held informally when you want to share concerns and accomplishments with your students' parents.

  - Student-led conferences with a teacher and parent allow students to talk about personal strengths and weaknesses and set goals for their next steps in learning, as well as help students become more aware of what to say and do about their learning.

- Conferencing about reading, writing, speaking, or listening or collections of work may include:

  - examining and discussing a reading response with comments about why its attributes meet a learning standard

  - analyzing and discussing how the traits on a written essay match the descriptions on a rubric

  - providing feedback about an inference skill or questioning strategy

  - explaining the reasons for a score on a vocabulary progress test

  - discussing a student's self-assessment reflection

  - evaluating a collection of work in a portfolio together with the student

- Evaluative communication provides feedback with a judgment about the quality of the work. This type of formal communication is typically shared by mark or symbol—check, score, or grade to designate the quality or level of learning. Symbols are often used on
  - checklists
  - continuums
  - assessment reports
  - report cards
- Narrative statements are often found on students' work, in portfolios, or as an addition to a report marked with symbols.

Student Portfolios

A portfolio is a collection of representative student work in reading, writing, speaking, and listening, serving as documentation of change and growth over a period of time. It centers discussion about learning among teachers, students, and parents on actual samples of work. The collection may be evaluated in process or as a completed product with narrative comments or symbols such as rubric scores, and it is a credible form of progress monitoring. A rubric is a valuable way to score entries in the portfolio because criteria in a rubric serve as a clear vision for students during the writing process, in drafting as well as the final product. The final rubric scores awarded in the portfolio contribute to an overall evaluation of learning along with other requirements for a grade.

What is the teacher's role?

- To make decisions with your students about the purpose, process, content, and timeline of the portfolio
- To consider options for the format of the portfolio (e.g., folder, binder, or electronic versions)
- To decide the method for evaluating the process and contents of the portfolio (e.g., conferencing with the student and parents, narrative feedback, scoring, grading, and perhaps review by other teachers or students)
- To share examples of portfolios to show students how portfolios might be organized and what might be kept in a portfolio
- To model metacognition (the awareness of the internal thinking that influences the choices for selection and revision of portfolio contents) by keeping a personal portfolio and sharing how you select and reflect on the pieces you include in it

What is the student's role?

- To add, change, or remove portfolio items demonstrating evidence of reading, writing, speaking, and listening to their portfolios with decreasing assistance from the teacher

- To explain and reflect about their collection of work

- To set and monitor goals for learning, as well as discuss strengths and weaknesses with teachers and family

- To participate in self-assessment and peer-assessment activities to improve their skills in collecting and learning from evidence in their portfolios

Tools and Techniques for Maintaining Portfolios

- **Student Portfolios** (See pages 94–95.)
  Maintaining a portfolio is a process that allows your students to use work samples to document and reflect on their growth in reading, writing, speaking, and listening.

- **Portfolio Guide** (See page 119.)
  This form helps you manage the contents of students' portfolios.

- **Portfolio Selection Slips** (See page 120.)
  These forms help your students select items to include in their portfolios and reflect on how the items demonstrate their growing skills in reading, writing, speaking, and listening.

- **Peer Assessment** (See page 71.)
  This form affords your students an opportunity to assess a peer's work and apply what they are learning about the quality of effective reading, writing, speaking, and listening.

- **Reading Log** (See page 75.)
  This form allows students to keep track of the literature they have read, as well as rate the quality of the selections.

- **About My Reading** (See page 76.)
  This form encourages your students to describe and evaluate their own reading progress.

- **Writing Log** (See page 77.)
  This form helps students keep track of and reflect on the pieces they have written.

- **About My Writing** (See page 78.)
  This form encourages your students to describe and evaluate their own writing progress.

Grading

- As mentioned earlier in this chapter, grading is a formal, summative form of communication about learning. Grading provides information for students, parents, teacher record-keeping, and sometimes district reporting, and it often leads to decisions about future learning goals for the student. Guidelines about grading attempt to ensure fairness to the student and sound grading practices.

What is a grade?

- A grade is the evaluative symbol reported at the end of an instructional unit of time. It is a summary of performance or achievement, showing whether the student met learning goals or standards. The symbol is usually a number or letter and answers, "How well is the student achieving at this point in time?" The primary purposes of grading are

  - to inform students, parents, teachers, and others about the student's current level of achievement

  - to support learning goals and inform progress of learning

  - to improve students' achievement by providing feedback that explains the criteria upon which the grade is based

  - to answer the question, "Has the student met the intended learning goals for this period?"

What are some general guidelines for grading?

- Base grades on academic achievement. Feedback on effort, behavior, ability, and attendance should be documented and reported separately.

- Communicate achievement of clear learning goals and standards with grades.

- Discuss expectations for grading with students and parents at the beginning of the instruction. Explain the criteria for grades in the classroom and school. Display models of graded work to students and parents at the beginning of the year to clarify and demonstrate expectations for students.

- Develop criteria for grades which may include test scores, rubric scores, completed work, and narrative records.

- Use rubrics as a lead-in to fair grading because of the clear descriptive criteria for scoring and the alignment to learning standards.

- Add narrative and descriptive feedback with grades whenever possible.

- Do not grade all work—some work is in draft form or for practice only.

- Use *recent* summative classroom assessments to measure achievement of learning goals.

- Determine marking period grades from multiple types of scores. Summarize overall achievement for a marking period into one score or grade.

- Check with the district's grading policy to ensure that your procedures are fair and consistent with the guidelines established by your school and district.

What are some opportunities for grading in Scott Foresman *Reading Street*?

The program offers many opportunities to grade students' work, including:

- activities and projects
- writing assignments
- pages from the Reader's and Writer's Notebook
- pages from the Fresh Reads for Fluency and Comprehension
- speeches and oral presentations
- Weekly Tests
- Unit Benchmark Tests
- End-of-Year Benchmark Test

Tools and Techniques for Grading

- **Rubrics in the Teacher's Editions**
  Your Scott Foresman *Reading Street* Teacher's Editions contain a variety of rubrics to help you assess your students' performances.

- **Creating a Rubric** (See page 121.)
  This form is used to identify criteria for assessing reading, writing, speaking, and listening and to evaluate how well students meet those criteria on various assignments.

- **Grading Writing** (See page 122.)
  Teachers can use the Creating a Rubric form to develop grading criteria for students' responses to writing prompts.

- **Grading Products and Activities** (See pages 123–124.)
  Teachers can use the Creating a Rubric form to develop grading criteria for a wide variety of students' products and activities.

Want to learn more about record keeping and grading?

If you are interested in learning more about record keeping and sharing assessment information, you will find the following resources interesting.

References

Afflerbach, P. *Understanding and Using Reading Assessment, K–12*. Newark, DE: International Reading Association, 2007.

Fisher, D., and N. Frey. *Checking for Understanding: Formative Assessment Techniques for Your Classroom*. Alexandria, VA: Association for Supervision and Curriculum Development, 2007.

Guskey, T. R. *How's My Kid Doing? A Parent's Guide to Grades, Marks, and Report Cards*. San Francisco, CA: Jossey-Bass, 2002.

Marzano, R. J. *Transforming Classroom Grading*. Alexandria, VA: Association for Supervision and Curriculum Development, 2000.

O'Connor, K. *How to Grade for Learning*. Arlington Heights, IL: Skylight Professional Development, 2002.

Stiggins, R.; J. Arter; J. Chappuis; and S. Chappuis. *Classroom Assessment for Student Learning: Doing It Right—Using It Well*. Portland, OR: Assessment Training Institute, 2004.

Teacher Forms
Teacher Summary Reports

What are they?
- Various forms that teachers can compile as a way of summarizing and assessing a student's literacy growth over time

What do they show?
- A student's reading, writing, speaking, and listening behaviors and strategies

How do I use them?
- In order to document a student's progress, compile and synthesize information from any or all of these sources:
  - Ongoing teacher observations
  - Behavior checklists
  - Profiles and inventories
  - Self, peer, and group assessments
  - Conference records
  - Reading and writing logs
  - Strategy assessments
  - Rubrics
  - Student portfolios
  - Cumulative folder form
  - Test scores
- Use what you have gathered when you prepare grades and as you get ready for conferences with students, parents, administrators, or resource teachers.

7 • Evidence of Learning

Teacher Form
Reading Strategy Assessment

What is it?

- A form to use at the end of each grading period to help synthesize the information gathered about a student's reading progress

What does it show?

- A student's knowledge and use of reading strategies, including self-assessment
- A student's reading proficiency levels at the end of a grading period

How do I use it?

- Use the checklist to summarize a student's progress in applying reading strategies or to help you transfer information to a more traditional reporting form.

A Criteria help you synthesize the information you've compiled from any of the forms and checklists you used throughout the grading period.

Teacher Form
Reading Strategy Assessment

Student _Kathy Noonan_   Date _11/3_
Teacher _Mrs. Hill_   Grade _4_

		Proficient	Developing	Emerging	Not showing yet
Building Background	Previews	✔	☐	☐	☐
Comments:	Ask questions	✔	☐	☐	☐
Is usually very interested in what she is reading.	Predicts	✔	☐	☐	☐
	Activates prior knowledge	✔	☐	☐	☐
	Sets own purposes for reading	✔	☐	☐	☐
A	Other:	☐	☐	☐	☐
Comprehension	Retells/Summarizes	✔	☐	☐	☐
Comments:	Questions and evaluates ideas	☐	✔	☐	☐
Needs to work on decoding skills. Kathy	Paraphrases	✔	☐	☐	☐
comprehends well	Rereads/reads ahead for meaning	☐	☐	✔	☐
unless vocabulary	Visualizes	✔	☐	☐	☐
is problematic. Is	Uses text structure to locate information	☐	✔	☐	☐
sometimes reluctant to	Uses decoding strategies	☐	✔	☐	☐
try new approaches	Uses vocabulary strategies	☐	✔	☐	☐
(e.g., reading ahead).	Understands key ideas in a text	☐	✔	☐	☐
	Relates text to other texts, experiences, or understanding	✔	☐	☐	☐
	Other:	☐	☐	☐	☐
Fluency	Adjusts reading rate	✔	☐	☐	☐
Comments:	Reads for accuracy	☐	✔	☐	☐
Reads dialogue with expression.	Uses expression	✔	☐	☐	☐
	Other:	☐	☐	☐	☐
Self-Assessment	Is aware of: Strengths	☐	✔	☐	☐
Comments:	Needs	☐	✔	☐	☐
Thinks that she reads	Improvement/Achievement	☐	✔	☐	☐
more than she does.	Sets and implements learning goals	✔	☐	☐	☐
Kathy shies away from	Maintains logs, records, portfolio	✔	☐	☐	☐
collaborative learning	Works with others	☐	☐	✔	☐
activities.	Shares ideas and materials	☐	✔	☐	☐
	Other: accepts suggestions for improvement	☐	✔	☐	☐

Form for reproduction is on page 149.

Teacher Form
Writing Strategy Assessment

What is it?
- A form to use at the end of each grading period to help synthesize the information gathered about a student's writing progress

What does it show?
- A student's knowledge and use of writing strategies
- A student's writing proficiency levels at the end of a grading period

How do I use it?
- Use the checklist to summarize a student's progress in applying writing strategies or to help you transfer information to a more traditional reporting form.

Ⓐ Criteria help you synthesize the information you've compiled from any of the forms and checklists you used throughout the grading period.

Teacher Form
Writing Strategy Assessment ✓

Student: Kari Snow   Date: 10/15
Teacher: Ms. Brewer   Grade: 4

Ⓐ

		Completed	Developing	Emerging	Not Showing Yet
Focus/Ideas Comments: *needs to expand details*	Addresses the writing task	✓			
	Demonstrates understanding of purpose	✓			
	States central idea		✓		
	Details support central idea		✓		
	Conclusion reinforces central idea		✓		
	Other:				
Organization Comments: *difficulty with conclusions*	Product of writing process	✓			
	Has a clear beginning, middle, and end		✓		
	Begins with a topic sentence	✓			
	Uses transitions between sentences and paragraphs		✓		
	Uses order words (first, then, after, finally)		✓		
	Other:				
Voice Comments: *doesn't have a grasp on voice*	Speaks directly to audience		✓		
	Voice matches writer's purpose		✓		
	Shows rather than tells		✓		
	Shows writer's feelings and personality		✓		
	Keeps reader's attention		✓		
	Other:				
Word Choice Comments:	Uses vivid words to elaborate ideas	✓			
	Avoids slang and jargon		✓		
	Uses strong images or figurative language		✓		
	Uses action verbs versus linking verbs		✓		
	Uses new words to express ideas		✓		
	Other:				
Sentences Comments:	Expresses thoughts in lively, varied sentences		✓		
	Mixes short and long sentences	✓			
	Includes questions, commands, and exclamations	✓			
	Sentences flow logically from one to another		✓		
	Avoids choppy and wordy sentences		✓		
	Other:				
Conventions Comments: *great spelling and grammar*	Uses subjects and verbs in agreement	✓			
	Uses correct punctuation for grade level	✓			
	Capitalizes proper nouns and sentence beginnings	✓			
	Forms noun plurals correctly	✓			
	Spells words correctly	✓			
	Other:				

© Pearson Education

Form for reproduction is on page 150.

Teacher Form
Cumulative Folder Form

What is it?
- A cumulative record of a student's reading progress, to be placed in the student's permanent record that follows him or her from year to year.

What does it show?
- The most basic and permanent information on how the student performed during each school year—namely, his or her score on the Baseline Group Test, scores for each Unit Benchmark Test, group placement, and any additional comments from the teacher.

How do I use it?
- Record scores and comments from unit to unit.
- Place the form into the student's cumulative folder at the end of the school year.

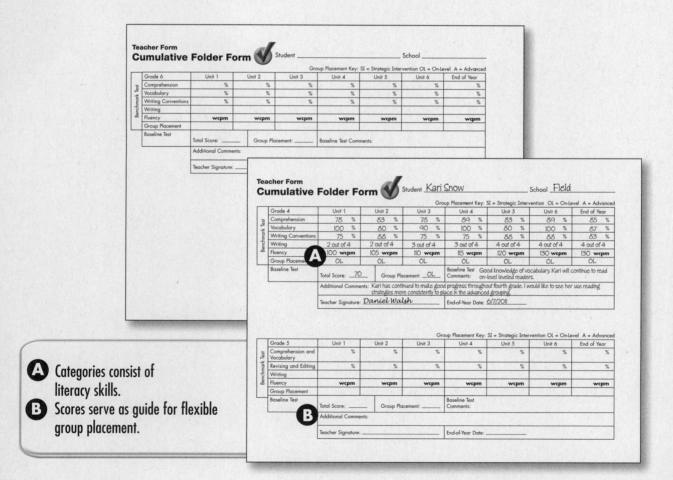

A Categories consist of literacy skills.
B Scores serve as guide for flexible group placement.

Form for reproduction is on page 151–152.

Teacher Form
Portfolio Guide

What is it?
- A form for managing the contents of a student's portfolio, whether teacher- or student- selected
- A cover sheet showing the portfolio contents at-a-glance

What does it show?
- An overall composite of a student's strengths, needs, interests, and attitudes throughout the year
- A student's selected work throughout the year

How do I use it?
- Track forms and work samples submitted at various times during the year.
- Fill in dates as a reminder of when items were submitted and when to collect additional submissions.

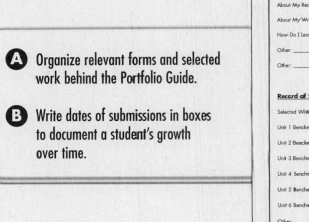

A Organize relevant forms and selected work behind the Portfolio Guide.

B Write dates of submissions in boxes to document a student's growth over time.

Form for reproduction is on page 147.

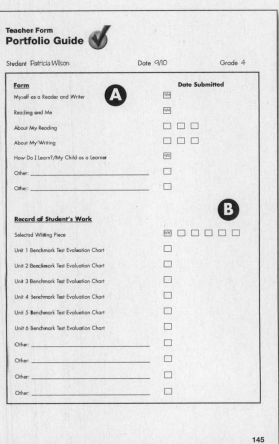

Student Form
Portfolio Selection Slips

What are they?
- Forms to help students select work samples to include in their portfolios
- Opportunities for students to think about what they have included in their portfolios and why they have chosen those items

What do they show?
- A student's rationale for including each piece in the portfolio
- What students think of their own work

How do students use them?
- Give students time to look over their work, decide which items to submit to their portfolios, and complete the forms.
- Attach one slip to each work sample and place it in the portfolio for future review of contents.

A Form gives students a chance to assess their work.

B Form gives students a chance to assess their own growth as learners.

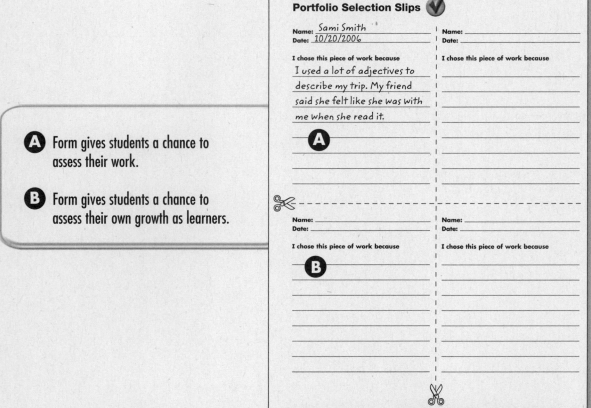

Form for reproduction is on page 148.

Teacher Form
Creating a Rubric

What is it?
- A form that may be used for evaluation of reading, writing, speaking, or listening assignments
- A tool that allows you to focus assessment on the key concepts emphasized during instruction

What does it show?
- How well a student exhibits his or her understanding of the key features of the assignment
- Areas in which a student may require additional instruction

How do I use it?
- Decide which assessment criteria are most relevant to a particular assignment. List them in the Features column.
- Rate and comment on those features as you assess the assignment.
- If desired, teacher may choose to convert the ratings into letter grades.

A The open-endedness of this form allows you to customize assessment features to meet the needs of every assignment.

B Your comments help you remember why you arrived at a rating and give you a starting point for discussing the assignment with the student or family.

C When desired, the rating may be turned into a letter grade.

Teacher Form
Creating a Rubric

Student Eriko Sato   Teacher Mr. Everett   Date 10/27

Assignment Make-believe story — The Beautiful Princess

Features	Rating	Comments
Entertaining **A**	4 ③ 2 1	Story shows a sense of humor. Needs to get to the point quicker.
	4 3 2 1	
Beginning, middle, end	④ 3 2 1	Understands sequence and story progression.
	4 3 2 1	
Interesting characters	4 ③ 2 1	Doing better at descriptions of characters.
	4 3 2 1	
Setting and plot	④ 3 2 1	Main character strives for goal and reaches it.
	4 3 2 1	
Use of dialogue	4 3 ② 1	Dialogue would bring story to life.
	4 3 2 1	
	4 3 2 1	
	4 3 2 1	
Total ③		

Key: **4** - Has more than expected
   3 - Has what was expected
   2 - Has less than expected
   1 - Did not fulfill assignment or did not complete the assignment

Read by:

Form for reproduction is on page 153.

7 • Evidence of Learning

Teacher Form
Grading Writing

Grading Responses to Writing Prompts

- Writing prompts occur in several places in Scott Foresman *Reading Street*:
  - Following each selection and in the end-of-unit writing-process activity in the Teacher's Edition
  - In the Unit Benchmark Tests and the End-of-Year Benchmark Test
- To grade students's writing, you can use the Creating a Rubric form. For your convenience, an example scale for a how-to response has been completed for you below. Actual determinations about what score equals which grade will, however, vary with different teachers and districts.

A List the features of a how-to article and add your own criteria if you wish.

B Comments help you remember why you arrived at a rating and give you a starting point for discussing the writing with the student.

C To determine the possible score, multiply the number of features by 4 (5 features x 4 = 20). Then add the ratings you've given the features to find the student's actual score. In this example 17 out of 20 = B.

Score	Grade
18–20	A
15–17	B
12–14	C
10–11	D
9 and below	F

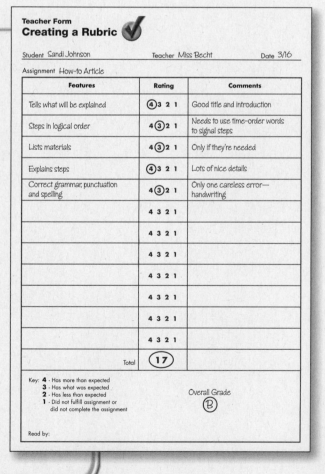

Teacher Form
Creating a Rubric

Student Sandi Johnson   Teacher Miss Becht   Date 3/16

Assignment How-to Article

Features	Rating	Comments
Tells what will be explained	④3 2 1	Good title and introduction
Steps in logical order	4③2 1	Needs to use time-order words to signal steps
Lists materials	4③2 1	Only if they're needed
Explains steps	④3 2 1	Lots of nice details
Correct grammar, punctuation and spelling	4③2 1	Only one careless error— handwriting
	4 3 2 1	
	4 3 2 1	
	4 3 2 1	
	4 3 2 1	
	4 3 2 1	
	4 3 2 1	
	4 3 2 1	
Total	⑰	

Key: **4** - Has more than expected
3 - Has what was expected
2 - Has less than expected
1 - Did not fulfill assignment or did not complete the assignment

Overall Grade Ⓑ

Read by:

Form for reproduction is on page 153.

Teacher Form
Grading Products and Activities

Grading Products and Activities

- The Creating a Rubric form lends itself to grading a variety of students' products and activities, including:
  - Class discussions
  - Speeches
  - Retellings
  - Oral readings and dramatizations
  - Drawings, sculptures, and other artwork
  - Graphic organizers such as Venn diagrams, story maps, concept maps, and KWL charts
- Two examples and grading scales—for a class discussion and for a graphic organizer—are provided here. Actual determinations about what score equals which grade will, however, vary with different teachers and districts.
- In determining the criteria on which to evaluate students' work, you may find it helpful to refer to the various teacher summary reports described earlier or to the other checklists in this handbook.

7 • Evidence of Learning

A Example for a CLASS DISCUSSION

B To get a grade:
5 features x 4 = 20;
18 out of 20 = A.

Score	Grade
18–20	A
15–17	B
12–14	C
10–11	D
9 and below	F

A

Teacher Form
Creating a Rubric

Student Dawn Kolak   Teacher Miss Bolt   Date 5/10

Assignment Class Discussion

Features	Rating	Comments
Gave detailed, thoughtful answers	④ 3 2 1	Came prepared to discuss
Backed up opinions with fact	④ 3 2 1	Great!
Asked questions to clarify	4 ③ 2 1	A little quiet but improving
Was supportive of others' ideas and opinions	4 ③ 2 1	Needs to show more outward reactions
Connected text to self	④ 3 2 1	Good—related to a family experience
	4 3 2 1	
	4 3 2 1	
	4 3 2 1	
	4 3 2 1	
	4 3 2 1	
	4 3 2 1	
	4 3 2 1	
B Total	⑱	

Key: **4** - Has more than expected
   3 - Has what was expected
   2 - Has less than expected
   1 - Did not fulfill assignment or did not complete the assignment

Overall Grade
Ⓐ

Read by:

C Example for a GRAPHIC ORGANIZER

D To determine a grade:
4 features x 4 = 16;
14 out of 16 = B.

Score	Grade
15–16	A
13–14	B
11–12	C
10	D
9 and below	F

Form for reproduction is on page 153.

C

Teacher Form
Creating a Rubric

Student Laura Damon   Teacher Ms. Dolan   Date 11/3

Assignment Graphic Organizer

Features	Rating	Comments
Set up clear categories	4 3 ② 1	Categories were mixed between general & specific
Showed relationships between parts	4 ③ 2 1	Some relationships shown nicely
Included all important information	④ 3 2 1	Synthesized information very well
Was neat and well drawn	4 3 ② 1	Needs to work on presentation
	4 3 2 1	
	4 3 2 1	
	4 3 2 1	
	4 3 2 1	
	4 3 2 1	
	4 3 2 1	
	4 3 2 1	
	4 3 2 1	
D Total	⑪	

Key: **4** - Has more than expected
   3 - Has what was expected
   2 - Has less than expected
   1 - Did not fulfill assignment or did not complete the assignment

Overall Grade
Ⓒ

Read by:

Teacher Form
Grading Group Activities

Grading Group Activities

- You can use the Creating a Rubric form to assign grades for group work. Students can be graded in one of two ways:

  – As group members working together

  – As individuals contributing to the group effort

- When evaluating the group as a unit, use criteria that emphasize students' ability to work together in an efficient and cooperative manner. Be mindful that cooperative or group grading can unfairly reward or penalize individual students.

- When assigning grades to individual students in a group, use criteria that emphasize the specific tasks the student must do. You might use students' reviews of their work on the Group Assessment form described in chapter 3.

- The examples provided here show ways to evaluate and grade groups as well as individual students within groups. Actual determinations about what score equals which grade will vary with different teachers and districts.

7 • Evidence of Learning

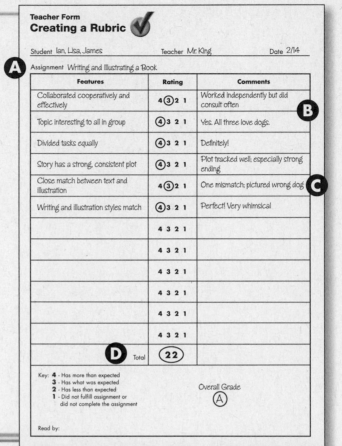

A Example for a COOPERATIVE GROUP ACTIVITY

B These criteria assess students' ability to work together cooperatively and effectively.

C These criteria assess the actual product that students created.

D To get a grade:
6 features x 4 = 24;
22 out of 24 = A.

Score	Grade
22–24	A
18–21	B
15–17	C
14–16	D
13 and below	F

Teacher Form
Creating a Rubric ✓

Student Ian, Lisa, James   Teacher Mr. King   Date 2/14

Assignment Writing and Illustrating a Book

Features	Rating	Comments
Collaborated cooperatively and effectively	4 ③ 2 1	Worked independently but did consult often
Topic interesting to all in group	④ 3 2 1	Yes. All three love dogs.
Divided tasks equally	④ 3 2 1	Definitely!
Story has a strong, consistent plot	④ 3 2 1	Plot tracked well; especially strong ending
Close match between text and illustration	4 ③ 2 1	One mismatch; pictured wrong dog
Writing and illustration styles match	④ 3 2 1	Perfect! Very whimsical
	4 3 2 1	
	4 3 2 1	
	4 3 2 1	
	4 3 2 1	
	4 3 2 1	
	4 3 2 1	
Total	㉒	

Key: **4** - Has more than expected
3 - Has what was expected
2 - Has less than expected
1 - Did not fulfill assignment or did not complete the assignment

Overall Grade Ⓐ

Read by:

E Example for an INDIVIDUAL IN A GROUP

F These criteria assess individual students according to the specific tasks they have performed.

G To get a grade:
3 features x 4 = 12;
10 out of 12 = B.

Score	Grade
11–12	A
10	B
9	C
8	D
7 and below	F

Teacher Form
Creating a Rubric ✓

Student Ian Murphy   Teacher Mr. King   Date 2/14

Assignment Writing/Illustrating a Book

Features	Rating	Comments
Created half of book illustrations	④ 3 2 1	Worked conscientiously; finished ahead of schedule
Created illustrations that hit highlights of text	④ 3 2 1	Ian's illustrations were right on target.
Participated in development of story line	4 3 ② 1	Less attention to this than to doing the art
	4 3 2 1	
	4 3 2 1	
	4 3 2 1	
	4 3 2 1	
	4 3 2 1	
	4 3 2 1	
	4 3 2 1	
	4 3 2 1	
	4 3 2 1	
Total	⑩	

Key: **4** - Has more than expected
3 - Has what was expected
2 - Has less than expected
1 - Did not fulfill assignment or did not complete the assignment

Overall Grade Ⓑ

Read by:

Form for reproduction is on page 153.

Classroom-based Assessment Tools

Myself as a Reader and Writer

		A Lot	Sometimes	Not at All
Name	Date			

1. I like to read

	A Lot	Sometimes	Not at All
realistic fiction	☐	☐	☐
fantasy stories (for example, tall tales, myths, science fiction)	☐	☐	☐
historical fiction	☐	☐	☐
plays	☐	☐	☐
biographies and autobiographies	☐	☐	☐
nonfiction articles	☐	☐	☐
other:	☐	☐	☐

2. The subjects I like to read about most are

	A Lot	Sometimes	Not at All
students my age	☐	☐	☐
sports	☐	☐	☐
famous people	☐	☐	☐
exploration and adventure	☐	☐	☐
how things work	☐	☐	☐
things that are funny	☐	☐	☐
other:	☐	☐	☐

3. I like to write

	A Lot	Sometimes	Not at All
made-up stories	☐	☐	☐
true stories	☐	☐	☐
letters	☐	☐	☐
poems	☐	☐	☐
reports	☐	☐	☐
plays	☐	☐	☐
other:	☐	☐	☐

4. The best book or story I have read in the last year is

_____

_____

5. The best thing I have written in the last year is a piece about

_____

_____

Student Form
Reading and Me

Name   Date

Mark the box next to the answer that tells how you feel.

1. How often do you like to read?

☐ All of the time
☐ Sometimes
☐ Not too often
☐ Never

2. When I read I

☐ always try my best.
☐ try my best most of the time.
☐ don't try very hard.
☐ often give up.

3. In general, when I read I

☐ really enjoy it.
☐ think it's OK.
☐ don't like it very much.
☐ dislike it a lot.

4. I think reading is

☐ my favorite thing to do.
☐ one of my favorite things to do.
☐ not one of my favorite things to do.
☐ my least favorite thing to do.

5. I read

☐ a lot better than my classmates.
☐ a little better than my classmates.
☐ about the same as my classmates.
☐ worse than my classmates.

6. When I am reading by myself, I understand

☐ most of what I read.
☐ some of what I read.
☐ not much of what I read.
☐ very little of what I read.

7. I am

☐ a great reader.
☐ a good reader.
☐ an OK reader.
☐ a poor reader.

8. I care what other kids think about my reading.

☐ Never
☐ Not too often
☐ Sometimes
☐ Always

9. I think that reading is

☐ very easy.
☐ kind of easy.
☐ kind of hard.
☐ very hard.

10. When I read in school I usually

☐ feel good about it.
☐ feel OK about it.
☐ feel not too good about it.
☐ feel terrible about it.

Reading and Me (continued)

Name   Date

Mark the box next to the answer that tells how you feel.

11. I talk with my friends about the things that I read

☐ all of the time.
☐ sometimes.
☐ not too often.
☐ never.

12. People who read a lot are

☐ very interesting.
☐ kind of interesting.
☐ not very interesting.
☐ pretty boring.

13. I think that reading in school is

☐ very important.
☐ important.
☐ somewhat important.
☐ not too important.

14. I think that reading at home is

☐ very important.
☐ important.
☐ somewhat important.
☐ not too important.

15. I like getting a book for a present.

☐ All the time
☐ Sometimes
☐ Not very often
☐ Never

16. I read newspapers

☐ very well.
☐ pretty well.
☐ not too well.
☐ not well at all.

17. I read schoolbooks

☐ very well.
☐ pretty well.
☐ not too well.
☐ not well at all.

18. I read comics

☐ very well.
☐ pretty well.
☐ not too well.
☐ not well at all.

19. I read magazines

☐ very well.
☐ pretty well.
☐ not too well.
☐ not well at all.

20. I read storybooks or novels

☐ very well.
☐ pretty well.
☐ not too well.
☐ not well at all.

Teacher Form

Profile of English Language Learners

Student:

Trait	Mostly	Unevenly	Rarely	Date/Comment
Oral Language				
Uses names of many objects				
Uses and understands basic everyday vocabulary				
Speaks hesitantly, searching for words				
Speaks fluently but makes errors				
Uses mostly present-tense verbs				
Has trouble with irregular forms (standed, more slower)				
Asks and answers simple questions				
Follows simple directions				
Is able to explain events or ideas				
Reading				
Recognizes basic sound/letter relationships in words				
Follows text being read aloud				
Needs pictures to comprehend text				

Profile of English Language Learners (continued)

Student:

Trait	Mostly	Unevenly	Rarely	Date/Comment
Joins in choral reading				
Retells predictable text				
Recognizes many words by sight				
Relies on print more than on illustrations				
Retells beginning, middle, and end of things read				
Writing				
Writes labels for pictures of people and actions				
Uses single words or phrases to express ideas				
Writes simple but understandable sentences				
Spells simple words correctly				
Makes up spellings showing correct sound/letter relationships				
Uses standard word order				
Adds endings (-s, -es, 's, -ed, -ing) correctly				
Understands basic capitalization and punctuation				
Writes sentences demonstrating fluency and control of vocabulary				

Student Form

How Do I Learn?

Name _____   Date _____

1. **Which statement is most true about you?**

   a. ☐ I nearly always understand things better if I see a picture or diagram.

   b. ☐ When someone explains something, I usually understand it just by listening.

   c. ☐ Sometimes I need pictures to help me understand; other times I don't.

2. **If you have a choice, you would rather work**

   a. ☐ in a group with three or four others.

   b. ☐ with one partner.

   c. ☐ by yourself.

3. **You want to remember a story you read. The best way for you to do this would be to**

   a. ☐ draw a picture of it.

   b. ☐ act out a scene from it.

   c. ☐ discuss it with a partner or group.

   d. ☐ do this instead:

   _____

   _____

4. **You go to a museum. The kind of exhibit you like best has**

   a. ☐ a film to go with it.

   b. ☐ levers and buttons you can play with.

   c. ☐ a book where you can write what you liked and didn't like.

   d. ☐ something else:

   _____

   _____

5. **Your group is planning a presentation about castles for younger students. The part you would like to do best is**

   a. ☐ design the invitations.

   b. ☐ build a model of the castle.

   c. ☐ talk to the students after the presentation to see how they liked it.

   d. ☐ something else:

   _____

   _____

Parent Form
My Child as a Learner ✓

Name _____   Date _____

Please comment and provide examples of your child's learning in the following areas.

My child	Yes	No	Comments/Examples
1. usually • reads daily • writes daily • watches TV daily	☐ ☐ ☐	☐ ☐ ☐	
2. often • is curious • keeps on with what he or she is doing • does things in new ways • becomes easily frustrated • likes trying new things • likes to express opinions	☐ ☐ ☐ ☐ ☐ ☐	☐ ☐ ☐ ☐ ☐ ☐	
3. understands what he or she is • reading • writing • watching	☐ ☐ ☐	☐ ☐ ☐	
4. explores ideas by • reading • writing • drawing • watching • talking	☐ ☐ ☐ ☐ ☐	☐ ☐ ☐ ☐ ☐	
5. enjoys working • with others • alone	☐ ☐	☐ ☐	
6. is someone who • is proud of achievement • recognizes his or her own growth • considers new possibilities • sets goals for himself or herself	☐ ☐ ☐ ☐	☐ ☐ ☐ ☐	
7. likes to read about			
8. likes to write about			
9. likes to watch			
10. Additional comments and reactions:			

My name _____   Relationship to child _____

I can be reached at _____

Teacher Form

Narrative Retelling Chart

Name _____ Date _____

Selection Title _____

Retelling Criteria/Teacher Prompt	Teacher-Aided Response	Student-Generated Response	Rubric Score (Circle one.)
Connections Has anything like this happened to you? How does this story remind you of other stories?			4 3 2 1
Author's Purpose Why do you think the author wrote this story? What was the author trying to tell us?			4 3 2 1
Characters Describe _____ (character's name) at the beginning and end of the story.			4 3 2 1
Setting Where and when did the story happen?			4 3 2 1
Plot Tell me what the story was about in a few sentences.			4 3 2 1

Summative Retelling Score 4 3 2 1

Comments _____

Teacher Form

Expository Retelling Chart

Selection Title _____

Name _____ Date _____

Retelling Criteria/Teacher Prompt	Teacher-Aided Response	Student-Generated Response	Rubric Score (Circle one)
Connections Did this selection make you think about something else you have read? What did you learn about as you read this selection?			4 3 2 1
Author's Purpose Why do you think the author wrote this selection?			4 3 2 1
Topic What was the selection mostly about?			4 3 2 1
Important Ideas What is important for me to know about _____ (topic)?			4 3 2 1
Conclusions What did you learn from reading this selection?			4 3 2 1

Summative Retelling Score 4 3 2 1

Comments _____

Teacher Form

Work Habits Conference Record

Student

Use the key at the bottom of the page to assess student's performance.

Date	Understands tasks	Sets priorities	Uses time appropriately	Solves problems effectively	Seeks help when needed	Completes tasks on time	Can explain process/ project effectively	Comments

4 Does more than expected   **3** Does what was expected   **2** Does less than expected   **1** Does not fulfill the assignment or does not complete the assignment

Teacher Form

Skills Conference Record ✓

Grade _____

Student _____   Teacher _____

		Proficient	Developing	Having difficulty	Not showing trait
Reading Comments:	Sets own purpose for reading	☐	☐	☐	☐
	Predicts and asks questions	☐	☐	☐	☐
	Retells/Summarizes	☐	☐	☐	☐
	Reads fluently	☐	☐	☐	☐
	Understands key ideas in a text	☐	☐	☐	☐
	Uses decoding strategies	☐	☐	☐	☐
	Makes text connections	☐	☐	☐	☐
	Other:	☐	☐	☐	☐
Writing Comments:	Follows writing process	☐	☐	☐	☐
	Develops central idea with details	☐	☐	☐	☐
	Organizes ideas logically	☐	☐	☐	☐
	Reveals purpose with voice	☐	☐	☐	☐
	Expresses ideas with word choice	☐	☐	☐	☐
	Uses varied sentence structure	☐	☐	☐	☐
	Uses language conventions appropriately	☐	☐	☐	☐
	Other:	☐	☐	☐	☐
Speaking and Listening Comments:	Follows instructions	☐	☐	☐	☐
	Asks questions	☐	☐	☐	☐
	Answers questions	☐	☐	☐	☐
	Paraphrases	☐	☐	☐	☐
	Participates in discussions	☐	☐	☐	☐
	Makes eye contact with audience	☐	☐	☐	☐
	Other:	☐	☐	☐	☐

Teacher Form

Observing English Language Learners

Student:

Behaviors Observed	Date:			Date:			Date:			Date:		
	Yes	No	Sometimes	Yes	No	Sometimes	Yes	No	Sometimes	Yes	No	Sometimes
The student												
• uses context clues to figure out new words												
• uses prior knowledge to figure out new words												
• uses visuals to decipher meaning												
• uses strategies to decipher meaning												
• can identify the strategies he or she is using												
• understands why he or she is using a particular strategy												
• assesses his or her own progress												
• generally understands what the class is reading												

General Comments

Student Self-Assessment

Name _____   Teacher _____   Date _____

Work or Project I'm Assessing: _____

Things I Did Well	Things I Need to Work On
How I Will Work on Them	**My Goals for the Future**

Student Form
Peer Assessment

My name is _____ Date_____

I'm looking at _____'s work.

The work I am looking at is _____.

Things I Especially Like About Your Work	Things I Had Trouble Understanding
_____	_____
_____	_____
_____	_____
_____	_____
_____	_____
_____	_____
_____	_____
_____	_____

Suggestions

_____

_____

_____

_____

_____

_____

_____

_____

Student Form

Group Assessment ✓

Teacher _____   Date _____

What the Group Did: _____

_____

_____

What I Did:

Member 1

Member 2

Member 3

Member 4

Problems We Had: _____

_____

_____

Our Goals for Next Time: _____

_____

Student Form
Reading Log

Name _____

Dates Read	Title and Author	What is it about?	How would you rate it?	Explain your rating.
From ___ to ___			**Great** 5 4 3 2 1 **Awful**	
From ___ to ___			**Great** 5 4 3 2 1 **Awful**	
From ___ to ___			**Great** 5 4 3 2 1 **Awful**	
From ___ to ___			**Great** 5 4 3 2 1 **Awful**	
From ___ to ___			**Great** 5 4 3 2 1 **Awful**	

About My Reading ✔

Name _____   Date _____

1. **Compared with earlier in the year, I am enjoying reading**

   ☐ more   ☐ less   ☐ about the same

2. **When I read now, I understand**

   ☐ more than I used to   ☐ about the same as I used to

3. **One thing that has helped me with my reading is**

   _____

   _____

   _____

4. **One thing that could make me a better reader is**

   _____

   _____

   _____

5. **Here is one selection or book that I really enjoyed reading:**

   _____

   _____

6. **Here are some reasons why I liked it:**

   _____

   _____

   _____

   _____

   _____

Student Form
Writing Log

Student _____

Date _____

Teacher _____

Grade _____

Date	Title	Type of Writing	How I felt about this piece	What I liked or disliked	Put in Portfolio
			4 3 2 1		
			4 3 2 1		
			4 3 2 1		
			4 3 2 1		
			4 3 2 1		
			4 3 2 1		

Key
4 = Excellent
3 = Good
2 = Fair
1 = Poor

About My Writing ✓

Name _____   Date _____

1. Compared with earlier in the year, I am enjoying writing

   ☐ more   ☐ less   ☐ about the same

2. When I write now, my writing is

   • clearer than it used to be   ☐ yes   ☐ no

   • more interesting than it used to be   ☐ yes   ☐ no

3. One thing that has improved my writing is

   _____

   _____

   _____

4. One thing that could make me a better writer is

   _____

   _____

   _____

5. Here is one piece that I wrote that I think is really good:

   _____

   _____

6. Here are some things that are good about it:

   _____

   _____

   _____

   _____

Teacher Form
Portfolio Guide ✓

Student _____ Date _____ Grade _____

Form	**Date Submitted**
Myself as a Reader and Writer	☐
Reading and Me	☐
About My Reading	☐ ☐ ☐
About My Writing	☐ ☐ ☐
How Do I Learn?/My Child as a Learner	☐
Other: _____	☐
Other: _____	☐

Record of Student's Work	
Selected Writing Piece	☐ ☐ ☐ ☐ ☐ ☐
Unit 1 Benchmark Test Evaluation Chart	☐
Unit 2 Benchmark Test Evaluation Chart	☐
Unit 3 Benchmark Test Evaluation Chart	☐
Unit 4 Benchmark Test Evaluation Chart	☐
Unit 5 Benchmark Test Evaluation Chart	☐
Unit 6 Benchmark Test Evaluation Chart	☐
Other: _____	☐
Other: _____	☐
Other: _____	☐
Other: _____	☐

Student Form
Portfolio Selection Slips

Name: _____

Date: _____

I chose this piece of work because

_____

_____

_____

_____

_____

_____

_____

Name: _____

Date: _____

I chose this piece of work because

_____

_____

_____

_____

_____

_____

_____

Name: _____

Date: _____

I chose this piece of work because

_____

_____

_____

_____

_____

Name: _____

Date: _____

I chose this piece of work because

_____

_____

_____

_____

_____

Reading Strategy Assessment

Student _____ Date _____

Teacher _____ Grade _____

		Proficient	Developing	Emerging	Not showing trait
Building Background Comments:	Previews	☐	☐	☐	☐
	Asks questions	☐	☐	☐	☐
	Predicts	☐	☐	☐	☐
	Activates prior knowledge	☐	☐	☐	☐
	Sets own purposes for reading	☐	☐	☐	☐
	Other:	☐	☐	☐	☐
Comprehension Comments:	Retells/Summarizes	☐	☐	☐	☐
	Questions and evaluates ideas	☐	☐	☐	☐
	Paraphrases	☐	☐	☐	☐
	Rereads/reads ahead for meaning	☐	☐	☐	☐
	Visualizes	☐	☐	☐	☐
	Uses text structure to locate information	☐	☐	☐	☐
	Uses decoding strategies	☐	☐	☐	☐
	Uses vocabulary strategies	☐	☐	☐	☐
	Understands key ideas of a text	☐	☐	☐	☐
	Relates text to other texts, experiences, or understanding	☐	☐	☐	☐
	Other:	☐	☐	☐	☐
Fluency Comments:	Adjusts reading rate	☐	☐	☐	☐
	Reads for accuracy	☐	☐	☐	☐
	Uses expression	☐	☐	☐	☐
	Other:	☐	☐	☐	☐
Self-Assessment Comments:	Is aware of: Strengths	☐	☐	☐	☐
	Needs	☐	☐	☐	☐
	Improvement/Achievement	☐	☐	☐	☐
	Sets and implements learning goals	☐	☐	☐	☐
	Maintains logs, records, portfolio	☐	☐	☐	☐
	Works with others	☐	☐	☐	☐
	Shares ideas and materials	☐	☐	☐	☐
	Other:	☐	☐	☐	☐

Teacher Form

Writing Strategy Assessment

Student _____ Date _____

Teacher _____ Grade _____

		Competent	Developing	Emerging	Not showing trait
Focus/Ideas Comments:	Addresses the writing task	☐	☐	☐	☐
	Demonstrates understanding of purpose	☐	☐	☐	☐
	States central idea	☐	☐	☐	☐
	Details support central idea	☐	☐	☐	☐
	Conclusion reinforces central idea	☐	☐	☐	☐
	Other:	☐	☐	☐	☐
Organization Comments:	Product of writing process	☐	☐	☐	☐
	Has a clear beginning, middle, and end	☐	☐	☐	☐
	Begins with a topic sentence	☐	☐	☐	☐
	Uses transitions between sentences and paragraphs	☐	☐	☐	☐
	Uses order words *(first, then, after, finally)*	☐	☐		☐
	Other:	☐	☐		☐
Voice Comments:	Speaks directly to audience	☐	☐	☐	☐
	Voice matches writer's purpose	☐	☐	☐	☐
	Shows rather than tells	☐	☐	☐	☐
	Shows writer's feelings and personality	☐	☐	☐	☐
	Keeps reader's attention	☐	☐	☐	☐
	Other:	☐	☐	☐	☐
Word Choice Comments:	Uses vivid words to elaborate ideas	☐	☐	☐	☐
	Avoids slang and jargon	☐	☐	☐	☐
	Uses strong images or figurative language	☐	☐	☐	☐
	Uses action verbs versus linking verbs	☐	☐	☐	☐
	Uses new words to express ideas	☐	☐	☐	☐
	Other:	☐	☐	☐	☐
Sentences Comments:	Expresses thoughts in lively, varied sentences	☐	☐	☐	☐
	Mixes short and long sentences	☐	☐		☐
	Includes questions, commands, and exclamations	☐	☐		
	Sentences flow logically from one to another	☐	☐	☐	☐
	Avoids choppy and wordy sentences	☐	☐	☐	☐
	Other:	☐	☐	☐	☐
Conventions Comments:	Uses subjects and verbs in agreement	☐	☐	☐	☐
	Uses correct punctuation for grade level	☐	☐	☐	☐
	Capitalizes proper nouns and sentence beginnings	☐	☐	☐	☐
	Forms noun plurals correctly	☐	☐	☐	☐
	Spells words correctly	☐	☐	☐	☐
	Other:	☐	☐	☐	☐

Teacher Form

Cumulative Folder Form

 Student _____ School _____

Group Placement Key: SI = Strategic Intervention OL = On-Level A = Advanced

Grade 4	Unit 1	Unit 2	Unit 3	Unit 4	Unit 5	Unit 6	End of Year
Comprehension	%	%	%	%	%	%	%
Vocabulary	%	%	%	%	%	%	%
Writing Conventions	%	%	%	%	%	%	%
Writing							
Fluency	wcpm	wcpm	wcpm	wcpm	wcpm	wcpm	wcpm
Group Placement							

Benchmark Test

Baseline Test

Total Score: _____   Group Placement: _____

Additional Comments:

Baseline Test Comments:

Teacher Signature: _____   End-of-Year Date: _____

Group Placement Key: SI = Strategic Intervention OL = On-Level A = Advanced

Grade 5	Unit 1	Unit 2	Unit 3	Unit 4	Unit 5	Unit 6	End of Year
Comprehension and Vocabulary	%	%	%	%	%	%	%
Revising and Editing	%	%	%	%	%	%	%
Writing							
Fluency	wcpm	wcpm	wcpm	wcpm	wcpm	wcpm	wcpm
Group Placement							

Benchmark Test

Baseline Test

Total Score: _____   Group Placement: _____

Additional Comments:

Baseline Test Comments:

Teacher Signature: _____   End-of-Year Date: _____

Teacher Form

Cumulative Folder Form

 Student _____ School _____

Group Placement Key: SI = Strategic Intervention OL = On-Level A = Advanced

Grade 6	Unit 1	Unit 2	Unit 3	Unit 4	Unit 5	Unit 6	End of Year
Comprehension	%	%	%	%	%	%	%
Vocabulary	%	%	%	%	%	%	%
Writing Conventions	%	%	%	%	%	%	%
Writing							
Fluency	wcpm	wcpm	wcpm	wcpm	wcpm	wcpm	wcpm
Group Placement							

Benchmark Test

Baseline Test		
Total Score: _____	Group Placement: _____	Baseline Test Comments:

Additional Comments:

Teacher Signature: _____   End-of-Year Date: _____

Teacher Form
Creating a Rubric

Student _____   Teacher _____   Date _____

Assignment _____

Features	Rating	Comments
	4 3 2 1	
	4 3 2 1	
	4 3 2 1	
	4 3 2 1	
	4 3 2 1	
	4 3 2 1	
	4 3 2 1	
	4 3 2 1	
	4 3 2 1	
	4 3 2 1	
	4 3 2 1	
	4 3 2 1	
Total		

Key: **4** - Has more than expected
     3 - Has what was expected
     2 - Has less than expected
     1 - Did not fulfill assignment or
         did not complete the assignment

Read by: _____

Fourth Grade Formal Assessment Tools

Form from Fourth Grade Baseline Group Test Teacher's Manual

Grade 4 Baseline Test Evaluation Chart

(including percentage conversion chart)

Student's Name _____ Date _____

Item	Score (circle one)		Item	Score (circle one)		Number Correct/ 25	Percent Correct/ 25	Total Number Correct/ 55	Total Percent Correct /55	Total Number Correct/ 55 (continued)	Total Percent Correct/ 55 (continued)
Vocabulary			**Reading**			1	4%	1	2%	32	58%
1.	0	1	1.	0	1	2	8%	2	4%	33	60%
2.	0	1	2.	0	1	3	12%	3	5%	34	62%
3.	0	1	3.	0	1	4	16%	4	7%	35	64%
4.	0	1	4.	0	1	5	20%	5	9%	36	65%
5.	0	1	5.	0	1	6	24%	6	11%	37	67%
6.	0	1	6.	0	1	7	28%	7	13%	38	69%
7.	0	1	7.	0	1	8	32%	8	15%	39	71%
8.	0	1	8.	0	1	9	36%	9	16%	40	73%
9.	0	1	9.	0	1	10	40%	10	18%	41	75%
10.	0	1	10.	0	1	11	44%	11	20%	42	76%
11.	0	1	11.	0	1	12	48%	12	22%	43	78%
12.	0	1	12.	0	1	13	52%	13	24%	44	80%
13.	0	1	13.	0	1	14	56%	14	25%	45	82%
14.	0	1	14.	0	1	15	60%	15	27%	46	84%
15.	0	1	15.	0	1	16	64%	16	29%	47	85%
16.	0	1	16.	0	1	17	68%	17	31%	48	87%
17.	0	1	17.	0	1	18	72%	18	33%	49	89%
18.	0	1	18.	0	1	19	76%	19	35%	50	91%
19.	0	1	19.	0	1	20	80%	20	36%	51	93%
20.	0	1	20.	0	1	21	84%	21	38%	52	95%
21.	0	1	21.	0	1	22	88%	22	40%	53	96%
22.	0	1	22.	0	1	23	92%	23	42%	54	98%
23.	0	1	23.	0	1	24	96%	24	44%	55	100%
24.	0	1	24.	0	1	25	100%	25	45%		
25.	0	1	25.	0	1			26	47%		
			26.	0	1			27	49%		
			27.	0	1			28	51%		
			28.	0	1			29	53%		
			29.	0	1			30	55%		
			30.	0	1			31	56%		

Vocabulary Score _____/25= _____%

TOTAL (Vocabulary + Reading Score) _____/55= _____%

Reading Score _____/30= _____%   **Placement:** _____

Alternate Baseline Test Placement: (Optional)

Strategic Intervention _____

On-Level _____   **Advanced** _____

Fluency Rate _____   (Optional)

Interim Overall Placement (circle one)   **Strategic Intervention   On-Level   Advanced**

Fluency Forms

Class Fluency Progress Chart

Student's Name	Initial		Unit 1		Unit 2		Unit 3		Unit 4		Unit 5		Unit 6	
	Date	WCPM	Date	WCPM	Date	WCPM	Date	WCPM	Date	WCPM	Date	WCPM	Date	WCPM
1.														
2.														
3.														
4.														
5.														
6.														
7.														
8.														
9.														
10.														
11.														
12.														
13.														
14.														
15.														
16.														
17.														
18.														
19.														
20.														
21.														
22.														
23.														
24.														
25.														
26.														
27.														
28.														
29.														
30.														
31.														
32.														
33.														
34.														
35.														

Fluency Progress Chart, Grade 4

Name _____

WCPM	1	2	3	4	5	6	7	8	9	10	11	12	13	14	15	16	17	18	19	20	21	22	23	24	25	26	27	28	29	30	31	32	33	34	35	36
165																																				
160																																				
155																																				
150																																				
145																																				
140																																				
135																																				
130																																				
125																																				
120																																				
115																																				
110																																				
105																																				
100																																				
95																																				
90																																				
85																																				
80																																				
75																																				
70																																				

Timed Reading/Week

161

Forms from Fourth Grade Weekly Tests Teacher's Manual

Scott Foresman *Reading Street*
Class Weekly Test Progress Chart—Grade 4

Teacher's Name: _____

Student Name	Weekly Test Total Score																													
	1	2	3	4	5	6	7	8	9	10	11	12	13	14	15	16	17	18	19	20	21	22	23	24	25	26	27	28	29	30
1																														
2																														
3																														
4																														
5																														
6																														
7																														
8																														
9																														
10																														
11																														
12																														
13																														
14																														
15																														
16																														
17																														
18																														
19																														
20																														
21																														
22																														
23																														
24																														
25																														
26																														
27																														
28																														
29																														
30																														

Scott Foresman *Reading Street*
Student Weekly Test Progress Chart—Grade 4

Student Name: _____

Test	Vocabulary	Phonics/Word Analysis	Comprehension	Multiple-Choice Total	Writing	TOTAL
Weekly Test 1	/7	/5	/8	/20		
Weekly Test 2	/6	/6	/8	/20		
Weekly Test 3	/7	/5	/8	/20		
Weekly Test 4	/7	/5	/8	/20		
Weekly Test 5	/7	/5	/8	/20		
Weekly Test 6	/7	/5	/8	/20		
Weekly Test 7	/5	/7	/8	/20		
Weekly Test 8	/7	/5	/8	/20		
Weekly Test 9	/7	/5	/8	/20		
Weekly Test 10	/7	/5	/8	/20		
Weekly Test 11	/7	/5	/8	/20		
Weekly Test 12	/6	/6	/8	/20		
Weekly Test 13	/5	/7	/8	/20		
Weekly Test 14	/6	/6	/8	/20		
Weekly Test 15	/7	/5	/8	/20		
Weekly Test 16	/7	/5	/8	/20		
Weekly Test 17	/7	/5	/8	/20		
Weekly Test 18	/7	/5	/8	/20		
Weekly Test 19	/7	/5	/8	/20		
Weekly Test 20	/7	/5	/8	/20		
Weekly Test 21	/7	/5	/8	/20		
Weekly Test 22	/7	/5	/8	/20		
Weekly Test 23	/7	/5	/8	/20		
Weekly Test 24	/7	/5	/8	/20		
Weekly Test 25	/7	/5	/8	/20		
Weekly Test 26	/7	/5	/8	/20		
Weekly Test 27	/6	/6	/8	/20		
Weekly Test 28	/7	/5	/8	/20		
Weekly Test 29	/6	/6	/8	/20		
Weekly Test 30	/7	/5	/8	/20		

Comprehension Target Skill Coverage

How can the Weekly Tests predict student success on Unit Benchmark Tests?

Each Unit Benchmark Test, as well as assessing overall student reading ability, concentrates on two skills taught and/or reviewed during the unit by including several questions on those skills. In order to ensure that comprehension target skill can be accurately learned and then tested, students learn each target skill through a combination of being taught and reviewing the skill multiple times before testing occurs. The charts below show the units/weeks where the target comprehension skills are taught and where they are tested on Weekly Tests. Based on the student's number of correct answers for each tested target skill, the teacher will know whether a student has gained the necessary skill knowledge before the Unit Test is given. A low score on the Weekly Tests probably indicates a need for closer review of the student's performance and perhaps additional instruction. It is important to understand that these tests provide only one look at the student's progress and should be interpreted in conjunction with other assessments and the teacher's observation.

Using the Comprehension Target Skill Coverage Chart

To score target skill knowledge, use the Comprehension Target Skill Coverage Chart.

1. Make a copy of the appropriate Comprehension Target Skill Coverage chart for each student.

2. To score, circle the number of correct answers the student had for that skill on the appropriate Weekly Test.

3. Using the total number of correct answers for a skill, check the appropriate box under *Student Trend* to indicate whether or not the student has acquired the target skill knowledge. We recommend 90% correct as the criterion for skill acquisition at this level. Add any notes or observations that may be helpful to you and the student in later instruction.

Grade 4 — Comprehension Target Skill Coverage Chart

Student Name _____

Unit 1 Tested Skills	Weekly Test Locations	Number Correct	Student Trend
Sequence	Weekly Test 1	0 1 2 3 4 5	_____ Skill knowledge acquired _____ Skill needs further review
	Weekly Test 2	0 1	
	Weekly Test 3	0 1	
Author's Purpose	Weekly Test 2	0 1 2 3 4 5	_____ Skill knowledge acquired _____ Skill needs further review
	Weekly Test 4	0 1 2 3 4 5	
	Weekly Test 5	0 1	

Unit 2 Tested Skills	Weekly Test Locations	Number Correct	Student Trend
Draw Conclusions	Weekly Test 1	0 1 2	_____ Skill knowledge acquired _____ Skill needs further review
	Weekly Test 3	0 1 2	
	Weekly Test 6	0 1 2	
	Weekly Test 7	0 1 2 3 4 5	
	Weekly Test 8	0 1 2 3 4 5 6	
	Weekly Test 9	0 1 2	
	Weekly Test 10	0 1 2	
Main Idea and Supporting Details	Weekly Test 5	0 1 2 3 4 5 6 7	_____ Skill knowledge acquired _____ Skill needs further review
	Weekly Test 7	0 1	
	Weekly Test 9	0 1	
	Weekly Test 10	0 1 2 3 4 5	

Grade 4 — Comprehension Target Skill Coverage Chart

Student Name _____

Unit 3 Tested Skills	Weekly Test Locations	Number Correct	Student Trend
Fact and Opinion	Weekly Test 9	0 1 2 3 4 5	____ Skill knowledge acquired ____ Skill needs further review
	Weekly Test 10	0 1	
	Weekly Test 11	0 1	
	Weekly Test 12	0 1 2 3 4 5	
Generalize	Weekly Test 13	0 1 2 3 4 5	____ Skill knowledge acquired ____ Skill needs further review
	Weekly Test 15	0 1 2 3 4 5	

Unit 4 Tested Skills	Weekly Test Locations	Number Correct	Student Trend
Compare and Contrast	Weekly Test 16	0 1 2 3 4 5	____ Skill knowledge acquired ____ Skill needs further review
	Weekly Test 17	0 1 2 3 4 5	
	Weekly Test 19	0 1	
	Weekly Test 20	0 1	
Cause and Effect	Weekly Test 1	0 1	
	Weekly Test 2	0 1 2	
	Weekly Test 6	0 1 2 3 4 5	
	Weekly Test 8	0 1	
	Weekly Test 13	0 1 2	
	Weekly Test 14	0 1 2 3 4 5	____ Skill knowledge acquired ____ Skill needs further review
	Weekly Test 16	0 1	
	Weekly Test 17	0 1 2	

Grade 4 — Comprehension Target Skill Coverage Chart

Student Name _____

Unit 5 Tested Skills	Weekly Test Locations	Number Correct	Student Trend
Author's Purpose	Weekly Test 2	0 1 2 3 4 5	
	Weekly Test 4	0 1 2 3 4 5	
	Weekly Test 5	0 1	
	Weekly Test 7	0 1	_____ Skill knowledge acquired
	Weekly Test 21	0 1 2 3 4 5	_____ Skill needs further review
	Weekly Test 23	0 1	
Literary Elements: Character/Plot/Theme	Weekly Test 3	0 1 2 3	
	Weekly Test 4	0 1 2 3	
	Weekly Test 6	0 1	
	Weekly Test 7	0 1 2	
	Weekly Test 8	0 1	
	Weekly Test 20	0 1 2 3 4 5	
	Weekly Test 22	0 1 2 3	_____ Skill knowledge acquired
	Weekly Test 23	0 1 2 3 4 5	_____ Skill needs further review
	Weekly Test 25	0 1	

Grade 4 — Comprehension Target Skill Coverage Chart

Student Name _____

Unit 6 Tested Skills	Weekly Test Locations	Number Correct	Student Trend
Fact and Opinion	Weekly Test 9	0 1 2 3 4 5	
	Weekly Test 10	0 1	
	Weekly Test 11	0 1	
	Weekly Test 12	0 1 2 3 4 5	____ Skill knowledge acquired
	Weekly Test 24	0 1	
	Weekly Test 27	0 1 2 3 4 5	____ Skill needs further review
Graphic Sources	Weekly Test 11	0 1 2 3 4 5	
	Weekly Test 12	0 1	
	Weekly Test 14	0 1	
	Weekly Test 18	0 1	
	Weekly Test 19	0 1 2 3 4 5	____ Skill knowledge acquired
	Weekly Test 21	0 1	
	Weekly Test 30	0 1 2 3 4 5	____ Skill needs further review

Weekly Test Item Analysis—Grade 4

TEST	SECTION	ITEMS	SKILL
Weekly Test 1	**Vocabulary**	1–7	Understand and use new vocabulary
	Word Analysis	8–12	Word ending *-ed*
	Comprehension	13–16, 18	◎ Sequence
		17, 19	Draw conclusions
		20	**R** Cause and effect
	Written Response	Look Back and Write	Respond to literature
Weekly Test 2	**Vocabulary**	1–6	Understand and use new vocabulary
	Word Analysis	7–12	Suffixes *-or, -er*
	Comprehension	15, 16, 18–20	◎ Author's purpose
		14, 17	Cause and effect
		13	**R** Sequence
	Written Response	Look Back and Write	Respond to literature
Weekly Test 3	**Vocabulary**	1–7	Understand and use new vocabulary
	Word Analysis	8–12	Word ending *-ing*
	Comprehension	13–16, 18	◎ Literary elements: Character, setting, plot
		19, 20	Draw conclusions
		17	**R** Sequence
	Written Response	Look Back and Write	Respond to literature

Weekly Test Item Analysis—Grade 4

TEST	SECTION	ITEMS	SKILL
Weekly Test 4	**Vocabulary**	1–7	Understand and use new vocabulary
	Word Analysis	8–12	Compound words
	Comprehension	14, 16, 18, 19, 20	⊙ Author's purpose
		13, 15–17	**R** Literary elements: Character, setting, plot
	Written Response	Look Back and Write	Respond to literature
Weekly Test 5	**Vocabulary**	1–7	Understand and use new vocabulary
	Word Analysis	8–12	Related words
	Comprehension	13, 14–16, 18–20	⊙ Main idea and details
		17	**R** Author's purpose
	Written Response	Look Back and Write	Respond to literature
Weekly Test 6	**Vocabulary**	1–7	Understand and use new vocabulary
	Word Analysis	8–12	Prefixes *un-, in-*
	Comprehension	14, 15, 17, 18, 19	⊙ Cause and effect
		16, 20	Draw conclusions
		13	**R** Literary elements: Character, setting, plot
	Written Response	Look Back and Write	Respond to literature

Weekly Test Item Analysis—Grade 4

TEST	SECTION	ITEMS	SKILL
Weekly Test 7	**Vocabulary**	1–5	Understand and use new vocabulary
	Word Analysis	6–12	Word origins
	Comprehension	15, 17–20	◉ Draw conclusions
		13, 14	Main idea and details; Literary elements: Character
		16	R Author's purpose
	Written Response	Look Back and Write	Respond to literature
Weekly Test 8	**Vocabulary**	1–7	Understand and use new vocabulary
	Word Analysis	8–12	Latin prefixes *dis-, re-, non-*
	Comprehension	13–16, 19, 20	◉ Draw conclusions
		17	Literary elements: Character
		18	R Cause and effect
	Written Response	Look Back and Write	Respond to literature
Weekly Test 9	**Vocabulary**	1–7	Understand and use new vocabulary
	Word Analysis	8–12	Compound words
	Comprehension	13, 15, 16, 18, 20	◉ Fact and opinion
		17, 19	Draw conclusions
		14	R Main idea and details
	Written Response	Look Back and Write	Respond to literature

Weekly Test Item Analysis—Grade 4

TEST	SECTION	ITEMS	SKILL
Weekly Test 10	**Vocabulary**	1–7	Understand and use new vocabulary
	Word Analysis	8–12	Suffix -*ly*
	Comprehension	13–15, 18, 19	◉ Main idea and details
		16, 20	Draw conclusions
		17	**R** Fact and opinion
	Written Response	Look Back and Write	Respond to literature
Weekly Test 11	**Vocabulary**	1–7	Understand and use new vocabulary
	Word Analysis	8–12	Word origins—Latin
	Comprehension	13–15, 18, 20	◉ Graphic sources
		17, 19	Main idea and details
		16	**R** Fact and opinion
	Written Response	Look Back and Write	Respond to literature
Weekly Test 12	**Vocabulary**	1–6	Understand and use new vocabulary
	Word Analysis	7–12	Greek roots *bio-, phon, graph*
	Comprehension	13, 16, 18–20	◉ Fact and opinion
		14, 17	Draw conclusions
		15	**R** Graphic sources
	Written Response	Look Back and Write	Respond to literature

Weekly Test Item Analysis—Grade 4

TEST	SECTION	ITEMS	SKILL
Weekly Test 13	**Vocabulary**	1–5	Understand and use new vocabulary
	Word Analysis	6–12	Related words
	Comprehension	13, 15, 16, 18, 19	◉ Generalize
		14, 17	Cause and effect
		20	R Draw conclusions
	Written Response	Look Back and Write	Respond to literature
Weekly Test 14	**Vocabulary**	1–6	Understand and use new vocabulary
	Word Analysis	7–12	Latin roots *struct, scrib, script*
	Comprehension	13–15, 17, 18	◉ Cause and effect
		16, 20	Draw conclusions
		19	R Graphic sources
	Written Response	Look Back and Write	Respond to literature
Weekly Test 15	**Vocabulary**	1–7	Understand and use new vocabulary
	Word Analysis	8–12	Related words
	Comprehension	14, 15, 17, 19, 20	◉ Generalize
		13	Sequence
		18	Main idea and details
		16	R Draw conclusions
	Written Response	Look Back and Write	Respond to literature

Weekly Test Item Analysis—Grade 4

TEST	SECTION	ITEMS	SKILL
Weekly Test 16	**Vocabulary**	1–7	Understand and use new vocabulary
	Word Analysis	8–12	Suffixes *-ian, -ist, -ism*
	Comprehension	13, 14, 15, 18, 19	⦿ Compare and contrast
		17, 20	Draw conclusions
		16	R Cause and effect
	Written Response	Look Back and Write	Respond to literature
Weekly Test 17	**Vocabulary**	1–7	Understand and use new vocabulary
	Word Analysis	8–12	Latin roots *aqua, dict*
	Comprehension	13, 14, 16, 18, 19	⦿ Compare and contrast
		17, 20	Cause and effect
		15	R Generalize
	Written Response	Look Back and Write	Respond to literature
Weekly Test 18	**Vocabulary**	1–7	Understand and use new vocabulary
	Word Analysis	8–12	Related words–prefixes *im-, in-*
	Comprehension	13, 15, 16, 18, 19	⦿ Sequence
		14	Graphic sources
		20	Draw conclusions
		17	R Generalize
	Written Response	Look Back and Write	Respond to literature

Weekly Test Item Analysis—Grade 4

TEST	SECTION	ITEMS	SKILL
Weekly Test 19	**Vocabulary**	1–7	Understand and use new vocabulary
	Word Analysis	8–12	Greek and Latin prefixes *trans-, tele-*
	Comprehension	13, 15, 16, 18, 19	◉ Graphic sources
		14, 20	Main idea and details
		17	R Compare and contrast
	Written Response	Look Back and Write	Respond to literature
Weekly Test 20	**Vocabulary**	1–7	Understand and use new vocabulary
	Word Analysis	8–12	Greek prefixes *amphi-, anti-*
	Comprehension	14, 15, 17, 18, 20	◉ Literary elements: Character and plot
		16, 19	Draw conclusions
		13	R Compare and contrast
	Written Response	Look Back and Write	Respond to literature
Weekly Test 21	**Vocabulary**	1–7	Understand and use new vocabulary
	Word Analysis	8–12	French word origins
	Comprehension	15–17, 19, 20	◉ Author's purpose
		14, 18	Draw conclusions
		13	R Graphic sources
	Written Response	Look Back and Write	Respond to literature

Weekly Test Item Analysis—Grade 4

TEST	SECTION	ITEMS	SKILL
Weekly Test 22	**Vocabulary**	1–7	Understand and use new vocabulary
	Word Analysis	8–12	Suffixes *-ous, -able, -ible*
	Comprehension	13, 15, 17–19	◉ Compare and contrast
		14, 16, 20	**R** Literary elements: Character and plot
	Written Response	Look Back and Write	Respond to literature
Weekly Test 23	**Vocabulary**	1–7	Understand and use new vocabulary
	Word Analysis	8–12	Related words
	Comprehension	13, 15, 16, 17, 20	◉ Literary elements: Character, plot, and theme
		14, 18	Sequence
		19	**R** Author's purpose
	Written Response	Look Back and Write	Respond to literature
Weekly Test 24	**Vocabulary**	1–7	Understand and use new vocabulary
	Word Analysis	8–12	Suffix *-ion*
	Comprehension	13, 14, 17, 18, 20	◉ Main idea and details
		15, 16	Draw conclusions
		19	**R** Fact and opinion
	Written Response	Look Back and Write	Respond to literature

Weekly Test Item Analysis—Grade 4

TEST	SECTION	ITEMS	SKILL
Weekly Test 25	**Vocabulary**	1–7	Understand and use new vocabulary
	Word Analysis	8–12	German word origins
	Comprehension	15–19	◉ Draw conclusions
		13, 14	Sequence
		20	R Literary elements: Character, plot, and theme
	Written Response	Look Back and Write	Respond to literature
Weekly Test 26	**Vocabulary**	1–7	Understand and use new vocabulary
	Word Analysis	8–12	Latin roots *gener, port*
	Comprehension	13, 15, 17, 19, 20	◉ Cause and effect
		14, 18	Draw conclusions
		16	R Main idea and details
	Written Response	Look Back and Write	Respond to literature
Weekly Test 27	**Vocabulary**	1–6	Understand and use new vocabulary
	Word Analysis	7–12	Latin roots *dur, ject*
	Comprehension	14–16, 18, 19	◉ Fact and opinion
		13, 20	Main idea and details
		17	R Draw conclusions
	Written Response	Look Back and Write	Respond to literature

Weekly Test Item Analysis—Grade 4

TEST	SECTION	ITEMS	SKILL
Weekly Test 28	**Vocabulary**	1–7	Understand and use new vocabulary
	Word Analysis	8–12	French word origins
	Comprehension	13, 14, 18–20	◎ Sequence
		16, 17	Draw conclusions
		15	R Compare and contrast
	Written Response	Look Back and Write	Respond to literature
Weekly Test 29	**Vocabulary**	1–6	Understand and use new vocabulary
	Word Analysis	7–12	Related words
	Comprehension	13–15, 17, 18	◎ Generalize
		19, 20	Draw conclusions
		16	R Sequence
	Written Response	Look Back and Write	Respond to literature
Weekly Test 30	**Vocabulary**	1–7	Understand and use new vocabulary
	Word Analysis	8–12	Prefixes *astro-*, Greek and Latin roots
	Comprehension	13, 15, 17, 18, 20	◎ Graphic sources
		14, 19	Draw conclusions
		16	R Generalize
	Written Response	Look Back and Write	Respond to literature

Forms from Grade 4 Unit and End-of-Year Benchmark Tests Teacher's Manual

CLASS RECORD CHART

Grade 4 Unit Benchmark Tests

Teacher Name _____ Class _____

Student Name	Unit 1		Unit 2		Unit 3		Unit 4		Unit 5		Unit 6	
	Pt 1–3	Pt 4	Pt 1–3	Pt 4	Pt 1–3	Pt 4	Pt 1–3	Pt 4	Pt 1–3	Pt 4	Pt 1–3	Pt 4
1.												
2.												
3.												
4.												
5.												
6.												
7.												
8.												
9.												
10.												
11.												
12.												
13.												
14.												
15.												
16.												
17.												
18.												
19.												
20.												
21.												
22.												
23.												
24.												
25.												
26.												
27.												
28.												
29.												
30.												

Evaluation Chart: Grade 4 — Unit 1 Benchmark Test

Student Name _____ Date _____

Reading – Parts 1–3			
Item	**Tested Skill**	**Item Type***	**Score** (circle one)
Reading – Part 1: Comprehension			
1.	Author's purpose	C	0 1
2.	Compare and contrast	I	0 1
3.	Draw conclusions	C	0 1
4.	Sequence	L	0 1
5.	Draw conclusions	I	0 1
6.	Draw conclusions	I	0 1
7.	Literary elements: character	I	0 1
8.	Sequence	L	0 1
9.	Draw conclusions	I	0 1
10.	Main idea and details	C	0 1
11.	Sequence	C	0 1
A.	Constructed-response text-to-self connection		0 1 2
12.	Main idea and details	I	0 1
13.	Main idea and details	I	0 1
14.	Fact and opinion	C	0 1
15.	Author's purpose	C	0 1
16.	Author's purpose	C	0 1
17.	Author's purpose	C	0 1
18.	Main idea and details	L	0 1
19.	Compare and contrast	I	0 1
20.	Compare and contrast	L	0 1
21.	Author's purpose	C	0 1
22.	Draw conclusions	C	0 1
B.	Constructed-response text-to-text connection		0 1 2
Reading – Part 2: Vocabulary			
23.	Word structure: suffixes		0 1
24.	Context clues: synonyms		0 1
25.	Word structure: suffixes		0 1
26.	Context clues: unfamiliar words		0 1
27.	Word structure: suffixes		0 1
28.	Word structure: suffixes		0 1
29.	Context clues: multiple-meaning words		0 1

Reading – Part 2: Vocabulary (continued)			
30.	Context clues: synonyms	0	1
31.	Context clues: multiple-meaning words	0	1
32.	Word structure: suffixes	0	1
Reading – Part 3: Writing Conventions			
33.	Imperative and exclamatory sentences	0	1
34.	Declarative and interrogative sentences	0	1
35.	Clauses and complex sentences	0	1
36.	Clauses and complex sentences	0	1
37.	Compound sentences	0	1
38.	Clauses and complex sentences	0	1
39.	Complete subjects and predicates	0	1
40.	Complete subjects and predicates	0	1
Student's Reading Total Score/Total Possible Score		_____ /44	

*L = literal   I = inferential   C = critical analysis

Reading — Parts 1–3 percentage score: _____ ÷ 44 = _____ × 100 = _____%

(student's total score)   (percentage score)

Writing – Part 4

Writing Score (Complete one.)   _____/6   _____/5   _____/4   _____/3

Notes/Observations:

Evaluation Chart: Grade 4 — Unit 2 Benchmark Test

Student Name _____ **Date** _____

Item	Tested Skill	Item Type*	Score (circle one)
Reading – Parts 1–3			
Reading – Part 1: Comprehension			
1.	Main idea and details	I	0 1
2.	Main idea and details	I	0 1
3.	Draw conclusions	I	0 1
4.	Fact and opinion	C	0 1
5.	Sequence	L	0 1
6.	Sequence	L	0 1
7.	Author's purpose	C	0 1
8.	Draw conclusions	I	0 1
9.	Draw conclusions	C	0 1
10.	Author's purpose	C	0 1
11.	Draw conclusions	I	0 1
A.	Constructed-response text-to-world connection		0 1 2
12.	Main idea and details	I	0 1
13.	Draw conclusions	C	0 1
14.	Sequence	L	0 1
15.	Main idea and details	L	0 1
16.	Main idea and details	L	0 1
17.	Draw conclusions	C	0 1
18.	Generalize	C	0 1
19.	Main idea and details	I	0 1
20.	Main idea and details	C	0 1
21.	Main idea and details	I	0 1
22.	Cause and effect	I	0 1
B.	Constructed-response text-to-text connection		0 1 2
Reading – Part 2: Vocabulary			
23.	Context clues: unfamiliar words		0 1
24.	Context clues: synonyms		0 1
25.	Word structure: suffixes		0 1
26.	Word structure: suffixes		0 1
27.	Context clues: unfamiliar words		0 1
28.	Word structure: prefixes		0 1
29.	Word structure: suffixes		0 1

Reading – Part 2: Vocabulary (continued)			
30.	Word structure: suffixes	0	1
31.	Context clues: unfamiliar words	0	1
32.	Word structure: prefixes	0	1
Student's Regrouping Multiple-Choice Score/Total Response Score		_____ /32	
Reading – Part 3: Writing Conventions			
33.	Regular plural nouns	0	1
34.	Common and proper nouns	0	1
35.	Irregular plural nouns	0	1
36.	Regular plural nouns	0	1
37.	Irregular plural nouns	0	1
38.	Common and proper nouns	0	1
39.	Singular possessive nouns	0	1
40.	Plural possessive nouns	0	1
Student's Reading Total Score/Total Possible Score		_____ /44	

*L = literal   I = inferential   C = critical analysis

Regrouping (Reading — Parts 1–2) percentage score: _____ ÷ 32 = _____ × 100 = _____%

(student's score)   (percentage score)

Reading — Parts 1–3 percentage score: _____ ÷ 44 = _____ × 100 = _____%

(student's total score)   (percentage score)

Writing – Part 4
Writing Score (Complete one.)   _____ /6   _____ /5   _____ /4   _____ /3
Notes/Observations:

Evaluation Chart: Grade 4 — Unit 3 Benchmark Test

Student Name _____ **Date** _____

	Reading – Parts 1–3		
Item	**Tested Skill**	**Item Type***	**Score** (circle one)
Reading – Part 1: Comprehension			
1.	Author's purpose	I	0 1
2.	Fact and opnion	C	0 1
3.	Author's purpose	C	0 1
4.	Main idea and details	C	0 1
5.	Generalize	I	0 1
6.	Fact and opinion	I	0 1
7.	Draw conclusions	I	0 1
8.	Author's purpose	C	0 1
9.	Draw conclusions	I	0 1
10.	Main idea and details	I	0 1
11.	Draw conclusions	I	0 1
A.	Constructed-response text-to-self connection		0 1 2
12.	Literary elements: character	I	0 1
13.	Fact and opinion	I	0 1
14.	Cause and effect	L	0 1
15.	Generalize	I	0 1
16.	Draw conclusions	I	0 1
17.	Author's purpose	I	0 1
18.	Generalize	I	0 1
19.	Cause and effect	I	0 1
20.	Main idea and details	C	0 1
21.	Generalize	I	0 1
22.	Generalize	C	0 1
B.	Constructed-response text-to-text connection		0 1 2
Reading – Part 2: Vocabulary			
23.	Context clues: homonyms		0 1
24.	Context clues: homonyms		0 1
25.	Context clues: unfamiliar words		0 1
26.	Context clues: unfamiliar words		0 1
27.	Word structure: suffixes		0 1
28.	Context clues: unfamiliar words		0 1
29.	Context clues: multiple-meaning words		0 1

Reading – Part 2: Vocabulary (continued)			
30.	Word structure: prefixes	0	1
31.	Context clues: unfamiliar words	0	1
32.	Context clues: multiple-meaning words	0	1
Student's Regrouping Multiple-Choice Score/Total Possible Score		_____**/32**	
Reading – Part 3: Writing Conventions			
33.	Past, present, and future verb tenses	0	1
34.	Past, present, and future verb tenses	0	1
35.	Action and linking verbs	0	1
36.	Past, present, and future verb tenses	0	1
37.	Past, present, and future verb tenses	0	1
38.	Main and helping verbs	0	1
39.	Past, present, and future verb tenses	0	1
40.	Subject-verb agreement	0	1
Student's Reading Total Score/Total Possible Score		_____**/44**	

*L = literal   I = inferential   C = critical analysis

Regrouping (Reading — Parts 1–2) percentage score: _____ ÷ 32 = _____ × 100 = _____%
      (student's score)   (percentage score)

Reading — Parts 1–3 percentage score: _____ ÷ 44 = _____ × 100 = _____%
      (student's total score)   (percentage score)

Writing – Part 4

Writing Score (Complete one.) _____/6   _____/5   _____/4   _____/3

Notes/Observations:

Evaluation Chart: Grade 4 — Unit 4 Benchmark Test

Student Name _____ Date _____

Reading – Parts 1–3			
Item	**Tested Skill**	**Item Type***	**Score** (circle one)
Reading – Part 1: Comprehension			
1.	Compare and contrast	I	0 1
2.	Compare and contrast	L	0 1
3.	Main idea and details	I	0 1
4.	Cause and effect	I	0 1
5.	Draw conclusions	I	0 1
6.	Compare and contrast	L	0 1
7.	Compare and contrast	L	0 1
8.	Draw conclusions	C	0 1
9.	Author's purpose	C	0 1
10.	Main idea and details	C	0 1
11.	Cause and effect	I	0 1
A.	Constructed-response text-to-world connection		0 1 2
12.	Literary elements: plot	C	0 1
13.	Literary elements: character	C	0 1
14.	Compare and contrast	I	0 1
15.	Draw conclusions	I	0 1
16.	Cause and effect	I	0 1
17.	Draw conclusions	I	0 1
18.	Draw conclusions	C	0 1
19.	Compare and contrast	I	0 1
20.	Cause and effect	I	0 1
21.	Author's purpose	C	0 1
22.	Cause and effect	I	0 1
B.	Constructed-response text-to-text connection		0 1 2
Reading – Part 2: Vocabulary			
23.	Context clues: synonyms		0 1
24.	Context clues: synonyms		0 1
25.	Context clues: antonyms		0 1
26.	Context clues: multiple-meaning words		0 1
27.	Context clues: antonyms		0 1
28.	Context clues: antonyms		0 1
29.	Context clues: unknown words		0 1

Reading – Part 2: Vocabulary (continued)			
30.	Context clues: antonyms	0	1
31.	Context clues: unknown words	0	1
32.	Context clues: multiple-meaning words	0	1
Student's Regrouping Multiple-Choice Score/Total Possible Score		_____/32	
Reading – Part 3: Writing Conventions			
33.	Subject and object pronouns	0	1
34.	Pronouns and antecedents	0	1
35.	Subject and object pronouns	0	1
36.	Singular and plural pronouns	0	1
37.	Pronouns and antecedents	0	1
38.	Contractions and negatives	0	1
39.	Pronouns and antecedents	0	1
40.	Singular and plural pronouns	0	1
Student's Reading Total Score/Total Possible Score		_____/44	

*L = literal   I = inferential   C = critical analysis

Regrouping (Reading — Parts 1–2) percentage score: _____ ÷ 32 = _____ × 100 = _____%
                                                     (student's score)   (percentage score)

Reading — Parts 1–3 percentage score: _____ ÷ 44 = _____ × 100 = _____%
                                        (student's total score)   (percentage score)

Writing – Part 4

Writing Score (Complete one.) _____/6   _____/5   _____/4   _____/3

Notes/Observations:

Evaluation Chart: Grade 4 — Unit 5 Benchmark Test

Student Name _____ Date _____

Item	Tested Skill	Item Type*	Score (circle one)		
Reading – Parts 1–3					
Reading – Part 1: Comprehension					
1.	Sequence	I	0	1	
2.	Author's purpose	C	0	1	
3.	Literary elements: plot	I	0	1	
4.	Literary elements: character	C	0	1	
5.	Literary elements: character	C	0	1	
6.	Literary elements: theme	I	0	1	
7.	Draw conclusions	I	0	1	
8.	Literary elements: plot	I	0	1	
9.	Literary elements: theme	I	0	1	
10.	Literary elements: plot	I	0	1	
11.	Draw conclusions	I	0	1	
A.	Constructed-response text-to-world connection		0	1	2
12.	Sequence	I	0	1	
13.	Author's purpose	C	0	1	
14.	Cause and effect	I	0	1	
15.	Main idea and details	I	0	1	
16.	Author's purpose	C	0	1	
17.	Fact and opinion	I	0	1	
18.	Cause and effect	I	0	1	
19.	Draw conclusions	I	0	1	
20.	Author's purpose	C	0	1	
21.	Main idea and details	C	0	1	
22.	Author's purpose	C	0	1	
B.	Constructed-response text-to-text connection		0	1	2
Reading – Part 2: Vocabulary					
23.	Context clues: homographs		0	1	
24.	Context clues: synonyms		0	1	
25.	Context clues: synonyms		0	1	
26.	Context clues: synonyms		0	1	
27.	Context clues: synonyms		0	1	
28.	Context clues: homographs		0	1	
29.	Context clues: synonyms		0	1	

Reading – Part 2: Vocabulary (continued)		
30.	Context clues: unfamiliar words	0 1
31.	Context clues: unfamiliar words	0 1
32.	Context clues: synonyms	0 1
Student's Regrouping Multiple-Choice Score/Total Possible Score		_____/32
Reading – Part 3: Writing Conventions		
33.	Adverbs	0 1
34.	Adjectives and articles	0 1
35.	Comparative and superlative adjectives	0 1
36.	Adverbs	0 1
37.	Adjectives	0 1
38.	Adverbs	0 1
39.	Prepositions	0 1
40.	Prepositions and prepositional phrases	0 1
Student's Reading Total Score/Total Possible Score		_____/44

*L = literal   I = inferential   C = critical analysis

Regrouping (Reading — Parts 1–2) percentage score: _____ ÷ 32 = _____ × 100 = _____%
                                       (student's score)   (percentage score)

Reading – Parts 1–3 percentage score: _____ ÷ 44 = _____ × 100 = _____%
                               (student's total score)   (percentage score)

Writing – Part 4

Writing Score (Complete one.)   _____/6   _____/5   _____/4   _____/3

Notes/Observations:

Evaluation Chart: Grade 4 — Unit 6 Benchmark Test

Student Name _____ Date _____

Reading – Parts 1–3			
Item	**Tested Skill**	**Item Type***	**Score** (circle one)
Reading – Part 1: Comprehension			
1.	Graphic sources	I	0 1
2.	Fact and opinion	C	0 1
3.	Graphic sources	I	0 1
4.	Fact and opinion	C	0 1
5.	Compare and contrast	L	0 1
6.	Draw conclusions	I	0 1
7.	Draw conclusions	I	0 1
8.	Sequence	L	0 1
9.	Main idea and details	C	0 1
10.	Author's purpose	C	0 1
11.	Cause and effect	L	0 1
A.	Constructed-response text-to-world connection		0 1 2
12.	Sequence	L	0 1
13.	Draw conclusions	I	0 1
14.	Main idea and details	I	0 1
15.	Fact and opinion	C	0 1
16.	Draw conclusions	I	0 1
17.	Graphic sources	I	0 1
18.	Author's purpose	C	0 1
19.	Fact and opinion	I	0 1
20.	Fact and opinion	C	0 1
21.	Graphic sources	C	0 1
22.	Graphic sources	I	0 1
B.	Constructed-response text-to-text connection		0 1 2
Reading – Part 2: Vocabulary			
23.	Word structure: root words		0 1
24.	Context clues: multiple-meaning words		0 1
25.	Word structure: root words		0 1
26.	Context clues: multiple-meaning words		0 1
27.	Context clues: multiple-meaning words		0 1
28.	Dictionary/glossary: unfamiliar words		0 1
29.	Dictionary/glossary: unfamiliar words		0 1

Reading – Part 2: Vocabulary (continued)		
30.	Dictionary/glossary: multiple-meaning words	0 1
31.	Dictionary/glossary: multiple-meaning words	0 1
32.	Dictionary/glossary: unfamiliar words	0 1
Student's Regrouping Multiple-Choice Score/Total Possible Score		_____ /32
Reading – Part 3: Writing Conventions		
33.	Quotation marks	0 1
34.	Commas	0 1
35.	Capitalization	0 1
36.	Commas	0 1
37.	Quotation marks	0 1
38.	Conjunctions and combining sentences	0 1
39.	Conjunctions and combining sentences	0 1
40.	Capitalization	0 1
Student's Reading Total Score/Total Possible Score		_____ /44

*L = literal   I = inferential   C = critical analysis

Regrouping (Reading — Parts 1–2) percentage score: _____ ÷ 32 = _____ × 100 = _____%
(student's score)   (percentage score)

Reading — Parts 1–3 percentage score: _____ ÷ 44 = _____ × 100 = _____%
(student's total score)   (percentage score)

Writing – Part 4

Writing Score (Complete one.) _____ /6   _____ /5   _____ /4   _____ /3

Notes/Observations:

Evaluation Chart: Grade 4 — End-of-Year Benchmark Test

Student Name _____ Date _____

Reading – Parts 1–3

Item	Tested Skill	Item Type*	Score (circle one)	Item	Tested Skill	Item Type*	Score (circle one)
Reading – Part 1: Comprehension				26.	Cause and effect	I	0 1
1.	Compare and contrast	L	0 1	27.	Main idea and details	I	0 1
2.	Compare and contrast	I	0 1	28.	Draw conclusions	I	0 1
3.	Graphic sources	I	0 1	29.	Main idea and details	C	0 1
4.	Fact and opinion	C	0 1	30.	Graphic sources	I	0 1
5.	Main idea and details	I	0 1	31.	Graphic sources	I	0 1
6.	Author's purpose	C	0 1	32.	Fact and opinion	C	0 1
7.	Cause and effect	L	0 1	33.	Draw conclusions	I	0 1
8.	Sequence	I	0 1	B.	Constructed-response text-to-text connection		0 1 2
9.	Fact and opinion	C	0 1	**Reading – Part 2: Vocabulary**			
10.	Draw conclusions	C	0 1	34.	Context clues: unfamiliar words		0 1
11.	Cause and effect	L	0 1	35.	Word structure: prefixes		0 1
12.	Cause and effect	L	0 1	36.	Context clues: multiple-meaning words		0 1
13.	Draw conclusions	I	0 1	37.	Context clues: homonyms		0 1
14.	Compare and contrast	I	0 1	38.	Context clues: unfamiliar words		0 1
15.	Sequence	C	0 1	39.	Context clues: antonyms		0 1
16.	Author's purpose	C	0 1	40.	Context clues: antonyms		0 1
17.	Literary elements: theme	C	0 1	41.	Context clues: unfamiliar words		0 1
18.	Literary elements: character	I	0 1	42.	Word structure: suffixes		0 1
19.	Main idea and details	I	0 1	43.	Context clues: synonyms		0 1
20.	Literary elements: plot	I	0 1	44.	Context clues: multiple-meaning words		0 1
21.	Literary elements: character	I	0 1	45.	Context clues: multiple-meaning words		0 1
22.	Sequence	I	0 1	46.	Context clues: synonyms		0 1
A.	Constructed-response text-to-text connection		0 1 2	47.	Dictionary: multiple-meaning words		0 1
23.	Author's purpose	C	0 1	48.	Dictionary: multiple-meaning words		0 1
24.	Sequence	I	0 1	**Reading – Part 3: Writing Conventions**			
25.	Sequence	I	0 1	49.	Imperative and exclamatory sentences		0 1

Reading – Part 3: Writing Conventions (continued)

50.	Adverbs	0 1	56.	Past, present, and future verb tenses	0 1	
51.	Capitalization	0 1	57.	Subject-verb agreement	0 1	
52.	Compound and complex sentences	0 1	58.	Pronouns and antecedents	0 1	
53.	Irregular plural nouns	0 1	59.	Comparative and superlative adjectives	0 1	
54.	Possessive nouns	0 1	60.	Commas	0 1	
55.	Action and linking verbs	0 1				

Student's Reading Total Score/Total Possible Score _____ **/64**

*L = literal   I = inferential   C = critical analysis

Reading — Parts 1–3 percentage score: _____ ÷ 64 = _____ × 100 = _____%

(student's total score)   (percentage score)

Writing – Part 4

Writing Score (Complete one.) _____/6 _____/5 _____/4 _____/3

Notes/Observations:

Monitor Progress Passages
from Fourth Grade Teacher's Editions

A Lasting Friendship

For as long as she could remember, Kim had felt more comfortable   12
with animals than people. She was shy and quiet at school and she was   26
quiet at home now, too, with her mother, who'd been sick. When Kim   39
found five abandoned kittens, she didn't feel shy at all. She talked to   52
them, petted them, and fed them milk.   59

Kim knew that she wouldn't be able to keep the kittens, though.   71
Instead, she brought them to a new animal shelter. As soon as she   84
arrived there, she felt comfortable with the sounds of the animals,   95
barking and meowing. They feel lonely, like me, she thought.   105

"May I come back," Kim asked a worker, "to help?" The next   117
Saturday, Kim went to the shelter to work. That's when she met Mira.   130
Mira was bent over talking to a sad-looking puppy. Kim watched as   142
Mira stroked the puppy and told it that she felt sad also. When Mira   156
saw Kim, she turned away, blushing.   162

"It's okay," said Kim. "I feel sad a lot too. Looks like we have a lot in   179
common—you and me and the animals." From then on, Kim and Mira   192
met at the shelter each Saturday. They talked to the animals and to each   206
other too. It was the beginning of a lasting friendship.   216

MONITOR PROGRESS   • Check Fluency

Because of Winn-Dixie **45k**

Name _____

Camp Grove

Bruce went to Camp Grove because his parents made him go. Camp Grove was an outdoor adventure camp. Bruce did not like the outdoors or adventures.

Still, July found Bruce in the mountains of South Carolina unpacking his bags at Camp Grove. He peeked around at the other boys in his cramped cabin. They all seemed so different from him. One drummed on his cot, singing a rap tune. Another grunted as he lifted hand weights. Two more argued about who had the best cell phone. Bruce was quiet, and he just liked to read and play cards. Why was he here?

Their counselor, a lanky guy named Tim, came into the cabin. "Cabin four is the best!" he said. "Let's gather round and get to know each other."

They played a get-to-know-you game. Bruce thought the game would be dumb, but he learned that the weight-lifting boy, Justin, had a grandfather who lived in Bruce's town. He also learned that another boy, Sam, liked to play cards too.

After they all went to the lake to canoe, Bruce and Sam came back to the cabin and played cards.

During his two weeks at camp, Bruce made many discoveries. He discovered that he did like the outdoors after all. He even discovered that meeting new people was not so bad. Justin taught him about lifting weights.

When camp ended, Justin said he'd call Bruce the next time he visited his Grandpa. Sam and Bruce agreed they'd be back to play card games next year.

MONITOR PROGRESS • Sequence

Because of Winn-Dixie **45m**

Always a Doctor

It can be hard to change who you are. Juan Romagoza of El   13

Salvador had a love for helping people. He was studying to be a   26

surgeon. Then, during a civil war in his country, the military kidnapped   38

him. They did not like that Juan had been giving care to farm workers.   52

The military treated him badly. They hurt him so that he would not be   66

able to do surgery any more.   72

Juan lived through the civil war. In the 1980s he fled from his   85

country and came to the United States. Here, he met a doctor in   98

Washington, D.C. The doctor found Juan to be a kind and caring man.   111

He hired Juan to run a free clinic one night a week. Juan would give   126

care to those who could not pay for it. Juan showed kindness toward the   140

people he cared for. He found that he loved his work.   151

Now, twenty years later, Juan's clinic gives care to people full time.   163

They even have a new building. Juan's clinic helps Latino people who   175

might not be able to pay for a doctor's care. They are grateful for his   190

help and see him as a hero. And Juan Romagoza is grateful to be a   205

doctor.   206

MONITOR PROGRESS   • Check Fluency

Eve Bunting: Hope in Hard Times

Eve Bunting's father often told her that life was hard. Life was hard for Eve at times. But this Irish immigrant used her experience to become a well-loved author. She wrote over two hundred books for children.

Eve was born in Northern Ireland in 1928. Her childhood was a happy one. Many nights were spent by the fireplace as her father read poems. Later, when Eve was at boarding school, World War II broke out. German planes bombed the city. Eve and her classmates hid in bomb shelters under the ground.

When she grew up, Eve got married and had three children. Life in Northern Ireland was not easy, though. There was much hatred. Groups with different religions and beliefs did not get along. Eve and her husband, Ed, made a hard choice. They would leave the troubles of Ireland and come to America.

They moved in 1958 with no money and no job. Eve missed Ireland, though, and felt lonely in her new home. Eve decided to take a class in writing. She rewrote an Irish tale about two giants that she had loved as a child and it became her first book for children.

After that, Eve found many ideas for books. She thought of her hard times growing up. Life was hard for other children too, she knew. When Eve read news about hard times, she wrote about them. She wrote one book about a homeless father and son. Another was about riots in Los Angeles. Eve hopes that her books will help give children hope when life is hard.

MONITOR PROGRESS • Author's Purpose

The Train Man

The steam locomotive whistled and began to move. "I can't wait to   12
visit Salt Lake City," Lilly told her younger brother Ted.   22

An older man in a seat across from them looked up. "Going to   35
Utah?" he asked. "We'll be crossing track I built with my own hands."   48

Ted's eyes widened.   51

"It wasn't easy, building the railroad," the man said. "We worked   62
every day, sometimes sixteen hours a day, laying track. Many lives were   74
lost. Mine was almost one of them."   81

Lilly and Ted waited for more, but the man fell silent and slept.   94

"It was in Omaha, Nebraska, near here, where we started the   105
tracks," the man said when he woke. "Thirty years ago, in 1865. The   118
Union Pacific built tracks west from Omaha. The Central Pacific built   129
them east from Sacramento. Both tried to reach Salt Lake City first."   141

The next day, when Nebraska's plains had turned to Wyoming's   151
hills, the man continued. "We were building a bridge," he said. "I   163
fell 50 feet into a canyon. Broke my back. It could have been worse,   177
though. Other men blasted through mountains. Those explosives were   186
touchy. Many men died."   190

Lilly and Ted learned much from the train man. By the time they   203
reached Salt Lake City, they appreciated the railway that had taken   214
them there.   216

MONITOR PROGRESS   • Check Fluency

On the Banks of Plum Creek   **109k**

Name _____

A Home On The Prairie

The oxen pulled the wagon to a stop near a grove of trees. Robert climbed out and looked around. Prairie stretched as far as he could see. "So this is Illinois," Robert said, as his little brother Jeff climbed out of the wagon. "I thought we'd never make it."

The three-month journey from Pennsylvania to Illinois had been long and dangerous. First their wagon had gotten stuck in mud. Then they'd gotten lost. Finally, though, on May 18, 1838, they'd arrived. "It'll be worth it," Pop said, unloading the wagon. "There's free land here to farm. And we'll have a home to call our own."

"First things first," Pop told Mom. "We'll plow the land and plant seeds for crops. Then we'll build a proper home."

As they built a temporary shelter in the grove, a neighbor rode up on his horse. The neighbor, Mr. Murphy, helped raise the shelter and told them about his farm not far away. "It's not easy to plow this land," he said. "You'll need a special metal plow."

The next day, Mr. Murphy and his family came by with food and a plow. Robert and Jeff played with Mr. Murphy's sons while Mr. Murphy showed Pop how to plow through the tough roots of the tall prairie grasses.

After a few weeks, Robert and his family had their land plowed and seeds planted. Using wood from the trees nearby, they built a home. Living on the Illinois prairie was hard work, Robert found. However, with neighbors to help and crops growing, it was beginning to feel like a real home.

Keeper of the Mesas

The morning shone brightly when Jen woke up and looked out at   12
the mesas of New Mexico. As always, the rolling plains and red mesas   25
seemed magical. Jen left her small cabin with her dog, Cloud, on their   38
daily walk. Even the breeze seemed enchanted. Cloud must have felt it   50
too. In a quick move, he pulled away from Jen and ran. "Cloud!" Jen   64
shouted, running after him.   68

On the far side of a mesa, Cloud entered a forest. Jen followed. The   82
forest was silent. She could not even hear Cloud's barking. She walked   94
deeper, until she was stopped by a voice from the treetops. "I am   107
the keeper of the mesas," said the smooth woman's voice. "I oversee   119
the land."   121

Jen nodded. Somehow she understood. "I am getting old," the voice   132
went on. "It will soon be time for another to take over. And you, I have   148
been watching you. You know the magic of the land. I would like you to   163
be the one."   166

Jen nodded again. She knew the voice was done speaking. She   177
knew, also, that she would be led back here when the time was right.   191
As Jen stepped out of the forest, Cloud came running toward her. They   204
walked back home slowly through the enchanted day.   212

MONITOR PROGRESS   • Check Fluency

The Sleeping Princess

Once upon a sunny Arizona day, a boy named Peter walked through a canyon, searching for shiny rocks and lizards. He'd chased a lizard into a cave, when he came upon a princess, fast asleep. "I know how this story goes," Peter said to the princess. "I kiss you, you wake up, and we get married." Peter caught the lizard he'd been chasing. "But I am not a prince," he said. "I am a boy, and I do not kiss girls."

Peter tickled the princess with the lizard's tail to wake her up, but she didn't move. He splashed her with water, but she only sighed. He even sang to her, but his howls did not wake her either.

Peter stomped his feet. "Why won't you wake up?" However, Peter knew why. "I will NOT kiss you," he argued. "I don't kiss girls." The princess just slept.

Finally, Peter put down the lizard and groaned. "Do I have to kiss your face?" He tried kissing her hand. The princess slept.

Finally, with a defeated sigh, Peter gave the princess a quick peck on the cheek.

She opened her blue eyes and looked at him. "Don't get any ideas," Peter said, backing away. "I'm just a boy. I'm not a prince. And I will not marry you."

The princess laughed and looked him over. "You're a cute boy," she said, "but, no prince. I'd rather marry a frog."

Relieved, Peter led the princess out of the cave. The two of them walked through the canyon together, looking for shiny rocks and enchanted frogs.

MONITOR PROGRESS • Author's Purpose

Reaching the Peak

On August 29, 1871, John Tileston got up early. He toasted some   12

bacon and boiled his tea. John had climbed nearly to the snow line of   26

Mount Lyell the day before. Now he was ready to climb the peak.   39

The lower part of Mount Lyell had been climbed by many. Mount   51

Lyell was the highest mountain in Yosemite National Park. However,   61

no one had climbed its peak. This part of the mountain was a piece of   76

granite that rose high above the snow. It had been described as sharp   89

and impossible to reach. Other climbers had tried and failed.   99

At 6 A.M., after breakfast, John left his campsite and began his climb.   112

John, from Boston, was on vacation for pleasure. Yet, he reached the   124

peak before 8 A.M.! Looking out, he saw the valleys and lakes below.   137

The land was rugged and lovely like much of the West.   148

John left his card at the peak for others to find. By 1 P.M. that day, he   165

had climbed back down and reached his camp. He felt tired, but well.   178

He later wrote to his wife that he had climbed the top (thought to be   193

"inaccessible").   194

MONITOR
PROGRESS   • Check Fluency

Letters Home **165k**

Name _____

Lynn Hill: Climbing the Mighty Stone

Lynn Hill woke up and stared at the huge rock above her. She had not been able to climb this section of rock the week before. Last night, though, she dreamed that she'd done it. Now, she felt sure that she could become the first person to free climb the nose of El Capitan. She called it Yosemite's mightiest stone.

El Capitan rose 3,000 feet above the valley. Many had climbed its peak, but Lynn was free climbing. She used only her body, and ropes to catch her if she fell. This, nobody had done before.

Since she was 13 years old, Lynn had found that she had a gift for climbing. She had spent the last few days studying this section of rock. At first she'd thought it would be hard for a small person like her. Now she knew, with the strange set of moves she'd found, it was just right for her small body. It would take all of her eighteen years of training.

That morning, Lynn started her climb. All her moves worked well, just like in her dream. High on the rock, she climbed smoothly. She put her small fingers into the tiny cracks. She found her footholds. She used friction on the soles of her shoes where there were no footholds. It took only one try, and she did it.

On the summit, Lynn and her partner camped out. They watched a night bright with stars. Lynn's climb up the rugged nose of El Capitan would not only make her famous. It brought back to her the strong spirit of climbing.

MONITOR PROGRESS • Main Idea and Details

The Doodler

Things were busy in Mrs. Green's fourth-grade class. Katie and Pam   11
made lists. Mike and Dave lettered signs. Everyone was getting ready   22
for the opening of the new school playground. Everyone except for Jeff,   34
that is. Jeff just doodled.   39

Jeff doodled on his schoolwork while the class planned games.   49

He doodled in his notebook while they wrote to the band.   60

No one noticed Jeff and his doodling. Then, one day at recess,   72
Katie and Pam had a problem. They needed posters to put up at school   86
about the playground opening.   90

"I can't draw," Katie said. "Can you?" Pam shook her head no.   102

Jeff, who had been doodling nearby, heard them. "I can draw," he   114
said quietly. But they did not hear him.   122

So, Jeff made a sketch of the new playground, which he had heard   135
them describe in class. When he was done, he showed the sketch to   148
Katie. She gasped and showed it to Pam. Pam showed it to Dave who   162
showed it to everyone else.   167

"Can we use this drawing for our poster?" they asked Jeff. Jeff   179
nodded. "Can you make some signs too?" they asked. Jeff nodded   190
again. "I can do it all," he said with a smile.   201

MONITOR PROGRESS   • Check Fluency

The Yo-Yo Show

Bev was the first one to arrive at day camp Monday morning. It didn't bother her, though, since she had her yo-yo. She spun it up and down and practiced her tricks.

The other campers watched as they arrived. "How do you do that?" Angie asked, as Bev did an *Around the World* trick.

"It just takes practice," Bev said. "I'll show you if you like." Bev gave Angie the yo-yo and showed her how.

In the locker room before swimming, she showed Ann how to do a *Rock the Cradle.*

The next day, Angie, Ann, Lisa, Sam, and Mark all came to camp with yo-yos.

Bev helped Lisa do spins at art time. Sam and Mark did *Walk the Dogs* in the field during their baseball game.

"Put those yo-yos away!" the counselors said. "They're disrupting the game."

After the game, the staff had a meeting about the yo-yos. The campers waited. They were worried. Would they get in trouble? Would their yo-yos be taken away?

When the staff came out, they said, "We have a deal. You put your yo-yos away during art. You put them away during baseball. We will have other practice times. Then, on Friday, we will put on a yo-yo show for your parents."

The campers cheered. They worked hard on their tricks. The show was a big hit.

The next Monday, Ann was the first to get to camp. It didn't bother her, though. Why? Because she had her juggling bags.

MONITOR PROGRESS   • Cause and Effect

What Jo Did **195m**

Name _____

Welcoming Mr. Lincoln

"Help me roll up this sign," I told Bev. "The train's coming at   13

2:00 P.M."   15

Our class had been planning for today for weeks. In only a few   28

hours, Abraham Lincoln would be here. We would give him the best   40

welcome ever.   42

It had to be good. We wanted Mr. Lincoln to remember our small   55

New York village. Even more, we wanted to show him support. He was   68

going to Washington to be sworn in as President. But, in this year of   82

1861, our whole country did not back him. Some southern states had left   95

the Union. President Lincoln would have a hard job.   104

At noon we walked to the train depot. There was a huge crowd,   117

maybe a thousand people! Cadets stood around a platform, holding   127

muskets. A band played. We squeezed through the crowd and waited.   138

At 2:00 P.M. the train came, covered in flags. Mr. Lincoln stepped   150

from the train to the platform. We held our signs high and cheered.   163

He looked tired. When he began to speak, though, his face lit up. He   177

thanked us for our welcome. He told us with our support he would be   191

able to face the hard times ahead.   198

His speech ended quickly, but I knew this was a moment I would   211

never forget.   213

MONITOR PROGRESS • Check Fluency

Better Than a Dance

It seemed as if everyone knew someone fighting in the war. My father said, "John, if we can't help there, we had best be helping here. This is a fight we must not lose."

After Japan bombed Pearl Harbor in 1941, a lot of soldiers went overseas to help in World War II. Farmers here raised extra crops. The factory made tanks for the war. We used coupons to buy meat and sugar. We even drove slower to save fuel. When I was not in school or helping at our store, I listened to the radio for news.

So when talk started in school about the fifth-grade dance, it didn't seem right. Why should we spend money on fun when those soldiers needed so much to survive?

"Billy," I said to my best friend, "the money for the dance has a better use."

"Yeah," he said. "I was thinking the same."

"You think the rest of the class might agree?" I asked. He nodded.

We told our idea to the teachers and they called a meeting. "Let's give the dance money to the soldiers instead of buying food and balloons," I said to the class.

"We can open up the gym that night," said Billy. "We'll ask people to bring in scrap metal. They need it for weapons."

"Folks can bring supplies and people can give money instead of buying party clothes," the class added. It was agreed.

The night of the dance, we opened the gym. Our school raised over a hundred dollars, plus supplies, for the soldiers. I must say, it felt good to do our part.

MONITOR PROGRESS • Draw Conclusions

Name _____

The Recyclers

    Steve and his best friend, Joe, had never thought much about   11

recycling. With baseball and school and hanging out with friends, they   22

had enough to do.   26

    When they visited the town dump, though, all of that changed. They   38

saw the huge amount of garbage piled there. "There isn't much room   50

left," the man in charge said. "If folks would recycle, we would have   63

room for years to come."   68

    Steve and Joe could see the glass and aluminum in the piles. People   81

had thrown them out, when they could have been recycled. "Are people   93

doing anything to help?" Steve asked. The man just shrugged.   103

    That's when Steve and Joe decided to do something. They rounded   114

up their friends. "Let's start a drive," they said. "Every week, we'll   126

collect things that can be recycled. We can bring them to the recycling   139

center. We can even earn money for aluminum cans."   148

    Their friends loved the idea. They made signs to let people know   160

what they would be collecting. Then each week, each of them went   172

to one apartment building. They picked up cans and newspapers and   183

bottles. Everyone was thankful for their help. Best of all, it felt great to   197

know that these things would be used again instead of taking up space   210

in the dump.   213

MONITOR PROGRESS   • Check Fluency

Scene Two **255k**

Name _____

Team Read

Mrs. Black stood in front of her fourth-grade class. "Go teams!" she said.

"Come on, team one," Kathy whispered to the students at her table. "Read fast."

Team one buried themselves in their books and read. Teams two and three all read too, worlds away in their stories. It didn't feel like a race, because the students enjoyed reading. Their school was trying to read 5,000 books in a month. The principal, Mr. Appelt, had promised the school a big prize, but it was secret. Mrs. Black said the winning team in her class would be the first to learn the secret.

On team one, Kathy was worried. One teammate, Sara, had only read six books. The rest had read ten.

"Sara, you need to read more," Kathy told her. "We're behind." She pointed to the chart that listed the books they had read. Team two was ahead.

"Don't worry," Sara said. "I am reading at home." Kathy hoped so. On the last day, all of the students came into the room. They showed Mrs. Black the books they had read. Sara looked at Kathy and smiled. She had read four books at home. Everyone looked as Mrs. Black updated the chart. Team one had won!

"Go to the office," Mrs. Black told team one. "Mr. Appelt will tell you the secret."

In the office, Mr. Appelt smiled. "The secret prize is a school carnival," he said. "You may tell the school what they won."

The next day, that is exactly what they did.

MONITOR PROGRESS   • Draw Conclusions

Scene Two **255m**

Name _____

Chase: An Instinct to Herd

"Chase!" shouts Kate. "What are you doing?" 7

Kate knows what Chase is doing, though. Chase, a Border Collie 18
puppy, is running in circles around a group of ducks. Kate knows that 31
Chase is trying to herd the ducks. Herding is gathering animals and 43
making them move. It is an instinct for Chase. Her ancestors have been 56
herding sheep for hundreds of years. 62

Even though Chase is born with the instinct to herd, she will still 75
need training. When Chase gets older, Kate will train her. She will 87
teach Chase to follow commands. "Come by" means to move in a circle 100
around the sheep. "Walk up" means to run toward the sheep and make 113
them move. Chase will learn to keep the sheep together. She will learn 126
to guide the sheep into their pen. She will learn to separate one sheep 140
from the rest if it needs medicine. Sheepherding dogs have a big job on 154
farms. Chase will be quite a help to Kate when she gets bigger. 167

Right now Kate laughs at Chase as she tries to herd the ducks. 180
"Come, Chase," she says. "You will have plenty of time for herding 192
later. Now, let's play!" 196

MONITOR PROGRESS   • Check Fluency

Keith's Lucky Star

Keith and his guide dog, Star, are stopped at a corner. They wait for the traffic light to turn. Keith can hear the cars stop. The signal beeps, telling him it is clear to go. "Forward," he tells Star. Star will not move. Then Keith hears a bike go past quickly. Star has saved him from being hurt.

Keith is blind, and he knows that getting around town would be much harder without Star. He knows this relationship is the result of years of training.

Star was trained by a guide-dog school. When she was a puppy, she was healthy and friendly and smart. The school decided that she would make a good guide dog. At three months old, Star was brought to a family to be raised. She learned to fetch and walk with a leash and come when she was called.

When Star got older, she returned to the guide-dog school. A trainer taught her commands, such as "forward" and "halt." She learned to wear a harness. She learned to walk next to her master and to watch for things that might hurt her master.

After her training, the school paired up Star with Keith. They worked together at the school for a month. Keith learned how to give Star commands. Star learned to respect Keith and obey his commands.

Now, they are a team. Every day, Keith is glad for the independence she gives him. At home at the end of the day, Keith and Star play fetch together. He is glad for her company too.

MONITOR PROGRESS • Fact and Opinion

Name _____

The Private Side of the President

Think of all the times you hear about the President of the United   13

States. Being President is a very public job. People look at everything   25

the President does. We see him giving speeches. We see him shaking   37

hands with leaders. We see the President waving and smiling as he gets   50

off a plane.   53

What people may not know is that there is a private side to each   67

President too. Being the President is hard work. Presidents must keep   78

up with news from around the world. They must know all sides of big   92

issues. They must make hard decisions. Presidents read and study to   103

learn about each issue. They have meetings with their staff to help them   116

make decisions. They also make time to relax. They get exercise, take   128

vacations, and do things with their families.   135

When President George W. Bush is on vacation, he clears brush   146

around his Texas ranch. He also runs to stay in shape. Bill Clinton, the   160

President before Bush, liked to run too. He played the saxophone. He   172

also liked to eat peanut butter and banana sandwiches.   181

Maybe it is the relaxing they get that helps each President smile   193

in public. It is often the work they do in private that helps them make   208

decisions that shape our country.   213

MONITOR PROGRESS   • Check Fluency

Name _____

A President's Job—At Home and Around the World

It is a big job, being the President of the United States. Presidents manage things in our own country. Plus, they play a part in what is going on all over the world.

In our country, the President oversees many things. What kind of things? There is our money system. There are the courts, the army, and government programs. There are schools and parks. There is energy and transportation. The President makes sure that the government is doing well with all of these jobs, and more.

What does the President do for the world? The President's job is to help the United States get along with other countries and help other countries when they need it.

Franklin D. Roosevelt was our President from 1933 to 1945. He helped our country get through the Great Depression. Many people had lost their jobs and did not have enough money. As President, he began the New Deal program to make new jobs. In the world, he was in charge of our soldiers who fought in World War Two.

Lyndon B. Johnson was President from 1963 to 1969. There were big fights about civil rights in our country. He helped African-Americans gain equal rights. He also sent soldiers across the world to help with the Vietnam War and end the fighting.

Each President has to deal with things going on in our own country and around the world. It is a mighty big job. Would you like to do it?

MONITOR PROGRESS • Main Idea and Details

Name _____

Alicia's Winter Prediction

Alicia and her sister Sharon lived in Michigan. In the winter, it often   13
snowed heavily there. Now it was late November. Alicia said, "Sharon,   24
we should lug our sleds out of the basement."   33

Alicia set down the book she was reading. "I don't think so,   45
Sharon," she said. "I really doubt that snowy, wintry weather will   56
start immediately."   58

"But!" Sharon started to exclaim.   63

Alicia continued talking right over Sharon. "I read recently that in   74
wintertime, rabbits change in color from gray to white. If rabbits stay   86
gray for a long time in autumn, that usually means winter will come late."   100

"So?" asked Sharon.   103

"Yesterday, I saw gray rabbits running around. Since it's late   113
November but still autumn, I don't think winter will be here soon. We   126
won't need the sleds yet."   131

Sharon said to her sister, "Allow me to invite you to the window."   144

Alicia raised her eyebrows in surprise. She guessed why Sharon   154
wanted her to look out the window. Alicia walked over and slowly   166
opened the window blinds.   170

It was really snowing hard outside! In fact, there appeared to be   182
three or four inches of snow on the ground already. Alicia smiled,   194
turned to her sister, and said, "Allow me to invite you to the basement   208
where we will get our sleds."   214

Both sisters laughed. They loved snow!   220

MONITOR PROGRESS   • Check Fluency

Name _____

Will It Snow?

Do you live in a hot, dry part of the United States? That probably means you've never seen snow in person. What if you had a week to travel in the winter? Where could you go to be fairly certain that you would experience snow?

Weather charts illustrate how weather has behaved in years past. They can also suggest what future weather might be. Want to try to guarantee you'll find snow? Do this. Look at average monthly snowfall amounts in various places you might visit. What do those averages suggest? Will snow be likely to fall during the week you plan to visit?

Remember that the figures you see are just averages. Even if the monthly total is high for the time you plan to visit, that doesn't mean it will actually snow while you are there.

	Aspen, Colorado	Alpine, Utah	Big Sky, Montana	Chicago, Illinois
December Average Snowfall	21.1 inches	19.3 inches	11.3 inches	8.3 inches
January Average Snowfall	27.2 inches	23.0 inches	12.7 inches	10.7 inches
February Average Snowfall	25.2 inches	17.8 inches	9.9 inches	8.1 inches
March Average Snowfall	24.3 inches	14.5 inches	16.2 inches	7.0 inches

If you find a good place for snow, don't forget to bring warm clothes!

MONITOR PROGRESS

• Graphic Sources

Journey of the Caribou

A cold wind blows across the coast of Alaska. There, the herd of   13

caribou senses the coming of the first fall storm. They have spent the   26

summer grazing here, as they do each year. Their babies have grown   38

strong. All of them have become fat and healthy. But the storm tells them   52

that winter is on the way. It is time for them to begin their journey to   68

their winter range near the mountains. They will be sheltered there from   80

the worst weather.   83

Mothers have formed strong bonds with their young. They know   93

each other by sound and smell. The calves will stay close to their   106

mothers during the long migration.   111

After a journey of hundreds of miles, they reach their winter home.   123

It is cold now, and snowy. The caribou have grown long hollow hair to   137

trap air and hold heat near their bodies. They spread the toes on their   151

hooves to act as snowshoes on the deep snow. They dig down under   164

the snow to find lichen to eat.   171

The caribou will live here until spring. Then, they will make their   183

way back to their summer range. Mothers will give birth to new babies.   196

The herd will eat, rest, and get ready for the same journey next year.   210

MONITOR PROGRESS   • Check Fluency

Name _____

The Whooping Crane: A Long Journey Home

It is early spring. Flowers bloom around the Texas ponds. The call of the whooping cranes fills the air. It is the time of year when these birds begin to court. Pairs of birds sing out their calls. Then, in the middle of March, these huge white birds begin their migration. They fly 2,500 miles north, from Texas to Canada. With necks forward and wings spread wide, they glide with the wind. They can fly many miles without stopping. Each year, they fly the same route. In the third week in April, they arrive.

Each pair builds a nest in a marsh or a low pond. They lay two eggs and guard them until they hatch. Over the summer, the parents feed their chicks, though only one will likely live. When summer turns to fall, the birds begin their trip south. They will stop several times along the way to feed for a few weeks. On this long journey back to their warm winter home, the young birds learn the route from their parents. They will fly it every year when the seasons change.

Because of hunting and loss of living space, the whooping crane almost became extinct. In 1860, there were about 1,400 birds in North America. In 1941, there were only 15. Since then, people have worked to protect these birds. Slowly the flock has grown. In 2001, a group of people, flying three gliders, led six cranes to a new winter home. They hope to teach these birds a new migration route. This will help them get used to a safe new place to live. It will help the flock to keep growing strong.

How Day and Night Were Divided:
A Creek Indian Story

One day, all of the animals held a meeting. Bear, who was biggest,   13

took charge. Their question was how to divide day and night.   24

Some of the animals liked day. They wanted the day to last all the   38

time. Other animals liked night. They wished it to always be night. After   51

much talk, the ground squirrel said, "I see that Coon has rings on his   65

tail that are divided equally. First there is a dark color and then a light   80

color. I think day and night ought to be divided like the rings on Coon's   95

tail."   96

The animals were surprised by Ground Squirrel's wisdom. They   105

liked his plan so much that they decided to use it. From that day on,   120

they divided day and night like the rings on Coon's tail. Day and night   134

would succeed each other in regular order.   141

Bear, who was supposed to be in charge of the meeting, was filled   154

with envy. In anger, he scratched Ground Squirrel's back. This made   165

stripes on his back. Now, all of Ground Squirrel's children, and their   177

children, have stripes going down their backs too. And now day follows   189

night in order, just like the rings on Coon's tail.   199

MONITOR PROGRESS   • Check Fluency

How Night Came   **401k**

Name _____

The Origin of Night and Day: A Menominee Tale

One time, Manabush, a rabbit, was traveling through a forest. He came to a clearing on the bank of a river. There, he noticed Saw Whet Owl, who was perched on a twig. It was almost dark, and Rabbit could hardly see. He said to Owl, "Why do you like it dark? I do not like it to be dark. I am going to make the daylight." Owl looked at Rabbit. He said, "If you think you are strong enough, then do it. But let us have a contest to see who is stronger. Whoever wins can have it the way that he likes."

Then, Rabbit and Owl called together all of the animals and birds of the forest. Some of them wanted Rabbit to win so that it would always be light. Others liked the dark and wanted Owl to win.

Once all of the animals had arrived, the contest began. Rabbit began to repeat, "Light, Light." Owl began to repeat, "Night, Night." If one of them made a mistake and said his opponent's word, he would lose. Rabbit kept saying, "Light, Light." Owl kept saying, "Night, Night." The birds and animals cheered on their heroes. They cheered and cheered for the one they wanted to win. Finally, Owl accidentally repeated Rabbit's word, "Light." He had lost the contest.

Rabbit decided that it should be light. Being a good fellow, though, he also decided that night should have a chance too. This would benefit the loser and all of the animals and birds who had cheered him on. His decision pleased everyone. This is how it came to be that there was day and there was night.

MONITOR PROGRESS   • Generalize

How Night Came **401m**

Name _____

After Katrina: Making Things Better

When Hurricane Katrina hit New Orleans in 2005, most folks   10

thought their city was ready. Their homes were strong. They had built   22

flood walls. Levees made the banks of the nearby lakes strong, so they   35

would not flood the city. People thought their city was safe.   46

They were wrong, though. Huge numbers of homes were destroyed   56

in the strong winds. The levees failed in over fifty places. The flood walls   70

did not hold. After the storm hit, over 80 percent of the city was under   85

water. In some places there was 20 feet of water!   95

Since then, New Orleans has been slowly rebuilding. The   104

government and the people are working with each other. Engineers   114

have figured out what went wrong. They have worked to find ways to   127

make things better and stronger. As they rebuild homes, they are using   139

better designs and stronger construction. The roofs and walls will be   150

able to stand up to higher winds. To protect the city, engineers have   163

built stronger flood walls. They have come up with new and better ways   176

to build the levees. This time they will stand up to heavier flood waters.   190

Nobody knows when and if another storm will hit. The people of   202

New Orleans, though, are working so that next time they will be ready.   215

MONITOR PROGRESS • Check Fluency

Name _____

The Mystery of El Niño

In California, too much rain was falling. Storms were making rivers flood. Homes were being lost in sliding mud. When would the rain stop?

Across the world, Australia was having a dry spell. Crops died. Big fires started. Where was the rain?

It may not seem as if these things are connected. However, they are both caused by a weather cycle called El Niño. El Niño is a warming of the waters in the ocean near the tropics. This warming sets off changes in weather all over the world.

El Niño happens every two to seven years. Scientists are trying to figure out what makes an El Niño cycle begin. They know that during El Niño, trade winds slow. Trade winds are winds that blow to the west. This causes many changes, such as the flow of the ocean. Less warm water flows west from the tropics. It flows east instead. With that warmer water comes more rain. El Niño often brings more rain to Peru, but less rain to Australia. In the United States, it changes the weather too.

Now scientists can tell when El Niño is starting. But they still do not know what sets it off. They hope one day to find the answers.

MONITOR PROGRESS   • Cause and Effect

A Ride with Mother Nature

They say most things are caused by Mother Nature. Well, I got to   13

meet Mother Nature, and she is some lady. She lives in the sky and   27

races around on a cloud.   32

It was last spring, when I was climbing the world's tallest tree, when   45

I met her. She zoomed up in her cloud and asked me if I wanted a ride.   62

She held out a tiny hand and smiled so wide that the wrinkles in her   77

face went away. I climbed onto the cloud and off we went. Boy, that   91

cloud went fast! It even had onboard steering. Mother Nature showed   102

me how she stirred up mountain storms. She showed me how she tickled   115

the oceans to make tides. We raced over huge forests. "The trees are   128

my children," she said. "When they get tired and drop their leaves, I   141

send down snow to help them sleep. When it's time for them to wake   155

again, I blow the warm breath of springtime." She blew a springtime   167

breath right there, and I saw those trees grow leaves. Flowers sprouted.   179

It was something!   182

When we got back, my tree was waiting. I climbed down and   194

told everyone about my ride with Mother Nature. I do not think they   207

believed me, though. You believe me, don't you?   215

MONITOR PROGRESS   • Check Fluency

Paul Bunyan **459k**

Big Joe

Joe is a big boy. He is so big that he uses trains for roller skates and a slice of the moon as a helmet. Sometimes Joe is a good boy. But when his parents did not let him have an elephant to keep in his pocket, he had a tantrum. When they did not let him play baseball with tree trunks and mountaintops, he had another.

Since Joe is big, his tantrums are big. When he cries, he causes floods. When he screams "NO" he causes cold winds to blow. When he kicks his feet, he makes earthquakes. People say that Joe's spring tantrums, when he wants to drink the ocean and his parents say no, make hurricanes. They say that his fall tantrums, when he wants to play leap frog over mountains, make Earth move farther from the sun.

People also say, though, that when Joe is happy, good things happen. Every morning, Joe's parents let him whistle to wake the birds around the world. Every night his parents let him paint the sky to say goodnight to the sun. In the winter, he throws the feathers of his huge pillows up, up into the air. When they come down, they make the snow. In the spring, he tickles the ground, until things begin to grow. Come summer, he lassos the sun and pulls it a bit closer to warm him as he rests on the beach. In the fall, he paints the leaves until they glow.

Joe is not always naughty and he is not always good. When he has his tantrums, he is very, very bad. And when he's happy, he can be very, very good. Does this sound like anybody else you know?

MONITOR PROGRESS • Generalize

Paul Bunyan **459m**

Sir Laugh-A-Lot

Sir Laugh-A-Lot was a knight. He was not a very good knight   12

though. He got lost on every adventure. He dropped his spear whenever   24

he went to battle.   28

Once Sir Laugh-A-Lot was riding along on his horse, Shoeless, when   39

he saw a castle on a far-off hill. The castle looked huge. Sir Laugh-A-Lot   53

blinked. He thought he saw a gleam from the tower. Was it the flash of   68

blonde hair from a princess, trapped in a locked room? Maybe this was   81

the chance he had been waiting for!   88

"Go," he shouted to Shoeless. "That-a-way!"   94

They rode and rode toward the castle. Thoughts of the beautiful   105

princess filled his mind. "The castle should be getting closer," Sir   116

Laugh-A-Lot said to Shoeless. They rode some more. He planned his   127

daring rescue. But when they got to the hill, Sir Laugh-A-Lot saw that his   141

castle was only a big black rock. And the flash of blonde hair was only   156

the gleam of the sun on its edge.   164

"My princess is not a princess at all," laughed Sir Laugh-A-Lot. He   176

rode up to the rock and admired its castle-like shape. Then he lay down   190

and took a long nap. When he climbed back on Shoeless, he looked   203

around and wondered which way to ride to get back home.   214

MONITOR PROGRESS   • Check Fluency

A Secret in the Forest

It was the rabbit that led Isi deep into the forest. There she saw Nab, a boy from her village. He was digging. Near him lay a pile of stone tools, finely carved. He pulled a bowl from the earth near a stream and washed it. He added it to the pile.

Isi, quiet as a field mouse, snuck away. Now she understood Nab's secret. For three days, Nab had gone into the forest at sunrise with a plain stone. He had come out before day was done with a finely carved bowl or tool. "How did you do it?" the village children asked. "Magic," he had said. Now Isi knew it was not magic at all.

Isi, who valued truth, knew what must be done. After Nab had gone home, she went back to his place of digging. She found his pile of bowls and tools, hidden under a bush. From this, she took two bowls and a knife.

That evening, as Nab showed off a fine stone bowl to his friends, Isi walked up behind him. "You carve by magic?" she asked Nab.

"Yes," he said. The others nodded.

"Then I do too," Isi said. She held out a stone bowl. "I carved this by magic."

Nab stared. "You did not...." He stopped. "Where did you get that?"

"In the same place you got that," Isi said, pointing to his newest bowl. She showed him the other bowl and the knife. The children stared. "Is she magic too?" they asked.

Nab stopped to think. Isi looked at him hard. "No," Nab finally said. "And neither am I." And then he told them the truth.

MONITOR PROGRESS • Compare and Contrast

Gasping Garbage **51m**

Name _____

Why Do Orb Weavers Eat Their Webs?

Have you seen the wheel-shaped web of an orb weaver? Orb webs   12

can be very beautiful. They also help these special spiders catch their   24

prey.   25

The orb weaver works hard to spin its web. Why, then, do many   38

of these spiders eat their webs and build new ones each morning? This   51

may seem strange, but there are many good reasons for it. Spiders'   63

webs can be damaged by wind and bad weather. They can also be   76

damaged by the struggles of prey. After a while, the web becomes less   89

sticky. The spiders rebuild their webs so that they will be in good shape 103

to catch prey.   106

By eating the old web, the spider recycles the silk from the web.   119

Silk is made mostly of protein. The web is broken down by juices in the 134

spider. The juices connect the pieces of silk again. Then the spider lets 147

out the silk to make a new web.   155

Often, the spider leaves the main thread of its old web in place. This   169

is the thread that holds up the web. It is the hardest one for the spider 185

to make. The spider builds a new web around this thread. Then its new   199

home is done.   202

The spider can rest now and wait for its next meal to come.   215

MONITOR PROGRESS   • Check Fluency

Name _____

Why Do Bats Sleep Upside Down?

Does it seem strange that bats sleep hanging upside down? If you slept that way, think about what might happen. All of your blood would rush to your head. It would be hard to hang on tight. When you fell asleep, you would probably fall on your head.

Although this strange way of sleeping would not work for humans, it does seem to work well for bats. These flying mammals can sleep way up high. Bats are built in a special way so they can hang upside down easily while they sleep. The weight of the bat's body pulls the tendons in its feet closed. Its toes lock into place around whatever the bat is holding. When the bat sleeps, it does not need to think about holding on. It will not fall when it sleeps.

Unlike birds, most bats cannot take off for flight from the ground. They need to launch by falling into flight. If they sleep hanging upside down, all they have to do is to let go. When a bat wakes up, it opens its toes, spreads its wings, and falls into flight. Being ready to fly can help a bat escape fast if it needs to.

Sleeping upside down allows bats to roost in spots where they will not be seen by predators. The roof of a cave or a spot under a bridge can be safe places to sleep. Most bats roost in groups. When they sleep close together, they help each other stay warm. Like many other mammals, some bats hibernate during the winter. Keeping warm helps all of the bats save energy.

MONITOR PROGRESS   • Compare and Contrast

Name _____

Your Body: Its Own Password

Passwords are used for many things. You may need a password to   12

join a secret club. You may need one to start your computer. Passwords   25

can be lost or stolen though. Now there is another choice. Your body   38

can be its own password.   43

There are many things about our bodies that make us different from   55

anyone else. No two people have the same fingerprints. The police   66

have used fingerprints for a long time to keep track of people who have   80

broken the law.   83

No two faces are alike. Computers can match your face with a   95

picture of you on file. It can also take a picture of your eye to see the 112

patterns in your iris. Your voice can be used as a password. Even the   126

shape of your hand can be used as a password.   136

In the United States government, many people know big secrets.   146

They use their bodies as passwords to show who they are when they go   160

to work. That way nobody can take their place. Even some theme parks   173

check the fingers of guests coming in. This tells them that tickets are used 187

by the same person from day to day.   195

Your body makes a good password. It cannot be lost. It cannot be   208

stolen. It is just right.   213

MONITOR PROGRESS   • Check Fluency

Name _____

The Zimmerman Telegram

Did you know that during World War I, a secret message changed history?

Germany wanted to cut off the supply lines to its enemy countries, France and Britain. To do this, the Germans planned to attack boats in the ocean. This would stop things from getting through to their enemies. The Germans were worried though. If they sank American boats, the United States might join World War I. Germany did not want that to happen. It came up with a plan.

Germany asked Mexico to start a war with the United States. It hoped that this would keep the United States busy. Then they would not join World War I. Germany told Mexico that it would give Mexico land in the United States in return.

Arthur Zimmerman of the German government sent this plan in a coded message to Mexico. The message is known as the Zimmerman Telegram. Britain caught the message as it went across the sea. Britain had people study the message to break the code. They found out what the message said. It was important! The British told the United States about the plan. Some members of the United States government did not believe Britain, but Britain knew that it was true. So they broke the code in front of members of the United States government. The United States believed them and joined the war against Germany. They helped Britain and other countries fight against and defeat the Germans. It was a good thing that the German message was caught. It changed the history of the world.

MONITOR PROGRESS   • Sequence

Name _____

A New Life

Jake McGinty is one of many young people who are doing   11
something special this year. He is an exchange student. Jake left   22
America to live for a year in Japan. He is staying with a host family 37
and going to high school in Japan.   44

Jake was excited about going to Japan, but he had to do a lot to   59
prepare. He worked on his Japanese, learned the customs, and decided   70
what to pack. On the day he left, he said good-bye to his friends and 85
family. He worried about not knowing the language well enough. He   96
hoped his host family would like him. But he could not wait for his   110
adventure to begin.   113

When Jake got to Japan, his host family met him. Everything felt   125
new and exciting. School started and Jake, who is tall with red hair, 138
was treated like a rock star. Everyone wanted to meet him. There were 151
times, after the newness wore off, when Jake felt homesick. In time,   163
though, he got used to a new language, a new culture, and a new life. 178

By the time Jake leaves Japan, it will feel like home. The exchange   191
program connects people from different countries. It leads to friendship 201
and understanding. With hope, it will lead to a world of peace.   213

MONITOR PROGRESS   • Check Fluency

Name _____

Laura Bertrone: Teaching Understanding

Laura Bertrone was born in Argentina and lives there today. Laura spent twenty years working in France as an interpreter, translating languages. Laura worked with companies to help people who spoke different languages understand each other. Laura met people from all over the world that way. The differences between languages and cultures interested her enough to study them. Now she teaches people how to better understand each other.

People from different places see the world in different ways. Laura asks people to think about their families. Each member has different goals, tastes, and ways of doing things. Each has different views about people, money, and values. These differences are even bigger in the world. This can make it hard for people to understand each other. The challenge is for both sides to understand that the other side has different views. If both sides do this, they can understand, trust, and get along.

Laura has seen troubles in her home country. The government was in debt, and people lost their trust. Many people lost their jobs and became poor. Laura felt that a lack of understanding led to these troubles. Things are better now, but Laura still teaches people to change the way they think, to understand each other, and to work together.

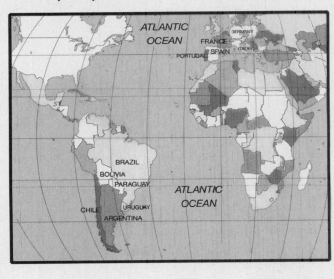

MONITOR PROGRESS • Graphic Sources

Name _____

Toad Troubles

"What's wrong with your toad?" Jen asked Sam. She bent over the   12
fish tank he had set up in his room.   21

"Nothing's wrong," said Sam. "He's doing great."   28

"He looks floppy," said Jen. "Is he eating?"   36

Sam shrugged. Sometimes his best friend could be annoying.   45

"What are you feeding him?" Jen asked.   52

"Dead insects," said Sam. "Toads eat insects, you know."   61

"Duh," said Jen. "Have you seen him eat since you caught him?"   73

"No," he said. "But maybe he eats at night. I don't know."   85

Jen gave Sam an annoyed look and turned on his computer. "You   97
need to know more about your new pet," she said. "How can you take   111
care of him?"   114

Sam shrugged.   116

"Here," Jen said, looking at a Web site. "Read this. Needs   127
moisture."   128

"I have a water bowl," said Sam.   135

"He needs wet dirt too," said Jen. "And look," she said. "Toads will   148
not eat food that is not moving. It says to try earthworms."   160

"Worms?" said Sam. He and Jen found a worm in the yard, along   173
with some wet soil. Then they came back and watched the toad eat   186
the worm.   188

"Cool!" Sam said.   191

MONITOR
PROGRESS
• Check Fluency

Encyclopedia Brown **165k**

The Glasses Detective

"Help!" cried Mark from his room.

Karen came running and saw her brother in bed, reaching toward his night table.

"Can't find your glasses?" Karen guessed. Mark could hardly see without them.

"No," said Mark. He began to cry.

Karen hated when Mark cried. "It's all right," she said. "Detective Karen is here. To find your glasses, we need to do some detective work." In her best detective voice, Karen said, "Where were you yesterday when you lost your glasses?"

"I don't know," said Mark. "I played."

"Well, where did you play?" asked Karen. "Details are important to detectives."

Mark sighed. "I played at Jim's house all day, and then I came home."

"And next?" asked Karen.

"We had dinner. I can't eat without seeing my food. Then I did homework. Then I...wait...I know where they are!"

"Go on," said Karen.

"I read a book on the couch and fell asleep."

Karen dashed away and came back holding Mark's glasses. Mark grinned as he put them on. "I can see!" he said.

"And I can see too," said Karen. "A little detective work goes a long way."

MONITOR PROGRESS • Character and Plot

Encyclopedia Brown **165m**

Name _____

Safe Rooms

Some parts of the country are often hit by hurricanes or tornadoes.   12

Many families living in these places are choosing to build safe rooms.   24

A safe room does what its name says. It keeps you safe, even in the   39

strongest winds.   41

Safe rooms are not very big. They usually can fit about eight   53

people who are sitting very closely together. Safe rooms can be in a   66

basement or on the first floor of a building. Safe rooms can also be   80

built underground, away from a building. The floor of a safe room is   93

anchored down. This way, the room cannot be turned over or lifted by   106

strong winds. The walls, ceiling, and door of a safe room are all built   120

in special ways. The wind cannot tear them up. Things blown against a   133

safe room by the wind will not hurt it. Where the parts of a safe room fit   150

together, very strong devices hold them tightly.   157

A safe room never has windows. It never shares the structure of the   170

building it is in. After a bad storm, you might see a safe room standing   185

by itself. The building around it has been destroyed. But the safe room   198

came through just fine!   202

Calling 911

Most of the time, life goes smoothly. However, if an emergency happens, you want to get help quickly. That is exactly what calling 911 is all about. Anyone can use this service. You just need to get to a safe place and make the call. By punching in these three numbers, you can reach the police, the fire department, or an ambulance.

When you dial 911, you are calling an emergency operator. This person is trained to connect you with the help you need. In order to do that, he or she must get some facts from you. You need to stay calm to answer the questions you are asked. Take a deep breath. Let the operator lead the talking.

All callers are asked many of the same questions. You will be asked to describe the emergency. You will be asked to give your name and to tell where you are. After that, the call will be about you and what is going on. The operator might tell you some things that you should do. Listen carefully. Do not hang up until you are told.

If you are calling on a cell phone, you might have to explain where you are in detail. When you call from a regular phone, the person on the other end of the call can see your address. The phone number and the address go together. With a cell phone, it is different. A cell phone is not hooked up at one place. That is why it is very important to know exactly where you are. Look for street signs or numbers on buildings.

Remember, call 911 only if a person is badly hurt or in danger. As soon as your call goes through, help will be on the way!

MONITOR PROGRESS   • Author's Purpose

The Arlington Springs Woman

In 1959, on Santa Rosa Island, a scientist named Phil Orr was   12

looking for signs of life from long ago. Orr found something important   24

buried 30 feet deep in a canyon. He found three human bones. Right   37

away, Orr knew the find was very important. He asked experts to help   50

him figure out how old the bones were.   58

Tests showed that the bones were 10,000 years old. This made   69

them the oldest remains ever found in North America. Still, Orr knew   81

that better ways of figuring out the age of remains were coming. He cut   95

out a block of earth where the bones were found. He wrapped it and   109

put it in a safe place. He named the bones "Arlington Springs Man."   122

Thirty years later, two scientists decided to test the bones again.   133

Amazing new methods for testing were then in use. The results showed   145

two new facts. First, the bones belonged to a woman, not a man.   158

Second, the bones were more than 13,000 years old! This meant   169

that humans could build boats and travel to islands much earlier than   181

we had thought. The remains of Arlington Springs Woman have led   192

to whole new ideas about when and how the first people reached   204

California.   205

MONITOR PROGRESS   • Check Fluency

Lost City **227k**

Name _____

A Life-Saving Island

Vitus Bering was born in Denmark around 1680. At age 23, he joined the Russian Navy. He became a great explorer. In 1724, the ruler of Russia wanted Bering to find the distance between Asia and North America. The ruler asked Bering to go east across Russia to a place called Kamchatka. There he was to build a ship and set sail in search of North America.

On his first trip, Bering found a large island. He realized that the two continents were not far apart. They were divided by a strait, not a sea. On his second trip, in 1741, Bering discovered Alaska. Since the weather was very rough and many men on the ship were ill, Bering did not explore it. Instead, he set sail back to Kamchatka. A terrible storm blew the ship all around what is now called the Bering Strait. More men became sick, and the ship's sails were ripped by the winds. Finally, someone saw land. The men wanted it to be Kamchatka. Yet, the man sent ashore soon knew it was not. This land was a small island, and no humans lived there. The man knew this because the animals did not fear him. He returned to the ship with the news.

Bering himself was dying. He gave orders for everyone to leave the ship and go to the island. He and half of his men would die there. Yet, the rest of the crew made it through the winter. They built a small ship and sailed to Kamchatka. Even in death, Bering had made a great discovery. He had discovered an island that offered food and water to save his men. That island today is known as Bering Island.

MONITOR PROGRESS • Compare and Contrast

Lost City **227m**

Stuck at the Top

"Kelsey will take me!" said Ashley. She turned toward her big sister.   12

Ashley had seen the Ferris wheel from far away. Ever since the   24
Cooley family had gotten to the fair, it was all she had talked about.   38

"Yes, I'll take you," said Kelsey. Ashley squealed with delight.   48

Soon the girls got into one of the swinging cages. They sat down   61
and put on the straps. They waved goodbye to their parents.   72

"Here we go!" said Kelsey as the cage began moving.   82

"Look at the fair!" cried Ashley. "You can see everything!"   92

As the cage reached the very top, the Ferris wheel stopped. The   104
cage rocked back and forth. A voice came over the speaker: "Sit tight.   117
We'll have you moving again soon."   123

"What is going on?" said Ashley. Her voice was very small. Her   135
eyes were very big. "I'm scared!"   141

Kelsey grabbed her hand. "Scared? Why, we have the best seats in   153
the world!" Kelsey started pointing things out to her little sister. Ashley's   165
fear soon turned back into excitement.   171

"These are great seats!" said Ashley as they began moving again.   182
The happy little girl never knew that her big sister was very scared   195
herself. She only knew that the Ferris wheel was the best ride in the   209
world.   210

MONITOR PROGRESS   • Check Fluency

Cliff Hanger **255k**

The Train Trap

As the train began moving, Alma felt a lump in her throat. She pressed her cheek against the window. Her parents grew smaller as the train picked up speed.

"It's okay," Alma's big brother Carlos said. "We'll have a great adventure."

Alma smiled shakily. It was not like her brother to be so kind. She guessed he was nervous too. It was their first trip to their grandparents' house without their parents.

Alma looked at the other passengers in their train car. There was no one her age. Alma decided that looking outside would be more interesting. Like Carlos, she put in her earphones, turned on her music, and looked at the sights rushing by.

Suddenly, Carlos nudged Alma and motioned for her to listen to him.

"I think something's wrong," he whispered as he pointed to a woman Alma had noticed earlier. The woman's eyes were wide, and she was grabbing at her throat with both hands.

"She's choking!" Alma gasped.

Carlos quickly stood up and ran to the woman. Using a move he had learned in health class, he soon got the woman to cough up a large nut that had lodged in her throat.

Alma brought the woman a bottle of water, and Carlos asked a man to find help. Very soon, someone arrived, and the woman was taken to another car where she could lie down. Before she left, she grabbed Carlos's hands. She said, "You saved my life!"

As Carlos and Alma went back to their seats, Alma looked at her brother. "I never thought we'd have this kind of adventure!" she grinned. "You are a hero!"

MONITOR PROGRESS

• Character, Plot, and Theme

Cliff Hanger **255m**

Name _____

Meg's Diary Entry for May 3rd

I have something really exciting to write about tonight, dear diary!   11
Today I was a cave explorer. I went with my class to Worley's Cave. It's   26
just across the state line in Tennessee. It was amazing!   36

I dressed like a cave explorer. I wore a helmet with a light on it. I   52
also wore gloves and kneepads. As our teacher suggested, I wore my   64
oldest warm clothes and a pair of boots. In my backpack I carried a set   79
of dry clothes, shoes, and water.   85

Worley's Cave is huge! It has about ten miles of passages and lots   98
of large rooms. It is also beautiful. The rooms, some with 100-foot   110
ceilings, are full of rock and crystal formations. Our guide led us   122
through many rooms. It was chilly—about 52 degrees—and muddy.   133
Sometimes we had to crawl. We all got soaked and dirty.   144

I think the guide saved the best part of the cave for last. We went   159
out beside a big underground stream! It was the bluest water I have   172
ever seen. I was hungry, cold, and tired by then, but that sight perked   186
me right up. Thank goodness for dry clothes and good food on the way   200
home. What a day!   204

MONITOR PROGRESS   • Check Fluency

Journal: My Trip to Mt. Everest Base Camp

September 12

It is the tenth day of my Mt. Everest adventure. I am now only three days from my goal of reaching the base camp.

Today is a day of rest in a tiny village in Nepal called Dingboche. The views from this place are beautiful! Since I am now 14,500 feet up, I am not surprised.

I know I need the day to rest. I have been having a bad headache. This can be the first sign of altitude sickness. Since this is a very serious condition, I must be careful. I feel jealous of my guide, who seems to feel great. I also know I am lucky that I do not feel worse. Yesterday I saw a very sick climber. He was dizzy. He did not even know his name. A helicopter had to get him off the mountain before it was too late.

So, for today, I will sit and look at the views. I will take photos. I will let my body get used to the height and the thin air. I will think about all the wonders I have seen.

September 13

This morning, all signs of my sickness were gone. We hiked through farms and meadows. Snow began to fall softly as we passed by stone markers. They are there in memory of climbers who did not make it off the mountain. As we reached our next stop, Lobuche, a full blizzard blew in. I feel very snug in my down sleeping bag, even though the temperature in my room is below freezing. It looks like we will not be able to leave for base camp tomorrow. Still, I know I am close. I know I will get there.

MONITOR PROGRESS

• Main Idea and Details

Name _____

Moon Games

It was finally Moon Games Week! The athletes had begun arriving   11

from Earth. The flags on their space suits told which countries they were   24

from. Most went right to the huge arena where the Games were held.   37

Lance was already seated there, ready to watch.   45

Lance was eager to see the pole vault event. He had heard that last   59

year's winner went so high up in the air that you could not see him for   75

a second or two. Lance also wanted to see the strange hopping motion   101

that racers used to move around the track in low gravity.   112

The pole vault event was all that Lance had hoped it would be. One   126

by one the athletes vaulted higher and higher. This year, the winner   138

vaulted so high that she disappeared for three seconds before coming   149

down! The long jump winner also set a record. He jumped the entire   162

length of the arena.   166

The races were slow. Because of the moon's low gravity, the athletes   178

could not run as they would on Earth. Their strange hopping was quite   191

a sight. But Lance decided that on the moon, the jumping events were   204

much more fun!   207

Copyright © by Pearson Education, Inc., or its affiliates. All Rights Reserved.

MONITOR PROGRESS   • Check Fluency

Moonwalk **315k**

A Hot Moon Walk

Xennah clicked the screen to zoom in on the moon Io. Her travel pod, *Flame*, had just passed through the wheel-shaped cloud that circled Io. Xennah could see that today only one of the many volcanoes had lava flowing. That was great news!

It was always hard to find a place to set down *Flame* on Io. *Flame* could handle all levels of heat, but Xennah's space suit could not be worn too close to lava. She had to land at a place where she could get out safely.

Xennah clicked the screen again to look closely at Io's surface. She chose a good landing spot and waited for the bump that meant she landed.

Xennah stepped into her suit. Once all the checks were done, she felt the puff that popped her out of *Flame* and onto Io.

Xennah was always happy to see the beauty of Jupiter while standing on the planet's fifth moon. Io belonged to Xennah. It was her job to learn all she could about it. Fifty-nine other moon scientists had been given the rest of Jupiter's moons. Those moons were dull to study. Unlike the hot, changing Io, they were dead, icy bodies.

Xennah saw a flash of red. Lava was heading toward her! One of the other volcanoes suddenly became active. Quickly Xennah pushed the button that popped her inside *Flame*. As the door shut, Xennah could see a red river racing beneath her. She had to lift off before *Flame* got carried away! Xennah spoke the words, "Lift off." Within seconds *Flame* took off. Her face dripped sweat. "I think I'll help out on a dull moon today."

MONITOR PROGRESS   • Draw Conclusions

Moonwalk **315m**

Tom Brokaw

On December 1, 2004, Tom Brokaw signed off as news anchor for   12

NBC. It would be his last time doing so. After more than twenty years,   26

his voice would no longer guide Americans through the daily news. His   38

voice had been smooth and full of charm. His voice had come from all   52

around the world. Brokaw believed in going where the news was. He   64

had brought war and peace into American living rooms. He had been   76

present at nearly every important world event. How could Americans   86

make sense of the world without him?   93

Tom Brokaw was among the first news reporters to become a true   105

star. He took his job very seriously. He also always looked for the   118

positive side of a story. He believed in goodness. Even in the worst   131

of times, people seemed to get comfort from Tom Brokaw. The nearly   143

sixteen million viewers who watched him sign off that final time were   155

surely happy to hear his last words, "I'll see you along the way." Since   169

then, Brokaw has kept his word to be there. He has done several   182

TV specials. For now, Americans can still count on hearing his voice   194

whenever something major happens in the world.   201

MONITOR PROGRESS

• Check Fluency

My Brother Martin **349k**

Shirley Chisholm

In 1968, history was made in the United States Congress. Shirley Chisholm became the first African American woman elected. She had already served at the state level of government for New York. Now she hoped to make a difference at the national level.

Chisholm believed her job was to serve the people. She especially wanted to represent people who did not have a voice. She spoke on behalf of women, the poor, and her fellow African Americans. She was a great speaker whose messages about equal rights and ending poverty were well received. Some important bills written by her were passed by Congress.

In 1972, Chisholm ran for President. She did not make it to the final race, but her voice was heard around the world. She continued to serve in Congress until 1983. More African American women joined her there. More important bills were passed to help children, workers in low-paying jobs, and women.

Chisholm continued to raise her voice for others after leaving government service. Her powerful words led many to join her in the fight for a fair way of life for all. One quote from Chisholm states her thoughts very clearly. "We need men and women ... who will dare to declare that they are free of the old ways that have led us wrong." Chisholm used her words to bring about change, and she did.

MONITOR PROGRESS • Cause and Effect

Name _____

Maya Lin

Maya Lin was born in 1959. As a child growing up in Ohio, she   14

enjoyed time alone. She loved to read. She liked to do art. She also   28

spent time outdoors, hiking, and studying birds.   35

Maya was always great at math. She decided she wanted to   46

be an architect. She went to Yale University. In her last year, she   59

had an interesting class project. The United States wanted to build a   71

memorial for the soldiers who fought and died in the Vietnam War.   83

The government decided to hold a contest. The best design would win.   95

Anyone could enter.   98

Maya Lin's design was chosen out of 1,421 entries. Not everyone   109

liked it at first. Maya's plan was to build a shiny black wall. The names   124

of the 58,000 killed or missing soldiers would be carved into it. It was a   139

simple and powerful idea. Once it was built, people saw its beauty.   151

When you visit the Vietnam Memorial, you walk down along the   162

wall. Then you walk up again, back into the light. It makes people feel   176

hopeful. Visitors also love to find and feel the names of their loved ones.   190

Maya Lin has designed other important projects, including the Civil   200

Rights Memorial. She still enjoys her time alone. She likes to stay out of   214

the public eye.   217

MONITOR PROGRESS   • Check Fluency

Name _____

Arthur Ashe

Famous tennis player Arthur Ashe was born in Virginia in 1943. As a boy, he did not look much like an athlete. "Skinny as a straw" was how some people described him. Yet, from the time he first picked up a racquet, he showed great talent. From the age of seven on, Arthur Ashe worked hard at playing tennis.

Ashe became good enough to go to college for free as a tennis player. He went to UCLA and in 1965 was the best college tennis player in the country. Two years earlier, he was the first African American to play for the United States in the Davis Cup.

Ashe was not just good *at* tennis. He was good *for* tennis. When he first started, no one could earn a living at the sport. Yet, lots of people wanted to watch the great players. In 1969, he helped form a group that made sure players earned more money.

Ashe also worked hard to make things better for people outside of tennis. When South Africa said he could not play there because of his skin color, Ashe made a bold move. He asked the Davis Cup to keep South Africa from playing in its matches. Those in charge agreed. When Ashe took his stand on this, many people became aware for the first time of what was going on in South Africa.

Ashe kept winning big tennis matches through the 1970s. He had chalked up more than 800 victories by the time he stopped playing. He knew that his talent could open doors for him. Arthur Ashe used his fame for good causes. He chose to speak out when he saw people being treated unfairly. He chose to make the world a better place.

MONITOR PROGRESS   • Fact and Opinion

Name _____

Pictures of Nature

Mr. Brown's class was spending the week outdoors. They were   10

taking pictures of nature. After two days, all of the students felt proud   23

of their work. They had taken pictures of trees and a meadow, a stream   37

and the clouds. The students thought the scenes were beautiful.   47

Mr. Brown just looked at the pictures and sighed.   56

"You are not really seeing nature," he said. "You must look harder."   68

On the third day, the students took pictures of a nest in a tree, a frog   84

on a lily pad, and a patch of blueberries.   93

"These are better," said Mr. Brown, "but you still need to look   105

harder."   106

On the fourth day, the students did not take any pictures. They could   119

not find anything new outside.   124

"Nature is different every day," Mr. Brown said. "Can't you see it?"   136

On the fifth day, the students silently put their pictures in front of Mr.   150

Brown. "What do you see?" they asked him.   158

Mr. Brown looked at the pictures. He smiled. The students had found   170

hidden things. There was a lizard that blended in with a tree's bark.   183

There was a butterfly fluttering near a wild rose. There were the eyes of   197

a deer hidden in the trees.   203

"Now you have seen it," said Mr. Brown. "Good job!"   213

MONITOR PROGRESS   • Check Fluency

Name _____

Kendra's Summer Job

Kendra needed to work the summer before her senior year. She had to earn money to help pay for the extras. She wanted a class ring. She had to buy her cap and gown. She hoped to have some great pictures taken of her.

The problem was that her small town did not have many jobs. But one night the phone rang. Kendra answered. It was Mrs. Bowman, and she was glad to hear Kendra's voice.

"Kendra," she began, "I must go back to work this summer. I have found a nursing shift for four hours each afternoon. I know how much Ellie loves to have you as her babysitter. Could you babysit every day this summer?"

Kendra was thrilled. "Yes!" she cried. "I would love to!"

At first, three-year-old Ellie cried when her mom left for work. Kendra felt terrible. She tried all kinds of fun ways to take Ellie's mind off of it. Over time, Ellie didn't cry at all. Kendra and Ellie really began to bond.

Kendra taught Ellie how to do new things. They read books and danced to music. They played games, baked bread, and planted a garden.

Ellie also taught Kendra some lessons. Ellie saw the world with so much excitement. Kendra began to notice things like leaves, rocks, and insects. She learned to laugh out loud again. Ellie taught her to enjoy simple things.

By the end of summer, Kendra had plenty of money. But that wasn't what she treasured most. She treasured the gifts Ellie had given her.

MONITOR PROGRESS • Sequence

Tía Lola **413m**

Name _____

Carmella's Decision

Carmella proudly looked at six plastic containers on the patio.   10
Each held a healthy tomato plant. Each plant had greenish-red,   20
reddish-green, or lovely red tomatoes. The red ones were begging to be   32
picked. Carmella had finally decided that today was the day she would   44
grant their wish. She was eager to taste juicy tomatoes that she had   57
grown on her own.   61

Weeks ago, Carmella didn't think she could grow tomatoes,   70
especially in containers on her patio. But she had. She initially put small   83
stones in the bottom of each container, plus good soil, fertilizer, and a   96
bit of gardening lime. Then she planted a little tomato seedling in each   109
container.   110

Carmella watered the plants daily and watched them grow. Later,   120
she stuck a stake in each container to support the plants and tomatoes.   133

Now it was picking time! On the patio, Carmella spread out this   145
morning's newspaper. She set her picked tomatoes on it. As she did,   157
she noticed an article in the paper. It said that the local food pantry was   172
running low on food for poor people. It really needed fresh vegetables   184
like tomatoes.   186

For Carmella, it was both a hard and an easy decision. She filled a   200
basket with tomatoes—her tomatoes. Then she asked Mom for a ride to   213
the food pantry.   216

MONITOR PROGRESS

• Check Fluency

The Peace Corps

In 1961, John F. Kennedy was inaugurated president of the United States. He was one of America's youngest presidents ever. He was also intelligent, handsome, and charming. His ideas and personality made many Americans, especially young Americans, feel optimistic about the future. He inspired many citizens to become involved in their country and the world.

One of Kennedy's first acts as president was to start the Peace Corps. He saw it as an ideal way for Americans to help people around the world. The plan was that American volunteers would go to countries that asked for help in education, business, farming, and so on. The volunteers would aid people in those countries by sharing with them skills and techniques that would improve their lives.

At first, some critics weren't sure that the Peace Corps would work. It was asking a lot of the volunteers. Before they were sent to another country, they would need to learn the country's language and history. They would have to be trained in the subject that they would teach. When they were in the country, volunteers wouldn't stay in hotels or fancy homes. They would be expected to live with the people they were helping. That meant, at times, that volunteers would have to live in housing without running water or electricity. Volunteers would also be expected to stay in a country for two years. That was a lot of time to sacrifice to help others.

Did the idea work? Yes! By the end of 1961, there were 900 Peace Corps volunteers working in 16 countries. Five years after that, there were more than 15,000 volunteers in 90 countries!

The Peace Corps is still very active. In its 50 or so years of existence, more than 170,000 American volunteers have served 136 different countries. The desire to help others that President Kennedy inspired still lives on.

MONITOR PROGRESS • Generalize

Name _____

America's First Woman Doctor

Elizabeth Blackwell was born in England in 1821. Her family
moved to the United States in 1832. Elizabeth's father wanted to help
end slavery. He worked hard for this and other social causes. He died
in 1838.

To earn a living, Elizabeth's mother opened a school. Elizabeth
became a teacher. However, she slowly felt herself drawn toward
becoming a doctor. It became "a great moral struggle," as she said.
None of the medical schools would accept her.

Finally, Geneva Medical College in New York agreed that she could
come there. Once there, Elizabeth found she was not readily accepted.
Yet she worked and studied very hard. She finished school at the top
of her class. In 1849, Elizabeth Blackwell became the first woman to
receive a medical degree in the United States.

Elizabeth's struggles were not over. No one would hire her as a
doctor. She went to London and Paris to find work. While there, she
lost the sight in one eye. She returned to the United States in 1851.
Still no one would hire her, so Elizabeth Blackwell opened her own
clinic. Her sister also became a doctor and joined her. In 1867, the
Blackwell sisters opened a medical college for women. Thanks to their
efforts, many more women could follow their dreams to become trained
doctors.

Line	Count
	10
	22
	35
	37
	47
	57
	69
	77
	88
	99
	112
	124
	132
	144
	157
	171
	183
	196
	207
	218
	219

MONITOR PROGRESS • Check Fluency

Name _____

Dreams of Driving Coast to Coast

Today, highways crisscross the United States. If you want to drive from the East Coast to the West Coast, you can choose from many different routes. This incredible web of roads is very young. In 2006, the American interstate highway system had its 50th anniversary.

The first person to really push for good roads was President Franklin D. Roosevelt. He felt that Americans should be able to go across their great country on a system of connected roads. In the late 1930s, Roosevelt planned three routes from east to west and five more from north to south.

Such dreams were grand, and World War II made it impossible to begin building roads. It fell to another President—Dwight D. Eisenhower—to make it possible. In 1956, Eisenhower signed an act into law that allowed work to begin.

Forty years and $425 billion later, the web of roads was finally done. By then, cars, trucks, and buses were going half a trillion miles a year on the roads!

The early plans for the interstate system were mostly followed. In the chart below, you can see exactly how big those ideas were.

Interstate Highway System Plans, 1956	
Lanes	Minimum of four, each 12 feet wide
Shoulders	10 feet wide
Total Miles	44,000
Entrances and Exits	16,000
Overpasses and Bridges	50,000
Completion Date	1972
Federal Budget	$25 billion

MONITOR PROGRESS • Graphic Sources

Far Side of the Moon **473m**

Assessment Charts and Student Progress Report

from

First Stop Fourth Grade

Fluency Progress Chart, Grade 4

Name _____

WCPM	1	2	3	4	5	6	7	8	9	10	11	12	13	14	15	16	17	18	19	20	21	22	23	24	25	26	27	28	29	30	31	32	33	34	35	36
165																																				
160																																				
155																																				
150																																				
145																																				
140																																				
135																																				
130																																				
125																																				
120																																				
115																																				
110																																				
105																																				
100																																				
95																																				
90																																				
85																																				
80																																				
75																																				
70																																				

Timed Reading/Week

Assessment Chart

Name _____   Date _____

Benchmark Score reflects grade-level target.

	Day 3 Retelling Assessment		Day 5 Fluency Assessment		Day 5 Comprehension Assessment		Reteach	Teacher's Comments
	Benchmark Score	Actual Score	Benchmark WCPM	Actual Score	Benchmark Score	Actual Score		
WEEK 1 *Because of Winn-Dixie* Sequence	3–4		95–105		3–4		✓	
WEEK 2 *Lewis and Clark and Me* Author's Purpose	3–4		95–105		3–4			
WEEK 3 *On the Banks of Plum Creek* Character, Setting and Plot	3–4		95–105		3–4			
WEEK 4 *The Horned Toad Prince* Author's Purpose	3–4		95–105		3–4			
WEEK 5 *Letters Home from Yosemite* Main Idea and Details	3–4		95–105		3–4			
Unit 1 Test Score								

- **RECORD SCORES** Use this chart to record scores for the Day 3 Retelling, Day 5 Fluency, Day 5 Comprehension, and Unit Test.

- **REGROUPING** Compare the student's actual score to the benchmark score and group flexibly or provide extra support as needed.

- **RETEACH** If a student is unable to complete any part of the assessment process, use the weekly Reteach lessons in the *First Stop* book for additional support. Record the lesson information in the space provided on the chart. After reteaching, you may want to reassess using the Unit Test.

Assessment Chart

Name _____ Date _____

	Day 3 Retelling Assessment		Day 5 Fluency Assessment		Day 5 Comprehension Assessment		Reteach	Teacher's Comments
Benchmark Score reflects grade-level target.	Benchmark Score	Actual Score	Benchmark WCPM	Actual Score	Benchmark Score	Actual Score		
WEEK 1 *What Jo Did* Cause and Effect	3–4		100–110		3–4		✓	
WEEK 2 *Coyote School News* Draw Conclusions	3–4		100–110		3–4			
WEEK 3 *Scene Two* Draw Conclusions	3–4		100–110		3–4			
WEEK 4 *Horse Heroes* Fact and Opinion	3–4		100–110		3–4			
WEEK 5 *So You Want to Be President?* Main Idea and Details	3–4		100–110		3–4			
Unit 2 Test Score								

- **RECORD SCORES** Use this chart to record scores for the Day 3 Retelling, Day 5 Fluency, Day 5 Comprehension, and Unit Test.

- **REGROUPING** Compare the student's actual score to the benchmark score and group flexibly or provide extra support as needed.

- **RETEACH** If a student is unable to complete any part of the assessment process, use the weekly Reteach lessons in the *First Stop* book for additional support. Record the lesson information in the space provided on the chart. After reteaching, you may want to reassess using the Unit Test.

Assessment Chart

Name _____ Date _____

	Day 3 Retelling Assessment		Day 5 Fluency Assessment		Day 5 Comprehension Assessment		Reteach	Teacher's Comments
Benchmark Score reflects grade-level target.	Benchmark Score	Actual Score	Benchmark WCPM	Actual Score	Benchmark Score	Actual Score		
WEEK 1 The Man Who Named the Clouds — Graphic Sources	3–4		105–115		3–4			
WEEK 2 Adelina's Whales — Fact and Opinion	3–4		105–115		3–4			
WEEK 3 How Night Came from the Sea — Generalize	3–4		105–115		3–4			
WEEK 4 Eye of the Storm — Predict	3–4		105–115		3–4			
WEEK 5 Paul Bunyan — Generalize	3–4		105–115		3–4			
Unit 3 Test Score								

- **RECORD SCORES** Use this chart to record scores for the Day 3 Retelling, Day 5 Fluency, Day 5 Comprehension, and Unit Test.

- **REGROUPING** Compare the student's actual score to the benchmark score and group flexibly or provide extra support as needed.

- **RETEACH** If a student is unable to complete any part of the assessment process, use the weekly Reteach lessons in the *First Stop* book for additional support. Record the lesson information in the space provided on the chart. After reteaching, you may want to reassess using the Unit Test.

Assessment Chart

Name _____ Date _____

Benchmark Score reflects grade-level target.	Day 3 Retelling Assessment		Day 5 Fluency Assessment		Day 5 Comprehension Assessment		Reteach	Teacher's Comments
	Benchmark Score	Actual Score	Benchmark WCPM	Actual Score	Benchmark Score	Actual Score		
WEEK 1 *The Case of the Gasping Garbage* — Compare and Contrast	3–4		110–120		3–4		✓	
WEEK 2 *Encantado* — Compare and Contrast, Summarize	3–4		110–120		3–4			
WEEK 3 *Navajo Code Talkers* — Sequence	3–4		110–120		3–4			
WEEK 4 *Seeker of Knowledge* — Graphic Sources	3–4		110–120		3–4			
WEEK 5 *Encyclopedia Brown* — Plot and Theme	3–4		110–120		3–4			
Unit 4 Test Score								

- **RECORD SCORES** Use this chart to record scores for the Day 3 Retelling, Day 5 Fluency, Day 5 Comprehension, and Unit Test.

- **REGROUPING** Compare the student's actual score to the benchmark score and group flexibly or provide extra support as needed.

- **RETEACH** If a student is unable to complete any part of the assessment process, use the weekly Reteach lessons in the *First Stop* book for additional support. Record the lesson information in the space provided on the chart. After reteaching, you may want to reassess using the Unit Test.

Assessment Chart

Name _____ Date _____

		Day 3 Retelling Assessment		Day 5 Fluency Assessment		Day 5 Comprehension Assessment		Reteach	Teacher's Comments
	Benchmark Score reflects grade-level target.	Benchmark Score	Actual Score	Benchmark WCPM	Actual Score	Benchmark Score	Actual Score		
WEEK 1	**Smokejumpers** Author's Purpose	3–4		115–125		3–4		✓	
WEEK 2	**Lost City** Compare and Contrast	3–4		115–125		3–4			
WEEK 3	**Cliff Hanger** Setting and Plot	3–4		115–125		3–4			
WEEK 4	**Antarctic Journal** Main Idea and Details	3–4		115–125		3–4			
WEEK 5	**Moonwalk** Monitor and Clarify	3–4		115–125		3–4			
	Unit 5 Test Score								

- **RECORD SCORES** Use this chart to record scores for the Day 3 Retelling, Day 5 Fluency, Day 5 Comprehension, and Unit Test.

- **REGROUPING** Compare the student's actual score to the benchmark score and group flexibly or provide extra support as needed.

- **RETEACH** If a student is unable to complete any part of the assessment process, use the weekly Reteach lessons in the *First Stop* book for additional support. Record the lesson information in the space provided on the chart. After reteaching, you may want to reassess using the Unit Test.

265

Assessment Chart

Name _____ Date _____

Benchmark Score reflects grade-level target.	Day 3 Retelling Assessment		Day 5 Fluency Assessment		Day 5 Comprehension Assessment		Reteach	Teacher's Comments
	Benchmark Score	Actual Score	Benchmark WCPM	Actual Score	Benchmark Score	Actual Score		
WEEK 1 *My Brother Martin* Cause and Effect	3–4		120–130		3–4		✓	
WEEK 2 *Jim Thorpe's Bright Path* Fact and Opinion	3–4		120–130		3–4			
WEEK 3 *Tía Lola* Sequence	3–4		120–130		3–4			
WEEK 4 *A Gift from the Heart* Generalize	3–4		120–130		3–4			
WEEK 5 *Far Side of the Moon* Graphic Sources	3–4		120–130		3–4			
Unit 6 Test Score								

- **RECORD SCORES** Use this chart to record scores for the Day 3 Retelling, Day 5 Fluency, Day 5 Comprehension, and Unit Test.

- **REGROUPING** Compare the student's actual score to the benchmark score and group flexibly or provide extra support as needed.

- **RETEACH** If a student is unable to complete any part of the assessment process, use the weekly Reteach lessons in the *First Stop* book for additional support. Record the lesson information in the space provided on the chart. After reteaching, you may want to reassess using the Unit Test.

Student Progress Report: Grade 4

Name _____

This chart lists the skills taught in this program. Record your student's progress toward mastery of the skills covered in this school year here. Use the chart below to track the coverage of these skills.

Skill	Date	Date	Date
Read aloud grade-level texts and understand what is read.			
Determine the meaning of English words derived from Greek, Latin, and other languages.			
Determine the meanings of unfamiliar words or multiple meaning words by using the context of the sentence.			
Complete analogies based on knowledge of synonyms and antonyms.			
Identify the meaning of common idioms.			
Use a dictionary or glossary to find the meanings of unknown words, the syllable rules for these words, and how to pronounce them.			
Understand that the lesson or message of a work of fiction is its theme.			
Compare and contrast the actions of characters in traditional and classic literature.			
Explain how a poem's structure influences its form.			
Describe the structural elements of dramatic literature.			

Skill	Date	Date	Date
Sequence and summarize the main events in the plot and explain their influence on future events.			
Describe how characters interact with each other and the changes they undergo.			
Identify whether the narrator or speaker of a story is first or third person.			
Identify similarities and differences between characters' experiences in fictional works and the actual experiences of the authors of these works.			
Identify the author's use of similes and metaphors to create imagery.			
Read independently for long periods of time and paraphrase the reading, including the order in which events occur.			
Explain the difference between a stated purpose and an implied purpose in expository texts.			
Summarize the main idea and supporting details.			
Distinguish fact from opinion in a text and explain how to verify a fact.			
Describe how ideas are related in texts that are organized by cause and effect, sequence, or comparison.			
Use text features to gain an overview of a text and to locate information.			
Explain how an author's use of language influences the reader.			

Skill	Date	Date	Date
Determine the sequence needed to follow a procedure.			
Explain information that is presented graphically.			
Explain the positive and negative effects of different advertising techniques and how they influence consumer behavior.			
Explain the effects of media techniques on the message being delivered.			
Compare the conventions used to communicate different kinds of digital information.			
Plan a first draft by choosing an appropriate genre for communicating ideas and generate ideas through a range of strategies.			
Develop drafts and organize ideas into paragraphs.			
Revise drafts to make them clear and well-organized for the audience and use simple and compound sentences.			
Edit drafts for grammar, mechanics, and spelling using a teacher-developed rubric.			
Revise a final draft based on comments from other students and the teacher, and publish the work for an audience.			
Write literary texts that are imaginative, build to an ending, and contain details about the characters and setting.			
Write poems that make use of sensory details and the conventions of poetry.			
Write about important life experiences.			

Skill	Date	Date	Date
Write brief compositions that establish a central idea in a topic sentence.			
Write brief compositions that include supporting sentences with simple facts, details, and explanations.			
Write brief compositions that contain a concluding statement.			
Write letters tailored for a specific audience and purpose and that use appropriate conventions.			
Write responses to texts using evidence to show understanding.			
Write persuasive essays for specific audiences on specific issues that include opinions and use supporting details.			
Use and understand verbs (irregular verbs).			
Use and understand nouns (singular/plural, common/proper).			
Use and understand adjectives as well as their comparative and superlative forms.			
Use and understand adverbs.			
Use and understand prepositions and prepositional phrases.			
Use and understand reflexive pronouns.			
Use and understand the function of correlative conjunctions.			
Use time-order transition words and transitions that indicate a conclusion.			
Use the complete subject and verb in a sentence.			
Show agreement between subjects and verbs in simple and compound sentences.			

Skill	Date	Date	Date
Write in script or print legibly.			
Use correct capitalization for historical events and documents.			
Use correct capitalization for titles of books, stories, and essays.			
Use correct capitalization for languages, races, and nationalities.			
Recognize and use commas in compound sentences.			
Recognize and use quotation marks.			
Spell words with plural rules.			
Spell words with irregular plurals.			
Spell words that double consonants in the middle.			
Spell words that spell the sound "sh" differently.			
Spell words that include silent letters.			
Spell base words and roots with affixes correctly.			
Spell commonly used homophones.			
Use spelling patterns and rules, as well as print and online dictionaries, to find and confirm the spellings of words.			
Develop research topics based on interests or the results of brainstorming sessions and then choose one idea and develop questions about it.			
Generate a plan for gathering information relevant to the research question.			
Collect information from surveys, on-site inspections, and interviews.			

Skill	Date	Date	Date
Collect information from experts, encyclopedias, and online searches.			
Collect information from visual sources of information.			
Skim and scan text features to locate information.			
Take notes and organize the information found during research.			
Identify the author, title, publisher, and publication year of sources.			
Differentiate between paraphrasing information and committing plagiarism and explain why it is important to cite reliable sources.			
Improve the focus of research by consulting expert sources.			
Draw conclusions through a brief written explanation and create a works-cited page.			
Listen attentively to speakers, ask relevant questions, and make relevant comments.			
Follow, restate, and give oral instructions.			
Express an opinion supported by accurate information, using eye contact, speaking rate, volume, and enunciation, and language conventions to communicate ideas.			
Participate in discussions, ask and answer questions, and offer suggestions that build upon the ideas of others.			

Skill	Date	Date	Date
Establish purposes for reading a text based on what students hope to accomplish by reading the text.			
Ask literal, interpretive, and evaluative questions of a text.			
Monitor and adjust comprehension using a variety of strategies.			
Make inferences about a text and use evidence from the text to support understanding.			
Summarize information in a text, maintaining meaning and logical order.			
Make connections between literary and informational texts with similar ideas and provide evidence from the text.			

Fifth Grade Formal Assessment Tools

Form from Fifth Grade Baseline Group Test Teacher's Manual

Grade 5 Baseline Test Evaluation Chart

(including percentage conversion chart)

Student's Name _____ Date _____

Item	Score (circle one)	Item	Score (circle one)	Number Correct/ 25	Percent Correct/ 25	Total Number Correct/ 55	Total Percent Correct /55	Total Number Correct/ 55 (continued)	Total Percent Correct/ 55 (continued)
Vocabulary		**Reading**		1	4%	1	2%	32	58%
1.	0 1	1.	0 1	2	8%	2	4%	33	60%
2.	0 1	2.	0 1	3	12%	3	5%	34	62%
3.	0 1	3.	0 1	4	16%	4	7%	35	64%
4.	0 1	4.	0 1	5	20%	5	9%	36	65%
5.	0 1	5.	0 1	6	24%	6	11%	37	67%
6.	0 1	6.	0 1	7	28%	7	13%	38	69%
7.	0 1	7.	0 1	8	32%	8	15%	39	71%
8.	0 1	8.	0 1	9	36%	9	16%	40	73%
9.	0 1	9.	0 1	10	40%	10	18%	41	75%
10.	0 1	10.	0 1	11	44%	11	20%	42	76%
11.	0 1	11.	0 1	12	48%	12	22%	43	78%
12.	0 1	12.	0 1	13	52%	13	24%	44	80%
13.	0 1	13.	0 1	14	56%	14	25%	45	82%
14.	0 1	14.	0 1	15	60%	15	27%	46	84%
15.	0 1	15.	0 1	16	64%	16	29%	47	85%
16.	0 1	16.	0 1	17	68%	17	31%	48	87%
17.	0 1	17.	0 1	18	72%	18	33%	49	89%
18.	0 1	18.	0 1	19	76%	19	35%	50	91%
19.	0 1	19.	0 1	20	80%	20	36%	51	93%
20.	0 1	20.	0 1	21	84%	21	38%	52	95%
21.	0 1	21.	0 1	22	88%	22	40%	53	96%
22.	0 1	22.	0 1	23	92%	23	42%	54	98%
23.	0 1	23.	0 1	24	96%	24	44%	55	100%
24.	0 1	24.	0 1	25	100%	25	45%		
25.	0 1	25.	0 1			26	47%		
		26.	0 1			27	49%		
		27.	0 1			28	51%		
		28.	0 1			29	53%		
		29.	0 1			30	55%		
		30.	0 1			31	56%		

Vocabulary Score _____ /25= _____ %   **TOTAL (Vocabulary + Reading Score)** _____ /55= _____ %

Reading Score _____ /30= _____ %   **Placement:** _____

Alternate Baseline Test Placement: (Optional)

Strategic Intervention _____

On-Level _____   **Advanced** _____

Fluency Rate _____   (Optional)

Interim Overall Placement (circle one)   **Strategic Intervention   On-Level   Advanced**

Fluency Forms

Reading Fluency Progress Chart

Student's Name	Unit 1		Unit 2		Unit 3		Unit 4		Unit 5		Unit 6	
	Date	WCPM	Date	WCPM	Date	WCPM	Date	WCPM	Date	WCPM	Date	WCPM
1.												
2.												
3.												
4.												
5.												
6.												
7.												
8.												
9.												
10.												
11.												
12.												
13.												
14.												
15.												
16.												
17.												
18.												
19.												
20.												
21.												
22.												
23.												
24.												
25.												
26.												
27.												
28.												
29.												
30.												
31.												
32.												
33.												
34.												
35.												

Fluency Progress Chart, Grade 5

Name _____

WCPM	1	2	3	4	5	6	7	8	9	10	11	12	13	14	15	16	17	18	19	20	21	22	23	24	25	26	27	28	29	30	31	32	33	34	35	36
175																																				
170																																				
165																																				
160																																				
155																																				
150																																				
145																																				
140																																				
135																																				
130																																				
125																																				
120																																				
115																																				
110																																				
105																																				
100																																				
95																																				
90																																				
85																																				
80																																				

Timed Reading/Week

281

Forms from Fifth Grade Weekly Tests Teacher's Manual

Scott Foresman *Reading Street*
Class Weekly Test Progress Chart—Grade 5

Teacher's Name: _____

Student Name	Weekly Test Total Score																													
	1	2	3	4	5	6	7	8	9	10	11	12	13	14	15	16	17	18	19	20	21	22	23	24	25	26	27	28	29	30
1																														
2																														
3																														
4																														
5																														
6																														
7																														
8																														
9																														
10																														
11																														
12																														
13																														
14																														
15																														
16																														
17																														
18																														
19																														
20																														
21																														
22																														
23																														
24																														
25																														
26																														
27																														
28																														
29																														
30																														

Scott Foresman *Reading Street*
Student Weekly Test Progress Chart—Grade 5

Student Name: _____

Test	Vocabulary	Phonics/Word Analysis	Comprehension	Multiple-Choice Total	Writing	TOTAL
Weekly Test 1	/7	/5	/8	/20		
Weekly Test 2	/7	/5	/8	/20		
Weekly Test 3	/7	/5	/8	/20		
Weekly Test 4	/7	/5	/8	/20		
Weekly Test 5	/6	/6	/8	/20		
Weekly Test 6	/7	/5	/8	/20		
Weekly Test 7	/7	/5	/8	/20		
Weekly Test 8	/7	/5	/8	/20		
Weekly Test 9	/7	/5	/8	/20		
Weekly Test 10	/7	/5	/8	/20		
Weekly Test 11	/5	/7	/8	/20		
Weekly Test 12	/7	/5	/8	/20		
Weekly Test 13	/7	/5	/8	/20		
Weekly Test 14	/7	/5	/8	/20		
Weekly Test 15	/6	/6	/8	/20		
Weekly Test 16	/7	/5	/8	/20		
Weekly Test 17	/5	/7	/8	/20		
Weekly Test 18	/6	/6	/8	/20		
Weekly Test 19	/6	/6	/8	/20		
Weekly Test 20	/7	/5	/8	/20		
Weekly Test 21	/7	/5	/8	/20		
Weekly Test 22	/7	/5	/8	/20		
Weekly Test 23	/6	/6	/8	/20		
Weekly Test 24	/6	/6	/8	/20		
Weekly Test 25	/5	/7	/8	/20		
Weekly Test 26	/7	/5	/8	/20		
Weekly Test 27	/7	/5	/8	/20		
Weekly Test 28	/6	/6	/8	/20		
Weekly Test 29	/6	/6	/8	/20		
Weekly Test 30	/7	/5	/8	/20		

Comprehension Target Skill Coverage

How can the Weekly Tests predict student success on Unit Benchmark Tests?

Each Unit Benchmark Test, as well as assessing overall student reading ability, concentrates on two skills taught and/or reviewed during the unit by including several questions on those skills. In order to ensure that comprehension target skill can be accurately learned and then tested, students learn each target skill through a combination of being taught and reviewing the skill multiple times before testing occurs. The charts below show the units/weeks where the target comprehension skills are taught and where they are tested on Weekly Tests. Based on the student's number of correct answers for each tested target skill, the teacher will know whether a student has gained the necessary skill knowledge before the Unit Test is given. A low score on the Weekly Tests probably indicates a need for closer review of the student's performance and perhaps additional instruction. It is important to understand that these tests provide only one look at the student's progress and should be interpreted in conjunction with other assessments and the teacher's observation.

Using the Comprehension Target Skill Coverage Chart

To score target skill knowledge, use the Comprehension Target Skill Coverage Chart.

1. Make a copy of the appropriate Comprehension Target Skill Coverage chart for each student.

2. To score, circle the number of correct answers the student had for that skill on the appropriate Weekly Test.

3. Using the total number of correct answers for a skill, check the appropriate box under *Student Trend* to indicate whether or not the student has acquired the target skill knowledge. We recommend 90% correct as the criterion for skill acquisition at this level. Add any notes or observations that may be helpful to you and the student in later instruction.

Grade 5 — Comprehension Target Skill Coverage Chart

Student Name _____

Unit 1 Tested Skills	Weekly Test Locations	Number Correct	Student Trend
Literary Elements: Character/Plot/Theme	Weekly Test 1	0 1 2 3 4 5	_____ Skill knowledge acquired _____ Skill needs further review
	Weekly Test 2	0 1	
	Weekly Test 3	0 1 2 3 4	
Cause and Effect	Weekly Test 2	0 1 2 3 4 5	_____ Skill knowledge acquired _____ Skill needs further review
	Weekly Test 4	0 1	
	Weekly Test 5	0 1 2 3 4 5	

Unit 2 Tested Skills	Weekly Test Locations	Number Correct	Student Trend
Compare and Contrast	Weekly Test 3	0 1 2	_____ Skill knowledge acquired _____ Skill needs further review
	Weekly Test 6	0 1 2 3 4 5	
	Weekly Test 7	0 1	
	Weekly Test 8	0 1 2 3 4 5	
	Weekly Test 9	0 1	
Sequence	Weekly Test 1	0 1	_____ Skill knowledge acquired _____ Skill needs further review
	Weekly Test 2	0 1 2	
	Weekly Test 7	0 1 2 3 4 5	
	Weekly Test 8	0 1	

Grade 5 — Comprehension Target Skill Coverage Chart

Student Name _____

Unit 3 Tested Skills	Weekly Test Locations	Number Correct	Student Trend
Main Idea and Supporting Details	Weekly Test 5	0 1	____ Skill knowledge acquired ____ Skill needs further review
	Weekly Test 12	0 1 2 3 4 5	
	Weekly Test 13	0 1	
	Weekly Test 14	0 1 2 3 4 5	
	Weekly Test 15	0 1	
Fact and Opinion	Weekly Test 4	0 1 2 3 4 5	____ Skill knowledge acquired ____ Skill needs further review
	Weekly Test 9	0 1	
	Weekly Test 11	0 1	
	Weekly Test 12	0 1	
	Weekly Test 13	0 1 2 3 4 5	
	Weekly Test 14	0 1	

Grade 5 — Comprehension Target Skill Coverage Chart

Student Name _____

Unit 4 Tested Skills	Weekly Test Locations	Number Correct	Student Trend
Generalize	Weekly Test 10	0 1 2	____ Skill knowledge acquired ____ Skill needs further review
	Weekly Test 14	0 1	
	Weekly Test 17	0 1 2 3 4 5	
	Weekly Test 19	0 1 2 3 4 5	
	Weekly Test 20	0 1	
Draw Conclusions	Weekly Test 1	0 1 2	
	Weekly Test 4	0 1 2	
	Weekly Test 5	0 1	
	Weekly Test 6	0 1 2	
	Weekly Test 7	0 1 2	
	Weekly Test 8	0 1 2	
	Weekly Test 11	0 1	
	Weekly Test 12	0 1 2	
	Weekly Test 13	0 1	
	Weekly Test 14	0 1	
	Weekly Test 15	0 1	
	Weekly Test 16	0 1 2 3 4 5	
	Weekly Test 17	0 1 2 3	____ Skill knowledge acquired ____ Skill needs further review
	Weekly Test 19	0 1	
	Weekly Test 20	0 1 2 3 4 5	

Grade 5 — Comprehension Target Skill Coverage Chart

Student Name _____

Unit 5 Tested Skills	Weekly Test Locations	Number Correct	Student Trend
Graphic Sources	Weekly Test 5	0 1	
	Weekly Test 13	0 1	
	Weekly Test 15	0 1 2 3 4 5	
	Weekly Test 18	0 1 2 3 4 5	
	Weekly Test 22	0 1 2 3 4 5	_____ Skill knowledge acquired
	Weekly Test 23	0 1	_____ Skill needs further review
	Weekly Test 25	0 1	
Author's Purpose	Weekly Test 6	0 1	
	Weekly Test 9	0 1 2 3 4 5	
	Weekly Test 10	0 1 2 3 4 5	
	Weekly Test 15	0 1	
	Weekly Test 16	0 1 2	
	Weekly Test 18	0 1	
	Weekly Test 21	0 1	_____ Skill knowledge acquired
	Weekly Test 23	0 1 2 3 4 5	_____ Skill needs further review
	Weekly Test 24	0 1	

Grade 5 — Comprehension Target Skill Coverage Chart

Student Name _____

Unit 6 Tested Skills	Weekly Test Locations	Number Correct	Student Trend
Sequence	Weekly Test 1	0 1	
	Weekly Test 2	0 1 2	
	Weekly Test 7	0 1 2 3 4 5	
	Weekly Test 8	0 1	_____ Skill knowledge acquired
	Weekly Test 11	0 1 2 3 4 5	
	Weekly Test 20	0 1 2	_____ Skill needs further review
	Weekly Test 30	0 1 2 3 4 5	
Draw Conclusions	Weekly Test 1	0 1 2	
	Weekly Test 4	0 1 2	
	Weekly Test 5	0 1	
	Weekly Test 6	0 1 2	
	Weekly Test 7	0 1 2	
	Weekly Test 8	0 1 2	
	Weekly Test 11	0 1	
	Weekly Test 12	0 1 2	
	Weekly Test 13	0 1	
	Weekly Test 14	0 1	
	Weekly Test 15	0 1	
	Weekly Test 16	0 1 2 3 4 5	
	Weekly Test 17	0 1 2 3	
	Weekly Test 19	0 1	
	Weekly Test 20	0 1 2 3 4 5	
	Weekly Test 21	0 1 2	
	Weekly Test 22	0 1 2	
	Weekly Test 24	0 1	
	Weekly Test 26	0 1 2 3 4 5 6	
	Weekly Test 27	0 1	_____ Skill knowledge acquired
	Weekly Test 28	0 1 2	
	Weekly Test 29	0 1	_____ Skill needs further review
	Weekly Test 30	0 1 2 3	

Weekly Test Item Analysis—Grade 5

TEST	SECTION	ITEMS	SKILL
Weekly Test 1	**Vocabulary**	1–7	Understand and use new vocabulary
	Word Analysis	8–12	Suffix -*ly*
	Comprehension	14–17, 20	◉ Literary Elements: Character and plot
		18, 19	Draw Conclusions
		13	R Sequence
	Written Response	Look Back and Write	Respond to literature
Weekly Test 2	**Vocabulary**	1–7	Understand and use new vocabulary
	Word Analysis	8–12	Greek and Latin roots
	Comprehension	14, 16–19	◉ Cause and effect
		13, 15	Sequence
		20	R Literary Elements: Character, setting, plot
	Written Response	Look Back and Write	Respond to literature
Weekly Test 3	**Vocabulary**	1–7	Understand and use new vocabulary
	Word Analysis	8–12	Compound words
	Comprehension	13, 14, 16, 18, 19	◉ Literary Elements: Theme and setting
		17, 20	Compare and contrast
		15	R Literary Elements: Character and plot
	Written Response	Look Back and Write	Respond to literature

Weekly Test Item Analysis—Grade 5

TEST	SECTION	ITEMS	SKILL
Weekly Test 4	**Vocabulary**	1–7	Understand and use new vocabulary
	Word Analysis	8–12	Shades of meaning
	Comprehension	13–15, 17, 19	◎ Fact and opinion
		18, 20	Draw Conclusions
		16	R Cause and effect
	Written Response	Look Back and Write	Respond to literature
Weekly Test 5	**Vocabulary**	1–6	Understand and use new vocabulary
	Word Analysis	7–12	Suffix *-ing*
	Comprehension	14–16, 18, 19	◎ Cause and effect
		13, 20	Draw conclusions, Main idea and details
		17	R Graphic sources
	Written Response	Look Back and Write	Respond to literature
Weekly Test 6	**Vocabulary**	1–7	Understand and use new vocabulary
	Word Analysis	8–12	Spanish word origin
	Comprehension	13, 14, 15, 17, 18	◎ Compare and contrast
		16, 19	Draw conclusions
		20	R Author's purpose
	Written Response	Look Back and Write	Respond to literature

Weekly Test Item Analysis—Grade 5

TEST	SECTION	ITEMS	SKILL
Weekly Test 7	**Vocabulary**	1–7	Understand and use new vocabulary
	Word Analysis	8–12	French word origins
	Comprehension	13, 14, 17–20	◉ Sequence
		15, 16	Draw conclusions
		19	**R** Compare and contrast
	Written Response	Look Back and Write	Respond to literature
Weekly Test 8	**Vocabulary**	1–7	Understand and use new vocabulary
	Word Analysis	8–12	Suffixes -*tion, -ion*
	Comprehension	14–17, 19	◉ Compare and contrast
		18, 20	Draw conclusions
		13	**R** Sequence
	Written Response	Look Back and Write	Respond to literature
Weekly Test 9	**Vocabulary**	1–7	Understand and use new vocabulary
	Word Analysis	8–12	Spanish word origins
	Comprehension	13–14, 18–20	◉ Author's purpose
		15, 17	Cause and effect, Fact and opinion
		16	**R** Compare and contrast
	Written Response	Look Back and Write	Respond to literature

Weekly Test Item Analysis—Grade 5

TEST	SECTION	ITEMS	SKILL
Weekly Test 10	**Vocabulary**	1–7	Understand and use new vocabulary
	Word Analysis	8–12	Word families
	Comprehension	13, 15, 17, 19, 20	◉ Author's purpose
		14, 18	Generalize
		16	**R** Literary Elements: Theme and setting
	Written Response	Look Back and Write	Respond to literature
Weekly Test 11	**Vocabulary**	1–5	Understand and use new vocabulary
	Word Analysis	6–12	Shades of meaning
	Comprehension	13–15, 16, 19	◉ Sequence
		17, 20	Fact and opinion, Draw conclusions
		18	**R** Cause and effect
	Written Response	Look Back and Write	Respond to literature
Weekly Test 12	**Vocabulary**	1–7	Understand and use new vocabulary
	Word Analysis	8–12	Greek and Latin roots
	Comprehension	13, 15, 18–20	◉ Main idea and details
		14, 17	Draw conclusions
		16	**R** Fact and opinion
	Written Response	Look Back and Write	Respond to literature

Weekly Test Item Analysis—Grade 5

TEST	SECTION	ITEMS	SKILL
Weekly Test 13	**Vocabulary**	1–7	Understand and use new vocabulary
	Word Analysis	8–12	Suffixes *-tion, -sion*
	Comprehension	13, 14, 16, 18, 19	◉ Fact and opinion
		15, 17	Graphic sources, Draw conclusions
		20	▣ R Main idea and details
	Written Response	Look Back and Write	Respond to literature
Weekly Test 14	**Vocabulary**	1–7	Understand and use new vocabulary
	Word Analysis	8–12	Suffix *-ous*
	Comprehension	14, 16–18, 20	◉ Main idea and details
		13	Draw conclusions
		19	Generalize
		15	▣ R Fact and opinion
	Written Response	Look Back and Write	Respond to literature
Weekly Test 15	**Vocabulary**	1–6	Understand and use new vocabulary
	Word Analysis	7–12	Compound words
	Comprehension	14, 15, 16, 18, 19	◉ Graphic sources
		13	Draw conclusions
		17	Main idea and details
		20	▣ R Author's purpose
	Written Response	Look Back and Write	Respond to literature

Weekly Test Item Analysis—Grade 5

TEST	SECTION	ITEMS	SKILL
Weekly Test 16	**Vocabulary**	1–7	Understand and use new vocabulary
	Word Analysis	8–12	Word endings *-ing, -ed, -s*
	Comprehension	13, 14, 15, 18, 19	⊙ Draw conclusions
		16, 17	Author's purpose
		20	R Literary Elements: Theme and setting
	Written Response	Look Back and Write	Respond to literature
Weekly Test 17	**Vocabulary**	1–5	Understand and use new vocabulary
	Word Analysis	6–12	Suffixes *-ly, -ian*
	Comprehension	13, 14, 17–19	⊙ Generalize
		15, 16, 20	R Draw conclusions
	Written Response	Look Back and Write	Respond to literature
Weekly Test 18	**Vocabulary**	1–6	Understand and use new vocabulary
	Word Analysis	7–12	Suffix *-ize*
	Comprehension	13–16, 18	⊙ Graphic sources
		19, 20	Main idea and details
		17	R Author's purpose
	Written Response	Look Back and Write	Respond to literature

Weekly Test Item Analysis—Grade 5

TEST	SECTION	ITEMS	SKILL
Weekly Test 19	**Vocabulary**	1–6	Understand and use new vocabulary
	Word Analysis	7–12	Prefixes *com-, pro-, epi-*
	Comprehension	13, 14, 16, 18, 19	◉ Generalize
		17, 20	Main idea and details
		15	**R** Draw conclusions
	Written Response	Look Back and Write	Respond to literature
Weekly Test 20	**Vocabulary**	1–7	Understand and use new vocabulary
	Word Analysis	8–12	Idioms
	Comprehension	13–17	◉ Draw conclusions
		18, 19	Sequence
		20	**R** Generalize
	Written Response	Look Back and Write	Respond to literature
Weekly Test 21	**Vocabulary**	1–7	Understand and use new vocabulary
	Word Analysis	8–12	Prefixes *im-, ate-*
	Comprehension	13–17	◉ Literary Elements: Character and plot
		19, 20	Draw conclusions
		18	**R** Author's purpose
	Written Response	Look Back and Write	Respond to literature

Weekly Test Item Analysis—Grade 5

TEST	SECTION	ITEMS	SKILL
Weekly Test 22	**Vocabulary**	1–7	Understand and use new vocabulary
	Word Analysis	8–12	Acronyms
	Comprehension	13–16, 18	◉ Graphic sources
		17, 19	Draw conclusions
		20	R Main idea and details
	Written Response	Look Back and Write	Respond to literature
Weekly Test 23	**Vocabulary**	1–6	Understand and use new vocabulary
	Word Analysis	7–12	Greek and Latin roots
	Comprehension	14, 16, 17, 19, 20	◉ Author's opinion
		13, 18	Main idea and details
		15	R Graphic sources
	Written Response	Look Back and Write	Respond to literature
Weekly Test 24	**Vocabulary**	1–6	Understand and use new vocabulary
	Word Analysis	7–12	Complex spelling patterns -ous, -ious, -eous
	Comprehension	14–16, 18, 20	◉ Cause and effect
		17	Draw conclusions
		19	Main idea and details
		13	R Author's purpose
	Written Response	Look Back and Write	Respond to literature

Weekly Test Item Analysis—Grade 5

TEST	SECTION	ITEMS	SKILL
Weekly Test 25	**Vocabulary**	1–5	Understand and use new vocabulary
	Word Analysis	6–12	Morphemes
	Comprehension	15–17, 19, 20	◉ Generalize
		14, 18	Main idea and details
		13	**R** Graphic sources
	Written Response	Look Back and Write	Respond to literature
Weekly Test 26	**Vocabulary**	1–6	Understand and use new vocabulary
	Word Analysis	7–12	Compound words
	Comprehension	13–15, 18–19	◉ Draw conclusions
		17	Draw conclusions
		20	Compare and contrast
		16	**R** Generalize
	Written Response	Look Back and Write	Respond to literature
Weekly Test 27	**Vocabulary**	1–7	Understand and use new vocabulary
	Word Analysis	8–12	Russian word origin
	Comprehension	15–18, 20	◉ Main idea and details
		13	Author's purpose
		14	Draw conclusions
		19	**R** Sequence
	Written Response	Look Back and Write	Respond to literature

Weekly Test Item Analysis—Grade 5

TEST	SECTION	ITEMS	SKILL
Weekly Test 28	**Vocabulary**	1–6	Understand and use new vocabulary
	Word Analysis	7–12	Complex spelling patterns ci= /sh/, ti=/sh/, ous=/us/
	Comprehension	13–15, 18, 19	◉ Compare and contrast
		16	Main idea and details
		17, 20	**R** Draw conclusions
	Written Response	Look Back and Write	Respond to literature
Weekly Test 29	**Vocabulary**	1–6	Understand and use new vocabulary
	Word Analysis	7–12	Word families
	Comprehension	14–16, 18, 20	◉ Fact and opinion
		13	Main idea and details
		17	Draw conclusions
		19	**R** Main idea and details
	Written Response	Look Back and Write	Respond to literature
Weekly Test 30	**Vocabulary**	1–7	Understand and use new vocabulary
	Word Analysis	8–12	Compound words
	Comprehension	13, 14, 18, 19, 20	◉ Sequence
		15–17	**R** Draw conclusions
	Written Response	Look Back and Write	Respond to literature

Forms from Grade 5 Unit and End-of-Year Benchmark Tests Teacher's Manual

CLASS RECORD CHART

Grade 5 Unit Benchmark Tests

Teacher Name _____ Class _____

Student Name	Unit 1		Unit 2		Unit 3		Unit 4		Unit 5		Unit 6	
	Pt 1–3	Pt 4	Pt 1–3	Pt 4	Pt 1–3	Pt 4	Pt 1–3	Pt 4	Pt 1–3	Pt 4	Pt 1–3	Pt 4
1.												
2.												
3.												
4.												
5.												
6.												
7.												
8.												
9.												
10.												
11.												
12.												
13.												
14.												
15.												
16.												
17.												
18.												
19.												
20.												
21.												
22.												
23.												
24.												
25.												
26.												
27.												
28.												
29.												
30.												

Evaluation Chart: Grade 5 – Unit 1 Benchmark Test

Student Name _____ Date _____

Reading – Parts 1–3			
Item	Tested Skill	Item Type*	Score (circle one)
Reading – Part 1: Comprehension			
1.	Literary elements: character	I	0 1
2.	Cause and effect	I	0 1
3.	Cause and effect	I	0 1
4.	Literary elements: character	L	0 1
5.	Literary elements: character	I	0 1
6.	Author's purpose	C	0 1
7.	Draw conclusions	I	0 1
8.	Sequence	L	0 1
9.	Compare and contrast	C	0 1
10.	Sequence	I	0 1
11.	Literary elements: theme	C	0 1
A.	Constructed-response text-to-text connection		0 1 2
12.	Literary elements: character	I	0 1
13.	Draw conclusions	I	0 1
14.	Draw conclusions	I	0 1
15.	Cause and effect	I	0 1
16.	Literary elements: setting	L	0 1
17.	Sequence	L	0 1
18.	Cause and effect	L	0 1
19.	Literary elements: character	C	0 1
20.	Literary elements: theme	C	0 1
21.	Author's purpose	I	0 1
22.	Literary elements: character	I	0 1
B.	Constructed-response text-to-text connection		0 1 2
Reading – Part 2: Vocabulary			
23.	Context clues: homonyms		0 1
24.	Context clues: antonyms		0 1
25.	Word structure: suffixes		0 1
26.	Word structure: suffixes		0 1
27.	Context clues: multiple-meaning words		0 1
28.	Context clues: homonyms		0 1
29.	Context clues: antonyms		0 1

Reading – Part 2: Vocabulary (continued)			
30.	Word structure: suffixes	0	1
31.	Context clues: multiple-meaning words	0	1
32.	Context clues: unfamiliar words	0	1
Student's Regrouping Multiple-Choice Score/Total Possible Score _____ /32			
Reading – Part 3: Writing Conventions			
33.	Declarative sentences	0	1
34.	Interrogative sentences	0	1
35.	Imperative sentences	0	1
36.	Subjects and predicates	0	1
37.	Subjects and predicates	0	1
38.	Complex sentences	0	1
39.	Compound sentences	0	1
40.	Proper nouns	0	1
Student's Reading Total Score/Total Possible Score _____ /44			

*L = literal   I = inferential   C = critical analysis

Regrouping (Reading — Parts 1–2) percentage: _____ ÷ 32 = _____ × 100 = _____%
(student's score)   (percentage score)

Reading — Parts 1–3 percentage score: _____ ÷ 44 = _____ × 100 = _____%
(student's total score)   (percentage score)

Writing – Part 4

Writing Score (complete one) _____ /6 _____ /5 _____ /4 _____ /3

Notes/Observations:

Evaluation Chart: Grade 5 – Unit 2 Benchmark Test

Student Name _____ Date _____

Reading – Parts 1–3			
Item	**Tested Skill**	**Item Type***	**Score** (circle one)
Reading – Part 1: Comprehension			
1.	Sequence	L	0 1
2.	Sequence	C	0 1
3.	Sequence	I	0 1
4.	Draw conclusions	I	0 1
5.	Compare and contrast	I	0 1
6.	Compare and contrast	I	0 1
7.	Fact and opinion	C	0 1
8.	Generalize	I	0 1
9.	Cause and effect	I	0 1
10.	Author's purpose	C	0 1
11.	Compare and contrast	I	0 1
A.	Constructed-response text-to-self connection		0 1 2
12.	Sequence	L	0 1
13.	Sequence	L	0 1
14.	Compare and contrast	L	0 1
15.	Compare and contrast	L	0 1
16.	Draw conclusions	I	0 1
17.	Compare and contrast	I	0 1
18.	Literary elements: character	I	0 1
19.	Literary elements: setting	I	0 1
20.	Author's purpose	C	0 1
21.	Literary elements: theme	I	0 1
22.	Literary elements: plot	C	0 1
B.	Constructed-response text-to-text connection		0 1 2
Reading – Part 2: Vocabulary			
23.	Word structure: prefixes		0 1
24.	Word structure: prefixes		0 1
25.	Context clues: unfamiliar words		0 1
26.	Context clues: unfamiliar words		0 1
27.	Dictionary/glossary: multiple-meaning words		0 1
28.	Dictionary/glossary: unknown words		0 1
29.	Context clues: synonyms		0 1

Reading – Part 2: Vocabulary (continued)		
30.	Word structure: prefixes	0 1
31.	Dictionary/glossary: unfamiliar words	0 1
32.	Context clues: unfamiliar words	0 1
Student's Regrouping Multiple-Choice Score/Total Possible Score		_____ /32
Reading – Part 3: Writing Conventions		
33.	Regular and irregular plural nouns	0 1
34.	Regular and irregular plural nouns	0 1
35.	Regular and irregular plural nouns	0 1
36.	Subject/verb agreement	0 1
37.	Abbreviations and titles	0 1
38.	Common and proper nouns	0 1
39.	Common and proper nouns	0 1
40.	Main and helping verbs	0 1
Student's Reading Total Score/Total Possible Score		_____ /44

*L = literal   I = inferential   C = critical analysis

Regrouping (Reading — Parts 1–2) percentage: _____ ÷ 32 = _____ × 100 = _____%

(student's score)   (percentage score)

Reading — Parts 1–3 percentage score: _____ ÷ 44 = _____ × 100 = _____%

(student's total score)   (percentage score)

Writing – Part 4

Writing Score (complete one) _____ /6   _____ /5   _____ /4   _____ /3

Notes/Observations:

Evaluation Chart: Grade 5 – Unit 3 Benchmark Test

Student Name _____ **Date** _____

Item	Tested Skill	Item Type*	Score (circle one)
Reading – Parts 1–3			
Reading – Part 1: Comprehension			
1.	Author's purpose	C	0 1
2.	Main idea and details	I	0 1
3.	Compare and contrast	I	0 1
4.	Author's purpose	I	0 1
5.	Fact and opinion	C	0 1
6.	Fact and opinion	C	0 1
7.	Main idea and details	L	0 1
8.	Draw conclusions	I	0 1
9.	Fact and opinion	C	0 1
10.	Main idea and details	L	0 1
11.	Generalize	I	0 1
A.	Constructed-response text-to-world connection		0 1 2
12.	Compare and contrast	L	0 1
13.	Main idea and details	I	0 1
14.	Cause and effect	I	0 1
15.	Draw conclusions	I	0 1
16.	Compare and contrast	L	0 1
17.	Fact and opinion	C	0 1
18.	Main idea and details	I	0 1
19.	Fact and opinion	C	0 1
20.	Sequence	L	0 1
21.	Author's purpose	C	0 1
22.	Generalize	I	0 1
B.	Constructed-response text-to-text connection		0 1 2
Reading – Part 2: Vocabulary			
23.	Context clues: homonyms		0 1
24.	Context clues: multiple-meaning words		0 1
25.	Context clues: antonyms		0 1
26.	Context clues: homonyms		0 1
27.	Context clues: multiple-meaning words		0 1
28.	Word structure: prefixes		0 1
29.	Context clues: multiple-meaning words		0 1

Reading – Part 2: Vocabulary (continued)		
30.	Context clues: multiple-meaning words	0 1
31.	Word structure: prefixes	0 1
32.	Context clues: homonyms	0 1
Student's Regrouping Multiple-Choice Score/Total Possible Score		_____ /32
Reading – Part 3: Writing Conventions		
33.	Principal parts of irregular verbs	0 1
34.	Past, present, and future tenses	0 1
35.	Past, present, and future tenses	0 1
36.	Troublesome verbs	0 1
37.	Troublesome verbs	0 1
38.	Past, present, and future tenses	0 1
39.	Prepositions and prepositional phrases	0 1
40.	Past, present, and future tenses	0 1
Student's Reading Total Score/Total Possible Score		_____ /44

*L = literal   I = inferential   C = critical analysis

Regrouping (Reading — Parts 1–2) percentage: _____ $\div$ 32 = _____ $\times$ 100 = _____%
(student's score)   (percentage score)

Reading — Parts 1–3 percentage score: _____ $\div$ 44 = _____ $\times$ 100 = _____%
(student's total score)   (percentage score)

Writing – Part 4

Writing Score (complete one) _____ /6 _____ /5 _____ /4 _____ /3

Notes/Observations:

Evaluation Chart: Grade 5 – Unit 4 Benchmark Test

Student Name _____ **Date** _____

Item	Tested Skill	Item Type*	Score (circle one)
Reading – Parts 1–3			
Reading – Part 1: Comprehension			
1.	Cause and effect	L	0 1
2.	Draw conclusions	I	0 1
3.	Sequence	L	0 1
4.	Author's purpose	C	0 1
5.	Generalize	C	0 1
6.	Draw conclusions	I	0 1
7.	Generalize	C	0 1
8.	Generalize	I	0 1
9.	Draw conclusions	C	0 1
10.	Draw conclusions	I	0 1
11.	Author's purpose	C	0 1
A.	Constructed-response text-to-text connection		0 1 2
12.	Author's purpose	C	0 1
13.	Main idea and details	C	0 1
14.	Fact and opinion	C	0 1
15.	Compare and contrast	I	0 1
16.	Cause and effect	I	0 1
17.	Generalize	C	0 1
18.	Main idea and details	I	0 1
19.	Fact and opinion	C	0 1
20.	Draw conclusions	L	0 1
21.	Draw conclusions	I	0 1
22.	Generalize	I	0 1
B.	Constructed-response text-to-text connection		0 1 2
Reading – Part 2: Vocabulary			
23.	Word structure: suffixes		0 1
24.	Word structure: suffixes		0 1
25.	Context clues: synonyms		0 1
26.	Context clues: synonyms		0 1
27.	Word structure: suffixes		0 1
28.	Context clues: synonyms		0 1
29.	Context clues: unfamiliar words		0 1

Reading – Part 2: Vocabulary (continued)		
30.	Context clues: unfamiliar words	0 1
31.	Context clues: synonyms	0 1
32.	Context clues: synonyms	0 1
Student's Regrouping Multiple-Choice Score/Total Possible Score _____ **/32**		
Reading – Part 3: Writing Conventions		
33.	Using *Who* and *Whom*	0 1
34.	Indefinite pronouns	0 1
35.	Pronouns	0 1
36.	Pronouns	0 1
37.	Pronouns	0 1
38.	Reflexive pronouns	0 1
39.	Pronouns	0 1
40.	Pronouns	0 1
Student's Reading Total Score/Total Possible Score _____ **/44**		

*L = literal   I = inferential   C = critical analysis

Regrouping (Reading — Parts 1–2) percentage: _____ ÷ 32 = _____ × 100 = _____%
$\qquad$ (student's score) $\qquad\qquad$ (percentage score)

Reading — Parts 1–3 percentage score: _____ ÷ 44 = _____ × 100 = _____%
$\qquad$ (student's total score) $\qquad\qquad$ (percentage score)

Writing – Part 4

Writing Score (complete one) _____ /6 _____ /5 _____ /4 _____ /3

Notes/Observations:

Evaluation Chart: Grade 5 – Unit 5 Benchmark Test

Student Name _____ Date _____

Reading – Parts 1–3			
Item	Tested Skill	Item Type*	Score (circle one)
Reading – Part 1: Comprehension			
1.	Author's purpose	C	0 1
2.	Draw conclusions	C	0 1
3.	Cause and effect	L	0 1
4.	Cause and effect	L	0 1
5.	Fact and opinion	C	0 1
6.	Author's purpose	C	0 1
7.	Draw conclusions	C	0 1
8.	Draw conclusions	I	0 1
9.	Main idea and details	I	0 1
10.	Graphic sources	I	0 1
11.	Graphic sources	C	0 1
A.	Constructed-response text-to-world connection		0 1 2
12.	Graphic sources	C	0 1
13.	Graphic sources	C	0 1
14.	Main idea and details	I	0 1
15.	Author's purpose	C	0 1
16.	Compare and contrast	I	0 1
17.	Cause and effect	L	0 1
18.	Generalize	I	0 1
19.	Draw conclusions	I	0 1
20.	Main idea and details	C	0 1
21.	Sequence	L	0 1
22.	Author's purpose	C	0 1
B.	Constructed-response text-to-text connection		0 1 2
Reading – Part 2: Vocabulary			
23.	Word structure: prefixes		0 1
24.	Word structure: prefixes		0 1
25.	Word structure: prefixes		0 1
26.	Context clues: unfamiliar words		0 1
27.	Word structure: prefixes		0 1
28.	Word structure: prefixes		0 1
29.	Context clues: unfamiliar words		0 1

Reading – Part 2: Vocabulary (continued)			
30.	Context clues: multiple-meaning words	0	1
31.	Word structure: Greek and Latin roots	0	1
32.	Word structure: suffixes	0	1
Student's Regrouping Multiple-Choice Score/Total Possible Score		_____ /32	
Reading – Part 3: Writing Conventions			
33.	Adverbs	0	1
34.	Adjectives	0	1
35.	Adjectives	0	1
36.	Adverbs	0	1
37.	Comparative and superlative adjectives	0	1
38.	Comparative and superlative adjectives	0	1
39.	Comparative and superlative adjectives	0	1
40.	Comparative and superlative adjectives	0	1
Student's Reading Total Score/Total Possible Score		_____ /44	

*L = literal   I = inferential   C = critical analysis

Regrouping (Reading — Parts 1–2) percentage: _____ ÷ 32 = _____ × 100 = _____%
(student's score)   (percentage score)

Reading — Parts 1–3 percentage score: _____ ÷ 44 = _____ × 100 = _____%
(student's total score)   (percentage score)

Writing – Part 4

Writing Score (complete one) _____/6   _____/5   _____/4   _____/3

Notes/Observations:

Evaluation Chart: Grade 5 – Unit 6 Benchmark Test

Student Name _____ Date _____

Item	Tested Skill	Item Type*	Score (circle one)		
Reading – Parts 1–3					
Reading – Part 1: Comprehension					
1.	Sequence	I	0	1	
2.	Sequence	I	0	1	
3.	Fact and opinion	C	0	1	
4.	Compare and contrast	L	0	1	
5.	Draw conclusions	I	0	1	
6.	Cause and effect	I	0	1	
7.	Draw conclusions	I	0	1	
8.	Draw conclusions	I	0	1	
9.	Main idea and details	I	0	1	
10.	Main idea and details	C	0	1	
11.	Author's purpose	C	0	1	
A.	Constructed-response text-to-world connection		0	1	2
12.	Sequence	L	0	1	
13.	Draw conclusions	I	0	1	
14.	Generalize	C	0	1	
15.	Draw conclusions	I	0	1	
16.	Literary elements: character	I	0	1	
17.	Literary elements: plot	I	0	1	
18.	Literary elements: plot	I	0	1	
19.	Draw conclusions	I	0	1	
20.	Sequence	I	0	1	
21.	Author's purpose	C	0	1	
22.	Literary elements: theme	I	0	1	
B.	Constructed-response text-to-text connection		0	1	2
Reading – Part 2: Vocabulary					
23.	Word structure: suffixes		0	1	
24.	Word structure: suffixes		0	1	
25.	Context clues: unfamiliar words		0	1	
26.	Dictionary/glossary: unfamiliar words		0	1	
27.	Word structure: suffixes		0	1	
28.	Word structure: suffixes		0	1	
29.	Context clues: homonyms		0	1	

Reading – Part 2: Vocabulary (continued)		
30.	Dictionary/glossary: unfamiliar words	0 1
31.	Word structure: suffixes	0 1
32.	Dictionary/glossary: unfamiliar words	0 1
Student's Regrouping Multiple-Choice Score/Total Possible Score		_____ /32
Reading – Part 3: Writing Conventions		
33.	Quotation marks	0 1
34.	Commas	0 1
35.	Commas	0 1
36.	Punctuation	0 1
37.	Commas	0 1
38.	Modifiers	0 1
39.	Commas	0 1
40.	Modifiers	0 1
Student's Reading Total Score/Total Possible Score		_____ /44

*L = literal   I = inferential   C = critical analysis

Regrouping (Reading — Parts 1–2) percentage: _____ ÷ 32 = _____ × 100 = _____%
(student's score)   (percentage score)

Reading — Parts 1–3 percentage score: _____ ÷ 44 = _____ × 100 = _____%
(student's total score)   (percentage score)

Writing – Part 4

Writing Score (complete one) _____ /6 _____ /5 _____ /4 _____ /3

Notes/Observations:

Evaluation Chart: Grade 5 – End-of-Year Benchmark Test

Student Name _____ Date _____

Reading – Parts 1–3

	Tested Skill	Item Type*	Score (circle one)	Item	Tested Skill	Item Type*	Score (circle one)
Reading – Part 1: Comprehension				27.	Compare and contrast	I	0 1
1.	Sequence	L	0 1	28.	Generalize	I	0 1
2.	Draw conclusions	I	0 1	29.	Fact and opinion	C	0 1
3.	Cause and effect	L	0 1	30.	Main idea and details	I	0 1
4.	Fact and opinion	C	0 1	31.	Graphic sources	C	0 1
5.	Draw conclusions	I	0 1	32.	Main idea and details	I	0 1
6.	Generalize	I	0 1	33.	Author's purpose	C	0 1
7.	Main idea and details	I	0 1	B.	Constructed-response text-to-text connection		0 1 2
8.	Compare and contrast	I	0 1	**Reading – Part 2: Vocabulary**			
9.	Main idea and details	I	0 1	34.	Word structure: prefixes		0 1
10.	Graphic sources	C	0 1	35.	Context clues: unfamiliar words		0 1
11.	Author's purpose	C	0 1	36.	Context clues: synonyms		0 1
12.	Sequence	I	0 1	37.	Dictionary/glossary: multiple-meaning words		0 1
13.	Literary elements: character	I	0 1	38.	Dictionary/glossary: multiple-meaning words		0 1
14.	Literary elements: plot	C	0 1	39.	Context clues: unfamiliar words		0 1
15.	Main idea and details	I	0 1	40.	Context clues: synonyms		0 1
16.	Literary elements: theme	C	0 1	41.	Word structure: suffixes		0 1
17.	Compare and contrast	I	0 1	42.	Dictionary/glossary: unfamiliar words		0 1
18.	Cause and effect	L	0 1	43.	Context clues: multiple-meaning words		0 1
19.	Draw conclusions	I	0 1	44.	Context clues: synonyms		0 1
20.	Draw conclusions	C	0 1	45.	Context clues: unfamiliar words		0 1
21.	Cause and effect	I	0 1	46.	Dictionary/glossary: unfamiliar words		0 1
22.	Author's purpose	C	0 1	47.	Context clues: synonyms		0 1
A.	Constructed-response text-to-text connection		0 1 2	48.	Word structure: Greek and Latin roots		0 1
23.	Cause and effect	C	0 1	**Reading – Part 3: Writing Conventions**			
24.	Draw conclusions	I	0 1	49.	Articles		0 1
25.	Draw conclusions	I	0 1	50.	Adverbs		0 1
26.	Fact and opinion	C	0 1	51.	Adjectives		0 1

Reading – Part 3: Writing Conventions (continued)					
52.	Pronouns	0 1	57.	Subject/verb agreement	0 1
53.	Dependent clauses	0 1	58.	Using *who* and *whom*	0 1
54.	Irregular verbs	0 1	59	Proper nouns	0 1
55.	Quotation marks	0 1	60.	Irregular plural nouns	0 1
56.	Commas	0 1			
Student's Reading Total Score/Total Possible Score					**_____ /64**

*L = literal   I = inferential   C = critical analysis

Reading — Parts 1–3 percentage score: _____ ÷ 64 = _____ × 100 = _____%

(student's total score)   (percentage score)

Writing – Part 4

Writing Score (complete one)   _____/6   _____/5   _____/4   _____/3

Notes/Observations:

Monitor Progress
Passages
from
Fifth Grade Teacher's Editions

Name _____

Journey Across the Ocean

America had been at war for two years when Nellie turned 18. She was   14

now old enough to join the war. The night before she left for Europe, she said   30

good-bye to her friends. Some understood why Nellie was leaving and some   42

did not. "My father fought in World War I," explained Nellie. "If he and the   57

men he fought with had not gone to war, we might not have all the freedoms   73

we have today. I want to do what I can to help the men fighting in the war."   91

"Aren't you afraid you will get hurt?" asked Catherine.   100

"That is possible, but it's a risk I'm willing to take," replied Nellie.   113

The next morning Nellie finished packing for her trip across the ocean.   125

She thought about all she was leaving behind so that she could go help   139

people she did not even know. For a minute, she began to worry that she   154

was making a mistake. She thought about how dangerous it would be on the   168

battlefield.   169

Then she began to think about why she decided to become a nurse in   183

the first place. Nellie wanted to help people, whether or not she knew them.   197

And what better people to help than those who were fighting for her country's   211

freedom? When she thought about it this way, Nellie once again became   223

confident in the decision.   227

Nellie said good-bye to her parents and brother. She promised that she   240

would write to them every day. Then she set out on her long journey across   255

the ocean, full of hope for the future.   263

MONITOR PROGRESS • Check Fluency

Red Kayak **49k**

320

Jeffrey's Home Run

Jeffrey and his friends were playing baseball in his back yard one Saturday afternoon. When it came time for Jeffrey to bat, he walked to the plate and looked towards the pitcher's mound. Stephen, one of the neighborhood's best pitchers, was winding up. A minute later, the ball came flying towards Jeffrey. He kept his eye on it and hit it with all he had.

As he ran to first base, Jeffrey watched the ball reach high into the air. It would be a home run if it made it to Mr. Bender's back yard! Jeffrey's happiness faded as he watched the ball sail into Mr. Bender's yard and crash into the bird feeder that he had made. The bird feeder cracked in half and all the seeds that were inside fell to the ground.

"Don't worry," said Stephen. "Mr. Bender's not home. But we better leave before he gets back. He loves to bird watch in his yard."

Jeffrey went inside when the other boys left. He felt bad about breaking Mr. Bender's bird feeder, but he thought he would be punished for breaking it. A few hours later, he saw Mr. Bender discover his broken bird feeder. The look on Mr. Bender's face made Jeffrey change his mind. He had to tell the truth, even though he might be punished.

Jeffrey walked over to Mr. Bender's house and told him what had happened. "I didn't do it intentionally. It was an accident," said Jeffrey.

Mr. Bender was glad that Jeffrey had told him the truth. He thought it was very brave of Jeffrey.

MONITOR PROGRESS • Character and Plot

Red Kayak **49m**

Thunder and Lightning

Nature can form dangerous weather. A thunderstorm   7
is one kind of weather that can become dangerous.   16
Thunderstorms begin to form when warm air with water   25
in it rises. As the air cools, the water becomes a cloud.   37
As the cloud moves higher in the sky, the water begins to   49
form drops of rain. As the cloud moves even higher, the   60
raindrops become charged. When all the raindrops in one   69
cloud begin to bounce off the raindrops in other clouds,   79
lightning forms. Lightning makes heat. When heat from   87
lightning hits the air around it, thunder is heard.   95

Once a storm begins, it is easy to tell how far away it   108
is. Light moves faster than sound, so lightning will be seen   119
before thunder is heard. For every three seconds between   128
seeing lightning and hearing thunder, the storm is about a   138
half mile away. Thunderstorms cause more than just thunder   147
and lightning. Rain, hail, and strong winds can also come   157
from these storms. These effects of a thunderstorm can   166
cause problems. Rain can cause flooding, and hail can   175
damage homes and cars. Strong wind can cause tree   184
branches to fall into the street and on homes.   193

It is important to stay inside during a thunderstorm since   203
it is possible to be hit by lightning. If someone is under   215
a tree or in an empty field, the chances of being hit by   228
lightning become higher. Thousands of people are hit by   237
lightning every year. Thunderstorms can be dangerous, but   245
they can also be beautiful. Lightning takes unique forms   254
and colors and every storm is different.   261

MONITOR PROGRESS   • Check Fluency

Thunder Rose **81k**

Name _____

Weather in Our Lives

Weather affects our lives in many ways. Weather can be one of the reasons that a person decides to live in a certain part of the country. Some people live in the South because it is warm all year round. Other people choose not to live in the Midwest because of the chance of a tornado forming. People who live in the Midwest have to be resourceful when a storm hits. Many homes have storm cellars. When a tornado hits, people have to be prepared to stay in the storm cellar until the storm passes. This means packing up some food and even clothes in case that storm lasts for a long time. A tornado can cause strong winds and rain.

The weather also has to do with the kind of clothes you wear. People who live in the North wear warm clothes in the winter because it is cold. Those who live in the South can wear shorts almost all year.

The food that people buy at the store is also affected by the weather. Some fruits and vegetables grow better in places with more sun or rain than others. This causes the price of certain foods to be higher in places where the fruits and vegetables do not grow.

Certain places in the world are popular vacation spots because of the weather. Many people have jobs at hotels and restaurants in these places. The islands in the Atlantic Ocean are popular vacation spots. These islands can also be hit by hurricanes. If a bad storm hits, people may not want to go there for a while, and the shops and hotels will lose money.

These are some of the ways that weather can affect our lives. It can have good and bad effects. The key is to be prepared.

MONITOR PROGRESS

• Cause and Effect

Thunder Rose **81m**

Name _____

Beware of Three Pointy Leaves!

John's little brother Matthew wanted to go camping with friends in the   12
woods near his home. John thought it would be a good idea to teach his   27
brother some survival tips before his trip.   34

So one afternoon, they went into the woods. John wanted to show   46
Matthew that there are some plants that are safe to eat and there are some   61
that he should stay away from. When the boys came to a patch of poison ivy,   77
John made sure that Matthew took a good look so he would remember it.   91

"Poison ivy has three pointy leaves. It can be hard to spot in the summer   106
because it looks the same as all the other green plants," said John. "But in the   122
fall and spring it turns to a deep red color."   132

John explained that Matthew could get a bad rash if he touched the   145
poison ivy or even if his clothes touched it and then he touched his clothes.   160

"What do I do if I get a rash?" asked Matthew.   171

"Well," said John, "the best thing to do is to go see a doctor."   185

He also explained that poison ivy has some good points. Birds and   197
animals are not affected by the oils in poison ivy, so they can eat it.   212

As they walked the rest of the way through the woods, John asked   225
Matthew to point out all the plants he had learned about that day. John was   240
happy that he could share some survival tips with his little brother.   252

MONITOR
PROGRESS

• Check Fluency

Name _____

Lost in the Woods

The air had become cooler during the past few days. The leaves were starting to turn colors. Max knew that summer was coming to an end. He loved the fall, but he had never been lost in the woods on a cold night.

Max was camping with his family. Max had wanted to set up one of the tents his family would sleep in, but he had not been able to do it by himself. His older brother had put the other tent together by himself in just a few minutes.

So Max decided to take a walk by himself while his father finished putting up the second tent. He had just wanted to walk through the woods around the campsite, but Max soon saw that he did not know how to get back to his family.

Max sat down and gathered his thoughts. He knew if he was not going to get back to the campsite soon, he would need water. He also knew that building a fire would not be a good idea because of all the dry leaves and twigs on the ground.

As he walked a little further, Max began to hear running water. He followed the sound and found a clearing in the woods and a ravine with fresh water running through it. After he had a drink, he decided it was safe to build a fire to stay warm. Once it was dark, Max knew he wouldn't get back to the campsite that night, so he tried to get some sleep.

The next morning a park ranger found Max and walked him back to the campsite. His family was not only relieved to have him back but very proud of Max's quick thinking. The ranger said Max had done exactly what he should have in that situation.

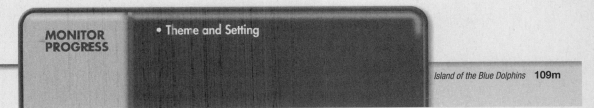

MONITOR PROGRESS

• Theme and Setting

Name _____

Pride of the Yankees

Lou Gehrig was born in 1903 in New York. Both of his parents were   14

from Germany. They worked hard so that their son would grow up to live the   29

American Dream. His mother, Christina, wanted her son to go to college and   42

get a job that would make him a good deal of money. He did go to college,   59

but he did not finish. Instead, Lou decided to use his skill for baseball. As a 75

lifelong New Yorker, he found a home with the New York Yankees in 1923.   89

In the beginning of his career, he played baseball under the shadow of the   103

great Babe Ruth. It was during the 1927 season that people began to notice   117

the younger player. He helped the Yankees win the World Series that year.   130

During the 1938 season, sports fans began to see a difference in Lou's   143

playing. He was not playing as well as he had in the past. When the 1939   159

season began, the once great player was having trouble with both hitting   171

and running. That year, he was told he had a sickness that was attacking the 186

nerves in his body. It was the last year that he would play baseball.   200

On July 4, 1939, the Yankees said good-bye to their teammate during a   213

double-header. Lou told the crowd that he was the luckiest man on the face of 228

the earth to have had the chance to play with the Yankees and to have such   244

supportive fans. Lou is still remembered as one of the best players in baseball. 258

He was elected to the Baseball Hall of Fame in 1939 at the age of 36.   274

MONITOR PROGRESS   • Check Fluency

Satchel Paige **139k**

Name _____

Fighting for Women's Rights

In 1872, Susan B. Anthony set out to gain the right to vote for women in the United States. Anthony first became interested in equal rights when her father began inviting friends to their home to talk about how important it was to free the slaves. She believed in ending slavery, and this was how she became involved in equal rights. Anthony began to write speeches for people who wanted equal rights for slaves and women.

Years later, she gathered a group of women who believed the same way that she did, and they tried to vote in Anthony's hometown. Two weeks later, she went to jail for doing this. Anthony was told to pay a fine as punishment for trying to vote. She refused and got away with not paying the fine. She believed this was a small success. So, Anthony kept trying to convince the government that women should be allowed to vote.

With the help of other women such as Elizabeth Cady Stanton, Anthony founded groups and a magazine about helping women gain the right to vote. These women had the opinion that if men who had come from other countries could vote, women should also have that right. For years, they tried to make their voices heard and gain equal rights.

Anthony and Stanton did not live to see women win voting rights in 1920, but they had spent most of their lives fighting for what they believed was right. These women were the greatest fighters for women's rights in history. They spoke against inequality and did not let others tell them that they could not reach their goals. Now they have a special place in history for their hard work.

MONITOR PROGRESS

• Fact and Opinion

Welcoming the Newcomers

During the late 1800s and early 1900s, millions of people came to the   13

United States. It was common for those who lived in Eastern Europe to work   27

on farms that were owned by rich land owners, and so the farmers did not   42

make much money. They came to America hoping to get better jobs and earn   56

more.   57

Another reason that people decided to leave their homes was so that they   70

could go to whatever church they chose. In many countries, the government   82

would not allow its people to attend the church of their choice.   94

Once they got to America, the poorest of the immigrants sometimes   105

ended up settling in or near the city they arrived in. This happened because   119

they did not have money when they arrived, so they had to find work right   134

away.   135

It was hard for some newcomers to feel at home in their new country.   149

People did not always make new immigrants feel welcome. Some made a life   162

here and brought other family members to the States once they were making   175

enough money to help them make the trip. Others only stayed long enough to   189

make the money they needed to return home and live comfortably.   200

Over time, the people who came to the United States from Eastern   212

Europe at the turn of the century spread out and settled all across the country. 227

Whatever their reasons for leaving home, the immigrants who arrived on the   239

shores of America added to the richness of its culture.   249

MONITOR PROGRESS   • Check Fluency

Ten Mile Day **169k**

Arriving at Ellis Island

In December of 1891, a young girl named Annie stepped on a ship with her two younger brothers. They would be at sea for twelve days making the trip from Ireland to America. They were sad to leave their home, but they would be happy to see their parents again.

Annie's parents and older brother had left Ireland two years earlier in search of a better life. In America, they had enough money for an apartment, clothes, and food.

When Annie and her brothers got off the ship on January 1, 1892, they were at Ellis Island. They were the first of hundreds of passengers to leave the ship. As Annie and her brothers walked towards the building, they heard the nearly deafening sound of bells and whistles. A man stopped her and gave her a ten dollar gold piece. Annie was told that she was the first person to walk through the newly opened building.

Because Annie and her brothers were the first people to make their way through Ellis Island, a statue of them now stands on the island. There is also a statue of them in Ireland, where their trip began.

Annie lived in New York City all her life. When she grew up, she married a man who had moved to America from Germany. They lived in New York City's Lower East Side. Some of Annie's descendants still live in New York City today.

Millions of immigrants followed Annie and her brothers through Ellis Island during the 60 years it was open. Now a museum, the island has become a symbol of America and new beginnings.

MONITOR PROGRESS
• Cause and Effect

Ten Mile Day **169m**

Name _____

The Right Change

My cousin Leah and I each had a ten-dollar bill that we could spend at   15
the school carnival. For weeks we had talked about the big day and what we   30
would do.   32

Leah had said, "I will spend two dollars on cotton candy, and two dollars   46
on a strawberry shake."   50

I knew that Leah would spend the remaining six dollars on carnival rides.   63
I would spend my ten dollars in the same way except that I would have a   79
peach shake instead of strawberry. I could almost taste the creamy sweetness   91
as Leah and I planned our day.   98

On the big day, Leah and I walked over to the park and went straight   113
to the fruit-shake man. Leah paid for her strawberry shake, took the change,   126
and walked over to the Bumper Boats while she waited for me. The peach   140
shake was cold in my hand as I gave the man my ten-dollar bill. He gave me   157
change and I began to walk away. Before stuffing the bills into my pocket, I   172
caught a quick glimpse of one. I should have had a five-dollar bill and three   187
one-dollar bills after paying for my two-dollar shake. But instead I had a ten- 201
dollar bill and three one-dollar bills. The shake man had given me too much   214
change. I began to think of all the things I could buy with the extra money.   230

I could ride even more rides and maybe take a chance on the Ring Toss   245
Game.   246

I took a sip of my shake and felt an ache in my stomach. I walked back   263
to the shake man and got the right change.   275

MONITOR PROGRESS   • Check Fluency

Upside Down Under

I spent the first ten years of my life living in upstate New York. My friends and I enjoyed summer days splashing in the lake, finding driftwood, and napping in hammocks. That changed the day my dad told us we were moving. He had accepted a job in some desert in Australia. What would I do there? Watch the dust blow? I felt my life turn upside down.

Really! I showed my dad my world globe. "We'll fall off!" I protested. I held a toy cowboy's feet on the green space that was Australia. His head pointed down and out into unknown space.

"Ever heard of gravity?" my dad asked. "The cowboy won't fall off and neither will you. But nice try!"

My only hope was to get my little sister stirred up into a huge fit. I showed her the globe and the cowboy. "See," I demonstrated. "Up here in New York we can stand up." I moved the cowboy down to our new home. "See, down here...." I let the cowboy drop to the floor and then shook my head slowly. "The rest of us might make it because we're heavier. But you're so small, there's no hope!" Her scream was all that I dreamed of and more.

"What did you tell her?" my dad asked. But he knew when he saw my sister. She was pale and screaming, standing next to the globe with the doomed cowboy at her feet.

She calmed down when my dad told her that at dinner I would explain gravity to her. For the next two hours I sat in my room writing a three-page report on gravity. I also had to include a poster that explained why we wouldn't fall off the Earth.

MONITOR PROGRESS • Compare and Contrast

At the Beach **201m**

Name _____

Runaway Car!

My grandfather frequently talks about an event that occurred when he   11
was a teenager. He wasn't old enough to legally drive, but he was aware of   26
how cars operated.   29

Grandfather was strolling down a slight hill. At the bottom of the hill   42
stood a cluster of youngsters chatting. As Grandfather approached them,   52
something made him glance back. He saw an old sedan coming down the   65
hill. He was surprised that he hadn't heard the car's engine. Then he saw   79
there wasn't a driver in the car! It was rolling down the hill on its own! It   96
appeared to be rapidly picking up speed.   103

Grandfather instantly thought of the kids down the hill. They couldn't hear   115
the car either. And it would roll faster and faster and probably hit them!   129

Just then, the car rolled past him. Grandfather chased it and in a few   143
strides, he caught up. When he put his hand on the driver's door handle, the   158
car nearly yanked him down. But Grandfather kept his balance and opened   170
the car door. He jumped into the seat and pushed the brake pedal hard.   184
The brakes squealed! The youngsters heard that and scattered. Grandfather   194
stopped the car. The kids were safe.   201

A woman ran up to Grandfather. "Young man," she shouted. "You're   212
driving too fast!"   215

The woman had not seen Grandfather's whole adventure. She had just   226
seen the end. But Grandfather didn't mind. He knew he had just saved the   240
lives of several youngsters.   244

MONITOR PROGRESS

• Check Fluency

The Battle Begins

In January 1944, World War II had been raging for more than five years. So much depended on who won. If the United States and its allies did, freedom would win too. If Nazi Germany and its partners did, freedom would die. No war had meant more.

American General Dwight Eisenhower understood that well. Starting that January, he led the preparation for a great battle. It would involve thousands of ships and airplanes. It would risk hundreds of thousands of lives. These forces would have to cross the English Channel. That was the unpredictable sea between Great Britain and France.

The goal was to attack the German army that hid on the cliffs and beaches of the French coast. This attack would begin a long series of battles that Eisenhower hoped would completely defeat Germany.

Over the first months of 1944, Eisenhower supervised the planning for the battle, training of troops, and assembling of ships and airplanes. In late May, he and his forces were ready. But the weather was not. Storms postponed the attack, day after day.

During the wait for better weather, Eisenhower had time to think. He knew that many soldiers who landed on the French beaches wouldn't live to see who won. Later, many more soldiers would die in other battles. There was no way to change that. In those waiting days, Eisenhower talked to the men about their homes. He knew that many men would never see those homes again. He hoped their sacrifices would be worth it.

Finally on June 5, Eisenhower got a promising weather forecast. Tomorrow morning the storms would briefly let up. On the morning of June 6, the English Channel was filled with 6,000 ships. Some were great battleships. Some were small landing craft carrying brave soldiers from the United States, Great Britain, and Canada. As the crafts neared the coast, soldiers peered out at the beaches and cliffs ahead. The great battle was about to begin.

MONITOR PROGRESS   • Sequence of Events

Name _____

A Happy Tune

Lars was the best musician in all the land. When he played his flute, no   15
one could resist the beautiful notes. If he played a happy tune, everyone who   29
heard the music smiled, and some even danced. If he played a sad tune,   43
everyone who heard shook their heads sadly and many cried. Lars played his   56
flute at every happy wedding and every sad funeral.   65

But it was a poor time and if Lars was paid at all, it was only with a few   84
coins. One day as Lars rested on a tree stump near the riverbank, he began   99
to play a sad tune. He was feeling lonely and hungry. He felt that his life   115
might never improve.   118

To Lars's surprise, the river began to churn around and around until a   131
white column rose up in the middle. The figure of a young maiden dressed in   146
river moss appeared before Lars. The maiden was crying and her tears turned   159
to silver minnows as they hit the river. Lars was upset to see the maiden cry   175
and he began to cry, too.   181

Finally, when they had both cried their limit of tears, the maiden asked   194
him, "Why are you so sad?" Lars told her about how lonely and hungry he   209
was. He said that he couldn't play at even one more wedding. "I'll only play   224
sad tunes for funerals."   228

The maiden reached into the river and began to toss the silver minnows   241
at Lars. As each minnow hit the ground, it turned to real silver. Soon, Lars was   257
standing in the middle of thousands of minnows made of real silver.   269

Lars and the river maiden married in June, and Lars played a happy tune!   283

MONITOR PROGRESS

- Check Fluency

How Tom Got Beautiful Feathers

In a long ago time, there lived a bird that had the most beautiful blue and green feathers. Her name was Mia and every day she would walk down to the edge of the river so that she could look at herself. High up in a tree, a peacock named Tom watched her. Every day, Tom was astonished at Mia's great beauty and vowed that one day he would marry her. But Mia was in love only with her shimmering blue and green reflection and had no time for Tom and his short, dull, brown feathers.

One day Mia stepped closer to the river bank so she could get a better look at herself. She tripped on an old tree root and fell into the river. She began to sputter and flap. Tom flew down to help her. He reached out to Mia but something in the river was pulling at her!

"Help me!" she screamed. Tom pulled hard but something in the river pulled even harder! Finally, with one great effort, Tom pulled Mia out of the river, where she fell to the ground. In the river, an old turtle with blue and green feathers in his mouth dove under the water, sorry that he had missed his chance to catch the bird.

Once the river was still, Mia looked at her reflection. She couldn't believe what she saw! Her blue and green feathers were gone, leaving behind short, dull, brown feathers. "I'm not beautiful!" Mia cried. "I'm as ugly as...." But before she could finish, Tom said, "You're beautiful and you always have been."

At that moment, blue and green feathers began to sprout on Tom. Mia spent the rest of her life in short, dull, brown feathers. They lived happily ever after.

MONITOR PROGRESS

• Compare and Contrast

The Ch'i-lin Purse **257m**

Tough Times

Times were challenging in Rudy's neighborhood. Many folks had lost   10
their jobs and struggled to pay bills.   17

Things were especially tough for Rudy's big family. His parents formerly   28
had good jobs, but now they were employed part-time and didn't earn much   41
money. Yet Rudy's family was an optimistic bunch. His parents hid their   53
worries and concerns. They made sure that their kids were decent students   65
and neighbors.   67

Elderly Mrs. Hendricks lived alone next door. She often watched Rudy   78
and his siblings as their parents worked. She seemed like a grandmother to   91
them.   92

During these hard times, neighbors put "share boxes" on their porches.   103
The boxes had extra food, books, DVDs, and other things that neighbors   115
shared with each other. Neighbors could take what they needed. When they   127
finished a book or a DVD, they put it in their share box for someone else to   144
use.   145

One Saturday, Rudy found a great DVD in Mrs. Hendricks' share box.   157
Mrs. Hendricks yelled through her screen door, "Enjoy it, Rudy! My son sent it   171
to me."   173

When Rudy got home, he discovered an open envelope in the DVD box.   186
The word Mom was printed on it. In it was $100! Rudy knew right away that   202
Mom was Mrs. Hendricks.   206

Some kids would think that their family could use $100 and keep it, but   220
not Rudy. He returned it immediately. Mrs. Hendricks hugged him and said,   232
"I'm not surprised that I lost it or that you, Rudy, returned it."   245

MONITOR PROGRESS   • Check Fluency

Blood

America needs blood! Experts say that about every two seconds someone in America urgently needs blood. Often it's a case of life or death. Why would people need blood? It can be for a variety of reasons, and none are good. A person may have been in a bad accident, need life-threatening surgery, have been badly burned, or may be fighting a horrible illness like cancer. People who need blood are usually in serious trouble.

How do these people obtain blood? Other people donate it to them. Occasionally donors know who will get their blood. But usually it goes to total strangers. It comes from people who voluntarily donated it.

Think about that. Volunteers donate a pint of their own blood to a total stranger! Why would someone do that? People donate because they know they're helping another human being. A donor is someone's hero. A donor can save another person's life!

Most people think donating blood is a good idea. They know that they, their families, or friends might even need blood. So donating makes sense. But there are problems.

First, only a little more than a third of the American population is eligible to donate. A lot of people who can't donate are kids. In most places, you must be 17 years old to donate.

Second, most people who are eligible to donate don't because they feel they don't have time. Others are afraid to donate. They think it will hurt. But donating only takes about an hour from start to finish. And if it hurts, it's no worse than a quick pinprick.

Do you think saving a life is worth an hour of your time? Do you think saving a life is worth the pain of a quick pinprick? You know the answer to both questions. Yes! Remember that when you turn 17!

MONITOR PROGRESS

• **Author's purpose**

A Summer's Trade **287m**

Name _____

Step Back in Time

It's fun to learn about how people lived a long time ago. Life was very   15

different for young people who lived during the historic time of the American   28

Revolution. Many families lived on farms. Even at a young age, children had   41

chores to do. They learned to sweep, sew, milk cows, and gather vegetables.   54

If they had a chicken coop, an important chore was to gather the eggs every   69

day.   70

Families often made what they needed. Wool was sheared from sheep,   81

spun into yarn, and woven to make clothes, blankets, and other useful items.   94

They made candles from hot wax that was melted and poured into molds.   107

Some people even made their own furniture such as tables, chairs, and beds.   120

Many towns and villages had schools but some areas did not. When   132

there was no teacher or school, parents would teach their children what they   145

needed to know at home.   150

Young people who lived long ago liked to have fun things to do just as   165

young people today do. One popular game was stick and ball. This game   178

was similar to what we know today as baseball. Some ways to have fun have   193

not changed much. Children long ago liked to fly kites, play checkers, and   206

play with dolls. These dolls were often made of scraps of fabric and buttons.   220

It is fun to imagine what people in the future will think about our lives   235

today.   236

MONITOR PROGRESS   • Check Fluency

Paul Revere **317k**

The Other Side of Edison

Thomas Edison is known as the greatest American inventor of all time. He received 1,093 patents. He developed many fabulous things, like movies and the electric light bulb. But that's only part of the story.

Edison set up a sort of factory. He built a group of labs, shops, and other buildings. He hired other inventors to work there. At one point, Edison had 10,000 people working for him. (Of course, not all of them were inventors.) He hardly ever worked on a project alone. But he always took sole credit for everything. If it came out of his factory, he put his name on it. He put his name on many things he had not worked on at all. All the patents were in his name. That's why he had so many.

There is one saying Edison is famous for. "Genius is one percent inspiration and ninety-nine percent perspiration." In other words, hard work is much more important than a good idea is. Look at his hard work on the electric light bulb. At the time, light bulbs cost a lot. They burned out quickly. Edison wanted to make a better bulb. He searched for something new from which to make the filament. He spent a year and a half testing thousands and thousands of materials until he found the right one.

Today, scientists inspecting the list of materials he tested are amused. There are many items that clearly wouldn't work. Edison went to school for only a short time. If he'd known a bit about chemistry or physics, he could have eliminated a lot of those materials without testing them. He wouldn't have had to "perspire" so much.

MONITOR PROGRESS • Author's Purpose

Bette Nesmith Graham

Bette Nesmith Graham dreamed of being an artist. But she was a single   13

mother. She had a young son to feed. So she took a job as a secretary.   29

This was the 1950s. There were no computers. Letters and documents   40

were written on typewriters. What was that like? Imagine you are sitting at   53

your keyboard. When you hit the keys, the words are printed on paper. There   67

is no computer in-between. What if you made a mistake? You had to   80

start over.   82

Bette knew there was a better way. Artists painted over their mistakes.   94

Maybe she could paint over typing mistakes. She mixed up a batch of paint   108

the same color as the paper at work. When she made a typing mistake, she   123

painted over it. The other secretaries wanted some too. Bette brought the   135

paint to work in small bottles.   141

In 1956, Bette started the Mistake Out Company. She mixed batches up   153

in her kitchen blender. Her son and his friends filled the bottles. And things   167

kept growing from there.   171

In 1968, Bette moved her company into a large factory. She sold one   184

million bottles of the paint that year alone.   192

In 1975, she moved to a larger plant. The following year, the company   205

made a profit of one and a half million dollars.   215

Bette retired. She sold her company for more than forty-seven million   226

dollars.   227

MONITOR PROGRESS   • Check Fluency

Perpetual Motion **353k**

Name _____

A Walk Through History

    A good way to learn about history is to visit the places where important events happened. The Freedom Trail in Boston gives visitors a chance to find out more about how the American Revolution began. This walking path is about two and a half miles long and is made up of red bricks. A guide leads the way. The guide takes visitors to sixteen different sites that are important to the history and fate of our country.

    The first stop is the Boston Common. This is one of the oldest public parks in the country. Before the war began, British soldiers camped in the park.

    Another important place a visitor will find is Faneuil Hall. This was a meeting room where many speeches were given leading up to the war.

    The next stop is the Paul Revere House. This is the oldest building in the downtown area. It was the home of Paul Revere. It was from this house that Paul Revere left for his famous midnight ride.

    As visitors follow the red brick path, they will soon come to the Old North Church. From the steeple of this church, Robert Newman held up two lanterns. This let Paul Revere know that the British were coming by sea so he could ride and warn people.

    Finally, visitors will see the Bunker Hill Monument. It marks the place of the first major battle of the war. From this amazing place, visitors can look out over the city of Boston.

MONITOR PROGRESS

• Sequence

Perpetual Motion **353m**

See How They Survive

A painting by a great artist can sell for millions of dollars. If you own one   16
of these original paintings, it could be worth a lot of money. Some people   30
who don't own an original painting want to make a lot of money anyway. So   45
they make fake paintings. A fake painting is called a forgery.   56

There are two aspects to a forgery. The first is artistic. You want people   70
to believe your painting was painted by a great artist. So you have to paint   85
very well. What's more, you have to paint in the style of that artist. You can   101
practice by copying real paintings. But eventually, you are going to have to   114
make up one of your own. (After all, you cannot paint a copy of, say, the   130
Mona Lisa and expect anyone to believe it's real. Everyone knows the real   143
Mona Lisa is in the Louvre.)   149

The second aspect of forgery is technical. Let's say you want to paint   162
a fake Rembrandt. Rembrandt lived 400 years ago. So you have to find a   176
canvas that is 400 years old. Then you have to make your paints the same   191
way people made paint 400 years ago. You might even have to find a   205
400-year-old brush.   207

After you paint the fake, you have to age it. Over hundreds of years,   221
paint dries up, shrinks, and cracks. Dirt and dust settles in the cracks. But you   236
don't want to wait hundreds of years. You have to find a way to make real-   252
looking cracks in the paint. You have to get real-looking dust and dirt into the   266
cracks.   267

Art forgery is a lot of work.   274

MONITOR PROGRESS   • Check Fluency

Leonardo's Horse **387k**

Do What You Want to Do

John Constable was one of the greatest English painters of all time. Sadly, he never achieved great success while he was alive.

John was born in 1776. His father made a lot of money in the wheat business. The plan was for John to take over the family business. But John wanted to paint.

In 1799 John began to study art. He took classes at the Royal Academy School. The school is run by The Royal Academy of Arts. The academy is like a club. Only the greatest English artists are members and you have to be invited to join.

Also at the school was a young man named J.M.W. Turner. He was only a year older than John. But the two never became friends. In fact, Turner became John's great rival.

Like most painters of the time, Turner painted mythological and biblical scenes. John painted fields and trees. Artists and critics loved Turner's work, but they ignored John's. In 1802 Turner was elected to the Royal Academy, but John wasn't asked to join until 1829. Turner achieved great success during his life, and yet John only sold twenty paintings in England while he was alive.

John could have painted things that other people liked. In fact, he sometimes painted portraits just to make some money. But he loved painting landscapes. At the time, other artists painted strange, imaginary landscapes. John painted real, actual landscapes. John thought that what he was painting was important. And history has proven him right.

MONITOR PROGRESS

• Main Idea and Supporting Details

Leonardo's Horse **387m**

Name _____

Dinos Alive!

Have you ever seen a dinosaur? In the movies, maybe. Have you ever   13

stood next to one? A full-size one that towered over you? One that moved   27

and roared? Some lucky people have.   33

A company in Texas makes dinosaurs. In four years it has made 80 of   47

them. And it is building more all the time. As soon as one is built, it is sent   65

out. Zoos and museums set them up to amaze visitors.   75

The animals start out as metal frames. Then "muscles" are added, and   87

finally, rubber "skin" is put in place. Motors make the animal move. Even the   101

eyes blink! Recorded grunts and roars bring everything to life. What's more,   113

each animal has its own voice. After all, why would an Apatosaurus sound   126

like a T-rex?   129

The dinosaurs offer a special opportunity. It's one thing to read that an   142

animal was three stories tall. But you do not really understand until you stand   156

next to one. Then you really know how big it is.   167

The dinosaurs are often set up in a group. A zoo, for example, might   181

rent eight or ten or twelve of them. Then it will set aside a forested space or   198

an open space that can be filled with replicas of ancient trees to put them in.   214

Once the dinosaurs are set up, the fun begins.   223

You really can believe that you are walking through a prehistoric forest.   235

Sure, you can tell the dinosaurs aren't real. They move, but they don't walk   249

around. If you look closely at the skin, you can tell it's rubber. But why would   265

you want to spoil the fun?   271

MONITOR PROGRESS   • Check Fluency

Changing the Way People Think

For more than a hundred years, people thought dinosaurs were just big and slow. Picture a T-rex with its head held high. Its tail drags on the ground. Its feet slam on the ground one after the other. Thump...Thump...Thump.

In the 1960s and 1970s, ideas began to change. It started in 1964 when a new kind of dinosaur was found. It was small, but in proportion with the others. And it had a huge claw on its foot. Not on its hand, but on its foot. How did it use a claw like that? It must have stood on one foot and kicked with the other. And to do that, it must have been fast.

A team of people discovered this dinosaur. One of the people was named John Ostrom. He was a teacher at Yale University. Another person was his student, Robert Bakker.

The two men had an idea. It seemed hard to believe. But it made sense. It fit the facts. What if all dinosaurs were fast?

Look at a bird when it walks. Its back is parallel to the ground. Maybe T-rex did not stand up straight. Maybe its tail did not drag on the ground. Maybe it ran with its back parallel to the ground. Then it could run fast.

Ostrom and Bakker were great scientists. The new picture of dinosaurs is much more accurate. It's also much more exciting.

MONITOR PROGRESS

• Fact and Opinion

Name _____

Scat!

It is not easy to say what jazz is. The word covers many different kinds of   16

music. One often-used definition is this: jazz music is played off the beat and   30

involves improvisation. That is a big word. It means "making things up as you   44

go along." But it is not as easy to do as it sounds.   57

Like most music, jazz starts with a tune. Imagine a group of jazz   70

musicians. They are playing a song. It is a song you know. But then the horn   86

player starts playing something new. The others keep playing the song. But   98

the horn player changes the rhythm. She plays something you have never   110

heard before. She is making it up as she plays. But she stays in the same key   127

as the other musicians. And though what she plays is not the tune of the song,   143

it is related to the tune. If you heard only the solo, you might be able to tell   161

what song she is improvising on.   167

But what about the singer? It is not easy for a singer to improvise. He has   183

to convey the meanings and feelings of the words.   192

This is where scat singing comes in. When he scats, a jazz singer sings   206

nonsense syllables. He uses his voice just like an instrument. He improvises.   218

Scat singing gives singers the same creative freedom the other musicians   229

have.   230

MONITOR PROGRESS   • Check Fluency

Name _____

America's First Lady of Song

There have been many great female American singers: Mahalia, Billie, Aretha. But surely the greatest of all was Ella Fitzgerald.

Ella's childhood was happy. But it was not easy. Her parents each worked two jobs. She went to school and studied hard. Then things got worse. When Ella was fifteen, her mother died in a car crash. A little later, her stepfather died too. Ella went to live with her aunt. She got into much trouble. She was sent to reform school, but eventually ran away.

One night she walked into the Apollo Theater. It was the best-known theater in Harlem. Every week it had Amateur Night. The Amateur Night crowds were rough. Ella signed up to dance. But the act before her was a dance team. She thought they were very good, too good to follow. So she sang a song instead. The crowd cheered. Now the music world knew about Ella Fitzgerald. Soon the rest of the world would too.

Ella made her first record in 1936. Two years later, she released a song called "A-Tisket, A-Tasket." It became a huge hit. She toured all over the world. She sang with great musicians. She appeared on TV. She was "The First Lady of Song."

The end of Ella's life was as rough as the beginning. By the 1980s, her voice was getting worn out. She suffered from diabetes, which made her blind. Later, she lost both legs to the disease.

Ella died peacefully in 1996. But for millions of music fans, her voice lives on.

MONITOR PROGRESS • Main Idea and Details

Name _____

The First Special Effects

The history of special effects is as old as the history of film. At first,   15

movies were made in just two places. Thomas Edison made movies in New   28

Jersey. The brothers Lumiere made movies in Paris.   36

The first movie theater opened in New York City, in 1894. The movies   49

were very short. They showed everyday life. A year later, things changed. A   62

man named Georges Melies made special effects films.   70

Other filmmakers were inventors. Melies was a magician. He thought like   81

one. He made movies like one.   87

The first effects were very simple. Imagine this: Cover the left half of the   101

lens. Film a person talking. Roll the film back to the beginning. Now cover the   116

right half of the lens. Film the same person listening. Play the film. The person   131

is listening to himself talk!   136

These effects are very simple. But people had never seen movies before.   148

To them, it all looked real. One of the Lumieres' first films showed a train   163

pulling into a station. When they showed the film, people screamed. The   175

people thought they were going to be hit by the train.   186

You can watch Melies' films online. How real do they look to you?   199

MONITOR PROGRESS

• Check Fluency

Name _____

Paint a (Motion) Picture

Imagine you are making a movie. It takes place in the Middle Ages. There is a scene of two knights walking toward a castle. How can you shoot it?

You could go somewhere where there is a castle. Take your actors and the film crew with you. But that costs a lot of money. Is there another way?

You could build a miniature landscape with small mountains, small trees, and a small castle. Or you could use special effects and put your real actors into the miniature landscape. But it would be expensive to build. Is there another way?

There is. All you need is paint, a sheet of glass, and a really good artist.

The artist paints the landscape on the glass: mountains, trees, and the castle. But she leaves part of the glass clear. Then you build a set that matches the painting. When you shoot the film, you set the painting up in front of the camera. All the camera sees is the painting. But through the clear part, it sees the set. The actors look as if they are in the painting!

MONITOR
PROGRESS   • Graphic Sources

Special Effects **473m**

Four Seasons

When Leo moved from the mountains of Georgia to sunny California, he   12
knew that he would miss the four seasons. But, he loved their home that was   27
the color of a mango.   32

The kitchen was painted seafoam green. The living room was painted   43
pumpkin orange. His mother's room was ripe-banana yellow. Leo's room was   54
white. And he didn't love his room with its four, boring, white walls.   67

"So, paint it," his mother said.   73

Leo did. On one wall, he painted a forest with pastel flowers just opening   87
up. He painted a pond with a mother duck and five babies.   99

On another wall, Leo painted a forest, but the trees were full of rich,   113
green leaves. On the pond bank, he painted himself holding a fishing pole.   126

On the third wall, Leo painted the same forest but this time the leaves   140
were orange, red, and yellow. Large, brown cattails grew around the pond.   152
Leo painted a flock of birds flying south.   160

On the fourth wall, Leo painted the same forest, but the trees were bare.   174
The pond was frozen, and Leo painted himself skating across the surface.   186

The boring, white walls were gone. And Leo could see the four seasons   199
anytime he wanted.   202

MONITOR PROGRESS

• Check Fluency

Weslandia **45k**

Name _____

The Sea Queen

Maria had only one week left before school started again and, so far, not one exciting thing had happened. Maria had been sure that something great, maybe something even magnificent, would happen to her. Each week she waited and watched with envy as exciting people got to do exciting things on her favorite reality television show.

"I bet if they made a reality show about me it would be called 'The Boring Life of Maria,'" she told her mom one evening.

"I think that might change," her mother said. "You get to spend this last week with Grandma Sandy in her beach house."

On Monday, Grandma Sandy told Maria to go exploring. Maria was walking across the warm sand thinking about her boring life when she spotted a large patch of sea grass. The sea grass seemed to be calling to her and beckoning her to come closer.

To Maria's surprise, the sea grass covered a hidden door. The handle was a seashell. She opened the door and found herself inside a cave painted blue and green. In the middle of the cave was a large chair made of woven sea grasses and decorated with shells.

Maria knew that she had to sit in the chair. As she sat down an amazing thing happened. Hundreds of sea creatures came forth. "Queen!" they called out to her.

Maria visited the sea cave every day. She learned the names of all the creatures who called her queen. So much for being bored, she thought. On her last day, the creatures presented her with the official notice that Maria would be their queen forever.

MONITOR PROGRESS

• Draw Conclusions

The President's Secret

In the 1932 election, when Franklin Roosevelt was chosen president of   11
the United States, he had a secret. He was disabled and couldn't walk on his   26
own. He spent most of his time in a wheelchair.   36

Roosevelt's disability was caused by a horrible disease called polio. He   47
came down with it when he was 39 years old. Polio killed many people, and   62
left many more disabled.   66

Roosevelt was a rich man who fought to find a way to walk unaided   80
again. He worked hard for other people's recovery too. Although he failed,   92
his battle with the disease made him a tougher, more determined person.   104

But why didn't Americans know that Roosevelt needed a wheelchair?   114
Roosevelt didn't want them to know. He and his advisers were afraid that   127
people would think he wasn't strong enough to be president.   137

Roosevelt had what was called a "gentlemen's agreement" with reporters   147
who worked for America's newspapers and radio networks. Reporters agreed   157
not to write or talk about Roosevelt's disability. Newspapers agreed not to   169
publish photographs that showed Roosevelt in a wheelchair. As a result,   180
during Roosevelt's years as president, no such story or photograph was   191
published. Even today, such photos are hard to find.   200

Many historians believe that Roosevelt was one of the greatest presidents.   211
He led the United States through tough times, including World War II. But the   225
big question still remains. In 1932, would Americans have voted for Roosevelt   237
if they had known that he used a wheelchair?   246

MONITOR PROGRESS   • Check Fluency

Lunch Lady **75k**

Mack's Solution

Mack yanked off his weighty winter coat and galoshes. He and two pals had been sledding like they always do on Saturdays in winter, but today they quit because the snow was melting rapidly into slush.

"Did you put the sleds away?" Mom inquired.

Mack frowned because he hadn't. He and his pals had used his family's three classic, old-fashioned sleds made out of wood with metal runners. They were so much better than plastic sleds and perfect for speeding down slick hills. But they were awkward to put away, so Mack left the sleds propped on the front porch.

"But it's my birthday," whined Mack. "That's why I shouldn't have to put sleds away," he said. "Today's special for me!"

"And that's why we're having a party," said Mom. "And that's why everything has to be just right. And . . . "

Before Mom could finish, Mack said, "That's why I should put away the sleds."

Mom smiled as Mack put back on his coat. Mack opened the front door and said, "Oh, no! The snow melted quickly. There's a river of water across our yard. How will people walk into our house for the party?"

Mom looked outside. "It is bad out front," she said.

Then Mack saw the sleds. "We'll use the sleds to make a wooden path over the water. The runners are high enough so people's feet won't get wet."

Mom thought about it and said. "That sounds a bit dangerous. Let's tell our guests to enter through the garage. The driveway isn't so wet."

Then she smiled at Mack and said, "But your suggestion was a clever one."

Mack grinned, and Mom added, "For finding another reason why *not* to put away the sleds."

Mack and Mom laughed. And Mack put the sleds away.

MONITOR PROGRESS   • Generalize

Lunch Lady **75m**

See How They Survive!

Survival for some animals means acting or looking like something else.	11
Brown-headed cowbirds, for instance, are the only birds in North America	22
that always lay their eggs in other birds' nests. More than 200 other species	36
are known to raise cowbirds' eggs.	42
The cowbird leaves a single egg in each nest. This egg usually hatches	55
before the other bird's eggs, giving the cowbird chick a good chance of	68
getting the most food. Some birds throw out the cowbird egg, but more raise	82
the chick along with their own.	88
In many insects, bright colors serve to scare away birds and other	100
animals. Large, black and orange Monarch butterflies, which migrate every	110
year between Mexico and breeding grounds in the north of North America,	122
feed on milkweed. These plants contain a poison. Any bird that fails to	135
heed the Monarch's bright orange warning color may learn too late that the	148
Monarch is not a treat but instead a dangerous meal.	158
The Viceroy butterfly looks so much like the Monarch that many people	170
can't tell them apart. Even though the Viceroy is not poisonous, its orange-	183
and-black warning colors protect it from most birds and other animals that	194
avoid the Monarch. This kind of defense, called *mimicry*, is common in the	207
insect world.	209
Survival in nature, then, is often more than meets the eye.	220

MONITOR PROGRESS

• Check Fluency

Exploding Ants **103k**

The Arctic Hare

The arctic hare lives in the frozen areas of North America, Newfoundland, and Greenland. The arctic hare's fur helps it survive both the cold winters.

The arctic hare's fur is its best defense against the freezing weather. In winter, the arctic hare grows two layers of fur. The short, thick bottom layer is called the underfur. On top of the underfur is another layer of long, silky fur. These two layers insulate the arctic hare.

The ever-changing color of the arctic hare's fur also protects the animal from predators. In the winter, it is bright white. The white fur blends perfectly with the snow and camouflages the arctic hare from its predators. In the cool summer, the arctic hare's color depends on where it lives. An arctic hare that lives where the summers are short has a sandy-brown or gray tone. An arctic hare that lives where the summers are longer has a brown and blue-gray tone. These colors help the arctic hare hide from its predators against the snow-free ground.

Although the arctic hare lives in a frigid and dangerous environment, its fur enables it to survive.

Climate in Eureka, Nunavut, Canada from 1971–2000				
	January	April	June	September
Daily Average Temperature (°C)	−37.1	−27.4	2.3	−7.7
Snowfall (cm)	3.2	4.3	3.5	11
Average Depth of Snow (cm)	15	18	5	3

MONITOR PROGRESS   • Graphic Sources

Name _____

Sad Cats Wink

Every member of the Wink family was happy about their new move   12

except one. Pop Wink was happy with his new bakery job. Mom Wink was   26

happy with her new coaching job. Jeff Wink was happy because his new   39

school had a swim team. Cats Wink was not happy.   49

He had not been the happiest of cats back in Ohio, but since the move   64

he looked absolutely miserable.   68

"He needs a job," Pop said. So Pop took him to the bakery. But that   83

didn't work out. A happy couple came in to order a wedding cake and the 98

sad look on Cat's face made them leave without choosing even a cookie.   111

Mom Wink took him to the soccer game. But that didn't work out either.   125

The fans didn't feel like cheering with the unhappy Cats Wink looking at 138

them.   139

Finally, Jeff took Cats to a swim meet. Jeff was swimming against Fins   152

Marin. At the signal, they jumped in. Fins inched ahead! He was almost to 166

the end of the pool where he would have to touch and race back. Cats sat 182

at the pool's edge, his face sadder than usual. When Fins touched the edge 196

of the pool, he saw the sorrowful face of Cats Wink. Fins paused and lost his 212

edge. Jeff touched, turned, and swam back faster than ever.   222

From then on, Cats attended every swim meet. And even though Cats   234

didn't look happy, he was.   239

MONITOR PROGRESS   • Check Fluency

Stormi Giovanni **135k**

Locker Trouble

Kiki Link stood at her new locker in her new school trying to remember her new combination. She tried ten to the right, fourteen to the left, and twenty to the right. She knew there was a twenty in there somewhere, but it was no use. Her locker would not open.

Murphy Jones walked up to Kiki. "Trouble?" she asked.

"I can't open it!" Kiki said, glancing at the clock in the hallway. "I've tried every combination I can think of."

"Is there a reason you want to open the locker?" Murphy asked.

Kiki looked at Murphy, wondering if she was crazy.

"Of course I have a good reason! My spelling book is in there! I need to get to class like right now!"

Murphy nodded her head. "Okay, I'm beginning to get the picture," she said. "You need to open the locker so that you can get your spelling book out. Am I right?"

Kiki wanted to scream!

"Let me see what I can do," Murphy said. She began to turn the dial.

"But how do you know my combination?" Kiki asked when the locker sprang open.

"I don't," Murphy said. "I know the combination to *my* locker."

"What?" Kiki asked.

Murphy pointed to the next locker over. "Try your combination there."

Kiki opened her locker, took out her spelling book, and rushed to class.

MONITOR PROGRESS

• Generalize

Stormi Giovanni **135m**

Jamal Makes Lemonade

Jamal walked into the kitchen and tripped over a box.   10

"Mom?" Jamal called.   13

"Over here! We finally got the rest of the boxes today," she said.   26

"No kidding," Jamal said. "I'm glad because I promised that I would   38
bring something for the school party tomorrow."   45

"What? You think I'm going to cook?" his mother said.   55

"It's just lemonade. I'll make it. I got the lemons already," Jamal told her. 69

Jamal had made lemonade before. He squeezed the lemons into a big   81
jug. He found the box that held tins of sugar, flour, salt, and coffee.   95

"One large scoop!" he said as he stirred the lemonade.   105

At the party the next day, Jamal began pouring the lemonade into cups.   118
Right away, he knew something was wrong. First came the frowns and then   131
sputters as the kids sipped the lemonade.   138

Jamal took a sip. It was salty. It was salted lemon water!   150

Jamal felt terrible. "I guess I got mixed up," he said.   161

Tomas, a boy who sat near Jamal, picked up his cup again. "It's not bad.   176
Really." Tomas took a sip and tried not to make a face. One by one, each   192
student sipped the lemonade.   196

Jamal knew that he was going to like the new school.   207

MONITOR PROGRESS   • Check Fluency

Name _____

Jenna Zorn, International Spy

As soon as the credits rolled on the spy movie, I knew what I wanted to be. I would be Jenna Zorn, International Spy. It had a nice ring to it. I was lucky to have a last name that began with a Z. I always knew on the first day of school to walk over to the last aisle and then back to the last seat. There's no hesitation about where to sit when your last name is Zorn.

Of course, when I became a spy, I would use lots of different names. I'd need lots of different costumes too. As I walked out of the theater, I remembered a used clothing store down the street.

I hit the jackpot. I found a black coat just my size once I pulled in the belt all the way to the first hole. It had to be black, of course, so that I could blend in anywhere. I also came across a pair of dark gray boots with rubber soles to help me make fast getaways. I found a black hat with a brim I could pull over one eye. The hat would help me look mysterious. Finally, the best score of all was a wig. It was kind of white blonde and it flipped up. I really looked pretty good in it.

I paid for my used spy outfit and then put it on before leaving the store. I pulled the hat down over one eye and then felt around for the door. It didn't take long to get used to walking around with one eye covered.

It was amazing! People would glance at me and then look quickly away. It was almost as if they didn't see me at all! I would be a great spy.

MONITOR PROGRESS   • Draw Conclusions

Name _____

My Sister is a Night Owl

I keep asking my mom if I can have my own room. That's because I'm   15
tired of sharing a room with my little sister.   24

Maria is my six-year-old sister and she's a night owl. If Maria were an   38
animal, you'd probably say that she was nocturnal. She's like a bat at night. 52
Every night, just as I close my eyes, Maria wants to talk. You might think that 68
she eats candy before bed, but no. My mom doesn't let us have sugar before 83
bed.   84

In our dark bedroom, we sound like this: 92

Maria: "Do you want to know who my best friend is?"   103

Me: "No."   105

Maria: "Can I tell you what Ethan did at recess?"   115

Me: "No."   117

Even as a baby, Maria had a hard time falling asleep. My mom would   131
rock her. My mom would sing to her. But Maria just babbled.   143

My mom was worried for a while. She wanted to know if Maria was   157
tired at school. But her teacher said, "No, she's a firecracker."   168

I've learned to fall asleep as Maria talks and talks. I asked my mom   182
again about having my own room. But my mom says that we don't have a   197
spare bedroom. I told her that I can sleep in the living room. But then again, 213
I'm so used to hearing Maria at night that the silence might be too much for 229
me!   230

MONITOR PROGRESS   • Check Fluency

The Skunk Ladder **197k**

Name _____

Camping for My First Time

Last summer my mom had this crazy idea that she would take me camping. If there's one thing you should know about my mom, it's this: she is not an outdoors person. My mom wears heels, not hiking boots. She doesn't like bugs. She doesn't know how to build a fire.

"Your Aunt Barb and her kids are coming too" my mom said.

Now she was making sense. Aunt Barb could tie knots and catch bait for fishing.

This was going to be a feat, but I could have a positive attitude. I didn't see my cousins that often because they lived across the country. Whenever we got together, we had lots of fun. Maybe we would roast marshmallows. Maybe we would look at the stars.

The plan was to go to the mountains for the weekend. When I asked my mom how big the cabin was, she said, "Cabin? We're sleeping in a tent."

"But we don't have a tent," I said.

That's when she opened the closet and a huge nylon thing with poles fell out. It spread across our living room floor. Mom laughed. I sighed.

My aunt arrived a day before we left. She made sure that Mom had a sleeping pad. We hadn't packed pillows, either. I did, however, remember my bird guide and wool hat.

I was going to grab my cordless video game. That's when my aunt shook her head.

"You're going to be so busy hiking and fishing, you won't need video games," she said. "Have you skinned a fish before?"

I made a face. But I was an outdoors person, right?

MONITOR PROGRESS • Character and Plot

Diving Into Shark Country

It must be a lot of fun to scuba dive. But scuba diving is not a game. If   18
you want to dive with sharks, for example, you must be trained. This means   32
that you must take classes. You must practice for hours.   42

Divers need to learn how to use special equipment. Divers use air tanks   55
and gear so they can stay in shark country for hours. They also must know the   71
rules about swimming with sharks.   76

All divers breathe through hoses that connect to tanks on their backs. The   89
tanks are full of oxygen. Divers have radios so they can talk to each other.   104
Of course, every diver also has a compass. A diver needs to know which   118
way to go.   121

Some people even take diving vacations just to see sharks. First, they   133
must prove that they know how to dive. After this, guides take the divers out   148
to sea in a boat.   153

Often there's a cage, and the divers can be suspended in the cage in the   168
water. This means they are floating in the sea. Sharks can swim all around   182
them, but the divers are safe inside the cage. Many divers bring cameras so   196
they can take photos.   200

If you saw a shark up close, what would you do? Would you smile at the   216
shark? Would you pull out your camera and take a picture? Or, would you   230
check to see that the cage door is closed good and tight?   242

MONITOR PROGRESS
• Check Fluency

Name _____

Why I Love Submarines

I have always loved submarines. When I was eight, I begged my mom to buy boat models for me to put together. Now, I check out books about how submarines work. I want to figure out how they can reach the sea floor and what they do once they are down there.

I am interested in every kind of "sub." Some of them are used during war, and others search for ships that went down. My uncle Jim mails stories to me about submarines. This week, I was surprised by the story he sent me. That's because it was about one of my favorite submarines in the world. Its name is *Newport News*. One of the reasons I like this one so much is because it started its first trip on March 15, 2001, which is also my birthday. It has been all around the world, but no one could have guessed what would happen to it.

A ship from another country was sailing right above where the *Newport News* was under the water. For some reason, this had a strange effect, and the *Newport News* was pulled to the surface of the ocean. That's when it hit the big ship. No one was hurt, which was a good thing.

When I get older, I want to make a submarine with the best technology ever.

But I'm not sure I want to live and work in a submarine. I already find it hard enough to live with two little sisters. It would be like living in a three-bedroom house underwater—with 120 roommates! That sounds like a very tight fit.

A Sailor's Vocabulary	
At Sea	On Land
deck	floor
bulkhead	wall
overhead	ceiling
aye, aye	I understand.

MONITOR PROGRESS   • Graphic Sources

Wreck of the Titanic **227m**

Name _____

How to Be an Astronaut

Have you ever thought about becoming an astronaut? It takes many years   12

of training and lots of hard work. But, if you love technology, science, and   26

adventure, it might be the perfect job for you.   35

First, you must love math and science. You need to do really well in those   50

subjects in school. When you get older, you will need to go to college. It is   66

also helpful to know a language other than English. In order to become an   80

astronaut, you need to be and stay in good shape. So, it is important that you   96

like to exercise. You also need to have good eyesight. Finally, you need to   110

become a pilot. You will have to have over 1,000 hours of experience flying   124

a plane.   126

Every two years, about 100 men and women are chosen for an astronaut   139

training program. If you are selected, you will take more classes in science,   152

technology, and space exploration. You will also learn how to live on a space   166

shuttle. And during your astronaut training program, you will learn how to   178

scuba dive too!   181

One of the NASA leaders said she was really excited about teachers going   194

into space because "they will help inspire a new generation of explorers."   206

What do you think?   210

MONITOR PROGRESS

• Check Fluency

Name _____

Becoming Someone's Role Model

My teacher asked us to write about one of our role models. I started to think about it, but my head went blank. I know what those words mean, but no one was coming to mind.

So, my teacher asked me to think about who I am and what I love to do. She asked me what my life is like. Well, I'm the oldest of four sisters. I love to read. Math and science are my favorite subjects. When I am not playing soccer, I love to study.

That's when my teacher told me about a woman named Aprille Ericsson. Like me, she is the oldest of four daughters. She was born in New York City. When she started high school, she knew that she was very good at math and science. I went to the library and checked out a book about her. I think that she's a very special and smart woman.

Today, Aprille is an aerospace engineer at NASA. She is the first African American woman to receive the highest degree in engineering at NASA.

I like what Aprille said in a speech that she gave to third-graders. She told them to "Read, read, read, and learn, learn, learn."

She said that knowing about important women from the past has helped her feel brave. She thinks about these women as she reaches her goals. For instance, she admires the first African American woman to earn a license to fly a plane.

One day, I hope to be a scientist. I would like to create inventions to help others. Maybe one day, people will look up to me too.

MONITOR
PROGRESS

• Author's Purpose

Name _____

Off to a Magic Land

My best friends and I have big plans. It all started Sunday when we were   15

talking. We wondered, "What would it be like to travel to another world?"   28

Have you ever wondered that too?   34

One of our favorite things to do is imagine the perfect world. We want to   49

go to a magic land where ten-year-olds rule. What, you haven't heard of this   63

place? But haven't you imagined it?   69

This is a land where fifth-graders make all the laws. We will decide what   83

time to go to bed. We will decide what time to eat dinner. When we want   99

dinner, we will imagine our meal. Magically, the food will appear.   110

We can turn serpents into pasta for dinner. We can change the music   123

from opera to pop. We can even grow wings and fly.   134

So, my friend and I are packing our bags. We will take extra warm   148

clothes for fear that we might run into icebergs. We will take flashlights. We   162

will bring my dog too. In this special land, dogs can talk. I can't wait to hear   179

what my dog will say to me.   186

But there is just one little problem: how will we get there? Maybe if we   201

close our eyes and do some imagining, we can get there quickly. I hope we   216

can get there quickly enough.   221

MONITOR PROGRESS

• Check Fluency

Name _____

Life-Saving Canaries

Deep underground, miners dig for coal. Working in a mine has always been extremely dangerous. It probably always will be. One of the biggest risks for miners is carbon monoxide. This gas can form in mines after an explosion or even a small fire. The gas has no taste, color, or smell. That makes it hard to tell if the gas is the air. Yet miners absolutely need to know. Carbon-monoxide fumes can be fatal to humans.

In ancient days of mining, there wasn't a good way to detect carbon monoxide. But somewhere in the long history of the mining industry, miners discovered one. They realized that small animals could be used to detect carbon monoxide. The way that the animals detected it, however, wasn't good for the little critters. It killed them.

At first, the animals used were mice. Their small bodies suffered much more quickly from carbon monoxide than bigger human bodies did. That meant carbon monoxide in the air would kill mice long before it hurt miners.

How did miners figure out that mice could help detect carbon monoxide? Mice have always lived everywhere, including in mines. Miners probably noticed that after they saw dead mice, miners often would die from carbon monoxide poisoning. Miners soon understood that dead mice in a mine meant it was time to get out!

After an explosion or a fire in a mine, miners who had to go back in began carrying mice in little cages. They watched the mice carefully. The miners left when they saw a mouse die.

Over time, miners started using canaries instead of mice. These yellow birds are the same size as mice and react to carbon monoxide the same way.

Miners preferred canaries because they died in a more noticeable fashion. Normally, canaries sat on perches in their cages. But when carbon monoxide poisoned them, they would fell off the perches dramatically. Miners then knew it was time to go!

Today, canaries aren't used for carbon-monoxide testing. Instead, miners use modern detecting gauges. That's good news for miners...and canaries.

MONITOR PROGRESS • Cause and Effect

Women Were Pioneers Too

Women had a very important role during the Gold Rush. But until   12
recently, there was little written about women's roles during the mid-1800s.   23
One woman decided that she was going to change this. Her name is JoAnn   37
Levy and she's a writer.   42

JoAnn Levy wanted to learn about women during the Gold Rush because   54
she was curious. But when she looked for books about this topic, she couldn't   68
find any. That's why she decided to write a book herself.   79

She read letters and diaries. She studied newspapers and court records.   90
In her books, she writes about what California looked like in the year 1850.   104
For instance, for every woman in the state that year, there were twelve men.   118

Still, many women came to California to start new lives. They, too,   130
wanted to open businesses—and find gold.   137

There was one woman who looked for gold in the creek alongside her   150
husband. She wore boots and a flannel shirt just like him. Day after day, she   165
worked quietly, panning gold. Another woman started a business to make   176
pies, and she sold them to the miners for their lunches.   187

During the Gold Rush, women were certainly pioneers too.   196

MONITOR PROGRESS   • Check Fluency

Ghost Towns **311k**

Name _____

Old Rough and Ready

This year, my fifth-grade class took a really cool field trip. We rode a bus to explore the old mining camps along Highway 49 in northern California. People came there from all over the world in the mid-1800s to discover gold. Most people hoped to strike it rich.

We had studied about the mining camps that sprouted up along the river. Most of these camps eventually turned into ghost towns. No one lives here now, as they did over 150 years ago. But we could still see where the restaurants, shops, and hotels once stood.

The miners often gave fun names to their towns. One town in the north was called "Rough and Ready." It was named after a captain during the Mexican War whose nickname was "Old Rough and Ready." The miners in Rough and Ready were lucky because they found a lot of gold in the river.

A town on the southern part of Highway 49 was named Mariposa. Mariposa is a Spanish word that means "butterfly." Our teacher told us that butterflies often flocked to this area. A priest who had lived in this camp wrote that during the day butterflies tried to find a place to hide from the strong sun. A butterfly even flew into one of the men's ears to hide.

Another town on the southern part of the highway was called Bear Valley. I imagine that miners saw a lot of bears wandering around there.

It was exciting to travel along Highway 49 and explore some of the vacant buildings. Even though no one lives in the mining camps now, I could still imagine what these towns were like many, many years ago.

MONITOR PROGRESS   • Generalize

Ghost Towns **311m**

Here Comes Pete

Jill sat on the front porch looking over her stack of baseball cards. She   14
loved to look at the stats of each player and try to memorize them. "Nothing   29
can ruin this great day," she thought.   36

Then her heart sank. Nothing could ruin her day, that is, except her   49
older brother, Pete. Her mind filled with dread as she saw him coming up the   64
walkway.   65

"What are you doing, Shrimp?" he asked as he bounded up the stairs   78
and swiped a baseball card from the top of her pile.   89

"Nothing," said Jill. "Just leave my stuff alone." Pete has always teased   101
Jill and called her names.   106

"What's this?" said Pete. "You collect baseball cards? Aren't you   116
supposed to play with dolls?" He grabbed a whole pile of cards and put them   131
in his pocket.   134

"They're mine!" yelled Jill. "That's it. I've had enough of this teasing.   146
Some brother you are. You always make fun of me and call me names. You   161
know we both like baseball. Why can't we just look at the cards together?"   175

Jill had never stood up to Pete before. Suddenly, he walked away.   187

About ten minutes later Pete quietly returned with a book of baseball   199
cards.   200

"You can have these," he said. Pete turned to walk away again.   212

"Oh, yeah," he added. "Sorry, I've been a mean brother. But, don't say I   226
never gave you anything."   230

MONITOR PROGRESS • Check Fluency

Project Paint Can

"We're ready," said Abby to her fellow students. "We can paint the wall Saturday."

The kids were part of an after-school program called Kids for the Community. This year the group had decided to paint over the graffiti on the wall around the park. They were confident that it would improve the look of the community.

"We will all have to bring some supplies," Abby said. "I have put them in groups of things to buy and things to bring from home."

"We all need to bring our own lunches, drinks, and snacks from home. We should also bring sunscreen because we'll be outside all day. Then there are things we need to buy. We need to call the hardware store to order paint and paint rollers for Saturday."

"I can do that," said Tanya. She looked up the phone number and quickly dialed.

"We need 100 gallons of white paint and 25 paint rollers," said Tanya over the phone.

"What are young kids going to do with so much paint?" asked Mr. Bleeker in disbelief. She explained the project to him and he agreed to set aside the supplies.

But Saturday did not go as planned. When the students arrived at the overpass they saw Mr. Bleeker standing in front of a solid wall of paint cans and a giant pile of rollers.

"What's going on, Mr. Bleeker?" asked Tanya.

"These supplies are a donation from Bleeker's Hardware. You kids should not have to pay for other people's poor behavior. We can paint over the graffiti together."

"Thanks!" said Tanya and Abby together. "Let's grab some rollers!"

MONITOR PROGRESS
• Draw Conclusions

Austin's Amazing Bats **343m**

Name _____

America's Eagle

Look at any American coin or dollar bill. Chances are you will see a   14

picture of the bald eagle. It has been on the Great Seal of the United States   30

since 1782. The bald eagle makes many people think of freedom.   41

But since the time it became an American symbol, the bald eagle started   54

to slowly disappear from the United States. By the late 1800s, towns and   67

cities had been built all the way across the country. This caused many of these 82

birds to lose their homes. In the 1900s, dangerous chemicals were used to kill   96

insects on farms. But animals as well as insects were affected. The chemicals   109

got into rivers and streams. Many eagles died from eating the fish from   122

these rivers and streams. Hunting was another reason the eagle was slowing   134

disappearing. By the 1970s, the bald eagle was almost gone forever.   145

Something had to be done to save our national bird. Laws were passed   158

that banned the use of certain chemicals. This kept many animals and their   171

homes much safer. Hunting the bald eagle is now against the law. People   184

set up special programs. They moved the few eagles that were left closer   197

together. This made it easier for the eagles to lay their eggs, keep their young 212

safe, and grow in number.   217

Efforts to save the bald eagle have paid off. The bird is no longer   231

endangered. But more work still needs to be done. Hopefully, one day there   244

will be as many bald eagles in America as there were when the country was   259

founded.   260

MONITOR PROGRESS   • Check Fluency

Saint Matthew Island **369k**

Name _____

Thanks to Trees

Think for a minute about all the things in your everyday life that come from trees. They provide shade on a hot, sunny day and supply us with fruits, nuts, and berries to eat. But trees give us even more than that.

We can thank trees for all of the wooden chairs, tables, homes, baseball bats, and other wooden items we see around us. We can thank trees for all of the paper we use for reading and writing. We even have handy products such as napkins and paper towels because of trees. Trees are one of the most useful natural resources in our modern world.

Cutting down trees for products is a big business. In fact, Americans alone use more paper each year than a forest can provide. It takes ten to twenty years for a tree to grow big enough to be harvested and used to make paper. During that time, the tree provides food and a home to many animals. When it is cut down, the ecosystem changes and the animals must find someplace else to live.

Fortunately, trees are a renewable resource, but it does take time for them to grow and be usable. There's a simple solution that keeps us from running out of forests. Plant more trees! Most companies in the United States that clear areas of the forests plant more trees than they cut down each year. While some areas are growing, others are being harvested for use. The forest can work in cycles for generations to come.

So, plant more trees! Not only do they help us meet our needs, they're also beautiful to look at. And the animals will thank you for it, too.

MONITOR PROGRESS

• Main Idea and Supporting Details

Saint Matthew Island **369m**

Judy's Wish

Judy was the receptionist at Mr. Knox's Box Factory. "If I had a nickel for   15
every time that phone rang I'd retire a very rich woman," she always said.   29

One day, a fairy came to her, right there in the factory lobby. "You're   43
on," said the fairy. "You get a nickel every time that phone rings."   56

"Mr. Knox's Boxes. How may I direct your call?" Judy said happily to the   70
next caller. The morning was as busy as ever. Her switchboard lit up. "Mr.   84
Knox's Boxes. Please hold," she told the next caller. She put them on hold and   99
pushed the next button.   103

By the time lunchtime rolled around, Judy was exhausted. She had even   115
forgotten about her wish until she saw the mound of nickels sitting on her desk.   130

"Maybe I can buy my lunch with that," she thought. But it took her the   145
entire lunch hour to tally up the coins. Lunchtime was over before she even left   160
her desk.   162

"Mr. Knox's Boxes," she started again sadly. "Please hold." By the time   174
the factory closed that day, Judy's desk had collapsed under the weight of the   188
nickels.   189

The next day, nickels rained down on the factory lobby. "Oh, what have I   203
done?" Judy said in despair.   208

Just then, the fairy appeared again. "You don't look like a satisfied   220
customer," said the fairy. "How about a refund?"   228

And suddenly, the nickels stopped falling. "But clean up this mess!" said   240
the fairy.   242

MONITOR PROGRESS   • Check Fluency

The Grass is Always Greener

George had a tiny patch of grass for a backyard. There were no trees to give the yard shade, so there were plenty of brown patches of grass that got burned from too much sun. Whenever George went in his yard, he always found himself gazing over the fence into his next-door neighbor's pristine yard.

"Guzman has the best yard I've ever seen," he told his wife at dinner one night. "It's about three times bigger than ours, and it has beautiful trees for shade and a great little vegetable garden. He keeps it in such good condition, too. It's much greener than ours."

"Well, why don't you tell him so yourself?" said his wife.

The next day, George told Guzman how much he admired his yard. "I would give anything to have a yard like that," said George.

"Be careful what you wish for," replied Guzman. "That yard drives me insane."

"What?" said George in surprise. He did not think that there could be unforeseen problems with something so beautiful. "Why wouldn't you want a yard like that?"

"Mowing is a definite chore because it's so big. It's unbearable in the middle of summer. Then fall rolls around and I'm out there raking leaves from those trees every weekend. And that vegetable garden is infested with pests. We'll be lucky if we get one tomato out of all of our efforts this year. And that lawn is so green because I spend a fortune on fertilizers. The outcome might be nice to look at, but I don't think it's worth my time."

"Wow!" said George. "Your yard actually doesn't look so good to me anymore."

MONITOR PROGRESS   • Compare and Contrast

Car Safety

What is the very first thing we do when we get into a car? We buckle up   17

for safety. We are lucky to live in an age when cars come with seat belts, air   34

bags, and other safety features. Still, each year about 40,000 people in the   47

United States die in car accidents.   53

Automobile safety has always been a concern. The first car accident   64

dates back to 1771. Just after the invention of a simple, steam-powered car,   77

the inventor crashed it against a wall.   84

The first seat belt was invented in 1849. It was like a harness that   98

attached the passenger to the back seat of the car.   108

In 1921, Henry Ford's Model T came with a child safety seat. But the   122

child seat did not look at all like the ones we have today. It was more like a   137

sack for putting the child in, with a drawstring that attached to the back seat   155

of the car.   158

Throughout the twentieth century, car safety became more and more of   169

a concern for carmakers. Car companies first started performing crash tests   180

in 1934. By 1989, all cars were required to have air bags as an additional   195

safety system. When the car is in an accident, the air bags quickly fill with air   211

and keep the passengers in place in the car.   220

It is hard to tell exactly how many lives seat belts and air bags save each   236

year. But they have definitely saved thousands of lives since they were first   249

invented.   250

MONITOR PROGRESS

• Check Fluency

The Titanic

In 1912, the rich and famous wished they could book a trip aboard the *R.M.S. Titanic.* It was the largest ocean liner ever built. People called the ship "practically unsinkable." However, the first voyage of the *Titanic* was a calamity. It hit an iceberg and sank before reaching its destination. About 1,500 people lost their lives.

The *Titanic* was a luxury cruise ship. There was a swimming pool on board as well as a gymnasium, bathhouses, libraries, and a squash court. The *Titanic's* passengers were some of the richest and most powerful people in world.

So what happened to this "unsinkable" ship? At 11:40 at night, the *Titanic* hit an iceberg. The collision damaged the hull, or outside, of the ship. Water entered the bottom of the ship. By 2:20 in the morning, the ship was gone.

For many years, people believed that the ship just filled with water and sank. However, in 1985, scientists had a new idea. They used new technology to reach the wreck at the bottom of the sea. They found that the ship broke into two pieces as it was sinking. One end rose up out of the water so high that its weight caused the ship to split in two.

Many believed this split happened first at the upper deck. In 2005, a newer theory suggested that the crack first happened at the bottom hull where the ship was damaged.

We are still learning from the disaster of the *Titanic.* Each new discovery is important. Each new idea brings us closer to knowing what really happened that night. When we know about the past, we can do better planning for safer ocean travel in the future.

MONITOR PROGRESS

• Fact and Opinion

The Hindenburg **433m**

Name _____

Louis Armstrong

When we think of our favorite jazz artists, a list of many wonderful   13
people comes to mind. Many of us would put Louis Armstrong on our list. This   28
cornet and trumpet player was born in New Orleans, Louisiana, in 1901. He   41
was well known for his deep and raspy singing voice.   51

Armstrong learned to play the cornet as a child and followed around   63
horn players in the New Orleans French Quarter. Then he became part of a   77
jazz band that went up and down the Mississippi River on a steamboat.   90

He played with different bands until 1925 when he began to record   102
songs under his own name. People loved to hear him play. He became   115
known as "Satchelmouth" because of the way he puffed up his cheeks while   128
playing horns. He was later known as just "Satchmo."   137

He made music during hard times in United States history. These times   149
included the Great Depression and the Second World War. His music was   161
always filled with a spirit that helped people forget their troubles. He was one   175
of the first jazz artists to sing instead of just play an instrument. Singing along   190
to the songs helped to make jazz music more popular than ever.   202

Armstrong died at the age of 69 in Queens, New York, in 1971. The   216
home where he died has been turned into a museum. In 2001, the New   230
Orleans airport was renamed in his honor. It is now the Louis Armstrong   243
International Airport.   245

MONITOR
PROGRESS
• Check Fluency

Copyright © by Pearson Education, Inc., or its affiliates. All Rights Reserved.

Name _____

Waking Up in a Swamp

Something really weird happened when I woke up this morning. First of all, when I opened my eyes, I saw that I wasn't in my bedroom. Instead, my bed was in a cave lit by burning torches. Secondly, there was a serpent sleeping on the ground next to me.

Moreover, I wasn't dressed in my pajamas. Instead, I was dressed like a knight. I even wore a chain vest, and it was very heavy. When I tried to sit up in my bed, my chains rattled. Eventually, I did stand up, and I was glad that I was wearing boots because the ground was like a swamp.

When I touched my head, I couldn't believe that I was wearing a helmet. It was not a bike helmet, but the kind you wear when you fight huge, living things. The next thing I knew, the serpent opened its eyes. Its eyes were red and sparkly. I was sure that this creature would lash out at me. It had teeth like a dragon. Instead, it smiled at me.

"Good morning," I said.

Then the serpent made a soft sound, but I couldn't make out the words.

"Would you like to be friends?" I said. I really hoped it wasn't going to put a spell on me.

Instead, the serpent nodded its head. At that moment, I was thankful that we wouldn't have to fight. I would definitely need a good breakfast before going into battle. Maybe it could direct me to a path that might take me home.

That's when I remembered that I had an English test first thing in the morning. I hoped that I would still get to school on time.

MONITOR PROGRESS • Sequence

Assessment Charts and Student Progress Report

from

First Stop Fifth Grade

Fluency Progress Chart, Grade 5

Name _____

WCPM	1	2	3	4	5	6	7	8	9	10	11	12	13	14	15	16	17	18	19	20	21	22	23	24	25	26	27	28	29	30	31	32	33	34	35	36
175																																				
170																																				
165																																				
160																																				
155																																				
150																																				
145																																				
140																																				
135																																				
130																																				
125																																				
120																																				
115																																				
110																																				
105																																				
100																																				
95																																				
90																																				
85																																				
80																																				

Timed Reading/Week

Assessment Chart

Name _____ Date _____

		Day 3 Retelling Assessment		Day 5 Fluency Assessment		Day 5 Comprehension Assessment		Reteach	Teacher's Comments
		Benchmark Score	Actual Score	Benchmark WCPM	Actual Score	Benchmark Score	Actual Score		
WEEK 1	**Red Kayak** Character and Plot	3–4		105–110		3–4		✔	
WEEK 2	**Thunder Rose** Cause and Effect	3–4		105–110		3–4			
WEEK 3	**Island of the Blue Dolphins** Setting and Theme	3–4		105–110		3–4			
WEEK 4	**Satchel Paige** Fact and Opinion	3–4		105–110		3–4			
WEEK 5	**Ten Mile Day** Cause and Effect	3–4		105–110		3–4			
	Unit 1 Test Score								

Benchmark Score reflects grade-level target.

• **RECORD SCORES** Use this chart to record scores for the Day 3 Retelling, Day 5 Fluency, Day 5 Comprehension, and Unit Test.

• **REGROUPING** Compare the student's actual score to the benchmark score and group flexibly or provide extra support as needed.

• **RETEACH** If a student is unable to complete any part of the assessment process, use the weekly Reteach lessons in the *First Stop* book for additional support. Record the lesson information in the space provided on the chart. After reteaching, you may want to reassess using the Unit Test.

Assessment Chart

Name _____ Date _____

Benchmark Score reflects grade-level target.

WEEK		Day 3 Retelling Assessment		Day 5 Fluency Assessment		Day 5 Comprehension Assessment		Reteach	Teacher's Comments
		Benchmark Score	Actual Score	Benchmark WCPM	Actual Score	Benchmark Score	Actual Score		
1	**At the Beach** Compare and Contrast	3–4		110–116		3–4		✓	
2	**Hold the Flag High** Sequence	3–4		110–116		3–4			
3	**The Ch'i-lin Purse** Compare and Contrast	3–4		110–116		3–4			
4	**A Summer's Trade** Author's Purpose	3–4		110–116		3–4			
5	**The Midnight Ride** Author's Purpose	3–4		110–116		3–4			
	Unit 2 Test Score								

- **RECORD SCORES** Use this chart to record scores for the Day 3 Retelling, Day 5 Fluency, Day 5 Comprehension, and Unit Test.

- **REGROUPING** Compare the student's actual score to the benchmark score and group flexibly or provide extra support as needed.

- **RETEACH** If a student is unable to complete any part of the assessment process, use the weekly Reteach lessons in the *First Stop* book for additional support. Record the lesson information in the space provided on the chart. After reteaching, you may want to reassess using the Unit Test.

Assessment Chart

Name _____ Date _____

		Day 3 Retelling Assessment		Day 5 Fluency Assessment		Day 5 Comprehension Assessment		Reteach	Teacher's Comments
		Benchmark Score	Actual Score	Benchmark WCPM	Actual Score	Benchmark Score	Actual Score		
WEEK 1	**Perpetual Motion Machine** Sequence	3–4		115–122		3–4		✓	
WEEK 2	**Leonardo's Horse** Main Idea and Details	3–4		115–122		3–4			
WEEK 3	**Dinosaurs of Waterhouse Hawkins** Fact and Opinion	3–4		115–122		3–4			
WEEK 4	**Mahalia Jackson** Main Idea and Details	3–4		115–122		3–4			
WEEK 5	**Special Effects in Film and Television** Graphic Sources	3–4		115–122		3–4			
	Unit 3 Test Score								

Benchmark Score reflects grade-level target.

- **RECORD SCORES** Use this chart to record scores for the Day 3 Retelling, Day 5 Fluency, Day 5 Comprehension, and Unit Test.

- **REGROUPING** Compare the student's actual score to the benchmark score and group flexibly or provide extra support as needed.

- **RETEACH** If a student is unable to complete any part of the assessment process, use the weekly Reteach lessons in the *First Stop* book for additional support. Record the lesson information in the space provided on the chart. After reteaching, you may want to reassess using the Unit Test.

Assessment Chart

Name _____ Date _____

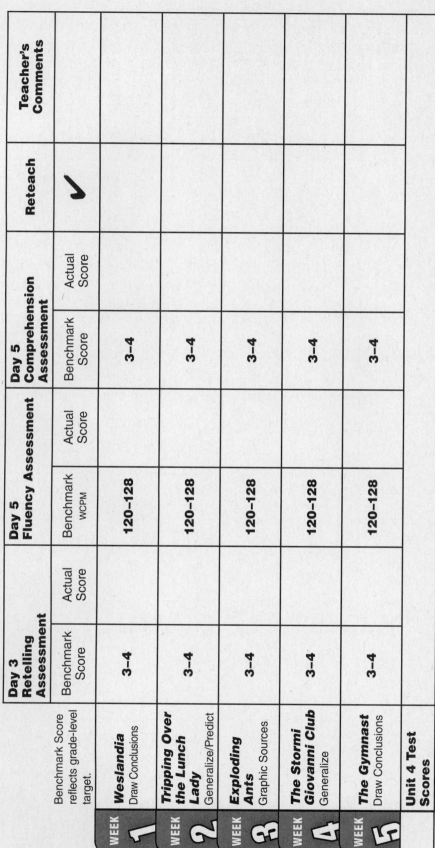

	Day 3 Retelling Assessment		Day 5 Fluency Assessment		Day 5 Comprehension Assessment		Reteach	Teacher's Comments
Benchmark Score reflects grade-level target.	Benchmark Score	Actual Score	Benchmark WCPM	Actual Score	Benchmark Score	Actual Score		
WEEK 1 **Weslandia** Draw Conclusions	3–4		120–128		3–4		✔	
WEEK 2 **Tripping Over the Lunch Lady** Generalize/Predict	3–4		120–128		3–4			
WEEK 3 **Exploding Ants** Graphic Sources	3–4		120–128		3–4			
WEEK 4 **The Stormi Giovanni Club** Generalize	3–4		120–128		3–4			
WEEK 5 **The Gymnast** Draw Conclusions	3–4		120–128		3–4			
Unit 4 Test Scores								

- **RECORD SCORES** Use this chart to record scores for the Day 3 Retelling, Day 5 Fluency, Day 5 Comprehension, and Unit Test.

- **REGROUPING** Compare the student's actual score to the benchmark score and group flexibly or provide extra support as needed.

- **RETEACH** If a student is unable to complete any part of the assessment process, use the weekly Reteach lessons in the *First Stop* book for additional support. Record the lesson information in the space provided on the chart. After reteaching, you may want to reassess using the Unit Test.

Assessment Chart

Name _____   Date _____

	Day 3 Retelling Assessment		Day 5 Fluency Assessment		Day 5 Comprehension Assessment		Reteach	Teacher's Comments
Benchmark Score reflects grade-level target.	Benchmark Score	Actual Score	Benchmark WCPM	Actual Score	Benchmark Score	Actual Score		
WEEK 1 **The Skunk Ladder** Character and Plot	3–4		125–134		3–4			
WEEK 2 **The RMS Titanic** Draw Conclusions	3–4		125–134		3–4			
WEEK 3 **Talk with an Astronaut** Author's Purpose	3–4		125–134		3–4			
WEEK 4 **Journey to the Center of the Earth** Cause and Effect	3–4		125–134		3–4			
WEEK 5 **Ghost Towns of the American West** Generalize	3–4		125–134		3–4			
Unit 5 Test Score								

- **RECORD SCORES** Use this chart to record scores for the Day 3 Retelling, Day 5 Fluency, Day 5 Comprehension, and Unit Test.

- **REGROUPING** Compare the student's actual score to the benchmark score and group flexibly or provide extra support as needed.

- **RETEACH** If a student is unable to complete any part of the assessment process, use the weekly Reteach lessons in the *First Stop* book for additional support. Record the lesson information in the space provided on the chart. After reteaching, you may want to reassess using the Unit Test.

Assessment Chart

Name _____ Date _____

	Day 3 Retelling Assessment		Day 5 Fluency Assessment		Day 5 Comprehension Assessment		Reteach	Teacher's Comments
Benchmark Score reflects grade-level target.	Benchmark Score	Actual Score	Benchmark WCPM	Actual Score	Benchmark Score	Actual Score		
WEEK 1 *The Truth About Austin's Amazing Bats* Draw Conclusions	3–4		130–140		3–4		✓	
WEEK 2 *Saint Matthew Island* Main Idea and Details	3–4		130–140		3–4			
WEEK 3 *King Midas* Compare and Contrast	3–4		130–140		3–4			
WEEK 4 *The Hindenburg* Fact and Opinion	3–4		130–140		3–4			
WEEK 5 *Sweet Music in Harlem* Sequence	3–4		130–140		3–4			
Unit 6 Test Score								

- **RECORD SCORES** Use this chart to record scores for the Day 3 Retelling, Day 5 Fluency, Day 5 Comprehension, and Unit Test.

- **REGROUPING** Compare the student's actual score to the benchmark score and group flexibly or provide extra support as needed.

- **RETEACH** If a student is unable to complete any part of the assessment process, use the weekly Reteach lessons in the *First Stop* book for additional support. Record the lesson information in the space provided on the chart. After reteaching, you may want to reassess using the Unit Test.

Student Progress Report: Grade 5

Name _____

This chart lists the skills taught in this program. Record your child's progress toward mastery of the skills covered in this school year here. Use the chart below to track the coverage of these skills.

Skill	Date	Date	Date
Read aloud grade-level texts and understand what is read.			
Determine the meaning of English words derived from Greek, Latin, and other languages.			
Determine the meanings of unfamiliar words or multiple meaning words by using the context of the sentence.			
Write analogies with known antonyms and synonyms.			
Identify and explain the meaning of common idioms, adages, and other sayings.			
Use a dictionary, a glossary, or a thesaurus to locate information about words.			
Students should analyze, make suggestions, and draw conclusions about the theme in different types of literature or genres, which derive from various cultural, historical, and contemporary content in the text. They should present evidence from the text to support their evaluations.			
Compare and contrast the themes of several works of fiction from various cultures.			
Describe the phenomena explained in origin myths from various cultures.			
Explain the effect of a historical event or movement on the theme of a work of literature.			
Analyze how poets use sound effects to reinforce meaning in poems.			

Skill	Date	Date	Date
Analyze the similarities and differences between an original text and its dramatic adaptation.			

Students should analyze, make suggestions, and draw conclusions about fiction writing, while keeping in mind the crafting of a story, such as the structure and elements used by an author, and present evidence from the content to support their analysis.

Skill	Date	Date	Date
Describe specific events in the story or novel that give rise to or hint at future events.			
Explain the roles and functions of characters, including their relationships and conflicts.			
Explain different forms of third-person points of view in stories.			
Identify the language and devices used in biographies and autobiographies, including how authors present major events in a person's life.			
Evaluate the impact of sensory details, imagery, and figurative language in literary text.			
Read independently for long periods of time and paraphrase the reading, including the order in which events occur.			
Draw conclusions about texts and evaluate how well the author achieves his or her purpose.			

Students should analyze, make suggestions, and draw conclusions about informative text, while presenting evidence from the content to support their analysis.

Skill	Date	Date	Date
Summarize the main ideas and supporting details in a text in ways that maintain meaning and logical order.			
Determine and verify the facts in a text.			

Skill	Date	Date	Date
Analyze how the organization of a text influences the relationships among the ideas.			
Use text features and graphics to gain an overview and locate information.			
Synthesize and make connections between ideas within a text and across two or three texts.			
Identify the author's viewpoint or position and explain the basic relationships among ideas in the argument.			
Recognize exaggerated, contradictory, or misleading statements in text.			
Interpret details from a text to complete a task, solve a problem, or perform procedures.			
Interpret information in maps, charts, illustrations, graphs, timelines, tables and diagrams.			
Explain how messages expressed in various forms of media are presented differently.			
Consider the different techniques used in media.			
Identify the point of view of media presentations.			
Analyze various digital media venues for levels of formality and informality.			
Plan a first draft by selecting a genre, deciding on suitable topics through a range of strategies, and developing a thesis or controlling idea.			
Develop drafts by choosing an organizational strategy and building on ideas to create a focused, organized, and coherent piece of writing.			

Skill	Date	Date	Date
Revise drafts to clarify meaning and enhance style.			
Edit drafts for grammar, mechanics, and spelling.			
Revise a final draft based on feedback from other students and the teacher, and publish the work for an audience.			
Write imaginative stories that include a clearly defined focus, plot, and point of view.			
Write imaginative stories that use sensory details to establish a believable setting.			
Write imaginative stories with dialogue to develop the story.			
Write poems using poetic techniques.			
Write poems using figurative language.			
Write poems using graphic elements.			
Write a personal narrative that conveys thoughts and feelings about an experience.			
Write essays with effective introductions and conclusions.			
Write essays that guide and inform the reader's understanding of key ideas and evidence.			
Write essays with specific facts, details, and examples in an appropriately organized structure.			
Write essays with a variety of sentence structures and transitions.			
Write letters that convey ideas, include important information, demonstrate a sense of closure, and use appropriate conventions.			

Skill	Date	Date	Date
Write responses to literary or expository texts and provide evidence from the text to demonstrate understanding.			
Write persuasive essays that establish a position and include sound reasoning, detailed and relevant evidence, and consideration of alternative.			
Use and understand the function of verbs (irregular verbs and active voice).			
Use and understand the function of collective nouns.			
Use and understand the function of adjectives and their comparative and superlative forms.			
Use and understand the function of adverbs.			
Use and understand the function of prepositions and prepositional phrases.			
Use and understand the function of indefinite pronouns.			
Use and understand the function of subordinating conjunctions.			
Use and understand the function of transitional words.			
Use the complete subject and verb in a sentence.			
Show agreement between subjects and verbs in simple and compound sentences.			
Use correct capitalization for abbreviations.			
Use correct capitalization for initials and acronyms.			
Use correct capitalization for organizations.			

Skill	Date	Date	Date
Recognize and use commas in compound sentences.			
Recognize and use proper punctuation and spacing for quotations.			
Use proper mechanics including italics and underlining for titles and emphasis.			
Spell words correctly with consonant changes.			
Spell words with vowel changes.			
Spell words with silent and sounded consonants			
Spell words with Greek roots.			
Spell words with Latin roots.			
Spell words with Greek suffixes.			
Spell words with Latin derived suffixes.			
Differentiate between commonly confused terms.			
Use spelling patterns and rules, as well as print and online dictionaries, to find and confirm the spellings of words.			
Know how to use the spell-check function in word processing while understanding its limitations.			
Brainstorm, discuss with others, decide on a topic, and formulate open-ended questions to apply to the major research topic.			
Generate a plan to gather information relevant to the research question.			
Collect information from print and electronic resources and data from experts.			

Skill	Date	Date	Date
Differentiate between primary and secondary sources.			
Record data using technology in order to see relationships between ideas and convert visual data into written notes.			
Identify the source of notes and record bibliographic information.			
Differentiate between paraphrasing information and committing plagiarism and explain why it is important to cite reliable sources.			

Students should clarify research questions and evaluate and put together the collected information. Students are expected to:

Improve the major research question, if needed, and then make a second set of questions from the answers collected.			
Evaluate the relevance, validity, and reliability of sources for the research.			

Compile important information from multiple sources.			
Develop a topic sentence, summarize information, and use evidence to support conclusions.			
Present the findings in a consistent format.			
Use quotations to support ideas and document the sources.			

Students are expected to listen and interpret a speaker's message and ask questions.			
Follow, restate, and give oral instructions.			
Determine main and supporting ideas in the speaker's message.			

Skill	Date	Date	Date
Give organized presentations that communicate ideas effectively.			
Participate in discussions by raising and considering suggestions from other group members and by identifying points of agreement and disagreement.			
Establish purposes for reading a text based on what students hope to accomplish by reading the text.			
Ask literal, interpretive, and evaluative universal questions of a text.			
Monitor and adjust comprehension using a variety of strategies.			
Make inferences about a text and use evidence from the text to support understanding.			
Summarize and paraphrase information in a text, maintaining meaning and logical order.			
Make connections between and among texts.			

Sixth Grade Formal Assessment Tools

Form from Sixth Grade Baseline Group Test Teacher's Manual

Grade 6 Baseline Test Evaluation Chart
(including percentage conversion chart)

Student's Name _____ Date _____

Item	Score (circle one)	Item	Score (circle one)	Number Correct/ 25	Percent Correct/ 25	Total Number Correct/ 55	Total Percent Correct /55	Total Number Correct/ 55 (continued)	Total Percent Correct/ 55 (continued)
Vocabulary		**Reading**		1	4%	1	2%	32	58%
1.	0 1	1.	0 1	2	8%	2	4%	33	60%
2.	0 1	2.	0 1	3	12%	3	5%	34	62%
3.	0 1	3.	0 1	4	16%	4	7%	35	64%
4.	0 1	4.	0 1	5	20%	5	9%	36	65%
5.	0 1	5.	0 1	6	24%	6	11%	37	67%
6.	0 1	6.	0 1	7	28%	7	13%	38	69%
7.	0 1	7.	0 1	8	32%	8	15%	39	71%
8.	0 1	8.	0 1	9	36%	9	16%	40	73%
9.	0 1	9.	0 1	10	40%	10	18%	41	75%
10.	0 1	10.	0 1	11	44%	11	20%	42	76%
11.	0 1	11.	0 1	12	48%	12	22%	43	78%
12.	0 1	12.	0 1	13	52%	13	24%	44	80%
13.	0 1	13.	0 1	14	56%	14	25%	45	82%
14.	0 1	14.	0 1	15	60%	15	27%	46	84%
15.	0 1	15.	0 1	16	64%	16	29%	47	85%
16.	0 1	16.	0 1	17	68%	17	31%	48	87%
17.	0 1	17.	0 1	18	72%	18	33%	49	89%
18.	0 1	18.	0 1	19	76%	19	35%	50	91%
19.	0 1	19.	0 1	20	80%	20	36%	51	93%
20.	0 1	20.	0 1	21	84%	21	38%	52	95%
21.	0 1	21.	0 1	22	88%	22	40%	53	96%
22.	0 1	22.	0 1	23	92%	23	42%	54	98%
23.	0 1	23.	0 1	24	96%	24	44%	55	100%
24.	0 1	24.	0 1	25	100%	25	45%		
25.	0 1	25.	0 1			26	47%		
		26.	0 1			27	49%		
		27.	0 1			28	51%		
		28.	0 1			29	53%		
		29.	0 1			30	55%		
		30.	0 1			31	56%		

Vocabulary Score _____/25=_____%   TOTAL (Vocabulary + Reading Score) _____/55=_____%

Reading Score _____/30=_____%   Placement: _____

Alternate Baseline Test Placement: (Optional)

Strategic Intervention _____

On-Level _____   Advanced _____

Fluency Rate _____   (Optional)

Interim Overall Placement (circle one) **Strategic Intervention   On-Level   Advanced**

Fluency Forms

Reading Fluency Progress Chart

Student's Name	Unit 1		Unit 2		Unit 3		Unit 4		Unit 5		Unit 6	
	Date	WCPM	Date	WCPM	Date	WCPM	Date	WCPM	Date	WCPM	Date	WCPM
1.												
2.												
3.												
4.												
5.												
6.												
7.												
8.												
9.												
10.												
11.												
12.												
13.												
14.												
15.												
16.												
17.												
18.												
19.												
20.												
21.												
22.												
23.												
24.												
25.												
26.												
27.												
28.												
29.												
30.												
31.												
32.												
33.												
34.												
35.												

Fluency Progress Chart, Grade 6

Name

WCPM	1	2	3	4	5	6	7	8	9	10	11	12	13	14	15	16	17	18	19	20	21	22	23	24	25	26	27	28	29	30	31	32	33	34	35	36
175																																				
170																																				
165																																				
160																																				
155																																				
150																																				
146																																				
140																																				
135																																				
130																																				
125																																				
120																																				
115																																				
110																																				
105																																				
100																																				
95																																				
90																																				
85																																				
80																																				

Timed Reading/Week

403

Forms from Sixth Grade Weekly Tests Teacher's Manual

Scott Foresman *Reading Street*
Class Weekly Test Progress Chart—Grade 6

Teacher's Name: _____

Student Name	\multicolumn{30}{c}{Weekly Test Total Score}
	1 2 3 4 5 6 7 8 9 10 11 12 13 14 15 16 17 18 19 20 21 22 23 24 25 26 27 28 29 30
1	
2	
3	
4	
5	
6	
7	
8	
9	
10	
11	
12	
13	
14	
15	
16	
17	
18	
19	
20	
21	
22	
23	
24	
25	
26	
27	
28	
29	
30	

Scott Foresman *Reading Street*
Student Weekly Test Progress Chart—Grade 6

Student Name: _____

Test	Vocabulary	Phonics/Word Analysis	Comprehension	Multiple-Choice Total	Writing	TOTAL
Weekly Test 1	/6	/6	/8	/20		
Weekly Test 2	/6	/6	/8	/20		
Weekly Test 3	/7	/5	/8	/20		
Weekly Test 4	/8	/4	/8	/20		
Weekly Test 5	/8	/4	/8	/20		
Weekly Test 6	/6	/6	/8	/20		
Weekly Test 7	/7	/5	/8	/20		
Weekly Test 8	/6	/6	/8	/20		
Weekly Test 9	/6	/6	/8	/20		
Weekly Test 10	/7	/5	/8	/20		
Weekly Test 11	/7	/5	/8	/20		
Weekly Test 12	/7	/5	/8	/20		
Weekly Test 13	/5	/7	/8	/20		
Weekly Test 14	/7	/5	/8	/20		
Weekly Test 15	/7	/5	/8	/20		
Weekly Test 16	/7	/5	/8	/20		
Weekly Test 17	/7	/5	/8	/20		
Weekly Test 18	/6	/6	/8	/20		
Weekly Test 19	/7	/5	/8	/20		
Weekly Test 20	/8	/4	/8	/20		
Weekly Test 21	/5	/7	/8	/20		
Weekly Test 22	/7	/5	/8	/20		
Weekly Test 23	/5	/7	/8	/20		
Weekly Test 24	/6	/6	/8	/20		
Weekly Test 25	/7	/5	/8	/20		
Weekly Test 26	/7	/5	/8	/20		
Weekly Test 27	/5	/7	/8	/20		
Weekly Test 28	/7	/5	/8	/20		
Weekly Test 29	/6	/6	/8	/20		
Weekly Test 30	/7	/5	/8	/20		

Comprehension Target Skill Coverage

How can the Weekly Tests predict student success on Unit Benchmark Tests?

Each Unit Benchmark Test, as well as assessing overall student reading ability, concentrates on two skills taught and/or reviewed during the unit by including several questions on those skills. In order to ensure that comprehension target skill can be accurately learned and then tested, students learn each target skill through a combination of being taught and reviewing the skill multiple times before testing occurs. The charts below show the units/weeks where the target comprehension skills are taught and where they are tested on Weekly Tests. Based on the student's number of correct answers for each tested target skill, the teacher will know whether a student has gained the necessary skill knowledge before the Unit Test is given. A low score on the Weekly Tests probably indicates a need for closer review of the student's performance and perhaps additional instruction. It is important to understand that these tests provide only one look at the student's progress and should be interpreted in conjunction with other assessments and the teacher's observation.

Using the Comprehension Target Skill Coverage Chart

To score target skill knowledge, use the Comprehension Target Skill Coverage Chart.

1. Make a copy of the appropriate Comprehension Target Skill Coverage chart for each student.

2. To score, circle the number of correct answers the student had for that skill on the appropriate Weekly Test.

3. Using the total number of correct answers for a skill, check the appropriate box under *Student Trend* to indicate whether or not the student has acquired the target skill knowledge. We recommend 90% correct as the criterion for skill acquisition at this level. Add any notes or observations that may be helpful to you and the student in later instruction.

Grade 6 — Comprehension Target Skill Coverage Chart

Student Name _____

Unit 1 Tested Skills	Weekly Test Locations	Number Correct	Student Trend
Literary Elements: Character/Setting	Weekly Test 1	0 1 2 3	_____ Skill knowledge acquired
	Weekly Test 2	0 1 2 3	
	Weekly Test 3	0 1	_____ Skill needs further review
Fact and Opinion	Weekly Test 2	0 1	_____ Skill knowledge acquired
	Weekly Test 4	0 1	_____ Skill needs further review

Unit 2 Tested Skills	Weekly Test Locations	Number Correct	Student Trend
Main Idea and Details	Weekly Test 5	0 1	
	Weekly Test 6	0 1 2 3 4 5	_____ Skill knowledge acquired
	Weekly Test 7	0 1 2 3 4 5	
	Weekly Test 10	0 1	_____ Skill needs further review
Graphic Sources	Weekly Test 5	0 1 2 3 4 5	
	Weekly Test 7	0 1	_____ Skill knowledge acquired
	Weekly Test 8	0 1 2 3 4 5	
	Weekly Test 10	0 1 2 3 4 5	_____ Skill needs further review

Grade 6 — Comprehension Target Skill Coverage Chart

Student Name _____

Unit 3 Tested Skills	Weekly Test Locations	Number Correct	Student Trend
Sequence	Weekly Test 1	0 1 2	
	Weekly Test 4	0 1	
	Weekly Test 9	0 1	
	Weekly Test 11	0 1 2 3 4 5	____ Skill knowledge acquired
	Weekly Test 12	0 1	
	Weekly Test 13	0 1 2 3 4 5	____ Skill needs further review
	Weekly Test 15	0 1	
Generalize	Weekly Test 6	0 1	____ Skill knowledge acquired
	Weekly Test 12	0 1 2 3 4 5	
	Weekly Test 13	0 1	____ Skill needs further review
	Weekly Test 14	0 1 2 3 4 5	

Unit 4 Tested Skills	Weekly Test Locations	Number Correct	Student Trend
Author's Purpose	Weekly Test 6	0 1	
	Weekly Test 16	0 1	____ Skill knowledge acquired
	Weekly Test 17	0 1 2 3 4 5	
	Weekly Test 18	0 1	____ Skill needs further review
	Weekly Test 20	0 1 2 3 4 5	
Cause and Effect	Weekly Test 1	0 1	
	Weekly Test 9	0 1	
	Weekly Test 11	0 1	
	Weekly Test 12	0 1	
	Weekly Test 14	0 1 2	
	Weekly Test 15	0 1	
	Weekly Test 16	0 1 2 3 4 5	____ Skill knowledge acquired
	Weekly Test 18	0 1 2 3 4 5	
	Weekly Test 20	0 1	____ Skill needs further review

Grade 6 — Comprehension Target Skill Coverage Chart

Student Name _____

Unit 5 Tested Skills	Weekly Test Locations	Number Correct	Student Trend
Literary Elements: Plot/Theme	Weekly Test 1	0 1 2	
	Weekly Test 2	0 1 2	_____ Skill knowledge acquired
	Weekly Test 11	0 1	_____ Skill needs further review
	Weekly Test 21	0 1 2 3 4 5	
Cause and Effect	Weekly Test 1	0 1	
	Weekly Test 9	0 1	
	Weekly Test 11	0 1	
	Weekly Test 12	0 1	
	Weekly Test 14	0 1 2	
	Weekly Test 15	0 1	
	Weekly Test 16	0 1 2 3 4 5	
	Weekly Test 18	0 1 2 3 4 5	
	Weekly Test 20	0 1	
	Weekly Test 21	0 1	_____ Skill knowledge acquired
	Weekly Test 23	0 1 2 3 4 5	_____ Skill needs further review
	Weekly Test 24	0 1	

Grade 6 — Comprehension Target Skill Coverage Chart

Student Name _____

Unit 6 Tested Skills, p.1	Weekly Test Locations	Number Correct	Student Trend
Compare and Contrast	Weekly Test 3	0 1 2 3 4 5	
	Weekly Test 4	0 1 2 3 4 5	
	Weekly Test 8	0 1	
	Weekly Test 9	0 1 2 3 4 5	
	Weekly Test 16	0 1	
	Weekly Test 17	0 1	
	Weekly Test 18	0 1	
	Weekly Test 26	0 1	_____ Skill knowledge acquired
	Weekly Test 28	0 1 2 3 4 5	
	Weekly Test 30	0 1	_____ Skill needs further review

Grade 6 — Comprehension Target Skill Coverage Chart

Student Name _____

Unit 6 Tested Skills, p.2	Weekly Test Locations	Number Correct	Student Trend
	Weekly Test 2	0 1 2	
	Weekly Test 3	0 1 2	
	Weekly Test 4	0 1	
	Weekly Test 5	0 1 2	
	Weekly Test 6	0 1	
	Weekly Test 7	0 1 2	
	Weekly Test 8	0 1 2	
	Weekly Test 9	0 1	
	Weekly Test 10	0 1 2	
	Weekly Test 11	0 1	
	Weekly Test 12	0 1	
Draw Conclusions	Weekly Test 15	0 1 2 3 4 5	
	Weekly Test 17	0 1	
	Weekly Test 19	0 1 2 3 4 5 6	
	Weekly Test 20	0 1 2	
	Weekly Test 21	0 1	
	Weekly Test 23	0 1 2	
	Weekly Test 24	0 1 2	
	Weekly Test 25	0 1 2	
	Weekly Test 27	0 1 2 3	
	Weekly Test 28	0 1	____ Skill knowledge acquired
	Weekly Test 29	0 1 2 3 4 5 6 7	____ Skill needs further review
	Weekly Test 30	0 1 2	

Weekly Test Item Analysis—Grade 6

TEST	SECTION	ITEMS	SKILL
Weekly Test 1	**Vocabulary**	1–6	Understand and use new vocabulary
	Word Analysis	7–12	Suffix *-ed, -ing*
	Comprehension	13, 14, 17, 18, 20	◉ Literary Elements: Setting and plot
		15, 19	Sequence
		16	**R** Cause and effect
	Written Response	Look Back and Write	Respond to literature
Weekly Test 2	**Vocabulary**	1–6	Understand and use new vocabulary
	Word Analysis	7–12	Shades of meaning
	Comprehension	13, 15, 16, 18, 20	◉ Literary Elements: Character and theme
		17, 19	Draw conclusions
		14	**R** Fact and opinion
	Written Response	Look Back and Write	Respond to literature
Weekly Test 3	**Vocabulary**	1–7	Understand and use new vocabulary
	Word Analysis	8–12	Spanish/Native American word origins
	Comprehension	13, 14, 17, 18, 20	◉ Compare and contrast
		16, 19	Draw conclusions
		15	**R** Literary Element: Character
	Written Response	Look Back and Write	Respond to literature

Weekly Test Item Analysis—Grade 6

TEST	SECTION	ITEMS	SKILL
Weekly Test 4	**Vocabulary**	1–8	Understand and use new vocabulary
	Word Analysis	9–12	Prefixes *ex-, re-*
	Comprehension	13–15, 18, 19	⊙ Compare and contrast
		17	Draw conclusions
		20	Fact and opinion
		16	R Sequence
	Written Response	Look Back and Write	Respond to literature
Weekly Test 5	**Vocabulary**	1–8	Understand and use new vocabulary
	Word Analysis	9–12	Multiple meaning words
	Comprehension	13–15, 18, 20	⊙ Graphic sources
		17, 19	Draw conclusions
		16	R Main idea and details
	Written Response	Look Back and Write	Respond to literature
Weekly Test 6	**Vocabulary**	1–6	Understand and use new vocabulary
	Word Analysis	7–12	Related works
	Comprehension	14, 15, 16, 19, 20	⊙ Main idea and details
		17	Author's purpose
		18	Draw conclusions
		13	R Generalize
	Written Response	Look Back and Write	Respond to literature

Weekly Test Item Analysis—Grade 6

TEST	SECTION	ITEMS	SKILL
Weekly Test 7	Vocabulary	1–7	Understand and use new vocabulary
	Word Analysis	8–12	Morphemes
	Comprehension	13, 14, 17, 18, 20	◉ Main idea and details
		15, 19	Draw conclusions
		16	R Graphic sources
	Written Response	Look Back and Write	Respond to literature
Weekly Test 8	Vocabulary	1–6	Understand and use new vocabulary
	Word Analysis	7–12	Spanish word origin
	Comprehension	13–17	◉ Graphic sources
		18, 20	Draw conclusions
		19	R Compare and contrast
	Written Response	Look Back and Write	Respond to literature
Weekly Test 9	Vocabulary	1–6	Understand and use new vocabulary
	Word Analysis	7–12	Shades of meaning
	Comprehension	13–15, 18, 19	◉ Compare and contrast
		17	Draw conclusions
		20	Cause and effect
		16	R Sequence
	Written Response	Look Back and Write	Respond to literature

Weekly Test Item Analysis—Grade 6

TEST	SECTION	ITEMS	SKILL
Weekly Test 10	**Vocabulary**	1–7	Understand and use new vocabulary
	Word Analysis	8–12	Greek or Latin word origins
	Comprehension	13–15, 18, 20	◉ Graphic sources
		17, 19	Draw conclusions
		16	**R** Main idea and details
	Written Response	Look Back and Write	Respond to literature
Weekly Test 11	**Vocabulary**	1–7	Understand and use new vocabulary
	Word Analysis	8–12	Shades of meaning
	Comprehension	13–17	◉ Sequence
		18	Cause and effect
		20	Draw conclusions
		19	**R** Plot
	Written Response	Look Back and Write	Respond to literature
Weekly Test 12	**Vocabulary**	1–7	Understand and use new vocabulary
	Word Analysis	8–12	Greek and Latin roots
	Comprehension	14–17, 20	◉ Generalize
		18	Cause and effect
		19	Sequence
		13	**R** Draw Conclusions
	Written Response	Look Back and Write	Respond to literature

Weekly Test Item Analysis—Grade 6

TEST	SECTION	ITEMS	SKILL
Weekly Test 13	**Vocabulary**	1–5	Understand and use new vocabulary
	Word Analysis	6–12	Suffixes *-ary, -ize*
	Comprehension	15, 17, 18–20	◉ Sequence
		14, 16	Literary Element: Character
		13	**R** Generalize
	Written Response	Look Back and Write	Respond to literature
Weekly Test 14	**Vocabulary**	1–7	Understand and use new vocabulary
	Word Analysis	8–12	Multiple meaning words
	Comprehension	13–15, 19, 20	◉ Generalize
		17	Cause and effect
		18	Main idea and details
		16	**R** Cause and effect
	Written Response	Look Back and Write	Respond to literature
Weekly Test 15	**Vocabulary**	1–7	Understand and use new vocabulary
	Word Analysis	8–12	Suffixes *-tion, -less*
	Comprehension	13–16, 19	◉ Draw conclusions
		18	Literary Element: Character
		20	Cause and effect
		17	**R** Sequence
	Written Response	Look Back and Write	Respond to literature

Weekly Test Item Analysis—Grade 6

TEST	SECTION	ITEMS	SKILL
Weekly Test 16	**Vocabulary**	1–7	Understand and use new vocabulary
	Word Analysis	8–12	French/Italian word origins
	Comprehension	13–17	◉ Cause and effect
		19	Author's purpose
		18	**R** Main idea and details
	Written Response	Look Back and Write	Respond to literature
Weekly Test 17	**Vocabulary**	1–7	Understand and use new vocabulary
	Word Analysis	8–12	Suffixes -*ship*, -*ence*
	Comprehension	13–17	◉ Author's purpose
		19	Compare and contrast
		20	Draw conclusions
		18	**R** Fact and opinion
	Written Response	Look Back and Write	Respond to literature
Weekly Test 18	**Vocabulary**	1–6	Understand and use new vocabulary
	Word Analysis	7–12	Suffixes -*en, -age, -ment*
	Comprehension	13, 15, 17, 19, 20	◉ Cause and effect
		14	Sequence
		18	Compare and contrast
		16	**R** Author's purpose
	Written Response	Look Back and Write	Respond to literature

Weekly Test Item Analysis—Grade 6

TEST	SECTION	ITEMS	SKILL
Weekly Test 19	**Vocabulary**	1–7	Understand and use new vocabulary
	Word Analysis	8–12	Greek/Latin roots
	Comprehension	13, 14, 16, 17, 20	◉ Draw conclusions
		15	Literary Element: Setting
		19	Draw conclusions
		18	R Sequence
	Written Response	Look Back and Write	Respond to literature
Weekly Test 20	**Vocabulary**	1–8	Understand and use new vocabulary
	Word Analysis	9–12	Shades of meaning
	Comprehension	13, 15, 17, 19, 20	◉ Author's purpose
		14, 18	Draw conclusions
		16	R Cause and effect
	Written Response	Look Back and Write	Respond to literature
Weekly Test 21	**Vocabulary**	1–5	Understand and use new vocabulary
	Word Analysis	6–12	Prefixes *ac-, de-*
	Comprehension	13, 14, 18–20	◉ Literary Elements: Theme and plot
		16	Draw conclusions
		17	Literary Element: Character
		15	R Cause and effect
	Written Response	Look Back and Write	Respond to literature

Weekly Test Item Analysis—Grade 6

TEST	SECTION	ITEMS	SKILL
Weekly Test 22	**Vocabulary**	1–7	Understand and use new vocabulary
	Word Analysis	8–12	Spanish word origins
	Comprehension	15, 17–20	◉ Fact and opinion
		13, 14	Literary Element: Character
		16	R Sequence
	Written Response	Look Back and Write	Respond to literature
Weekly Test 23	**Vocabulary**	1–5	Understand and use new vocabulary
	Word Analysis	6–12	Greek and Latin roots
	Comprehension	13, 14, 17, 19, 20	◉ Cause and effect
		15, 18	Draw conclusions
		16	R Sequence
	Written Response	Look Back and Write	Respond to literature
Weekly Test 24	**Vocabulary**	1–6	Understand and use new vocabulary
	Word Analysis	7–12	Shades of meaning
	Comprehension	14, 15, 17, 18, 20	◉ Main idea and details
		13, 19	Draw conclusions
		16	R Cause and effect
	Written Response	Look Back and Write	Respond to literature

Weekly Test Item Analysis—Grade 6

TEST	SECTION	ITEMS	SKILL
Weekly Test 25	**Vocabulary**	1–7	Understand and use new vocabulary
	Word Analysis	8–12	Affixes *un-, -able*
	Comprehension	14, 15, 17, 19, 20	◉ Sequence
		13, 18	Draw conclusions
		16	**R** Main idea and details
	Written Response	Look Back and Write	Respond to literature
Weekly Test 26	**Vocabulary**	1–7	Understand and use new vocabulary
	Word Analysis	8–12	Greek/Latin roots
	Comprehension	14, 15, 17–19	◉ Author's purpose
		13	Literary Element: Setting
		20	Literary Element: Character
		16	**R** Compare and contrast
	Written Response	Look Back and Write	Respond to literature
Weekly Test 27	**Vocabulary**	1–5	Understand and use new vocabulary
	Word Analysis	6–12	Greek/Latin roots
	Comprehension	14, 15, 17, 19, 20	◉ Graphic sources
		13, 18	Draw conclusions
		16	**R** Draw conclusions
	Written Response	Look Back and Write	Respond to literature

Weekly Test Item Analysis—Grade 6

TEST	SECTION	ITEMS	SKILL
Weekly Test 28	**Vocabulary**	1–7	Understand and use new vocabulary
	Word Analysis	8–12	Prefixes *pro-, uni-, dis-, (re-)*
	Comprehension	13, 15, 17–19	◉ Compare and contrast
		14, 20	Literary Element: Character
		16	**R** Draw conclusions
	Written Response	Look Back and Write	Respond to literature
Weekly Test 29	**Vocabulary**	1–6	Understand and use new vocabulary
	Word Analysis	7–12	French word origins
	Comprehension	14, 15, 17, 19, 20	◉ Draw conclusions
		13, 18	Draw conclusions
		16	**R** Author's purpose
	Written Response	Look Back and Write	Respond to literature
Weekly Test 30	**Vocabulary**	1–7	Understand and use new vocabulary
	Word Analysis	8–12	Shades of meaning
	Comprehension	14, 15, 16, 18, 20	◉ Generalize
		13, 19	Draw conclusions
		17	**R** Compare and contrast
	Written Response	Look Back and Write	Respond to literature

Forms from Grade 6 Unit and End-of-Year Benchmark Tests Teacher's Manual

CLASS RECORD CHART

Grade 6 Unit Benchmark Tests

Teacher Name _____   Class _____

Student Name	Unit 1		Unit 2		Unit 3		Unit 4		Unit 5		Unit 6	
	Pt 1–3	Pt 4	Pt 1–3	Pt 4	Pt 1–3	Pt 4	Pt 1–3	Pt 4	Pt 1–3	Pt 4	Pt 1–3	Pt 4
1.												
2.												
3.												
4.												
5.												
6.												
7.												
8.												
9.												
10.												
11.												
12.												
13.												
14.												
15.												
16.												
17.												
18.												
19.												
20.												
21.												
22.												
23.												
24.												
25.												
26.												
27.												
28.												
29.												
30.												

Evaluation Chart: Grade 6 – Unit 1 Benchmark Test

Student Name _____ Date _____

Reading – Parts 1–3

Item	Tested Skill	Item Type*	Score (circle one)
Reading – Part 1: Comprehension			
1.	Literary elements: character	I	0 1
2.	Literary elements: character	C	0 1
3.	Compare and contrast	C	0 1
4.	Literary elements: character	I	0 1
5.	Literary elements: setting	I	0 1
6.	Literary elements: setting	C	0 1
7.	Cause and effect	I	0 1
8.	Literary elements: plot	C	0 1
9.	Literary elements: character	I	0 1
10.	Literary elements: character	L	0 1
11.	Compare and contrast	C	0 1
A.	Constructed-response text-to-world connection		0 1 2
12.	Main idea and details	I	0 1
13.	Cause and effect	I	0 1
14.	Fact and opinion	C	0 1
15.	Compare and contrast	C	0 1
16.	Graphic sources	C	0 1
17.	Fact and opinion	C	0 1
18.	Graphic sources	L	0 1
19.	Author's purpose	C	0 1
20.	Fact and opinion	C	0 1
21.	Author's purpose	C	0 1
22.	Cause and effect	L	0 1
B.	Constructed-response text-to-text connection		0 1 2
Reading – Part 2: Vocabulary			
23.	Word structure: suffixes		0 1
24.	Word structure: Greek and Latin roots		0 1
25.	Word structure: endings		0 1
26.	Word structure: endings		0 1
27.	Word structure: suffixes		0 1
28.	Word structure: Greek and Latin roots		0 1
29.	Context clues: unfamiliar words		0 1

Reading – Part 2: Vocabulary (continued)			
30.	Thesaurus: synonyms	0	1
31.	Thesaurus: synonyms	0	1
32.	Context clues: unfamiliar words	0	1

Reading – Part 3: Writing Conventions			
33.	Common and proper nouns	0	1
34.	Common and proper nouns	0	1
35.	Imperative sentences	0	1
36.	Subjects and predicates	0	1
37.	Subjects and predicates	0	1
38.	Compound and complex sentences	0	1
39.	Independent and dependent clauses	0	1
40.	Compound and complex sentences	0	1
Student's Reading Total Score/Total Possible Score _____		/44	

*L = literal   I = inferential   C = critical analysis

Reading — Parts 1–3 percentage score: _____ ÷ 44 = _____ × 100 = _____%

(student's total score)   (percentage score)

Writing – Part 4

Writing Score (complete one) _____/6 _____/5 _____/4 _____/3

Notes/Observations:

Evaluation Chart: Grade 6 — Unit 2 Benchmark Test

Student Name _____ Date _____

Reading – Parts 1–3			
Item	Tested Skill	Item Type*	Score (circle one)
Reading – Part 1: Comprehension			
1.	Main idea and details	I	0 1
2.	Generalize	C	0 1
3.	Compare and contrast	C	0 1
4.	Main idea and details	L	0 1
5.	Graphic sources	C	0 1
6.	Compare and contrast	C	0 1
7.	Main idea and details	L	0 1
8.	Graphic sources	C	0 1
9.	Sequence	C	0 1
10.	Main idea and details	C	0 1
11.	Sequence	I	0 1
A.	Constructed-response text-to-world connection		0 1 2
12.	Sequence	I	0 1
13.	Sequence	L	0 1
14.	Compare and contrast	C	0 1
15.	Main idea and details	I	0 1
16.	Compare and contrast	L	0 1
17.	Graphic sources	I	0 1
18.	Generalize	C	0 1
19.	Main idea and details	I	0 1
20.	Graphic sources	C	0 1
21.	Generalize	C	0 1
22.	Generalize	C	0 1
B.	Constructed-response text-to-text connection		0 1 2
Reading – Part 2: Vocabulary			
23.	Context clues: unfamiliar words		0 1
24.	Word structure: suffixes		0 1
25.	Word structure: Greek and Latin roots		0 1
26.	Dictionary/glossary: unknown words		0 1
27.	Word structure: suffixes		0 1
28.	Word structure: suffixes		0 1
29.	Dictionary/glossary: unknown words		0 1

Reading – Part 2: Vocabulary (continued)		
30.	Dictionary/glossary: unknown words	0 1
31.	Dictionary/glossary: unknown words	0 1
32.	Word structure: Greek and Latin roots	0 1
Student's Regrouping Multiple-Choice Score/Total Possible Score		_____ /32
Reading – Part 3: Writing Conventions		
33.	Past, present, and future tenses	0 1
34.	Action and linking	0 1
35.	Regular and irregular plural nouns	0 1
36.	Subject-verb agreement	0 1
37.	Possessive nouns	0 1
38.	Subject-verb agreement	0 1
39.	Regular and irregular plural nouns	0 1
40.	Possessive nouns	0 1
Student's Reading Total Score/Total Possible Score		_____ /44

*L = literal   I = inferential   C = critical analysis

Regrouping (Reading — Parts 1–2) percentage score: _____ ÷ 32 = _____ × 100 = _____%
                                                             (student's score)   (percentage score)

Reading — Parts 1–3 percentage score: _____ ÷ 44 = _____ × 100 = _____%
                                                   (student's total score)   (percentage score)

Writing – Part 4

Writing Score (complete one)   _____ /6   _____ /5   _____ /4   _____ /3

Notes/Observations:

Evaluation Chart: Grade 6 — Unit 3 Benchmark Test

Student Name _____ Date _____

Reading – Parts 1–3			
Item	**Tested Skill**	**Item Type***	**Score** (circle one)
Reading – Part 1: Comprehension			
1.	Sequence	I	0 1
2.	Draw conclusions	I	0 1
3.	Draw conclusions	I	0 1
4.	Literary elements: plot	C	0 1
5.	Draw conclusions	I	0 1
6.	Literary elements: character	I	0 1
7.	Literary elements: plot	I	0 1
8.	Literary elements: plot	C	0 1
9.	Literary elements: character	I	0 1
10.	Cause and effect	L	0 1
11.	Sequence	L	0 1
A.	Constructed-response text-to-world connection		0 1 2
12.	Generalize	I	0 1
13.	Draw conclusions	I	0 1
14.	Sequence	I	0 1
15.	Cause and effect	L	0 1
16.	Generalize	C	0 1
17.	Cause and effect	I	0 1
18.	Draw conclusions	C	0 1
19.	Sequence	I	0 1
20.	Draw conclusions	I	0 1
21.	Generalize	C	0 1
22.	Generalize	C	0 1
B.	Constructed-response text-to-text connection		0 1 2
Reading – Part 2: Vocabulary			
23.	Word structure: word endings		0 1
24.	Context clues: antonyms		0 1
25.	Context clues: synonyms		0 1
26.	Context clues: synonyms		0 1
27.	Word structure: suffixes		0 1
28.	Word structure: word endings		0 1

Reading – Part 2: Vocabulary (continued)			
29.	Word structure: prefixes	0	1
30.	Word structure: prefixes	0	1
31.	Context clues: antonyms	0	1
32.	Word structure: suffixes	0	1
Student's Regrouping Multiple-Choice Score/Total Possible Score		_____/32	
Reading – Part 3: Writing Conventions			
33.	Verbs, objects, and subject complements	0	1
34.	Verbs, objects, and subject complements	0	1
35.	Troublesome verbs	0	1
36.	Principal parts of regular verbs	0	1
37.	Troublesome verbs	0	1
38.	Troublesome verbs	0	1
39.	Verbs, objects, and subject complements	0	1
40.	Verbs, objects, and subject complements	0	1
Student's Reading Total Score/Total Possible Score		_____/44	

*L = literal   I = inferential   C = critical analysis

Regrouping (Reading — Parts 1–2) percentage score: _____ ÷ 32 = _____ × 100 = _____%
                                                              (student's score)   (percentage score)

Reading — Parts 1–3 percentage score: _____ ÷ 44 = _____ × 100 = _____%
                                                              (student's total score)   (percentage score)

Writing – Part 4

Writing Score (complete one)   _____/6   _____/5   _____/4   _____/3

Notes/Observations:

Evaluation Chart: Grade 6 — Unit 4 Benchmark Test

Student Name _____ Date _____

	Reading – Parts 1–3		
Item	**Tested Skill**	**Item Type***	**Score** (circle one)
Reading – Part 1: Comprehension			
1.	Sequence	I	0 1
2.	Cause and effect	C	0 1
3.	Cause and effect	I	0 1
4.	Fact and opinion	C	0 1
5.	Draw conclusions	I	0 1
6.	Main idea and details	I	0 1
7.	Main idea and details	I	0 1
8.	Generalize	I	0 1
9.	Draw conclusions	C	0 1
10.	Author's purpose	C	0 1
11.	Cause and effect	L	0 1
A.	Constructed-response text-to-world connection		0 1 2
12.	Cause and effect	L	0 1
13.	Cause and effect	L	0 1
14.	Sequence	L	0 1
15.	Sequence	I	0 1
16.	Cause and effect	C	0 1
17.	Literary elements: setting	L	0 1
18.	Literary elements: character	I	0 1
19.	Compare and contrast	I	0 1
20.	Author's purpose	C	0 1
21.	Draw conclusions	I	0 1
22.	Author's purpose	C	0 1
B.	Constructed-response text-to-text connection		0 1 2
Reading – Part 2: Vocabulary			
23.	Context clues: unfamiliar words		0 1
24.	Context clues: unfamiliar words		0 1
25.	Dictionary/glossary: multiple-meaning words		0 1
26.	Dictionary/glossary: multiple-meaning words		0 1
27.	Dictionary/glossary: multiple-meaning words		0 1
28.	Word structure: prefixes		0 1
29.	Dictionary/glossary: unfamiliar words		0 1

Reading – Part 2: Vocabulary (continued)		
30.	Context clues: unfamiliar words	0 1
31.	Context clues: unfamiliar words	0 1
32.	Context clues: multiple-meaning words	0 1
Student's Regrouping Multiple-Choice Score/Total Possible Score _____		/32
Reading – Part 3: Writing Conventions		
33.	Subject and object pronouns	0 1
34.	Subject and object pronouns	0 1
35.	Subject and object pronouns	0 1
36.	Pronouns and antecedents	0 1
37.	Pronouns and antecedents	0 1
38.	Indefinite pronouns	0 1
39.	Possessive pronouns	0 1
40.	Reflexive pronouns	0 1
Student's Reading Total Score/Total Possible Score _____		/44

*L = literal   I = inferential   C = critical analysis

Regrouping (Reading — Parts 1–2) percentage score: _____ ÷ 32 = _____ × 100 = _____%

(student's score)   (percentage score)

Reading — Parts 1–3 percentage score: _____ ÷ 44 = _____ × 100 = _____%

(student's total score)   (percentage score)

Writing – Part 4

Writing Score (complete one)   _____/6   _____/5   _____/4   _____/3

Notes/Observations:

Evaluation Chart: Grade 6 — Unit 5 Benchmark Test

Student Name _____ Date _____

Reading – Parts 1–3			
Item	**Tested Skill**	**Item Type***	**Score** (circle one)
Reading – Part 1: Comprehension			
1.	Sequence	L	0 1
2.	Literary elements: plot	I	0 1
3.	Cause and effect	L	0 1
4.	Literary elements: plot	I	0 1
5.	Literary elements: theme	C	0 1
6.	Author's purpose	C	0 1
7.	Cause and effect	I	0 1
8.	Literary elements: plot	C	0 1
9.	Cause and effect	C	0 1
10.	Literary elements: theme	C	0 1
11.	Literary elements: characters	C	0 1
A.	Constructed-response text-to-self connection		0 1 2
12.	Cause and effect	L	0 1
13.	Cause and effect	L	0 1
14.	Cause and effect	L	0 1
15.	Sequence	C	0 1
16.	Author's purpose	C	0 1
17.	Literary elements: setting	I	0 1
18.	Literary elements: character	I	0 1
19.	Literary elements: plot	L	0 1
20.	Literary elements: plot	I	0 1
21.	Literary elements: theme	C	0 1
22.	Main idea and details	I	0 1
B.	Constructed-response text-to-text connection		0 1 2
Reading – Part 2: Vocabulary			
23.	Context clues: antonyms		0 1
24.	Context clues: synonyms		0 1
25.	Context clues: homonyms		0 1
26.	Context clues: unfamiliar words		0 1
27.	Context clues: antonyms		0 1
28.	Context clues: unfamiliar words		0 1
29.	Context clues: homonyms		0 1

	Reading – Part 2: Vocabulary (continued)		
30.	Context clues: homonyms	0	1
31.	Context clues: synonyms	0	1
32.	Context clues: antonyms	0	1
Student's Regrouping Multiple-Choice Score/Total Possible Score		_____ /32	
Reading – Part 3: Writing Conventions			
33.	Contractions and negatives	0	1
34.	Contractions and negatives	0	1
35.	Predicate adjectives	0	1
36.	Proper adjectives	0	1
37.	Demonstrative pronouns	0	1
38.	Comparative and superlative adjectives	0	1
39.	Adjective clauses	0	1
40.	Adverb phrases	0	1
Student's Reading Total Score/Total Possible Score		_____ /44	

*L = literal   I = inferential   C = critical analysis

Regrouping (Reading — Parts 1–2) percentage score: _____ ÷ 32 = _____ × 100 = _____%
 (student's score)   (percentage score)

Reading — Parts 1–3 percentage score: _____ ÷ 44 = _____ × 100 = _____%
 (student's total score)   (percentage score)

Writing – Part 4

Writing Score (complete one)   _____/6   _____/5   _____/4   _____/3

Notes/Observations:

Evaluation Chart: Grade 6 — Unit 6 Benchmark Test

Student Name _____ Date _____

Item	Tested Skill	Item Type*	Score (circle one)		
Reading – Parts 1–3					
Reading – Part 1: Comprehension					
1.	Compare and contrast	I	0	1	
2.	Compare and contrast	I	0	1	
3.	Draw conclusions	I	0	1	
4.	Cause and effect	I	0	1	
5.	Main idea and details	I	0	1	
6.	Compare and contrast	L	0	1	
7.	Compare and contrast	I	0	1	
8.	Generalize	C	0	1	
9.	Draw conclusions	I	0	1	
10.	Author's purpose	C	0	1	
11.	Literary elements: theme	C	0	1	
A.	Constructed-response text-to-world connection		0	1	2
12.	Draw conclusions	C	0	1	
13.	Compare and contrast	I	0	1	
14.	Compare and contrast	I	0	1	
15.	Draw conclusions	I	0	1	
16.	Sequence	I	0	1	
17.	Compare and contrast	L	0	1	
18.	Main idea and details	I	0	1	
19.	Fact and opinion	C	0	1	
20.	Author's purpose	C	0	1	
21.	Main idea and details	I	0	1	
22.	Draw conclusions	C	0	1	
B.	Constructed-response text-to-text connection		0	1	2
Reading – Part 2: Vocabulary					
23.	Context clues: multiple-meaning words		0	1	
24.	Context clues: unfamiliar words		0	1	
25.	Context clues: multiple-meaning words		0	1	
26.	Context clues: multiple-meaning words		0	1	
27.	Context clues: synonyms		0	1	
28.	Context clues: unfamiliar words		0	1	
29.	Context clues: unfamiliar words		0	1	

Reading – Part 2: Vocabulary (continued)		
30.	Context clues: multiple-meaning words	0 1
31.	Context clues: synonyms	0 1
32.	Context clues: unfamiliar words	0 1
Student's Regrouping Multiple-Choice Score/Total Possible Score		_____ /32
Reading – Part 3: Writing Conventions		
33.	Commas	0 1
34.	Quotations	0 1
35.	Commas	0 1
36.	Conjunctions	0 1
37.	Commas	0 1
38.	Commas	0 1
39.	Commas	0 1
40.	Conjunctions	0 1
Student's Reading Total Score/Total Possible Score		_____ /44

*L = literal   I = inferential   C = critical analysis

Regrouping (Reading — Parts 1–2) percentage score: _____ $\div$ 32 = _____ $\times$ 100 = _____%
                                      (student's score)   (percentage score)

Reading — Parts 1–3 percentage score: _____ $\div$ 44 = _____ $\times$ 100 = _____%
                               (student's total score)   (percentage score)

Writing – Part 4

Writing Score (complete one)   _____/6   _____/5   _____/4   _____/3

Notes/Observations:

Evaluation Chart: Grade 6 — End-of-Year Benchmark Test

Student Name _____ Date _____

Reading – Parts 1–3

Item	Tested Skill	Item Type*	Score (circle one)	Item	Tested Skill	Item Type*	Score (circle one)
Reading – Part 1: Comprehension				25.	Compare and contrast	I	0 1
1.	Literary elements: character	I	0 1	26.	Main idea and details	I	0 1
2.	Literary elements: setting	L	0 1	27.	Cause and effect	L	0 1
3.	Literary elements: character	I	0 1	28.	Graphic sources	I	0 1
4.	Literary elements: plot	C	0 1	29.	Author's purpose	C	0 1
5.	Sequence	I	0 1	30.	Sequence	L	0 1
6.	Draw conclusions	I	0 1	31.	Author's purpose	C	0 1
7.	Literary elements: character	I	0 1	32.	Graphic sources	I	0 1
8.	Cause and effect	I	0 1	33.	Graphic sources	I	0 1
9.	Draw conclusions	I	0 1	B.	Constructed-response text-to-text connection		0 1 2
10.	Literary elements: plot	C	0 1	**Reading – Part 2: Vocabulary**			
11.	Sequence	L	0 1	34.	Word structure: suffixes		0 1
12.	Fact and opinion	C	0 1	35.	Dictionary/glossary: unfamiliar words		0 1
13.	Author's purpose	C	0 1	36.	Dictionary/glossary: multiple-meaning words		0 1
14.	Sequence	I	0 1	37.	Context clues: unfamiliar words		0 1
15.	Generalize	C	0 1	38.	Word structure: prefixes		0 1
16.	Main idea and details	L	0 1	39.	Word structure: prefixes		0 1
17.	Cause and effect	L	0 1	40.	Word structure: base words		0 1
18.	Draw conclusions	C	0 1	41.	Context clues: homonyms		0 1
19.	Main idea and details	C	0 1	42.	Context clues: synonyms		0 1
20.	Compare and contrast	I	0 1	43.	Context clues: synonyms		0 1
21.	Draw conclusions	C	0 1	44.	Context clues: unfamiliar words		0 1
22.	Main idea and details	I	0 1	45.	Dictionary/glossary: multiple-meaning words		0 1
A.	Constructed-response text-to-text connection		0 1 2	46.	Dictionary/glossary: multiple-meaning words		0 1
23.	Draw conclusions	I	0 1	47.	Word structure: prefixes		0 1
24.	Fact and opinion	C	0 1	48.	Word structure: base words		0 1

Reading – Part 3: Writing Conventions						
49.	Sentences	0 1	55.	Subject-verb agreement	0 1
50.	Compound and complex sentences	0 1	56.	Irregular verbs	0 1
51.	Action and linking verbs	0 1	57.	Possessive nouns	0 1
52.	Subject and object complements	0 1	58.	Quotation marks	0 1
53.	Irregular plural nouns	0 1	59.	Proper nouns and adjectives	0 1
54.	Comparative and superlative adjectives	0 1	60.	Pronouns	0 1
Student's Reading Total Score/Total Possible Score _____ **/64**					

*L = literal   I = inferential   C = critical analysis

Reading — Parts 1–3 percentage score: _____ ÷ 64 = _____ × 100 = _____%

                           (student's total score)   (percentage score)

Writing – Part 4

Writing Score (complete one) _____/6 _____/5 _____/4 _____/3

Notes/Observations:

Monitor Progress Passages

from

Sixth Grade Teacher's Editions

Name _____

Black Hills Adventure

Jim had been on more difficult bicycle rides than this, but Custer   12
State Park in South Dakota was still pretty strenuous. The rolling plains   24
were a nice break after the hard ride down from the Needles. His   37
sister Barb had loved the rock spikes and the magnificent view from the   50
Black Hills, but it was the open plains that caught Jim's imagination.   62
The grasses stood almost to his waist. They made a rustling sound in   75
the wind that filled his ears the way the endless sky seemed to make his   90
eyes feel too small.   94

This is incredible!" he exclaimed as they stopped next to a small   106
stream. The hills ahead were dotted with big, brown boulders. "Let's ride   118
up there!"   120

Barb agreed. The trail curved gently around the base of a hill,   132
blocking the boulders from sight. They rode quickly along the trail.   143
Then Jim came to a sudden stop.   150

"Those aren't rocks," he breathed. "They're bison!" Just fifty   159
yards ahead, a herd of the massive animals roamed the hillside.   170
From a distance, they had looked like boulders. Closer, they just   181
looked *gigantic*.   183

"This is close enough," Barb said. The bison were strong and   194
wild-looking. She stared at their curved black horns. "Let's get out   205
of here!"   207

Just as Jim started to argue, two males started snorting and driving   219
their giant foreheads together. Great clods of dirt flew in the air.   231
"Good idea," Jim said quickly. "Yes. Time to get going, like, now!"   243

MONITOR PROGRESS • Check Fluency

Old Yeller **49k**

A Night in the Desert

Mom paused and looked around. The sky overhead was turning from crimson to almost purple. The dark red sandstone of Utah's Capitol Reef National Park glowed in the fading sunlight. "We have to stop," she said with a long sigh as she turned to her daughter.

"What do you mean? We're certainly not going to spend the night out here, are we? That's impossible. We cannot do that!" Maggie exclaimed, startled and more than a little scared.

Maggie and her very athletic mom had hiked a considerable distance away from the trail into the dry hills. It had been Maggie's idea to keep climbing higher and higher to see the panoramic view of the desert below. All around were magnificent, wind-carved cliffs in countless shades of red, gray, tan, and brown that accentuated their beautiful folds and turns. The soft smell of juniper in the air made Maggie and her mom forget themselves in the afternoon sun. Soon, they were too far from the campground to return before night.

"It's much too dangerous to hike in the dark," Mom said. "If we stay here, it will be easy to find the trail in the morning. Besides, it is the smart thing to do. Imagine what would happen if one of us fell in the dark."

"But the temperature drops in the desert at night, and it will get too cold," Maggie protested. "We won't even be able to make a fire because we won't have enough wood."

Mom nodded in agreement. When Maggie shivered at the thought of spending the night, Mom gently squeezed her shoulder. "Don't worry, honey. We have plenty of water, and we have our raincoats in our packs. We'll huddle together and wait it out. Let's find someplace out of the wind before we lose the light."

They sat with their backs against a smooth sandstone wall. They heard the wind moaning through the canyon, but the air barely stirred in their sheltered place. Maggie counted falling stars in the brilliant night sky until she fell asleep with her head in Mom's lap.

Serving Breakfast at the Shelter

"How are you today, Mr. Jackson?" Sheila asked as she carried a   12
carton of plastic forks into the church basement. The twelve-year-old girl   23
flashed an open-hearted smile as she paused to wait for Mr. Jackson's   35
reply. He stood in a line of raggedly dressed people, part of a small   49
group anticipating a free breakfast at the homeless shelter.   58

"I feel fine this morning," Mr. Jackson answered with a grateful nod.   70
"Thanks for asking." He stood a little straighter, his posture just a tiny bit   84
more erect, and adjusted his tattered clothes as he returned her smile.   96

As the girl whirled away on her daily task, the old man glanced at a   111
younger man who stood, weary and uncomfortable, behind him. "There   121
goes a quality person," Mr. Jackson said, nodding at Sheila's retreating   132
back and glancing at the younger man to be sure he was attentive.   145
"She serves breakfast in this shelter every day, and she always has a   158
kind word ready, even for an old, down-on-his-luck man like me."   169

The younger man's eyes narrowed a little as he thought about it,   182
the hardships of his life making him generally suspicious. "I wonder   193
why," he said at last, finally consenting to add his portion of the   206
conversation.   217

"I asked her once," Mr. Jackson answered with an air of satisfaction,   228
as if he had been anticipating the question and had his reply always   242
ready at the tip of his tongue. "She just believes in helping folks."   244

MONITOR
PROGRESS

• Check Fluency

Mother Fletcher's Gift **79k**

Taking Time for What's Really Important

Grandma Miriam carried the mound of dirty laundry through the narrow living room, carefully stepping around her granddaughter Noemi. Noemi had just turned three years old and was intensely curious about many things. The little girl held a book upside down in her hands. Carefully, Noemi turned the book over and examined the pictures.

"Read this?" she asked her grandmother, her dark brown eyes hopeful and questioning.

Grandma Miriam smiled but shook her head regretfully. "I'm sorry, sweetheart," she answered, "but I can't right now. I have to get this laundry started, and then we've got to go to the grocery store. Maybe we can read something a little later on." She walked to the utility room, set the laundry basket on the floor, and then moved into the kitchen of the small house to check on the teakettle, which wasn't boiling yet.

She looked back into the living room, where little Noemi had dropped the book to one side and was now staring at the television instead. Grandma Miriam was reminded of her own children, now grown up, back when Miriam was younger and even busier than she was now. There had never seemed to be enough time for anything but the endless cycle of cleaning, shopping, cooking, and getting the kids ready for school. The years had flown by in a blur of coats flying on and off, without a clear memory of the days that had disappeared into the past.

The kettle whistled, and Miriam turned to shut off the stove. She untied her apron, hung it on a hook on the kitchen door, and then walked back into the living room. She sat on the floor with a grunt and picked up Noemi's book. The girl grinned and leaned against Grandma Miriam so she could see and listen at the same time.

"Let's read right now," Grandma Miriam said. "I can do the laundry later."

MONITOR PROGRESS • **Character and Theme**

Name _____

Fun Food from El Salvador

Fifty years ago you would not have been able to experience the   12
taste of a *pupusa* unless you traveled to the Central American country   24
of El Salvador. Now this luscious treat is popping up all across the   37
United States. A pupusa is a thick, heavy, corn dough disk. It looks   50
entirely different from the flat, crisp tortillas sold in American grocery 61
stores. Pupusas are thick because they are stuffed with other foods,   73
so they look like fat miniature cakes. Some are filled with cheese and   86
some with meat. Other fillings include squash, refried beans, and even   97
some flower buds. Americans are used to filling tortillas by just rolling or 109
folding other foods inside them. But pupusas are stuffed by building up   121
the dough around the filling so that there is no opening. The pupusa is   135
then fried in a pan until it is brown on both sides. Another way to think   151
of a pupusa is as a different kind of grilled cheese sandwich.   163

The first pupusas were created almost two thousand years ago by   174
the Pipil people who lived in what is now called El Salvador. How do   188
we know? Scientists found a village buried by a volcano's explosion   199
long ago. The ashes from the volcano preserved food as it was being   212
cooked. The food was pupusas.   217

El Salvador's best-known dish now has its own holiday.   226
November 13 is National Pupusa Day. That must be a great day for   239
eating everywhere in the country!   244

MONITOR PROGRESS • Check Fluency

Name _____

Life for a Teenage Girl in Cuba

Even though their countries have different forms of government, teenage girls in the United States and in Cuba are more similar than they are dissimilar. Both groups enroll in school, although in Cuba, girls are required to attend school only through the ninth grade. As in most U.S. communities, Cuban school is in session from September through June. In Cuba, each girl studies nine or ten subjects in a single day, as opposed to six or seven for American girls.

Like teenagers everywhere, Cuban girls enjoy a variety of entertainments after school. They might watch television or play softball or volleyball. Like girls in the United States, Cuban girls might follow their favorite soap operas. In Cuba, all of the major soap characters are teens. American teens are influenced by the commercials on TV and may buy products as a result in Cuba, no consumer products are advertised on television.

Cuban girls on a first date might attend a school function or neighborhood party, just like in the United States. A second date might be eating ice cream or seeing a movie, again like in the United States. But it is a rare Cuban parent who will allow a teenage girl to have a boyfriend before she is 15.

While American girls take driver's education to earn their licenses at age 16, Cuban girls must wait until they are 21. For enjoyment, many girls in Cuba go to the beach. They talk and listen to music from a tape recorder or car radio rather than an MP3 player. They love "island" and "Latin" music, like salsa, but, like many girls in the U.S., Cubans also enjoy American pop music and rap. Most Cuban girls love to dance, and for a small entrance fee, they can go to discos that are open just for teenagers. Dancing also takes place at almost all family parties, outside on the neighborhood streets, and, of course, at the beach. Whatever their differences, the average teenage girl likes to have fun and talk about her future.

All About Mountain Gorillas

Mountain gorillas are magnificent animals that live in the rain   10
forest highlands of East Africa. They are the largest of the three   22
types of great apes—orangutans, chimpanzees, and gorillas. Adult   31
males are about six feet tall and may weigh up to 500 pounds. Females   45
are smaller, standing four to five feet tall and weighing less than half as   59
much as grown males.   63

Like all gorillas, mountain gorillas are covered in thick black   73
hair. When a gorilla male is ten or eleven years old, the hair on his   88
back turns silver. These grown males are called "silverbacks." They   98
lead their family groups. They defend the females and young gorillas   109
from their only enemies—leopards and people. Almost unbelievably   118
strong, gorillas can easily protect their babies against leopards. Their   128
luck against people is not as good.   135

Of the three types of gorillas in the world, mountain gorillas are   147
in the most immediate danger of extinction—there are not even 700   159
of the animals left in the world. Their habitat has been destroyed,   171
and local poachers kill them. A silverback will defend his group   182
with his life. When someone wants to capture a baby, usually the   194
silverback and the baby's mother are killed first. This can destroy the   206
family group forever. With so few of the animals left in the wild, the   220
remaining populations are more precious than ever.   227

We have to save these marvelous animals! If we do not act soon,   240
they will be lost.   244

Name _____

Medicines from the Rain Forest

As rain forests disappear all over the world, one of the greatest tragedies is the possible new knowledge that is disappearing with them. Thousands of plants and animals may be gone before science even finds out what they are. Perhaps worst of all, some of those unknown plants could have medicinal properties that might save many human lives.

Many rare plants that can be used as medicine have already been discovered, and the vast majority of these plants have been found in tropical rain forests. The World Health Organization (WHO) has been studying these plants since May of 1978. The organization came up with a list of 20,000 plants that people have traditionally used to improve their health. Of these, the WHO studied 200 plants more closely. Everything science has learned about the medical uses of these plants makes researchers eager to discover more of them. The plants could be real lifesavers, even curing cancer!

One example is a tree often called "kamala." Every part of the kamala tree can be used to treat skin infections from parasites. Parts of the fruit can treat parasites in the intestines. Another tropical tree, called "tofu balsam" or "Peru balsam," is used to fight infections of many kinds. A third plant, called "red periwinkle," comes from the forests of Southeast Asia. It may help treat such cancers as leukemia and Hodgkin's lymphoma.

Altogether, hundreds of plants that can help fight diseases have been identified so far. Many have been clinically tested to see if they work. At least 30 rain forest plants have parts that can help relieve pain, from the Brazilian pepper tree to passionflowers and guavas. Tests have been done to prove the anti-cancer powers of at least 20 tropical plants. More than 35 different rain forest plants can be used to fight bacteria. The list goes on and on. Science has barely scratched the surface of this promising new field of study.

Considering the benefits that could come from rain forest plants, it is almost unbelievable that the rain forests themselves are being destroyed.

Borias, the Wonder Dog

When people think of service animals, they usually picture dogs   10
leading the blind. Dogs, though, are smart enough to help people in all   23
kinds of ways. Take the fine team of Borias and Tamandra, for example.   36
Borias is a large, loving seven-year-old German shepherd dog who   46
looks like he was made for police work. Tamandra is an active young   59
woman who must use a wheelchair to get around.   68

Borias was only nine weeks old when Tamandra brought him home.   79
The FBI had been testing Borias for work as a search dog, but they   93
decided Borias would make a great service dog instead because he   104
was so calm and patient. After only a week with Tamandra, this small   117
puppy had learned to pick up her car keys. Now he can unzip her   131
backpack and add or remove items, and he runs errands for her all over   145
her house. One day in the grocery store, Tamandra says, she cried out   158
because she could not find her wallet. Instantly Borias dashed from her   170
side and soon returned, wagging proudly and carrying her wallet in his   182
mouth. Because Borias is so smart and gentle, Tamandra has trained   193
him to assist others as well. He passed the therapy-dog test so he can   207
visit elderly people confined to nursing homes, and some schools invite   218
Borias to visit so children can read aloud to him.   228

Tamandra says Borias not only makes her life easier, but he also   240
enables her to reach out to others. Doesn't he seem perfect?   251

MONITOR PROGRESS   • Check Fluency   *Hachiko* **169k**

Working Dogs of Alaska

Imagine yourself at 55 pounds pulling an 800-pound load while running. That sounds impossible! People cannot, but for an Alaskan sled dog, it's easy. Sled dogs are one of the best dogs. They have been used for ages by people in arctic areas to help make life easier in cold and snow. The Gold Rush of 1896 meant that more of these dogs were needed for transportation and to get supplies to the mining camps. Modern sled dogs came from many different kinds of dogs. Most look like the huskies you may have seen.

Some people believe that sled dogs are small because at that size the lungs, heart, and muscles get blood and oxygen more easily. But the right size alone is not enough to make a sled dog. People who work with these dogs think that curiosity and a desire to pull are most important. Still, it takes months of training to get a dog ready to be on a sled team. During races, sled dogs eat about six times as much as an ordinary dog.

When airplanes were developed, people thought they did the jobs of sled dogs better. However, an historic event in 1925 proved that sled dogs can, at critical times, be more valuable than airplanes. In the town of Nome, there was an epidemic of diphtheria, a serious illness that could take the lives of many children if they didn't get the right medicine. The closest place to get this medicine was the town of Nenana, 674 miles away. The problem was that it was 40 degrees below zero, and no one could safely fly a plane in that severe cold. Also, a plane crash would mean that all the medicine would be lost. The solution was to use dogsleds. The journey came to be called "The Great Race of Mercy to Nome." More than 100 dogs and 20 drivers were needed. In less than five-and-a-half days, the dogs made the dangerous journey and delivered the medicine. Today a famous dogsled race, The Iditarod, is held yearly along this same trail in honor of the mercy run.

MONITOR PROGRESS   • Fact and Opinion

Hachiko **169m**

Name _____

Is There Life on Mars?

There is only one place in the universe where we can say we know	14
with absolute certainty that life exists. That is on Earth. But for centuries	27
people have convinced themselves that living things might be found	37
on Mars.	39

Mars is smaller than Earth, but it is nearby. It is the closest planet to   54
our own and near enough in size to Earth to seem similar to us. It also   70
has an atmosphere that provides protection against the sun's brutal rays.   81

Most importantly, Mars seems to have water. For as long as people   93
have been able to observe details on the surface of the planet, we have   107
seen signs of erosion from flowing water. We know that there is ice at   121
the poles of Mars. There may be large amounts of ice frozen beneath   134
the surface of the planet. Scientists believe there could be "hot spots" on   147
the surface, like the hot pools at Yellowstone National Park, which could   159
support life. But no such spots have yet been found.   169

It may be that nothing has ever lived on Mars. Probes on the surface   183
have looked for signs of life in the soil. None have been found so far.   198
The planet is very cold, and the atmosphere is not rich with the gases   212
that living things on Earth need. And the lack of liquid water means life   226
as we know it on Earth could not survive on Mars.   237

But we will keep looking, and someday living things—people—will   248
visit the planet.   251

What Is a Black Hole?

They sound like something imaginary that a science fiction writer might make up, but scientists agree that they are real. A black hole is an invisible area in space that is so dense that nothing can escape the pull of its gravity. Its gravity is so strong that not even light can get away from it, which is why it is called a "black hole." Its density is infinite, with no limit. Yet it has no volume at all. Scientists call this a "singularity."

Black holes are the remains of stars. At the end of its life, a star with a mass that is at least ten or fifteen times greater than that of the sun may explode in a supernova. This may leave a large, burned-out remnant behind. Gravity makes this fall in on itself, so it becomes denser and denser. Finally, it is so dense that even the light rays it emits bend back inward. The edge where the black hole's gravity pulls in everything is called the "event horizon."

Many people believe wrongly that black holes are like giant vacuum cleaners in space, sucking up everything around them. This isn't true at all. In the first place, most black holes are quite small. The event horizon of a black hole that formed from a star the size of the sun would have a radius of only three kilometers, compared with the sun's radius of 700,000 km. If the sun suddenly became a black hole, Earth's orbit would not change. Only if you approached the event horizon would you be sucked into the black hole. Of course, you would plunge into the black hole at the speed of light!

Because no light escapes from a black hole, no one has ever actually seen one. Just the same, black holes can be detected in space. As matter is pulled into the black hole, it becomes so hot that it sends out X rays before it crosses the event horizon. We can detect these X rays as a jet that flows away from the black hole.

MONITOR PROGRESS   • Main Idea and Details

Name _____

Dressing for War

The soldiers of ancient China were like warriors everywhere in the   11
ancient world. They were caught up in an arms race. They needed to   24
cover their bodies with protective armor. On the one hand, they wanted   36
to obtain as much protection as they could from whatever weapons their   48
enemies were using. These could be swords, spears, clubs, rocks, or   59
arrows. But the soldiers also needed to be able to move without undue   72
effort. They needed to be able to use their own weapons. So armor   85
designers had to achieve a balance between maximum protection,   94
which meant very heavy, thick materials, and the need for light weight   106
and flexibility.   108

Chinese armor-makers tried to solve the problem with what is called   119
"lamellar-type" armor. This kind of armor is made of many small plates   131
that are sewn in overlapping layers. The pieces were attached to a vest   144
that covered the torso, shoulders, and upper arms. Although the vest   155
was heavy, the overlapping pieces of metal or stone would move with   167
the soldier's arms or torso. It would block the tip of an arrow, and a   182
sword would not cut through it. With a helmet to protect his head and   196
stiff boots for his lower legs, the soldier was as well protected as he   210
could be.   212

Of course, none of their armor would work against guns or   223
explosives. But at the time, their vests prevented arrows from killing the   235
soldiers just like Kevlar vests protect soldiers against bullets today.   245

Name _____

China's Last Emperor

The last emperor of China led what could be called an incredibly eventful life. His name was Puyi. He ruled under the name Xuantong. In addition to being China's last emperor, he may also have been its youngest. Born in 1906, he was an ordinary baby for fewer than three years. His great aunt Cixi was an extremely powerful woman who was basically the empress of China. Puyi's uncle was the ruler at the time, but Cixi really was the power behind the throne. When Puyi's uncle died in November 1908, Cixi selected Puyi to be the next emperor of the country. At the time, Cixi was seriously ill. She did not live to see Puyi ascend the throne on December 2, 1908, at the age of two years and ten months.

The tiny boy was introduced to his new role by officials who went to his house and dragged him screaming and crying to the palace, where he would now live. Puyi was accompanied to the throne by his nurse, and she was the only one who could console the young emperor.

The new emperor's reign was not peaceful. After just about three years, part of the army revolted. They demanded that China become a republic. In 1912, the young emperor was forced to give up the throne. In return, he was allowed to live in the palace as he had before he lost his title.

In 1917, a warlord restored the empire and put Puyi back on the throne, but only for a short while. Less than two weeks later, another warlord forced the emperor from power once again. In 1924, still another warlord threw Puyi out of China's capital. But Puyi had one last chance at power. After Japan invaded Manchuria in 1931, the Japanese made Puyi emperor of the conquered region in 1934. This time his reign name was Kangde. When Japan was defeated in World War II, Puyi was forced to give up his throne for the final time.

Name _____

Meet Sue the *Tyrannosaurus rex*

Standing at one end of the main hall of Chicago's Field Museum of   13
Natural History is a giant fossil of a *Tyrannosaurus rex* dinosaur. It is the   27
largest, most complete *T. rex* ever uncovered. It stands 13 feet tall at its   41
hips. From the tip of its monstrous, five-foot head to the end of its tail,   57
the entire dinosaur is 42 feet long. Almost all of the display is of the real   73
fossilized bones that were discovered in 1990. However, the skull is a   85
model. The real head is too heavy for the steel frame of the display to   100
hold it up. Visitors see the actual skull on a balcony above the hall.   114

The fossil is named "Sue" after the woman who found it. During the   127
summer of 1990, an amateur fossil hunter named Susan Hendrickson   137
was working with a team of fossil hunters near the town of Faith, South   151
Dakota. On August 12, most of the team left the area where they were   165
searching for fossils to fix a flat tire on their truck. Susan stayed behind   179
to search in some nearby sandstone bluffs. She found some small fossil   191
bones on the ground and searched the cliff overhead. Sticking out were   203
three very large bones from a *T. rex* that had died and been buried in   218
mud some 67 million years earlier.   224

No one knows if Sue was a male or female dinosaur, but the name   238
is here to stay.   242

Name _____

What Tree Rings Tell Us

If you want to know about a region's climate, ask a tree. Yearly changes in climate conditions are recorded in a tree's rings. Those rings can also show how old the tree is because a new ring is added every year. The rings are a result of the way trees grow, with a new layer of wood added each year under the bark. New growth in the spring is made up of larger cells. The cells that grow in the fall are smaller. One ring is made up of a light (spring) band and a dark (fall) band. This makes a clear line between years.

The study of tree rings is called *dendrochronology*, from *dendro*, meaning "trees," and *chronology*, which means "time." If you know the year a tree was felled, you can find its age simply by totaling the rings. But the rings reveal a more complex story than just age. An abundance of rain means good growing conditions. At these times, a tree's new cells are larger, and the rings are wider. Dry years are followed by two or three narrower rings.

What else can tree rings tell us? We can find a calendar of forest fires because scars from fires show up in the rings. We can also see how the weather patterns we have recorded compare with weather patterns in the past because many trees live for a long time.

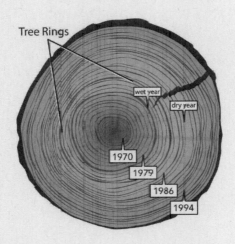

Tree Rings

wet year

dry year

1970

1979

1986

1994

MONITOR PROGRESS   • Graphic Sources

Name _____

Temperature Derby: Earth vs. the Moon

Unlike Earth, the moon has no atmosphere. Without an atmosphere,   10
it can have no weather. However, that doesn't mean its surface doesn't   22
have a constantly changing environment. Quite to the contrary,   31
conditions on the moon can change considerably. On Earth, the   41
atmosphere acts like the roof of a greenhouse, trapping the energy from   53
the sun. This helps maintain temperatures at the surface in a range that   66
will support life. No matter how uncomfortably hot or cold you may feel   79
at different times of the year, Earth's temperatures always fall within a   91
relatively narrow band. On the moon, the opposite is true.   101

Every day, the surface temperature on the moon ranges from an   112
average of 101° Centigrade (214° Fahrenheit) to –184°C (–300°F),   121
depending on whether or not sunlight is striking the surface. That means   133
you could go from heat great enough to boil water to cold intense   146
enough to freeze you solid simply by stepping into a shadow.   157

On Earth, on the other hand, the average temperatures are much   168
more moderate. Even the extremes on Earth come nowhere near   178
the daily temperatures on the moon. The highest temperatures ever   188
recorded on Earth were 58°C (136°F) at El Azizia, Libya, in 1932 and   201
57°C (134°F) in the United States' Death Valley in 1913. The coldest   213
temperature ever recorded on Earth's surface was –89°C (–129°F) at   223
Vostok, Antarctica, in 1983. Compared to the moon, that temperature   233
is balmy!   235

Name _____

Tapping the Power of the Sun

Solar energy is the fuel that has always powered life on Earth. Plants use the power of sunlight to make their own food through photosynthesis. As plants produce food, animals eat plants, so sunlight feeds animals as well as plants. What's more, without the sun, plants could not make oxygen, which animals need to breathe. Without solar energy, we would not exist!

Today, the world faces growing energy shortages and pollution problems. For help, we are turning more and more to a clean source of power that will never be used up. Solar energy is free and causes no air pollution. In contrast, oil, gas, and coal must be taken from the ground, and all produce pollutants when they are burned. Solar energy will be around as long as the sun continues to shine, but fossil fuels will eventually be used up. Finally, many solar energy systems that individuals can use are able to stand alone. There is no need to be connected to a supply source like pipes or wires.

People have been heating their homes with solar energy for thousands of years. The ancient Greeks arranged their houses so the sun would heat them in the winter. Today, special glass is used to achieve the same goal.

Photovoltaic solar cells use sunlight to directly generate electricity. Another option is to concentrate the sun's rays to produce heat to drive turbine generators that work like ordinary power plants.

Home water is usually heated with electricity or a flame. Solar power can heat water in pipes on, say, a roof. Hot water then costs nothing to produce, and no pollution is created.

In the United States, we usually cook food on electric or gas stoves. For us, solar cooking isn't really necessary. But in other parts of the world, where people may cook over a campfire, solar cookers are a great idea. They save money, and no trees need to be cut down. No pollution from burning wood is added to the air. Of course, the cookers can only be used when the sun is shining.

Beware the Dead Queen's Curse!

Marissa stood nervously stamping her feet on the limestone in   10
the cold air. This morning she would finally enter the unknown   21
pharaoh's tomb. She should be excited. Instead, she was filled   31
with a sense of dread.   36

The treasure Marissa hoped to find was for archaeology   45
rather than wealth. She was a scientist who did not believe in   57
curses. Just the same, the warning hidden in the strange writing   68
outside the tomb had unsettled her.   74

Any unopened tomb was dangerous, with risks from poisonous   83
gases, collapsing walls or tunnels, and pitfalls and blind turns   93
designed by the original builders. Those were the sorts of threats   104
Marissa was usually worried about. So why was the inscription   114
promising a horrific fate for anyone who violated this mysterious   124
queen's grave causing such fear in her? The cryptic glyphs at   135
the entrance indicated that this queen had returned to life at   146
least three times, always with terrible consequences for those who   156
disturbed her rest. Perhaps it was the tomb's location. Hidden far   167
from the other gravesites in the Valley of the Kings, the stone   179
slab that sealed this entrance was like nothing Marissa had ever   190
seen. The measurements she had made showed that the doorway   200
led into a tunnel that dove deep beneath the cliffs.   210

"Something about this just feels wrong," she muttered. But   219
she pressed the hidden release and held her breath as, with a   231
grinding sound, the rock began to slide.   238

MONITOR PROGRESS • Check Fluency

The Nile

For most of us, Africa's Nile River is wrapped in myth and magic.   13
We picture Cleopatra and other ancient Egyptian rulers floating on   23
golden ships as the great river rolls to the sea. The Nile is more than   38
just a character in Egypt's storied past, though. It has been the country's 51
lifeline for more than 5,000 years.   57

The Nile, which flows from south to north, is the world's longest   69
river at nearly 4,200 miles. Not one, but two, great civilizations arose   81
on the banks of the Nile—Nubia and ancient Egypt. Almost all of the   95
commerce of these two empires was conducted on the Nile. And every   107
year, between June and September, the river's floods restored the farms   118
along its banks. Even the ancient Egyptian calendar was based on the   130
river's flood cycle.   133

To this day, the Nile remains an invaluable resource for this desert   145
country. The Aswan Dam, built in the 1960s, now controls the river's   157
flood cycles and harnesses its power. Hydroelectric power stations at   167
the dam provide most of the country's electricity. Today, more than 100   179
million people reside along its banks, most of them in Egypt.   190

MONITOR PROGRESS   • Graphic Sources   *Egypt* **323m**

First Solo Flight

Eddie held his hands comfortably on the controls, his grip tight   11

but not taut. He listened to the muted roar of the small plane's engine.   25

He glanced through the side windows and kept his cockpit "sterile,"   36

speaking to no one while he was taxiing. "If you're going to collide   49

with something, odds are it will be while you taxi," his instructor had   62

often repeated.   64

Eddie glanced at the windsock and adjusted his ailerons for a   75

crosswind. As the tower gave him clearance, Eddie rolled faster and   86

faster down the runway. Then he pulled back on the controls and slid   99

effortlessly into the air. He was flying solo at last!   109

He checked the instruments every now and then, but he kept his   121

eyes on the distant edge of the horizon to avoid motion sickness.   133

As he circled above the field, he realized he was grinning so   145

intensely that his cheeks ached. Flying was the best feeling in the   157

world! He had spent many hours in the air, but never alone at the   171

controls like this afternoon. It was amazing how different it felt to be   184

in total control. Eddie wished it would never end, but he had promised   197

to make his first solo flight brief. After just 15 minutes, he adjusted the   211

elevators and ailerons and then used both feet on the rudder pedals to   224

line up with the center line of the runway as he eased the aircraft back   239

onto the ground.   242

MONITOR PROGRESS   • Check Fluency   *Hatchet* **359k**

Name _____

Lost in the Woods

Just off the trail you spot an unusual bird and take a few steps in its direction, but it flits to another tree. You follow, but suddenly the trail has disappeared behind you, and you're living every hiker's worst nightmare. What should you do to rediscover your path? First, remember the acronym S.T.O.P., which reminds you to first *sit*, next *think*, then *observe*, and finally *plan*. Following this method will help you avoid panic. After you calm down, think about the direction of your original route. If it is a sunny day, you can use a stick to check your current orientation. Find a level place where a shadow can be cast. Put a meter-long stick in the ground, look for the shadow, and mark the shadow's tip on the ground. About 15 minutes later, mark the shadow tip again. A line between the two marks will be an east-west pointer where the first mark will always be at the western end. Now stand at the second mark and face the first mark. (You'll be facing west.) Turn your head to the right, and you'll be looking north.

Suppose, though, that the sun is setting and the moon is rising. The lighted side of the moon will always point to the west early in the night. But if the time of the moon's rising is after midnight, the east side of the moon will be illuminated.

Next, study the stars. Pick out the brightest star in the handle of the "Little Dipper" constellation (also called *Ursa Minor*). This is Polaris, the North Star, and if you're facing it, you're also facing north.

Observing vegetation can help a little. You may have heard that moss only grows on a tree's north side. This legend is false because moss grows all the way around a tree, and it will be thicker and bushier on the side of the tree that faces the equator.

Of course, you can remember to bring a compass. Then all you have to do is check it! Use any of these methods to retrace your steps, and then you can continue your hike in your original direction.

MONITOR PROGRESS   • Sequence

Hatchet **359m**

Arthur Ashe

If you grow up on the grounds of a park with four tennis courts, 14
three baseball diamonds, and a pool, chances are that athletics will 25
figure in your future. That was the case for Arthur Ashe, who was 38
born in 1943 and became the first African American ever to excel 50
internationally in professional tennis. 54

Ashe began playing tennis when he was just six. He was 65
exceptionally good at it. He studied under a coach who believed that 77
showing respect, being well-groomed, and never cheating were the 86
hallmarks of good sportsmanship. 90

In 1960, Ashe won the National Interscholastics tournament. This 99
earned him a scholarship to UCLA. He won several championships and 110
led UCLA to the college title in 1965. Before beginning his professional 122
career, he served his country for two years in the army. He followed that 136
with a successful effort to create a national tennis program in America's 148
inner cities. Today that program includes over 150,000 kids. 157

In 1973, Ashe became the only African American man to win the 169
singles championship at Wimbledon and be ranked first in the world. 180
Six years and many successes later, Ashe suffered a heart attack. But he 193
didn't stop working to help others. He developed foundations to foster 204
minority athletes, help poor children, and stop substance abuse. 213

After Ashe died in 1993, the stadium at the National Tennis Center 225
in New York was named after this remarkable athlete. 234

MONITOR PROGRESS   • Check Fluency   *When Marian Sang* **389k**

The Marian Anderson Award

In 1998, five years after Marian Anderson died at age 96, a group of people in Philadelphia created the Marian Anderson Award to honor her memory. The award is given to an artist "whose leadership on behalf of a humanitarian cause or issue benefits society." The prize makes sense because Anderson was not only admired for her beautiful voice but she was also well-known for helping others.

The Marian Anderson Award was designed with two main goals. First, it underlines the importance of the arts in all of our lives. Second, it recognizes the work and commitment of a distinguished individual who has not only used his or her talent for artistic expression but has also worked toward the betterment of all people.

In keeping with its objectives, the award has these three programs:

1. The Marian Anderson Award recognizes the humanitarian work of a great artist.

2. The Marian Anderson Prize for Emerging Classical Artists recognizes the talents of a young musical artist from Pennsylvania, New Jersey, and Delaware—the states around Philadelphia.

3. The Marian Anderson Art Study-Grant Program provides financial assistance to gifted young artists from the Greater Philadelphia area. It helps high school-aged artists develop their talent.

There are only two requirements for an artist to be eligible to receive the Marian Anderson Award. First, he or she must be a critically acclaimed artist. Second, he or she must be a leader in a cause or issue that is not directly related to his or her performing career.

Since 1998, the award has been given out every year, with the exception of 2004. Almost all of the recipients have been actors, musical performers, or others connected to the entertainment industry, including such people as Harry Belafonte, Oprah Winfrey, Elizabeth Taylor, and Sidney Poitier. In 2008, writer and poet Maya Angelou was honored. It was the first time a writer had ever received the award. Angelou once eloquently described Anderson's voice as "notes of melted silver on lace." When she was given the award, Angelou defined it with just one word: "Humbling."

MONITOR PROGRESS • Generalize

Crossing the English Channel

Many obstacles stood in the way of Gertrude Ederle's dream of   11
swimming across the English Channel, but on August 6, 1926, she   22
became the first woman to complete the feat, shattering the previous   33
record holder's time.   36

Ederle was born in New York City on October 23, 1906. A bout   49
of childhood measles caused her to lose some of her hearing. Doctors   61
warned her that swimming would worsen her condition, but she refused   72
to stay out of the pool. In fact "Trudy," as she was called, became a   87
competitive swimmer and started breaking records at the age of 12.   98

In 1924, she competed in the Olympics in Paris, France, where   109
she took home a gold and two bronze medals. The following year,   121
she made her first attempt at swimming the 21-mile distance across the   133
channel. Nine miles into her swim, however, Ederle was disqualified. A   144
trainer, who thought Gertrude was drowning, reached out to save her,   155
breaking the rule against any physical contact with another person.   165

Ederle set out again a year later, from Cape Griz-Nez, France.   176
Undeterred by choppy seas and strong winds that drove her miles   187
off course, she reached Kingsdown, England, in just 14 hours   197
31 minutes—nearly 2 hours less than the standing record. Ederle's   208
record held for almost 25 years.   214

By the 1940s, just as doctors had predicted, Ederle completely lost   225
her hearing. Following this loss, Ederle began training a new generation   236
of athletes. She taught swimming to deaf children at a New York City   249
school for many years. Ederle passed away on November 30, 2003,   260
at age 97, but her well-earned fame continues to inspire young athletes   272
everywhere.   273

MONITOR PROGRESS   • Check Fluency   *Learning to Swim* **419k**

Name _____

The History of Muscle Beach

In southern California near the town of Venice, you can visit a sandy stretch along the Pacific Ocean with the odd name of Muscle Beach. Today it is a place where people gather to work out, climb ropes, and lift weights. They also play basketball. However, this is not how Muscle Beach started.

It began during the Great Depression just two miles north in the town of Santa Monica. There, the government's Works Progress Administration built platforms as a place for people to gather. Soon, however, the area was filled every day with circus acrobats, movie stuntmen, tumblers, and gymnasts. If you happened to be visiting the beach back then, you would have seen a free show that would have cost several dollars at a circus. Throughout the 1930s, 1940s, and early 1950s, physically fit men and women somersaulted and built human towers. Weightlifting meant strong men lifting pretty girls instead of barbells. Some of the sights included a water-skiing elephant, a trumpet player making music with one hand and lifting a dumbbell with the other, and the world's first female weightlifter.

Some of the early professionals in the physical fitness movement got their start at Muscle Beach. Jack LaLanne and Vic Tanney went on to have television shows, exercise books, and national health clubs.

In the 1950s, the city of Santa Monica began charging dues of $3.00 per year to take control of beach activities. Supervision was added, and the Muscle Beach Weightlifting Club was formed with 500 members. Money from dues allowed the club to buy Olympic weightlifting equipment and fence the space. Still, city officials worried they couldn't control the activities and the crowds.

In 1959, Muscle Beach was moved down the coast to a smaller area in Venice. The new Muscle Beach focused on bodybuilding. It attracted bodybuilders like Steve Reeves, who went on to become the original television "Superman" actor, and Arnold Schwarzenegger, a movie star, and later, governor of California. Today Muscle Beach is thought of as a family recreation center. Only memories of its golden years remain.

MONITOR PROGRESS   • Sequence

Maya Wonders

One of the greatest civilizations in the history of the world flourished   12
over 500 years ago in Central America. The Maya lived from Mexico   24
south to Honduras. Some of their beautiful cities are found in Mexico's   36
Yucatan area. We have learned a lot about the Maya from the remains   49
of those cities.   52

The Maya were some of the world's greatest astronomers, and they   63
were great architects. They built large towns of stone, with temples,   74
courts, and giant pyramids rising above the thick tropical rain forest.   85
They were such skilled builders that some of their buildings can be   97
used as calendars. Some show exactly where stars, like Venus, rise at   109
different times of year.   113

One of the most famous Mayan buildings is the Pyramid of Kukulcan   125
at Chichén Itzá, in the Yucatan. It is dedicated to the Feathered Serpent,   138
Kukulcan. The building is also called El Castillo, or "the Castle." It   150
includes many symbols related to the Mayan calendar. Each of the four   162
sides has 91 stairs. Combined with the central platform at the top, these   175
represent the 365 days of the year. Statues of the Feathered Serpent go   188
down the sides of the northern stairway. On the days of the spring and   202
autumn equinoxes, these snakes "come to life." As the sun sets on those   215
two days, shadows form a diamond pattern, like a snake's scales. As   227
the sun goes down, the snake slowly slithers down into the earth.   239

MONITOR PROGRESS   • Check Fluency   *Juan Verdades* **447k**

Name _____

Riding the Range: Past and Present

If a cattle rancher from the 1850s was suddenly transported into the present day, he or she would scarcely recognize the industry. Ranchers from bygone years might conclude that the only thing that was the same was the cattle.

Early ranching was done on open grazing lands, where pastures weren't owned by individual ranchers. A "ranch" was just a headquarters shack on open range, and the cattle were nearly wild. To deliver their cattle to the markets, ranchers drove the herds to railroad stations, which means that cowboys riding horses walked along as the cattle ate their way across open range. The key to favorable grazing for cattle herds was water. Even as ranchers began to buy up large sections of land, having a good water supply was the key to their success.

To keep track of their stock, ranchers branded calves with red-hot irons. This left a mark on the animal's hide that made its ownership clear. Cowboys on horseback rounded up young calves, roped the animals, tied their feet together, and held them down while they were branded. You can see the basic technique today at a rodeo in the calf-roping competition.

Today, a rancher might own a few horses, but they aren't used to drive or round up cattle. If a rancher now needs to check fences in far-flung parts of the ranch, he or she jumps into a pickup truck or rides an all-terrain vehicle. A modern ranch has miles and miles of barbed wire enclosing good pastures. Water supplies are regulated, and hay to feed the cattle probably is raised on the ranch. The ranch has lots for the cattle and chutes to load the animals into trucks, which the rancher might also own. From the ranch cattle are taken to feedlots where they eat corn.

Cattle today are branded with electric branding irons, and helicopters may be used to drive the herds into corrals. Computers are used to manage the ranch and to check prices. Even more amazing to a rancher from 150 years ago, today's ranch might raise zebras, bison, or ostriches instead of cattle!

Chess Parks

Old "Abuelo Horace," as everyone called Horace Gonzales, was   9
practically purple with rage. Horace was a fixture in San Antonio's   20
downtown parks, and no one had ever seen him angry before. And it   33
had been prompted by a sudden thunderstorm.   40

Almost every Tuesday, Horace and his best friend, Manny, met   50
near the riverfront to play long, intense chess games. Horace carried   61
a folding chair in one hand and a cardboard chessboard in the other,   74
his pockets bulging with chess pieces. Manny carried two more folding   85
chairs, one to be used as a table. Thanks to San Antonio's typically   98
sunny weather, the games were uneventful. But today, the downpour   108
had destroyed the chessboard. Horace stamped away and was not   118
seen again for two weeks.   123

When Horace reappeared, he and Manny were pushing a   132
wheelbarrow. In it was a stone chessboard made of marble and granite   144
tile scraps. Horace had glued the pieces onto a slab from a stone   157
countertop. Also in the wheelbarrow were four iron pipes and a handful   169
of bolts.   171

Horace and Manny drove the pipes into the ground. They bolted   182
the chessboard to the top. Horace took their usual pieces from his   194
pockets, and they sat down to play. Soon a crowd gathered, and   206
envious chess players who admired the outdoor board demanded   215
permanent chessboards of their own.   220

And that's how "chess parks" came to be located in cities   231
throughout America. At least, that's what Horace's grandchildren insist.   240

MONITOR PROGRESS   • Check Fluency   *Morning Traffic* **479k**

Toni's Tough Decision

Toni Marcone was as perplexed as she had ever been. She had been offered not one but two jobs for the summer. Now she was in a quandary about which to select. Since Toni was going to summer school, her mother had insisted that the teenager accept only one of the options.

Her neighbor, Marcus Robbins, needed assistance every day, and he was willing to pay handsomely for it. All Toni had to do was ride the Robbinses' mower around their yard for two boring hours, or weed the lawn, or mulch the garden for about half of each day. Toni knew the job would be tedious, but the pay would be good enough to buy a new wardrobe. It was almost impossible to turn it down.

Yet her second opportunity was so appealing that she felt she would hate herself if she didn't grab it. Leah Tompkins was going to be away the entire summer, and she needed someone to give her horse, Brandy, daily exercise. It was Toni's dream job! Every morning, before the day's heat rose, she would ride her bike to the stable, walk Brandy, then saddle her for a quick trot or a good run, whichever Toni wanted. If someone had asked Toni to describe what she would most like to do with her summer vacation, she could hardly have come up with a more attractive plan. There was just one problem, and it was a big one: the job paid nothing at all. She would be doing it partially as a favor for Leah, mainly as a pleasure for herself.

Now, she had to decide. If she agreed to take care of Brandy, it would be a commitment she could not shirk. Leah would be counting on her. At the end of the summer, she would be happy but unable to afford new clothing. If she helped Mr. Robbins, she would earn a lot of money over the course of the summer, but she would miss what felt like a once-in-a-lifetime opportunity.

"What should I do?" she wailed as she flopped onto her bed.

MONITOR PROGRESS • Draw Conclusions

Morning Traffic **479m**

Name _____

Penguins On the Move

In the heart of Antarctica's incredibly harsh winter, when   9
temperatures fall as low as –100°F (–73°C), the world's largest   21
penguins, the emperors, begin to lay their eggs. And these birds that 33
depend entirely on the sea lay their eggs far from open water, leading 46
to an amazing trek through one of Earth's worst climates.   56

Emperor penguins stand nearly four feet tall. Like all penguins, they 67
are designed for swimming with their powerful wings. As graceful as   78
they are in the water, they are equally ungainly on land, walking very 91
awkwardly. Yet parent birds walk as much as 50 miles in one direction 104
to feed their chicks.   108

Female emperors lay one egg. The male immediately rests the egg   119
on his feet, covering it with a flap of skin at the base of his belly. To 136
keep warm in the bitter winter wind, the males all huddle together in 149
a large mass.   152

While the males incubate the eggs, the females march off to the sea 165
for a hunting trip that might last two months. Because it is winter, the 179
sea ice extends far from land. The females trudge many miles to reach 192
open water. They feed for weeks before making the return trip. By now, 205
they may have to walk 50 miles to reach the colony. When they finally 219
arrive, the starving males set out in search of food, leaving the females 232
to feed and care for the newborn chicks.   240

Name _____

Up Close to the Giants of the Sea

You stand on the ship's deck looking across the quiet ocean waters of Alaska's Glacier Bay when a geyser seems to burst in front of you, causing you to lift your binoculars to your eyes. The fountain of water is interrupted by a long black back breaking the surface. A giant fin follows, and then, just as quickly, the creature dives, and its 15-feet-wide flukes stand above the water for a moment before disappearing. You have just experienced the thrill of whale-watching.

The most common whales seen during Alaska whale-watching are either humpback whales or orcas. Your boat will head toward the places where they feed for a few months each year. One of the most interesting feeding habits of humpback whales is called the bubble net. Think of how you may have tried blowing bubbles underwater while you were swimming or even in the bathtub. The humpbacks do this while swimming in a wide circle around a school of fish. When the bubbles rise up, they create a kind of net that forces the fish to move into a tight bunch. As a result, the whales are able to push forward into the ball of fish with their mouths open and gobble up enormous meals.

Salmon is a favorite food of orcas, sometimes inaccurately called "killer whales." Each year during the time salmon lay their eggs, they swim through the waters in huge numbers. The effect of this salmon run is that orca pods show up to eat them.

Whale-watching may be affecting whale pods, groups of female whales and their babies. Each pod has its own series of songs used to "talk" to one another. A pod's favorite call might sound like a kitten or even a whistle. Scientists have found that the pods' calls get longer when there are a lot of whale-watching boats around. They believe that the boats create so much noise underwater that the orcas need longer songs to be heard by one another, just as you sometimes have to shout when there is too much noise.

Saving the Whooping Crane

Trong clearly remembered the first time he saw a whooping crane. It   12
was back in 1995 at the Arkansas National Wildlife Refuge on the Gulf   25
Coast of Texas. Who could miss such a sight? The bird was more than   39
five feet tall and bright white, with huge wings with black tips, a long,   53
slim neck, and a long, sharp, narrow yellow bill. Even if it had not had   68
red splashes of feathers on its forehead and cheeks, Trong would never   80
have forgotten the bird.   84

When he learned that the bird was critically endangered, Trong   94
decided to dedicate himself to helping save the species. He learned that   106
in the 1940s fewer than 20 whooping cranes survived. The tiny flock   118
made a yearly journey between their nesting grounds in Canada and   129
Texas. Thanks to the efforts of many dedicated people, the flock grew   141
to more than 180 birds by year 2000, but they all lived in the same   156
places, just Canada and Texas.   161

Trong joined the effort to introduce another flock of migrating   171
whooping cranes. After years of study, scientists created a flock in   182
southern Wisconsin. Trong traveled north to help. Because Trong knew   192
how to fly an ultralight plane, he joined the team that would guide   205
young cranes on their flight to Florida. They led the birds on a 1,200-mile   220
trip in the fall, and the cranes returned to Wisconsin in the spring. At last,   235
there was real hope that the species would be saved.   245

Why You Should Adopt a Dog or Cat

In a small animal shelter, a nine-year-old dog sits inside a small wire cage, forlornly waiting for its master to somehow rescue it from this terrifying place. But no one ever comes. This little dog's owner was elderly and ill and is unable to have a pet in the continuing-care facility where she now lives. Now, if the dog does not find a new home soon, its fate is assured.

Every day across America, homeless dogs and cats roam the streets, and every day across America some people decide they no longer want or no longer can care for their pets. Consequently, every day across America thousands of animals are euthanized—put to sleep. The Humane Society of America says that half of the eight to ten million cats and dogs in shelters last year were destroyed, which means that five million animals lost their lives because no one could give them a home.

Deciding to get a pet means you first need to consider your reasons. When your family gets a pet for the household, in many ways it is like adding a new brother or sister. The pet will need food, a place to sleep, and care and love every day for years to come. Pets are not just things we own. They should be part of the family. Why not give your family's love to a stray, abused, or homeless animal that so very much needs your love and attention?

Sure, you could pay hundreds of dollars for a purebred dog. But for a small donation, you could instead find a cute, loving animal in any shape or size in the many shelters located in or near your town. You would be helping that shelter meet its responsibility to find homes for pets. You would be making room in the shelter for another homeless dog or cat. And most importantly, you would be saving a life. That special dog or cat, puppy or kitten is looking longingly out of a cage right now, hoping someone will walk through the door and say, "Yes, we are going home together."

The Boys Stake a Claim

Robinson looked up at his partner, Billings, dirt falling from the 11
rough flannel of his shirt sleeves. He beamed enthusiastically as he 22
displayed the dented metal grid in his muddy hands. "I think we've 34
found our mother lode," Robinson said, his teeth flashing a broad grin 46
in the late-afternoon sun, his excited voice trembling with joy. 56

"Let me see," Billings answered, his eyes eager for the sight of 68
gold in the sifting tray. There it was, a bright nugget in the gravel 82
in the tray, gleaming its message of riches to the weary eyes of the 96
weather-worn men. 98

They leaped away from their trench with a whoop and danced a jig 111
together, dust flying around them. Then they immediately got to work, 122
staking their claim. 125

Billings drove a stake into the ground where they stood. It would 137
be the "discovery monument" that the law required. A lode claim 148
can be 1,500 feet long and 600 feet wide, so Billings and Robinson 161
paced along the path of the vein of quartz they had found. They each 175
walked 750 feet and put a marker stake in the ground. Then each man 189
marched 300 feet to the corner of their claim. 198

Robinson posted a "notice of location" at one end of the claim, and 211
they were ready to file their claim in town. "But first," he said, "let's buy 226
a really fine meal to celebrate." 232

Billings agreed, but with one condition: "I want a good hot 243
bath first." 245

MONITOR PROGRESS • Check Fluency

Name _____

The Final Spikes

James Washington wiped the sweat from his forehead and squinted in the morning sunlight. He was proud to be a part of this historic day, May 10, 1869, when the last pairs of long steel rails would be laid. The Atlantic and Pacific Oceans would at last be connected by the railroad.

Washington had been with the huge task almost from the very beginning. He had baked in the summer sun laying track west from Omaha, Nebraska, for the Union Pacific Railroad. At the same time, another team of workers for the Central Pacific Railroad cut through the mountains from California. Washington remembered blasting away a track bed in the cliffs of the mountains. Many men perished as a result of the harsh working conditions in the mountains.

Now, at Promontory in Utah, the tracks would finally be joined. The effect would be instantaneous: the time it took to travel from coast to coast across America would be instantly reduced from months to about a week, starting this morning.

As the last 100 feet of the track were placed, it seemed that everyone wanted to be a part of it. One man borrowed Washington's shovel and threw some dirt onto the track bed. "I want to be able to say I helped finish the transcontinental railroad," the man said to Washington. Washington, who really had helped, just smiled.

When the rails were almost in contact, the presidents of the railroad companies and the governors of the western states all began to make speeches. They went on and on, and Washington nearly fell asleep three times. Governors from different states had brought spikes of gold and silver to be the final spikes holding the rails in place. The governor of California, also the president of Central Pacific, went first. He swung the hammer and missed. A huge laugh went up from the crowd. Then a vice president of the Union Pacific Railroad also missed his spike. Men fell down laughing.

But Washington just bowed his head, awestruck by what had been accomplished with his help.

MONITOR PROGRESS • **Cause and Effect**

Black Frontiers **109m**

Name _____

Swimming With the "Red Devils"

Of the hundreds of species of squid in the world, it is impossible to   14

pick the one that is the most interesting. Every one is a carnivore that   28

has no bones but a skeleton of cartilage. Each has a large head with a   43

large brain and may be very smart. All squid have eight arms covered   56

with suckers near their mouths plus two longer tentacles that have rows   68

of suckers with razor-sharp hooks for grabbing prey. They tear their   79

food apart with powerful jaws that are shaped like the beak of a parrot.   93

The smallest known squid is less than one inch (0.025 meters) long,   105

and the largest is up to 60 feet (18 meters) long with its tentacles. The   120

giant squid's eyeball is the size of a basketball!   129

And although people all over the world eat squid, there is one type   142

that, in turn, sometimes attacks people. Called the Humboldt squid, it   153

can be more than six feet (2 meters) long and weigh up to 100 pounds   168

(99 kg). Fishermen in Mexico's Sea of Cortez call them *"diablos rojos,"*   180

or "red devils," because they can change their color from white to red   193

as quickly as several times per second.   200

Divers have been bitten by Humboldt squid. Some have been   210

dragged deep underwater. Some divers now wear armor around them.   220

Researchers think these squid are generally harmless. But, they agree,   230

these big, intelligent creatures can also be dangerous at times.   240

Would you swim with them?   245

MONITOR PROGRESS   • Check Fluency   *Deep-Sea Danger* **141k**

Name _____

Our "Neighbor" Venus

For several reasons, the planet Venus is often called Earth's "twin." The two planets are almost the same size, with Earth's diameter a mere 400 miles (644 km) larger than that of Venus. The orbit of Venus comes closer to Earth than any other planet in our solar system. Since it is so close, Venus is also the brightest planet or star in the night sky.

Yet what seems quite similar is really very different in almost every way but size. For one thing, although it has an atmosphere like Earth, its atmosphere is made up mostly of carbon dioxide with dense clouds of sulfuric acid blanketing the surface. Our knowledge comes mainly from a U.S. space probe called *Magellan*, which orbited Venus and mapped its surface using radar.

The surface has some features that resemble Earth's. For example, around 65 percent of the planet's surface is made up of flat, smooth plains that are dotted with thousands of volcanoes. Most of the remainder of the planet's surface is made up of six mountain ranges. There are also canyons and valleys on Venus.

Yet Venus has features that are completely unlike anything on Earth. Venus has "coronae," or crowns, which are huge structures like rings that are from 95 to 360 miles (155 to 580 km) across. Scientists think molten material inside the planet formed them. The planet also has "tesserae," or tiles, which are raised areas. Ridges and valleys have formed in these tiles, but they go in many different directions.

It is very hot and dry at ground level on Venus. How hot? It is about 870° F (455° C) on the surface of Venus, which is hotter than any other planet. No liquid water exists at that temperature. Nothing on Earth could survive at the surface temperature of Venus. We may have named the planet after the Roman goddess of love, but there is nothing lovable about Venus for any Earthling.

Venus seems similar to Earth, but in truth, it's as foreign as anything can be.

MONITOR PROGRESS • Draw Conclusions

Deep-Sea Danger **141m**

Name _____

From Telephones to Cell Phones

Telephones send electric signals over wires, but cell phones use radio   11
waves, and that has made all the difference. Alexander Graham Bell was   23
one of two different people who invented the telephone, but he was the   36
first to patent it in 1876. His invention meant the death of the telegraph, 50
and now cell phones are rapidly replacing land-line phones that use   61
wires from poles or underground cables.   67

Back in 1947, people began thinking about ways to improve "car   78
phones." These crude phones were little more than two-way radios   88
with very poor sound quality that broke up while people talked. One   100
company came up with the idea of cell towers to send and receive   113
signals, but the electronics for the phones themselves weren't developed   123
until the 1960s. At that time, a caller had to stay in one cell area.   138
By 1971, a call could continue through two or more areas without   150
being dropped. Still, cellular phone service had to be approved by   161
the government, and that took about another ten years. Meanwhile,   171
scientists worked on the phones.   176

The first really portable phone came from research costing   185
100 million dollars, and it weighed 28 ounces and was as large as   198
a brick. They were too big to be carried but could be put in cars. By   214
1991, though, dialed phones were replaced by digital circuits and   224
became much smaller because of computer chips. And as you probably   235
know, today's cells do much more than make calls.   244

Grayson Rosenberger, Teen Inventor

In 2007 fifteen-year-old Grayson Rosenberger of Nashville, Tennessee, learned that a boy his age named Daniel had lost a leg in an accident. Daniel lives in Ghana, a poor African country where few citizens can afford more than the basics. An artificial, or prosthetic, leg with a skin-like covering to make it look real costs about $1,000. The fact that a realistic-looking leg was unaffordable for some people got Grayson to thinking.

It was Daniel's story that led Grayson to invent a covering that gives the prosthetic the shape and look of a real leg. Even better, the prosthetic with Grayson's covering costs only $15.

Grayson's invention is a plastic packing wrap and packing-tape "skin" that has been molded with a heat gun. It won, the young man the title of Teen Inventor of 2007 and a $10,000 first prize from the company that manufactures the plastic wrap. In many poorer countries, people look down on others who have artificial limbs. That's why Grayson's inexpensive invention is doubly good. It helps those with prosthetics fit in better.

Inventors say their ideas for products often grow out of the situations in their everyday lives. When Grayson's mother was a teenager, she lost both of her legs in an automobile accident. That led her and Grayson's father, to start an organization called Standing with Hope. This charity gives prosthetics to people who need them, but the artificial limbs don't have "skins." All of these facts played a part in Daniel's invention.

During the spring following Grayson's award-winning invention, his parents went back to Ghana to continue the work of Standing with Hope. This time Grayson went with them. He had a special gift for a young man named Daniel.

Name _____

The Art of the Wedding Cake

"You don't really intend to bake it yourself, do you?" whined her   12
sister, dramatically rolling her eyes.   17

"It will never work," warned her mother with a cautionary glance.   28
But Fran just smiled inwardly. She wanted her wedding to be absolutely   40
perfect, and the proof would shine in the cake. The wedding cake   52
would be more than just a dessert, she asserted to herself, convinced   64
that the cake she would make for her marriage to Jim would represent   77
all the good things their future might hold.   85

Despite her family's protests, Fran baked a layer each morning   95
during the week before the wedding. The cake itself was chocolate,   106
deep and dark for the adventurous mystery she hoped lay in store for   119
the two of them. The day of the rehearsal she frosted the three layers.   133
The first was pale yellow, a dream of sunny hopes for the years ahead.   147
The second layer was the blue of calm oceans to help them sail safely   161
through life. The final layer was green like spring so that she and Jim   175
might grow in wisdom and love. Finally, she decorated the cake with the   188
titles of beloved books. Fran and Jim had met working in a bookstore,   201
and their lives, she knew, would continue to be filled with reading.   213

When Jim cut the cake at the reception, he whispered, "This looks   225
like a recipe of us." And everyone clapped as the bride and groom   238
tasted the future.   241

MONITOR PROGRESS   • Check Fluency   *The View from Saturday* **213k**

Name _____

Letters on a Window

As Belinda locked the door of the shop, she glanced at the gold letters that gleamed in the glow of the streetlight. She recalled the first time those letters had enthralled her.

It wasn't the message that had caught her attention. That was just an offer to make invitations and announcements by hand. Her eye was seized by the ornate calligraphy, the careful precision of each character and the intriguing lines and curves of each letter's decorations. Until then, she would not have believed a simple letter "a" could be so beautiful.

Belinda had imagined the person who had applied the gold letters, picturing someone as tall, slender, and elegant as the lettering she so admired. She saw a graceful, elderly woman whose perfect handwriting was a holdover from her youth in a different time, when the art of lovely lettering was appreciated in a slower-moving world.

Belinda had walked home as darkness fell, filling in ever more details of the unknown calligrapher's life. She gave the woman a privileged childhood far away, perhaps overseas. By the time Belinda fell asleep, she had constructed a whole life story for the person whose shop she had seen. In the morning, she had decided, she would return to the shop to confirm her predictions.

Life rarely matches a fantasy, Belinda now knew. The artist sat on a tall stool behind an old wooden drafting table. He was shaped like a pear, with narrow shoulders and clothing that desperately needed ironing. He was neither old nor elegant. His fingernails were long, and his hair was standing at weird angles all over his head. She might have pitied him if he had looked just a tiny bit less eccentric.

Yet on a sheet of paper in front of him was the most beautiful lettering in the world. Belinda felt like a moth near a candle. She could not take her eyes off the man's work. The little man looked up with a knowing smile, gestured to Belinda, and offered her the pen from his hand.

Belinda reached out and accepted the invitation to her future.

Name _____

Julio's Arbor

Ever since he had harvested grapes in southern California as a   11
young man, Julio had dreamed of raising luscious table grapes on some   23
land of his own. So he scrimped and saved and finally returned to his   37
birthplace in Texas with four bare-root vines. He lovingly planted them   48
where they would feed on solar energy. In California, Julio had played   60
the role of mere laborer, but he had watched and learned. Now he   73
knew how to make cuttings for new vines. He knew how to fatten the   87
grapes and precisely when to harvest the sweet fruit.   96

For years, he patiently pruned his vines each winter. He trained   107
some vines over an arbor behind his house, but he planted new   119
cuttings in rows along a wire. Each spring, he and his growing children   132
watched the buds appear, and they watched the flowers form. The   143
small green berries followed the flowers on the vines, and Julio girdled   155
the stems so that all the energy of the roots and vines would go into   170
the growing fruit. He gave his vines water, and he waited again   182
as the berries grew plump with water and sugar. When the grapes   194
looked like clusters of green-gold marbles glowing in the morning sun,   205
Julio harvested his crop, using sterile clippers that he used only to   217
harvest grapes.   219

And when Julio shared his bounty with his family and friends, he felt   232
that his life was complete, and that nothing could improve it.   243

Name _____

The History of the Mexican Flag

Two North American countries are officially known as the United States. These are the United States of America and the United States of Mexico. But there is no tale of a character like Betsy Ross making Mexico's first flag. Just adopted in 1968, the flag is based on a design from 1821 that supposedly tells the story of the Aztec people who lived in what is now modern Mexico back in 1325. The rectangular flag's background is three equal vertical stripes of green, white, and red. Its center depicts an eagle perched on a cactus holding a rattlesnake in its talons.

Supposedly, a god told the Aztecs that when they saw an eagle doing those things on an island, they should build their city on that spot. Some histories claim that such a vision appeared on an island in the middle of Lake Anahuac, and the Aztecs began to build Tenochtitlan. Today this place is known as Mexico City.

The first Mexican flag was only a tri-color flag and was called the *sierra* (mountain range), a name it received from the Indians who lived on the sierra of Veracruz. But there are many opinions about the meaning of the three colors. Some have said that the green stands for victory and hope, the white for purity, and the red for the blood of Mexican heroes in battle. Still others claim green is for the earth's fertility. More commonly, it is believed that the green is for independence, white for the largest religion in Mexico—Roman Catholicism—and red for union.

The flag had no eagle until 1968 when Mexico hosted the Olympic summer games. Mexico's president at the time was concerned because Italy's flag had the same three stripes of green, white, and red. The eagle emblem was added to avoid confusion. Maybe the government hurried to get the new design in their constitution because the description said the eagle faced left. That meant that viewed from the back, the eagle faced right. Finally, in 1995, the flag's legal description was changed to take care of this problem.

Name _____

A Timeless Drama

Predators and their prey are locked in an eternal struggle for 11
advantage. Their relationship is survival at its most stark, with one animal 23
seeking to eat the other, while the other seeks to not be eaten. This 37
violent drama plays out every day on the plains of Africa, as it does in 52
all other wild places. In Africa, though, it seems more raw and wilder 65
than elsewhere. Perhaps this is because the animals are often larger, 76
more numerous, or faster than other places. 83

And no predator anywhere is faster than the cheetah. For short 94
bursts, cheetahs can run nearly 70 miles per hour (112 kmh). They 106
reach a speed of 45 mph (72 kmh) in just two-and-a-half seconds. 118
With this acceleration, cheetahs can run down any animal that is small 130
enough for them to overpower. 135

Among the favorite meals of cheetahs are Thomson's gazelles. 144
Cheetahs can easily outrun Tommies, as the small gazelles are known. 155
Yet cheetahs fail to catch a meal more often than they succeed. Why? 168
The answer is in the endless struggle between predator and prey. The 180
cheetah has the advantage of speed. The Tommie counters with an 191
ability to leap ten feet into the air and 30 feet in a single bound. This 207
helps, but what saves most Tommies is their ability to turn very quickly. 120
Usually, cheetahs are unable to cut back and forth behind the fleeing 232
animal. Most Tommies escape. 236

And the life-or-death contest goes on at another time. 245

Name _____

Seasonal Weather Cycles vs. Drought

East and Southern Africa experience distinct annual cycles of rainy and dry seasons. You may have seen documentary films about great herds of animals migrating on the plains of Kenya or Tanzania. The movements of these animals are driven by the changing pattern of rain that falls on that part of the continent every year. In East Africa, there is one lengthy dry season from June through October, or basically through the winter. Then there are two rainy seasons. One is called the "short rains," which lasts from the middle of October until the middle of December. The "long rains" fall from March through May. When the rains cease, the plants wither, and animals move away in search of green grasses. When the rains return, the land again becomes green. This causes the great herds of plant-eating animals to return.

The pattern of dry and wet seasons isn't the same everywhere, though. A little further south, in Malawi and Zimbabwe for example, there are not two rainy seasons. In the Southern African countries, the dry season is approximately from April through October. Every year the rains fall from November through March. Farmers and animals in the region both have adapted to these cycles of dry weather and rainfall.

There are important differences between a dry season and a drought. A dry season is any period of time experiencing low rainfall. A drought is a period in which water is insufficient to support plant life, especially agriculture. A drought does not have to be caused by a shortage of rain. Destruction of the environment can also cause drought. If the soil has been degraded so it cannot hold water, then that can cause drought conditions when rainfall is below average.

El Niño, which happens in the Pacific Ocean, can also cause drought in Africa. During El Niño years, the eastern tropical part of the Pacific Ocean becomes abnormally warm. This changes weather patterns all over the world. One of the effects can be drought in Africa, southern India, Indonesia, Australia, parts of South and Central America, and other places.

What Makes a Gemstone Precious?

Emerald, ruby, sapphire, and amethyst—the words sound like | 9
names of crayons, but they are four of the five stones called precious | 22
gemstones. Just add one more, diamond, and you have them all. | 33
Gemstones are rated by their beauty, rarity, durability or hardness, and | 44
desirability. Some are used to make jewelry. Some are used in industry, | 56
and some are traded between interested collectors. | 63

Of course, beauty depends on what pleases your own taste, but | 74
most people agree that these five kinds of minerals are beautiful. How | 86
do we know a stone is rare? Each is rated by the quality of the stone | 102
and its source. Not all diamonds are rare because there are many large | 115
deposits of diamonds available on Earth. But diamonds of certain size | 126
and color are worth great amounts of money. The same can be said of | 140
emeralds. As for durability, scientists have a measuring system called | 150
the Mohs scale. It rates the hardness of minerals. It runs from 10 for | 164
very hard down to 1. Diamonds rate 10 because they are the hardest | 177
substance known. In terms of jewels, durability simply means the stone | 188
can be bumped, banged, or dropped without damage. The Mohs scale | 199
answers that question. | 202

Not all precious gemstones are equally desirable. Most diamonds, | 211
for example, are industrial diamonds used in tools. Gemologists study | 221
color, cut, and clarity to determine desirability. | 228

Is there a precious gemstone in your future? | 236

MONITOR PROGRESS · Check Fluency   *Gold* **289k**

Name _____

A Golden Gift

Michael had contemplated Grandpa's gift for months, examining and then rejecting one idea after another. Grandpa was retiring after 43 years of employment. Michael understood that a traditional retirement gift was a gold watch, but he had only twenty dollars, and he was certain a watch would cost considerably more than that. Nonetheless, Michael wanted his gift to be gold.

Then he hit on a perfect solution to his dilemma.

All through spring, Grandpa had spent every weekend building a small pond in his garden. Michael had helped with the excavation, shoveling dirt away to make a hole about four feet deep at one end and about twelve feet long by six feet wide. The pond was surrounded by small mounds that Grandpa was going to cover with rocks and plants. Grandpa had lined the hole they dug with a rubber liner. They had put in a skimmer box with a pump to collect the water at the deep end of the pond, and they buried a hose from the pump to a small waterfall about fifteen feet away. They used sand and more of the pond liner to build a short stream to run from the little waterfall to the pond. Grandpa put a variety of round rocks in the bottom of the pond and planted water lilies, and he put flat rocks around the rim of the pond so he could walk around it.

When it was completed, the flow of water over the little waterfall and splashing from the stream into the pond made a delightful gurgling sound in the backyard. Michael researched fish online and immediately learned that koi were out of his price range. He also learned that he should not combine different types of fish in the pond, because flat-tailed fish would eat slower-moving fantailed fish. So he selected carefully.

When Michael presented a clear bowl containing three small Ryukin goldfish along with a printout from the Internet of tips for caring for the triangle-shaped fantailed fish, Grandpa got it instantly. "Instead of a gold watch," he laughed, "I'll be watching goldfish!"

MONITOR PROGRESS • Main Idea and Details   *Gold* 289m

Name _____

Talking Trash

How much trash do you personally create each day?　　9
Think about all of the garbage you generate, from a　　19
broken pencil to a cardboard juice box to an apple core.　　30
Altogether, it's probably fewer than five pounds of garbage　　39
if you produce about the same amount as other Americans.　　49
The national average per person is about 4.6 pounds　　58
daily, according to the Environmental Protection Agency.　　65
That may not seem like much, but remember it's just your　　76
output for a single day. Multiply the figure by 365 to figure　　88
out how much you add to the waste stream each year.　　99

The number is looking a bit larger now, isn't it? What　　110
happens when you multiply it by the number of people who　　121
live in your city? It's immediately clear why waste disposal　　131
is such an important issue in most cities. On average, every　　142
American contributes about 1,680 pounds of solid waste　　150
every year. That means a city of one million people will　　161
generate 850,000 tons annually. Our largest cities pile up　　170
an astonishing amount of trash. No wonder an old landfill　　180
north of Chicago is the highest point in Cook County, the　　191
county where Chicago is located in Illinois.　　198

Even after we recycle, on average every person in the　　208
United States still adds about three pounds of solid waste to　　219
the ever-growing piles every day. Do the math for your city　　230
or town. What reduction, reuse, and recycling strategies　　238
can you introduce today?　　242

Name _____

Saving the River of Grass

Few ecosystems in the United States have changed as dramatically in about one hundred years as Florida's Everglades. The vast wetland once covered four million acres of south Florida. It was part of an immense, 8.9-million-acre watershed that extended from Lake Okeechobee in the center of the state all the way south to Florida Bay. Water flowed from the Kissimmee River into the lake and then south to the ocean. The shallow moving water made the tall undulating sawgrass that grows in the Everglades ripple like a wave. For this reason, the Everglades is also called "the River of Grass."

When Americans began to settle in the southern parts of Florida around 1900, they set out to change the ecosystem. In 1905, efforts to drain the Everglades began. The goal was to make the region suitable for farming and development. Cities, such as Fort Lauderdale and Miami, began to develop along the coast.

As more people made their homes in or near the Everglades, they wanted to control the flooding that occurred almost every year. Bad floods in 1926 and 1928 led to the construction of levees around Lake Okeechobee.

In 1948, the United States Congress approved a giant drainage project. Canals were dug, levees and dams were built, and 1.7 billion gallons of water every day were directed out into the ocean.

As the vast marsh began to dry out, the entire ecosystem was badly damaged. Countless birds and other animals lost their habitat. Invasive plants began to take over the degraded landscape. By the 1990s, the Everglades was smaller than half of its original size, and people began to call for a plan to save the national treasure.

In 1992, the U.S. Army Corps of Engineers was asked to come up with a rescue plan. The proposal, called the Comprehensive Everglades Restoration Plan, was submitted to Congress in 1999 and approved in 2000. It will cost more than ten billion dollars, and it will take 30 years to complete, but the ecosystem of the Everglades will eventually be made healthy again.

Knights in Training

    Allow me to introduce myself. I am Edeldred, a page to the great   13

mounted knight Sir Galahad. Sir Galahad's manor is adjacent to my   24

father's. I am in training here, as is my eldest brother, Morton. He   37

is Sir Galahad's squire, an important role that will lead to his own   50

knighthood. He attends to Sir Galahad and serves his meals. Where I   62

train with a wooden sword and spear against the revolving dummy, my   74

brother develops his strength with real weapons, preparing to ride a   85

massive charger while wearing more than 40 pounds of armor.   95

    Morton helps the great knight with his armor and wears armor   106

himself. When Sir Galahad rides his huge horse armed with his long   118

lance and wielding his 32-pound broadsword, Morton attends with   127

replacement weapons. Morton will fight as a foot soldier himself, if   138

need be.   140

    Yet we train for more than battle. I take my lessons weekly to read   154

and write. Our lady, Sir Galahad's wife, has taught us to sing and   169

dance. Sir Galahad is strict about our behavior, insisting that we learn   181

the code of chivalry so well that not even the king could have taught   195

us better. Already my brother follows the code. He is always humble,   207

merciful, and respectful to all, and he is quick to protect the weak   220

against the strong. I can tell that Sir Galahad is proud of him.   233

    If I achieve my fondest wish, it will be to mimic my brother in   247

every way!   249

Name _____

The World-Champion Hog Caller

For as long as he could recollect, Davey had wanted to be the best at something. Only superlatives would do, as far as he was concerned. "Excellent" was fine, but it might as well be "competent" or "mediocre" or even "lousy" if the phrase "world's best" wasn't included in the same sentence. It wasn't sufficient to be very good at something. Davey's urge was to be better than anyone else.

The problem was, Davey lacked talent. He was hopeless as an athlete, so clumsy he could scarcely climb a flight of stairs without stumbling at least once. He was smart enough for ordinary purposes, but he couldn't look in a mirror and call himself a genius without collapsing onto the floor with laughter. He knew how to use a computer, but he had no clue as to how to create a new program.

It looked as though Davey was doomed to a lifetime of disappointment. But then his very clumsiness revealed his true prowess.

One day in late winter, Davey was walking gloomily down the lane that separated his family's farm from their neighbor's when a small rock rolled under his foot. Davey practically somersaulted backwards into an icy mud puddle. As he flipped, a high-pitched sound came out of his mouth like nothing he had ever heard before. Then he landed with a splash and the fall knocked the wind out of him. As he gathered himself, he noticed that he was surrounded by his neighbor's hogs. He stared at the pigs. They stared back, looking expectant. Davey made the connection.

All spring, Davey practiced in secret, hiding in the barn as he tried to consistently duplicate the eerie sound that had escaped his throat as he fell. He knew his determination had paid off when he emerged to find every pig within earshot outside the barn door, their tails wagging.

Naturally, Davey won the hog-calling contest at the state fair that year. He also won every year after that. And he traveled to other states, where he also won. Quite by accident, Davey had become the world's best hog caller!

MONITOR PROGRESS • Author's Purpose

Name _____

The Greatest Runner of All Time

    We found a scrap of parchment beneath a rock in the ruins of the   14

original Olympics stadium at the Temple of Hera in Olympia, Greece.   25

It tells the tale of Demetrios, who seems to have been the greatest of   39

all Olympic runners. His accomplishments might have been lost in the   50

mists of time. Only rumors of his greatness might have drifted across   62

the centuries from ancient Greece to the present-day Olympics. But we   73

found an eyewitness account.   77

    "I was the training partner and friend of Demetrios the Great. I gave   90

him water when he returned, victorious, from every contest. No athlete   101

could match his greatness.   105

    "In four consecutive Olympiads, from year 8 through year 20,   115

Demetrios competed in all of the running events. He sprinted in the   127

192-meter run that covered the length of the stadium. He won every   139

time. He also ran the two-length race and the longer distances, the   151

seven- to 24-length races. He likewise won every competition. Even in   162

the most grueling of all races, the four-length armored race, Demetrios   173

was never defeated. In this run, the athletes wore full hoplite battle   185

armor, a load weighing at least 50 pounds.   193

    "We proudly carried the olive branches that he was awarded   203

all across Greece, and we were greeted as heroes in every town. In   216

Athens, Demetrios received 500 drachma for every olive branch! This   226

was a small fortune by itself, and we received the reward sixteen times."   239

    I'll bet you thought only today's athletes were rich!   248

MONITOR PROGRESS   • Check Fluency   *Ancient Greece* **385k**

Name _____

Story of the Seasons

Demeter, Greek goddess of the harvest, was blessed with a beautiful daughter, Persephone. So great was Demeter's bliss that crops grew, flowers bloomed, and the earth sparkled with green fertility. So gorgeous was Persephone that Hades, god of the underworld, was captivated and abducted the terrified maiden. Hearing her daughter's screams, Demeter rushed to find her, but there was no trace.

Demeter searched the world night and day asking if anyone had seen Persephone. While she sought her daughter, crops withered and died in the cold, parched ground.

With their crops in ruin, the starving people appealed to the king of the gods, Zeus, for help. He commanded Hades to release Persephone, but Hades was sly. Not wanting to defy Zeus, but also not wanting to lose Persephone, he offered her a pomegranate, knowing that anyone who eats in the underworld can never leave. Persephone had eaten nothing for months, so she accepted the fruit. But she ate only three seeds. Thus she was able to leave but had to return for three months each year, one month for each seed she had eaten.

Demeter wept with joy when she saw her daughter again, and as she cried, gentle rains fell, and spring returned to the land. The people rejoiced as their crops sprouted. But every year, when Persephone must return to Hades, winter descends.

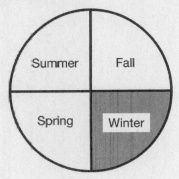

Key

 Persephone's time in the underworld each year

Celebrating Cinco De Mayo

The United States is constantly enriched by the celebrations and	10
traditions of people from all of the countries of the world. Americans	22
from all over the world celebrate days of independence and other	33
national holidays from their home countries. Particularly fascinating are	42
holidays that are more important in the United States than in the country	55
from which they came. One such celebration is the Fifth of May.	67

All across America today, the Fifth of May is dedicated to food,   79
music, and dancing of Mexico. People of Mexican heritage honor the   90
customs of their home country as well as the spirit of independence and   103
freedom that links the nations of North America.   111

May 5 commemorates the victory of a greatly outnumbered force   121
of Mexican militia over an invading French Army in the Battle of Puebla   134
in 1862. Many people now believe that the Fifth of May celebrates   146
Mexico's independence from Spain, but that is incorrect. Mexico's   155
Independence Day is September 16.   160

Interestingly, the Fifth of May is a very popular holiday in Puebla,   172
which is about 100 miles east of Mexico City, but it is not really   186
observed elsewhere in Mexico. It is a much more popular holiday in   198
the United States. In American cities, the Fifth of May is celebrated with   211
parades and a week of concerts and parties involving tasty Mexican   222
food and colorfully dressed dancers.   227

However, because the Fifth of May is so popular north of the   239
border, it is becoming more popular in Mexico as well.   249

Name _____

Hold the Utensils

A diplomatic experiment led to a sloppy but happy meal today in a cafeteria near the United Nations. Tourists were sampling the different foods offered at the 'Round the World in 80 Plates restaurant, when two visiting groups from Italy and China decided to switch utensils. They asked that dishes normally served with a fork be served with chopsticks, and other plates ordinarily eaten with chopsticks be served with plastic forks. Not only did many diners end up hungry, but food ended up in a few people's laps along the way.

A woman from China laughingly gave up on her fork at last, after ten minutes of watching glass noodles slide back onto her plate. "Chopsticks are like extensions of your fingers," she said, "able to pinch together and pick up any food that is on your plate. For everything else, a spoon is all you need."

A man from Italy who held one chopstick in each hand groaned for help. "Someone please teach me how to use these," he moaned. "I need a fork, with its pointed tines, so I can slice and stab my lasagna to lift it from the plate."

As the restaurant owner showed the man how to hold his chopsticks, she pointed out that chopsticks are at least 5,000 years old. Supposedly, she said, as Chinese cuisine changed so that food was chopped into small pieces before it was cooked, knives became unnecessary at the table. Therefore, chopsticks became the standard utensils, used for cooking and eating alike. Because chopsticks could be quickly made from bamboo, everyone carried them.

Forks, on the other hand, were developed around 3,000 years ago to hold a piece of meat in place so it could be easily carved. However, they were not widely used for eating until perhaps 1,000 years ago, and ordinary people did not use the implements until the 1800s. Forks with widely separated tines worked poorly with small pieces of food, and better forks were luxury items.

"Well, at least we all have spoons," one diner said as he reached for a bowl of tomato soup. The restaurant's owner let both groups eat for free, declaring, "Adventurous eaters should be rewarded!"

The Lincolnwood School Weekly Times

Mr. Cullen stood beaming at the sixth-grade students getting settled   10
before their afternoon journalism class. What kind crazy project, they   20
wondered, would Mr. Cullen have them tackle today?   28

"I have a special surprise for you," their teacher said. "Today we're   40
going to start developing a newspaper that will cover the coming week   52
in our school. First, you'll have to make some important decisions.   63
What will you call the paper? Who will be your audience? And, most   76
importantly, what kinds of stories will you include?"   84

Intrigued, the students set about the task of figuring out who would   96
be the editor in charge. Next, they assigned reporters to cover news   108
stories, write features, and create puzzles. Maggie volunteered to be the   119
copy editor and check all the work for spelling and grammar. Zack was   132
sure he could turn some of his doodles into comics, and Cameron pulled   145
out her camera to start taking photos. Then, they established deadlines   156
and contemplated the layout.   160

"Hey, if we give everyone in the school a copy of our newspaper,   173
who will pay for the paper we print it on?" asked Hiro.   185

"Sounds like you might have to talk the Parents Booster Club into   197
taking out an ad in your paper," suggested Mr. Cullen.   207

Ten days and one giant journalism lesson later, the class published   218
the first, but not the last, issue of the *Lincolnwood School Weekly*   230
Times. The headline read, "Lincolnwood School Inaugurates First   238
Student-Run-and-Managed Newspaper."   240

MONITOR PROGRESS   • Check Fluency

Name _____

Montezuma

People often ask me, was Montezuma the unlucky last ruler of a great empire whose brief indecision led to catastrophe for his people? Or was he a superstitious weakling, as many in Spain now like to imagine him? People ask me this question because I was there. My name is Aguilar, and I was an eyewitness from the very beginning.

Some have said that Montezuma was overcome by a small force of soldiers led by my master, Hernando Cortés. In a way, this is true. But from another perspective, it is not. We did defeat the armies of the Aztecs, but it was not without help.

Aztec superstition may have played a part. When we first reached this land, Montezuma had just been named the ninth emperor of the Aztecs. That was twenty years ago, in 1502. Evidently a legend said that the Aztec empire would fall when the god of wisdom, Quetzalcoatl, returned. Quetzalcoatl was said to have pale skin and a beard, like us Spaniards. This coincidence may explain why Montezuma was hesitant about fighting us. I know he first sent gifts instead of warriors to my master.

The gifts did not deter us. We advanced to the great city and made a captive of Montezuma. This meant we held the entire nation hostage, and they were unable to destroy us despite their huge advantage in numbers. But the Aztec people rebelled, and we forced Montezuma to address them. The people threw stones and arrows at their unfortunate emperor, fatally injuring him. He cursed us as we fled.

But there was vast wealth in gold there, and we would not return to Spain without it. So we came back to the city of the Aztecs. And with us came thousands of allies who were only too happy to help us destroy it.

Thus fell a vast empire, and a way of life was destroyed. In return, we gained a fortune in gold beyond imagination. The Aztecs' enemies who had helped us defeat them gained their freedom from harsh overlords. Montezuma may have cursed us, but he could not save himself or his city.

Miranda's Miraculous Monday

Glancing at the coming week on her school calendar, Miranda	10
noticed that Monday was labeled "Non-Attendance Day." She felt	19
buoyant, as if she had been handed a small, square gift. On her twelfth	33
birthday, her mother had agreed that they could take the train into the	46
city the next free weekday, and Miranda could plan every detail of the	59
day's events.	61
"Look out, Chicago!" she whispered as she flopped onto her bed to	73
develop the itinerary.	76
Outside of the station they hailed a cab, a first for Miranda, and	89
she told the driver, "Millennium Park, please." At that marvel of green	101
space built over a train yard, Miranda studied her reflection in the	113
polished stainless steel of the "Cloud Gate" sculpture before splashing	123
barefoot through the water. By eleven, they had crossed the street to	135
the Art Institute because Miranda wanted to see in person the famous	147
paintings. As she stood before one giant masterpiece, Miranda realized	157
it was composed of thousands of small dots of paint. Amazing!	168
Next on her agenda was lunch from a street vendor. They walked	180
to State Street and settled on hamburgers and fries. Their last stop was	193
the river, where they climbed aboard an excursion boat for a tour of	206
Chicago's architectural gems, some of the finest buildings in the nation.	217
By day's end, Miranda knew she would always enjoy seeking out	228
new places to explore.	232

MONITOR PROGRESS • Check Fluency

Where Opportunity Awaits **475k**

Name _____

The Great Depression

New Year's Eve, 1929, was as lavish and extravagant as the entire decade known as the Roaring Twenties had been. But only ten months later, on October 29, the stock market crashed, and life in America, and soon throughout the world, changed drastically.

This was the Great Depression. Stock prices collapsed until they were worth only 20 percent of their value. By 1933, one-fourth of the nation's workers were unemployed, and only half of the banks had survived. People who had held on to their jobs saw their wages cut by 43 percent.

Mills, mines, and factories were idle or even abandoned. Farms became almost worthless, and many farmers went hungry after losing their land. These newly homeless people began moving around the nation, living in temporary shantytowns and searching for work. Some jumped aboard train boxcars and traveled around the countryside.

As if the economic situation wasn't trouble enough, dust storms and drought plagued the Great Plains, taking lives and destroying agriculture and ranching in several states. Citizens turned to the government for help, and when President Herbert Hoover's plans didn't work, they elected Franklin D. Roosevelt in 1932. Roosevelt wasted no time, quickly assembling advisors who became known as the "Brain Trust." It took this group only 100 days to develop a program called the New Deal. Suddenly, there were several new government agencies that tried to get the country moving again. Unemployed young men were put to work in the Civilian Conservation Corps (CCC) doing outdoor jobs to improve the environment. The Works Progress Administration (WPA) created jobs in construction and the arts. Another agency tried to get industry going by devising new farming methods, building dams, and extending electrical power throughout much of the country.

People's spirits rose, and Franklin D. Roosevelt became the only President ever elected to four terms in office.

MONITOR PROGRESS   • Generalize

Assessment Charts and Student Progress Report

from

First Stop Sixth Grade

Fluency Progress Chart, Grade 6

Name _____

WCPM (vertical axis, bottom to top): 80, 85, 90, 95, 100, 105, 110, 115, 120, 125, 130, 135, 140, 145, 150, 155, 160, 165, 170, 175

Timed Reading/Week (horizontal axis): 1, 2, 3, 4, 5, 6, 7, 8, 9, 10, 11, 12, 13, 14, 15, 16, 17, 18, 19, 20, 21, 22, 23, 24, 25, 26, 27, 28, 29, 30, 31, 32, 33, 34, 35, 36

504

Assessment Chart

Name _____ Date _____

		Day 3 Retelling Assessment		Day 5 Fluency Assessment		Day 5 Comprehension Assessment		Reteach	Teacher's Comments
		Benchmark Score	Actual Score	Benchmark WCPM	Actual Score	Benchmark Score	Actual Score		
WEEK 1	**Old Yeller** Setting and Plot	3–4		115–120		3–4		✔	
WEEK 2	**Mother Fletcher's Gift** Character and Theme	3–4		115–120		3–4			
WEEK 3	**Viva New Jersey** Compare and Contrast	3–4		115–120		3–4			
WEEK 4	**Saving the Rain Forests** Fact and Opinion	3–4		115–120		3–4			
WEEK 5	**Hachiko: The True Story of a Loyal Dog** Fact and Opinion	3–4		115–120		3–4			
	Unit 1 Test Score								

Benchmark Score reflects grade-level target.

- **RECORD SCORES** Use this chart to record scores for the Day 3 Retelling, Day 5 Fluency, Day 5 Comprehension, and Unit Test.

- **REGROUPING** Compare the student's actual score to the benchmark score and group flexibly or provide extra support as needed.

- **RETEACH** If a student is unable to complete any part of the assessment process, use the weekly Reteach lessons in the *First Stop* book for additional support. Record the lesson information in the space provided on the chart. After reteaching, you may want to reassess using the Unit Test.

Assessment Chart

Name _____ Date _____

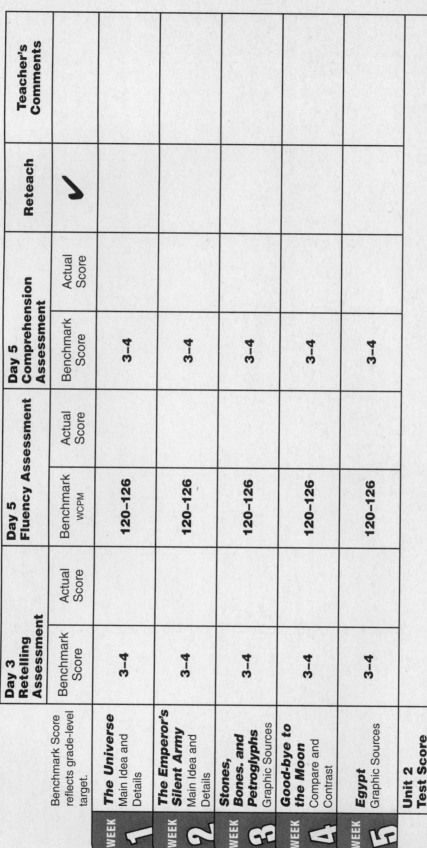

Benchmark Score reflects grade-level target.	Day 3 Retelling Assessment		Day 5 Fluency Assessment		Day 5 Comprehension Assessment		Reteach	Teacher's Comments
	Benchmark Score	Actual Score	Benchmark WCPM	Actual Score	Benchmark Score	Actual Score		
WEEK 1 *The Universe* Main Idea and Details	3–4		120–126		3–4		✔	
WEEK 2 *The Emperor's Silent Army* Main Idea and Details	3–4		120–126		3–4			
WEEK 3 *Stones, Bones, and Petroglyphs* Graphic Sources	3–4		120–126		3–4			
WEEK 4 *Good-bye to the Moon* Compare and Contrast	3–4		120–126		3–4			
WEEK 5 *Egypt* Graphic Sources	3–4		120–126		3–4			
Unit 2 Test Score								

• **RECORD SCORES** Use this chart to record scores for the Day 3 Retelling, Day 5 Fluency, Day 5 Comprehension, and Unit Test.

• **REGROUPING** Compare the student's actual score to the benchmark score and group flexibly or provide extra support as needed.

• **RETEACH** If a student is unable to complete any part of the assessment process, use the weekly Reteach lessons in the *First Stop* book for additional support. Record the lesson information in the space provided on the chart. After reteaching, you may want to reassess using the Unit Test.

Assessment Chart

Name _____ Date _____

Benchmark Score reflects grade-level target.

	Day 3 Retelling Assessment		Day 5 Fluency Assessment		Day 5 Comprehension Assessment		Reteach	Teacher's Comments
	Benchmark Score	Actual Score	Benchmark WCPM	Actual Score	Benchmark Score	Actual Score		
WEEK 1 **Hatchet** Sequence	3–4		125–132		3–4			
WEEK 2 **When Marian Sang** Generalize	3–4		125–132		3–4			
WEEK 3 **Learning to Swim** Sequence	3–4		125–132		3–4			
WEEK 4 **Juan Verdades: The Man Who Couldn't Tell a Lie** Generalize	3–4		125–132		3–4			
WEEK 5 **Morning Traffic** Draw Conclusions	3–4		125–132		3–4			
Unit 3 Test Score								

- **RECORD SCORES** Use this chart to record scores for the Day 3 Retelling, Day 5 Fluency, Day 5 Comprehension, and Unit Test.

- **REGROUPING** Compare the student's actual score to the benchmark score and group flexibly or provide extra support as needed.

- **RETEACH** If a student is unable to complete any part of the assessment process, use the weekly Reteach lessons in the *First Stop* book for additional support. Record the lesson information in the space provided on the chart. After reteaching, you may want to reassess using the Unit Test.

Assessment Chart

Name _____ Date _____

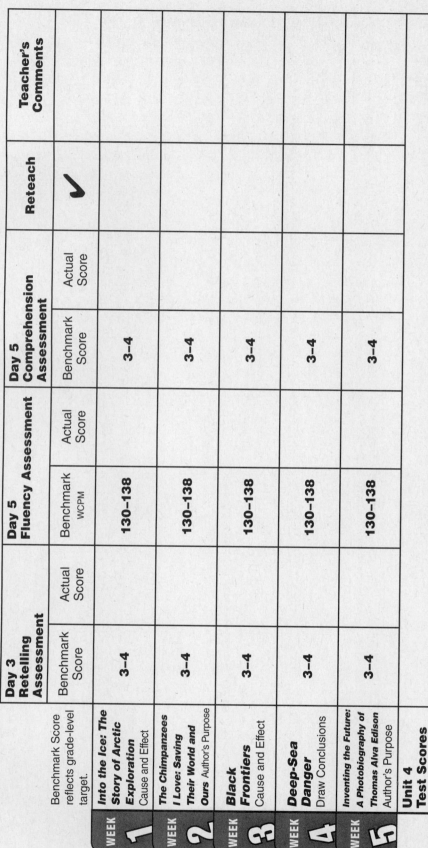

Benchmark Score reflects grade-level target.	Day 3 Retelling Assessment		Day 5 Fluency Assessment		Day 5 Comprehension Assessment		Reteach	Teacher's Comments
	Benchmark Score	Actual Score	Benchmark WCPM	Actual Score	Benchmark Score	Actual Score		
WEEK 1 *Into the Ice: The Story of Arctic Exploration* Cause and Effect	3–4		130–138		3–4		✓	
WEEK 2 *The Chimpanzees I Love: Saving Their World and Ours* Author's Purpose	3–4		130–138		3–4			
WEEK 3 *Black Frontiers* Cause and Effect	3–4		130–138		3–4			
WEEK 4 *Deep-Sea Danger* Draw Conclusions	3–4		130–138		3–4			
WEEK 5 *Inventing the Future: A Photobiography of Thomas Alva Edison* Author's Purpose	3–4		130–138		3–4			
Unit 4 Test Scores								

- **RECORD SCORES** Use this chart to record scores for the Day 3 Retelling, Day 5 Fluency, Day 5 Comprehension, and Unit Test.

- **REGROUPING** Compare the student's actual score to the benchmark score and group flexibly or provide extra support as needed.

- **RETEACH** If a student is unable to complete any part of the assessment process, use the weekly Reteach lessons in the *First Stop* book for additional support. Record the lesson information in the space provided on the chart. After reteaching, you may want to reassess using the Unit Test.

Assessment Chart

Name _____

Date _____

	Day 3 Retelling Assessment		Day 5 Fluency Assessment		Day 5 Comprehension Assessment		Reteach	Teacher's Comments
	Benchmark Score	Actual Score	Benchmark WCPM	Actual Score	Benchmark Score	Actual Score		
Benchmark Score reflects grade-level target.								
WEEK 1 *The View From Saturday* Theme and Plot	3–4		135–144				✔	
WEEK 2 *Harvesting Hope: The Story of César Chávez* Fact and Opinion	3–4		135–144		3–4			
WEEK 3 *The River That Went to the Sky: A Story from Malawi* Cause and Effect	3–4		135–144		3–4			
WEEK 4 *Gold* Main Idea and Details	3–4		135–144		3–4			
WEEK 5 *Greensburg Goes Green* Sequence	3–4		135–144		3–4			
Unit 5 Test Score								

- **RECORD SCORES** Use this chart to record scores for the Day 3 Retelling, Day 5 Fluency, Day 5 Comprehension, and Unit Test.

- **REGROUPING** Compare the student's actual score to the benchmark score and group flexibly or provide extra support as needed.

- **RETEACH** If a student is unable to complete any part of the assessment process, use the weekly Reteach lessons in the *First Stop* book for additional support. Record the lesson information in the space provided on the chart. After reteaching, you may want to reassess using the Unit Test.

Assessment Chart

Name _____ Date _____

Benchmark Score reflects grade-level target.

	Day 3 Retelling Assessment		Day 5 Fluency Assessment		Day 5 Comprehension Assessment		Reteach	Teacher's Comments
	Benchmark Score	Actual Score	Benchmark WCPM	Actual Score	Benchmark Score	Actual Score		
WEEK 1 *Don Quixote and the Windmills* Author's Purpose	3–4		140–150		3–4		✓	
WEEK 2 *Ancient Greece* Graphic Sources	3–4		140–150		3–4			
WEEK 3 *The All-American Slurp* Compare and Contrast	3–4		140–150		3–4			
WEEK 4 *The Aztec News* Draw Conclusions	3–4		140–150		3–4			
WEEK 5 *Where Opportunity Waits* Generalize	3–4		140–150		3–4			
Unit 6 Test Score								

- **RECORD SCORES** Use this chart to record scores for the Day 3 Retelling, Day 5 Fluency, Day 5 Comprehension, and Unit Test.

- **REGROUPING** Compare the student's actual score to the benchmark score and group flexibly or provide extra support as needed.

- **RETEACH** If a student is unable to complete any part of the assessment process, use the weekly Reteach lessons in the *First Stop* book for additional support. Record the lesson information in the space provided on the chart. After reteaching, you may want to reassess using the Unit Test.

Student Progress Report: Grade 6

Name _____

This chart lists the skills taught in this program. Record your child's progress toward mastery of the skills covered in this school year here. Use the chart below to track the coverage of these skills.

Skill	Date	Date	Date
Word Structure			
Decode multisyllabic words with common word parts and spelling patterns			
Decode base words and inflected endings: plurals			
Decode contractions and compound words			
Decode words with prefixes and suffixes			
Decode words with Greek and Latin roots			
Use context along with sound-letter relationships and knowledge of syllabification rules and word structure to decode words while self-monitoring and self-correcting			
Fluency			
Read aloud grade level text fluently with accuracy, comprehension, appropriate pace/rate; with expression/intonation (prosody); with attention to punctuation and appropriate phrasing			
Practice fluency in a variety of ways, including choral reading, partner/paired reading, Readers' Theater, repeated oral reading, and tape-assisted reading			
Read regularly and with comprehension in independent-level material			
Read silently for increasing periods of time			
Vocabulary and Concept Development			
Recognize and understand selection vocabulary			
Understand content-area vocabulary and specialized, technical, or topical words			
Use knowledge of word structure to figure out meanings of words			
Use context clues for meanings of unfamiliar words, multiple-meaning words, homonyms, homographs			
Use grade-appropriate reference sources to learn word meanings			
Create and use graphic organizers to classify and categorize, study, and retain vocabulary			
Extend academic language			
Extend knowledge of abbreviations, antonyms and synonyms, prefixes and suffixes, homographs and homophones, related words and derivations, compound words, figurative language and idioms, and time and order words			

Skill	Date	Date	Date
Extend knowledge of word origins: etymologies/word histories; words from other languages, regions, or cultures			
Extend knowledge of analogies			
Reading Comprehension			
Predict and set purpose to guide reading			
Use background knowledge before, during, and after reading			
Monitor and clarify by using fix-up strategies to resolve difficulties in meaning: adjust reading rate, reread and read on, seek help from reference sources and/or other people, skim and scan			
Question before, during, and after reading			
Visualize—use mental imagery			
Summarize text; recall and retell stories			
Identify important ideas that provide clues to a nonfiction author's meaning			
Identify elements of text structure in nonfiction, such as cause/effect, chronology, compare/contrast, description			
Identify elements of story structure in fiction, such as plot, problem/solution			
Create and us graphic and semantic organizers, including outlines, notes, summaries			
Identify author's purpose, and author's viewpoint and bias			
Categorize and classify			
Identify causes and effects			
Compare and contrast			
Identify facts and details			
Distinguish between statements of fact and opinion			
Follow directions or steps in a process			
Use graphic sources such as illustrations, photos, maps, charts, graphs, font styles, etc. to enhance meaning			
Identify main idea and supporting details			
Identify persuasive devices and propaganda			
Identify sequence of events			
Analyze text with various organizational patterns			
Describe and connect the essential ideas, arguments, and perspectives of a text			
Evaluate and critique ideas and text			
Draw inferences, conclusions, or generalizations; support them with textual evidence and prior knowledge			

Skill	Date	Date	Date
Make connections (text to self, text to text, text to world)			
Organize and synthesize ideas and information			
Literary Response and Analysis			
Identify types of everyday print materials (novels, poems, newspapers, signs, labels)			
Identify characteristics of literary texts, including drama, fantasy, traditional tales			
Identify characteristics of nonfiction texts, including biography, interviews, newspaper articles			
Identify characteristics of poetry and song, including rhymes, limericks, blank verse			
Recognize and describe traits, actions, feelings, and motives of characters; analyze characters' relationships, changes, and points of view; analyze characters' conflicts; analyze the effect of character on plot and conflict			
Identify the goal and outcome or problem and solution or resolution of a story			
Identify the rising action, climax, and falling action/denouement and/or setbacks in the plot of a story			
Relate a story's setting to its problem and solution; explain ways setting contributes to mood			
Analyze and evaluate author's use of setting, plot, character, and compare among authors			
Identify similarities and differences of characters, events, and settings within or across selections/cultures			
Identify use of dialect			
Identify the speaker or narrator in a selection			
Identify figurative language in a selection such as idiom, jargon, metaphor, simile, and slang; exaggeration and/or hyperbole; imagery and sensory words; personification; and symbolism			
Identify flashbacks and foreshadowing in a selection			
Distinguish between formal and informal language			
Identify and explain the use of humor, puns, and wordplay in a selection			
Identify point of view in a selection (first-person, third-person, omniscient)			
Identify sound devices and poetic elements such as alliteration, assonance, onomatopoeia, rhyme, rhythm, repetition, cadence, and word choice in selected works			
Identify the mood and tone of a selection			

Skill	Date	Date	Date
Recognize and analyze author's and illustrator's craft or style; evaluate author's use of various techniques to influence readers' perspectives			
Reflect on reading and respond (through talk, movement, art, and so on) by asking and answering questions about text; writing about what is read; using evidence from the text to support opinions, interpretations, or conclusions; locating materials on related topic, theme, or idea			
Choose text by drawing on personal interests, relaying on knowledge of authors and genres, estimating text difficulty, and using recommendations of others			
Comprehend basic plots and classic tales from around the world by comparing and contrasting tales from different cultures, developing abilities to interact with diverse groups and cultures, connecting experiences and ideas with those from diverse cultures and perspectives			
Compare language and oral traditions (family stories) that reflect customs, regions, and cultures, recognizing themes that cross cultures and bind them together in their common humanness			
Language Arts: Writing			
State a clear purpose and maintain focus; sharpen ideas			
Use sensory details and concrete examples; elaborate			
Delete extraneous information			
Use strategies such as tone, style, consistent point of view, to achieve a sense of completeness			
Use graphic organizers to group ideas			
Write coherent introductory, supporting, and concluding paragraphs that develop a central idea and have topic sentences and facts and ideas; use transitions to connect sentences and paragraphs and establish coherence			
Select an organizational structure such as comparison and contrast, categories, spatial order, climactic order, based on purpose, audience, length			
Organize ideas in a logical progression, such as chronological order or order of importance			
Use strategies of note-taking, outlining, and summarizing to impose structure on composition drafts			

Skill	Date	Date	Date
Develop personal, identifiable voice and an individual tone/style that is consistent and maintains its point of view; that is appropriate to audience, message, and purpose; that uses clear, precise, appropriate language, figurative language, and vivid words			
Prewrite using various strategies; develop first drafts of single- and multiple-paragraph compositions; revise drafts for varied purposes, including to clarify and to achieve purpose, sense of audience, improve focus and coherence, precise word choice, vivid images, and elaboration; edit and proofread for correct conventions (spelling, grammar, usage, and mechanics); and publish own work			
Write narrative compositions such as personal narratives, stories, biographies, autobiographies			
Write expositive compositions such as comparison and contrast, problem and solution, essays, directions, explanations, news stories, research reports, summaries			
Write descriptive compositions such as labels, captions, lists, plays, poems, response logs, songs			
Write persuasive compositions such as ads, editorials, essays, letters to the editor, opinions, posters			
Write notes and letters such as personal, formal, and friendly letters; thank-you notes; and invitations			
Write a response to literature			
Write on a daily basis as a tool for learning; write independently for extended periods of time			
Write legibly, with control over letter size and form; letter slant; and letter, word, and sentence spacing; write lowercase and uppercase letters in both manuscript and cursive			
Language Arts: Written and Oral English Language Conventions			
Use correct word order in written sentences			
Identify types of sentences (declarative, interrogative, exclamatory, imperative)			
Identify structure of sentences (complete, incomplete, simple, compound, complex, compound-complex)			
Identify sentence parts (subjects/predicates: complete, simple, compound; phrases; clauses)			
Identify and correct fragments and run-on sentences			
Combine and rearrange sentences; use appositives, participial phrases, adjectives, adverbs, and prepositional phrases			
Use transitions and conjunctions to connect ideas; independent and dependent clauses			

Skill	Date	Date	Date
Use a variety of sentence types and sentence openings to present effective style			
Identify parts of speech such as nouns (singular and plural), verbs and verb tenses, adjectives, adverbs, pronouns and antecedents, conjunctions, prepositions, interjections, and articles			
Use contractions correctly			
Identify and understand principles of usage such as subject-verb agreement and pronoun agreement and referents			
Identify and explain how to correct errors such as misplaced modifiers, misused words, and double negatives			
Use correct capitalization (first word in sentence, proper nouns and adjectives, pronoun I, titles, months, days of the week, holidays, and so on)			
Use correct punctuation (period, question mark, exclamation mark, apostrophe, comma, quotation marks, parentheses, colon, and so on)			
Spell independently, using knowledge of word structure to spell, including irregular words and frequently misspelled words such as homophones and homonyms; Use meaning relationships to spell			
Listening and Speaking			
Listen to a variety of presentations attentively and politely; self-monitor comprehension while listening, using a variety of skills and strategies such as asking questions			
Determine and listen for a purpose such as to enjoy and appreciate, to expand vocabulary and concepts, to obtain information and ideas, to follow oral directions, to answer questions and solve problems, to participate in group discussions, to identify and analyze literary language, to gain knowledge of your own and others' cultures, to respond to persuasive messages with questions or affirmations			
Recognize formal and informal spoken language			
Connect prior experiences to those of a speaker			
Listen critically to distinguish fact from opinion and to analyze and evaluate ideas, information, experiences			
Paraphrase, retell, or summarize information that has been shared orally			
Evaluate a speaker's delivery; identify tone, mood, and emotion			
Interpret and critique a speaker's purpose, perspective, persuasive techniques, verbal and nonverbal messages, and use of rhetorical devices; draw conclusions			

Skill	Date	Date	Date
Speak clearly, accurately, and fluently, using appropriate delivery for a variety of audiences and purposes; sustain audience interest and attention; use proper intonation, volume, pitch, modulation, and phrasing; speak with a command of standard English conventions; use appropriate language for formal and informal settings; stay focused and on topic; use appropriate verbal and nonverbal elements such as facial expression, gestures, eye contact, and posters			
Organize ideas and convey information in a logical sequence or structure with a beginning, middle, and end and an effective introduction and conclusion; support ideas and opinions with detailed evidence and with visual or media displays			
Speak for a purpose such as to ask and answer questions, to give directions and instructions, to explain information, to communicate needs and share ideas and experiences, to describe, to participate in conversations and discussions, to express an opinion, to recite poems or dramatic recitations, to deliver oral response to literature, to present oral reports			
Viewing Media			
Analyze and evaluate media; compare and contrast print, visual, and electronic media; recognize bias and propaganda in media messages; recognize purpose and persuasion in media messages			
Research Skills			
Know and use organizational features and parts of a book to locate information			
Use alphabetical order			
Understand purpose, structure, and organization of reference sources (print, electronic, media, Internet)			
Use accurate computer terminology and skills to create, name, locate, open, save, delete, and organize files; use input and output devices and basic keyboarding skills			
Work cooperatively and collaboratively with others; follow acceptable use policies			
Use electronic Web (nonlinear) navigation, online resources, databases, keyword searches			
Conduct Internet inquiry by identifying questions; locating, selecting, and collecting information; analyzing information; synthesizing information, and communicating findings; respect intellectual property and recognize hazards of Internet searches			
Use technology resources for solving problems and making informed decisions			

Skill	Date	Date	Date
Identify research topics; ask and evaluate questions; develop ideas leading to inquiry, investigation, and research			
Choose and evaluate appropriate reference sources; locate and collect information including using organizational features of electronic text			
Take notes; record findings; combine and compare information; evaluate, interpret, and draw conclusions about key information			
Paraphrase and summarize information; organize content systematically in an outline			
Communicate information in a written research report that includes citations and respects intellectual property and avoids plagiarism